RUS

Isaac Deutscher was born near C   , in 1907. After a varied education he launched, in 1924, into a literary career and worked with the Polish press until 1939 as journalist, economist, and literary critic. He joined the Polish Communist Party in 1926 but was expelled in 1932 for his activities as leader and spokesman of the anti-Stalinists. In 1939 he came to London and in the same year began writing for the *Economist*. During the years of the war and shortly afterwards Isaac Deutscher worked on the editorial staffs of both the *Observer* (under the pen-name Peregrine) and the *Economist* – holding among other positions that of chief European correspondent. After that time he concentrated more on his historical studies but he also lectured and broadcast on radio and television. In 1966–7 he was G. M. Trevelyan Lecturer at Cambridge University.

Isaac Deutscher's many published works include: *A Trotsky Trilogy: The Prophet Armed* (1954), *The Prophet Unarmed* (1959), *The Prophet Outcast* (1963); *Soviet Trade Unions* (1950); *Russia After Stalin* (1953); *Heretics and Renegades* (1955); *The Great Contest* (1960); and *Ironies of History, Essays on Contemporary Communism* (1966). His book, *Stalin, a Political Biography*, is also available in Pelicans.

Isaac Deutscher, who was married and had a son, lived in Hampstead until his death in 1967.

ISAAC DEUTSCHER

Russia, China, and the West

A Contemporary Chronicle, 1953–1966

Edited by
FRED HALLIDAY

PENGUIN BOOKS

Penguin Books Ltd, Harmondsworth,
Middlesex, England
Penguin Books Inc., 7110 Ambassador Road,
Baltimore, Maryland 21207, U.S.A.
Penguin Books Australia Ltd, Ringwood,
Victoria, Australia

First published in hardback by Oxford University Press and in
paperback by Penguin Books, 1970
This selection, Introduction, Commentaries and Chronology
© Oxford University Press, 1970

Made and printed in Great Britain by
Richard Clay (The Chaucer Press) Ltd,
Bungay, Suffolk
Set in Monotype Baskerville

CONTENTS

INTRODUCTION

This volume contains an edited selection of Isaac Deutscher's writings on current affairs from 1953 to 1966. They have been selected from a much larger number of pieces written over the same period, which were published irregularly in numerous journals and newspapers across the world.

These writings form part of Deutscher's total analytic work, and are of permanent importance both for students of this period of history and for students of Marxism. Other pieces of similar importance have appeared in collections such as *Russia in Transition*, *Heretics and Renegades*, and *Ironies of History*; but, while these were collections of separate articles, this book is an attempt to present the texts in a narrative sequence so that they form, in as far as is possible, a continuous commentary on the developments to which they refer. Since Deutscher did not write a systematic history of the period and did not produce a comment on every major event, it has been impossible to create a comprehensive narrative from his different writings; but by arranging the pieces in chapters and by introducing each chapter by a short summary of the historical background to the events described, a considerable degree of continuity has been achieved. In these introductory passages I have tried to show how the events appeared at the time, and for those who are familiar with this period the introductions will be unnecessary; but for those who never experienced, or who have forgotten, the developments of this period the introductory pieces and the chronological table at the end should be of some help.

The full total of Deutscher's writings on current affairs in this period came to about 300,000 words of which about a third is included in this volume. In the first place, no texts that have appeared in other volumes of essays have been included although they would have been of considerable interest. Secondly, I have tried to select those texts that deal with the central themes of Russia, China, and their relations with the West and have thereby had to exclude interesting material on such topics as Russian military strategy, the Korean events of 1960, and the 'thaw' in the United States around 1964–65.

Thirdly, repetitious passages and pieces of short-term interest have been excluded.

The material has been assembled in a number of ways. In some cases the articles that Deutscher wrote have been reprinted as they were written, with a few stylistic changes. In other cases articles have been substantially cut and such cuts have been marked by three dots. Several of the articles that he wrote at one time were divided into two parts and these divisions have in some cases been preserved; in others I have run the two articles together. The titles given to pieces are in some cases those of Deutscher himself and in other cases, where he did not give a title or where a less contemporary title was required, I have provided a new one. The chapter headings and the arrangement into chapters are my own.

These writings form an integral part of Deutscher's work, covering as they do many of the major developments in the communist world over recent years. He was one of the greatest Marxist writers of our time and it was his aim to provide a thorough Marxist analysis of the Soviet Union, from its beginnings up to the present day. For many who had originally supported the Russian Revolution the development of Stalinism seemed to discredit Marxism and entailed its rejection. Others who remained Marxists managed to do so only by shutting their eyes to what was occurring in the Soviet Union. For the former, an honest analysis of Russia was incompatible with Marxism; for the others, every development in the first socialist state was to be defended and loyally supported. It was Deutscher's achievement to transcend the intellectual and political dichotomies of his time. His writings showed not only that the evolution of Soviet Russia did not invalidate Marxism; nor just that Marxists could afford to recognize what was happening in Russia for what it was; but rather that it was only through Marxism and a Marxist analysis of political events that the course of Soviet history could be understood and individual events seen in their historical perspective.[1]

[1] 'I am a Marxist, of course. Those critics who call me "unrepentant", or say that I "will never learn", are for the most part people who once allowed themselves to be well taught by Stalin, and who later became anti-communists. I did not allow myself to be taught by Stalin, nor by Khrushchev, nor even by Mao Tse-tung, and certainly not by Western anti-

Deutscher's major works were his biographies of Trotsky and Stalin, but although his main emphasis lay in explaining the Revolution itself and the leaders of it, he was always conscious of the continuity of the Soviet experience. In analyzing the Russia of the 1950s and 1960s he is constantly aware of the meaning of contemporary events in terms of the Revolution itself. For Deutscher Khrushchev and Kosygin were not only the successors of Lenin and Trotsky but were continuing to fulfil or betray the policies of these earlier leaders. He entitled his Trevelyan lectures *The Unfinished Revolution*: this title summed up his perspective and central concern. The historical meaning of events in contemporary Russia could only be fully understood by a Marxist observer conscious both of the problems and the failure of the first 'socialist' state. Russia today has still to complete the tasks that the Bolsheviks set themselves in 1917. Some commentators analyzed Russia as a static totalitarian monster; others concentrated on trying to show that Russia was getting nearer to capitalism and the bourgeois West. Deutscher rejected both of these approaches and located the development of Russia firmly in the context of socialist history. Marxism as a theoretical system was to be vindicated not only by an analysis of its enemy, capitalism, but also by an analysis of those who claim to be its friends, in Russia or elsewhere.

These writings on post-Stalin Russia and China are complementary to his biographies. The relationship between the two is analogous to that between Marx's journalistic writings on France—*The Class Struggles in France* and *The Eighteenth Brumaire* —and the weightier volumes of *Capital*. In these more analytic works society and historical developments are fully examined and their theoretical implications are investigated; in the

communism. Marxism for me is no infallible theory—such a thing cannot exist. However, as a view of the world and a method of analysis, Marxism in my opinion is in no sense outdated or "surpassed". Probably this will happen one day to Marxism too, but we are still a long way away from that. The people who talk today about "anachronistic Marxism" have not yet offered us anything which is intellectually and politically superior to Marxism.' (From an interview Isaac Deutscher gave to Hamburg Television, 23 July 1967. This translation appeared in *New Left Review*, 47, January–February 1968.)

slighter texts the theoretical elements appear less systematically
but are used to illumine contemporary events.

In addition to this great historical and theoretical sense that
Deutscher brings to his work, these pieces are also important
because they discuss issues that are recurrent and unsolved. The
problems of the unfinished revolution in Russia and of the
legacies of Stalin's rule still remain. The 'socialist' camp has
still not effected a successful transition from monolithic unity
under Russian leadership to a more democratic alliance system.
The events in Czechoslovakia in 1968 would have provided him
with a magnificent opportunity to discuss both the historical
possibilities of a de-Stalinized socialism and the obstacles
created by Stalin's heirs to such a fulfilment. The first publication in a communist country of Deutscher's works was when the
Czech magazines *Student* and *Literary Listy* serialized *The Unfinished Revolution* and excerpts from his *Stalin*. Plans to publish a
full text of the *Stalin* were stopped by the August invasion.[1] The
Sino-Soviet dispute is still of immense importance for the
politics of the whole world and its theoretical issues are central
to the evolution of a socialist policy on revolution and the nature
of post-revolutionary society. When the German problem comes
up again for discussion the issues and interest of the debates of
the 1950s will remain.

When Deutscher's analyses of current events first appeared,
many of them were rejected with disbelief as they contradicted
the prevailing orthodoxy of the day. Bertrand Russell tells how
his immediate scepticism about Deutscher's analysis was later
dispelled:

In the period before Hungary and Suez, the late Isaac Deutscher
used to visit me at my home in Richmond. I would sit silently as he
propounded his views on the cold war. His scrupulous weighing of
the evidence and his balanced presentation of opposing views were
always scholarly, but I remained unconvinced. For me, Stalin's
terror and the introduction of the one-party state throughout
Eastern Europe, following the purges and mock trials of the Thirties,

---

[1] *Pravda,* in its famous editorial of 22 August 1968, wrote *inter alia*:
'The Czechoslovak press willingly opened their columns to writings of
outright adversaries of Marxism-Leninism. It is enough to recall the publication in many Czechoslovak periodicals of articles by the well-known
Trotskyite Isaac Deutscher, as well as excerpts from his book.'

made unorthodoxy unpalatable, even unthinkable. Ten years later, however, Deutscher was more persuasive. At a teach-in at Berkeley, California, in May 1965, he summarized his view of the cold war. Russia had lost 20 million dead in the Second World War and countless millions wounded. The war had been fought over its territory backwards and forwards, with a ferocity unknown in the West, and its industry and economy were in ruins. This was the nation supposedly poised to overrun the rest of Europe to the Atlantic.[1]

His analysis of the Sino-Soviet dispute was also greeted with disbelief by those who were confident of the permanent unity of the communist bloc; today his analysis has been clearly justified.

Deutscher was not always correct in his predictions; no writer on current affairs ever could be. But the value of his analysis and predictions, true or false, lay in his constant awareness of the broader significance of individual events and of their relationship to underlying political trends in Soviet history. In the Introduction to *The Great Contest* Deutscher himself described his approach to issues of current foreign policy which contrasted with those who viewed international politics in an immediate day-to-day perspective:

. . . the foreign policy of any government, especially of the Soviet Government, is a prolongation of its domestic policy. This is all too often forgotten in a period of 'summit' meetings, when the public is led to believe that three or four Big Men solve, or fail to solve, the world's predicaments according to whether they have or do not have the wisdom, the good will, or the magic wand needed to their task. I have endeavoured to concentrate attention on the essential motives and long-term aspirations of Soviet policy and to probe the 'stalemate of fears' that characterizes the present state of world diplomacy.

This concern for the 'essential motives and long-term aspirations' behind current events runs through the writings in this volume. The immediacy and freshness of current affairs is fused with the long-term perspective of history.

In conclusion I would like to express my gratitude to Tamara Deutscher for all her help in editing these papers of her

[1] *New Statesman*, 15 March 1968.

late husband and for her original offer to me that I should attempt such an edition. Her advice, encouragement, and patience have been of invaluable assistance.

The pieces reprinted in this volume are drawn from Deutscher's syndicated articles. The articles were not necessarily printed by any of the papers and magazines to which they were sent, and those that did publish them may have altered and edited them. These publications included the following: *The Sydney Morning Herald* (Australia); *Estado de São Paulo* (Brazil); *Winnipeg Free Press* and *Montreal Star* (Canada); *Ceylon Daily News*; *L'Express* and *Nouvel Observateur* (France); *Deutsche Zeitung* (Germany); *To Vima* (Greece); *The Statesman* (India); *Davar* (Israel); *Corriere della Sera* and *L'Espresso* (Italy); *Asahi Shimbun* (Japan); *The Press* (New Zealand); *Dagbladet* (Norway); *The Times*, *The Observer*, and *New Statesman* (U.K.); *The Reporter* and *The Nation* (U.S.A.).

London, 18 April 1969   Fred Halliday

1
The Fall of Beria

On Stalin's death in March 1953, the Soviet leaders established a collective leadership, with Malenkov as Prime Minister and Khrushchev as Party Secretary. This was followed at the end of March by the announcement of a limited amnesty and on 3 April the charges brought against the Kremlin doctors were dropped.

These moves represented a lessening of the power of the secret police, headed since 1938 by Lavrenti Beria. Known as 'the man who purged the purgers', he had been a close associate of Stalin's. On 10 July it was announced that he had been dismissed from his post as Minister of the Interior and arrested. He was accused in general of being an 'enemy of the people'; more specifically he was alleged to have worked for British Intelligence since 1919 when it supposedly contacted him in Azerbaijan; he was also accused of fostering bourgeois nationalism, of undermining the collective leadership, and of attempting to use the secret police to seize power for himself. It soon emerged that the abortive rising in East Germany in the previous month was also a contributory factor in Beria's fall, and that he had probably advocated a more liberal policy there. Whatever the truth of this accusation, there was no mention of it at the time.

Although arrested in July, Beria and his associates were not tried until December. His trial began on 12 December; it was announced on 23 December that he had been found guilty and executed at once.

1 BEFORE THE TRIAL

In 1938, when Beria became the Chief of the Soviet political police (N.K.V.D. as it was then called), Trotsky, in his Mexican refuge, made the grim forecast that Beria would not escape the fate of Yagoda and Yezhov, Beria's two predecessors in office who had been purged by Stalin. The prediction has now come true. Charged with high treason, terroristic acts, and attempts to wreck his country's defences, Beria is about to take his place in the dock.

The indictment of Beria and his associates follows closely the pattern established in the great purge trials of 1936–38. Not only is the defendant declared guilty of unimaginable crimes committed recently. His 'moral depravity' is traced back to the earliest stages of his political career. Beria is now said to have played a dual role almost all his adult life. Like, for example, Bukharin before him he is alleged to have been in the pay of the British and other foreign intelligence services, since at least 1919. And, as if to throw into relief the element of continuity with the previous purge trials and their nightmarish confessions, the Soviet State Prosecutor has hastened to announce that Beria and his co-defendants have already confessed their crimes.

Even in this era of universal witch-hunting the fantastic nature of the charge that Stalin's friend, countryman, relative, biographer, chief bodyguard, and chief security officer has for thirty-five years been in the pay of foreign espionage services should be evident to every thinking person. From the advance summary of the accusation it is already clear that this charge will to the end sound empty and hollow, because the State Prosecutor cannot substantiate it with any specific piece of evidence, direct or circumstantial. . . .

In the indictment of Beria only one count, the one speaking of his terroristic acts, is formulated with a slight touch of realism. It is indeed quite possible that Beria climbed the ladder of the political police over the dead body of Kedrov, Dzerzhinsky's assistant in the early days of the Soviet political police. It is also plausible that he intrigued against Ordjonikidze, another Georgian and Stalin's old friend and Commissar of Heavy Industry, who is now said to have distrusted Beria and opposed his promotion. (About Ordjonikidze's death in 1937 and its mysterious circumstances the most lurid versions have circulated for many years.) But if Beria climbed over corpses of rivals and opponents, so did Stalin and all his associates including Molotov, Kaganovich, Voroshilov, Malenkov, and others. How was it that Beria was not unmasked in Stalin's lifetime? Did Stalin perhaps know about his crimes? Was he himself perhaps Beria's abetter?

In the charges about Beria's terroristic acts there is another element of truth, although its meaning is quite different from that given to it by the Soviet Prosecutor. Beria has undoubtedly planned and committed many terroristic acts. But these acts were not directed against the ruling group. On the contrary, they were committed on its behalf and directed against the people. Malenkov, Molotov, and their friends are therefore broadly co-responsible for all of Beria's offences on this count.

This precisely may be the reason why they have decided to stage his trial. By blackening Beria they hope to whitewash themselves.[1] He is to be their scapegoat. On his head they try to put all their iniquities and 'all their transgressions and all their sins'. . . . They are aware that the masses are yearning to see the police state undone and replaced by a more democratic form of government. They know that the people will applaud them for the victimization of Beria and his associates.

Unfortunately, there is every reason to suspect that the Soviet ruling group is at present merely cheating the popular hope for more freedom. Even while it is staging a spectacle which looks like the burial of Stalin's political police, the spirit of Stalinism at its worst can be felt in this spectacle.

Note, in the first instance, that most of the defendants are Georgians and Ukrainians accused of being hostile towards Russia. It will be remembered that, during his Hundred Days after Stalin's death, Beria proclaimed an end to the policy of Russification and dismissed Russifiers from high office in Kiev, Kharkov, and Tiflis. His trial is the Russifiers' revenge. Malenkov evidently appeals not only to popular hopes for freedom and to the popular hatred of the police; he appeals also to Great Russian pride and prejudice, the emotions which Stalin so

[1] When Khrushchev and Bulganin visited London in 1956 they were asked by Isaac Deutscher at a press conference whether Beria was also responsible for the assassination of Trotsky. They gave no reply.

unscrupulously whipped up and exploited. It should not be forgotten, however, that the humiliation of the smaller nationalities always goes hand in hand with the oppression of everybody including the Great Russians.

The spirit of Stalinism at its worst shows itself even more strikingly in the announcement that the defendants have already confessed their guilt. Only a short time ago the Soviet people were led to believe that Stalin's successors were doing away with the 'confession', that characteristic feature of Stalinist 'justice'. The government then stated that the Ministry of State Security had invented the plot of the Kremlin doctors and by lawless methods coerced the doctors to admit their guilt. The rehabilitation of the doctors was the most telling blow ever inflicted on the political police, inflicted while Beria was in power and largely by Beria himself. But the die-hards of the political police, who have had allies in other quarters, have apparently refused to resign the 'right' to extort confessions, for this has been the most effective weapon by means of which they have kept the Soviet people in awe and subjection. . . .

17 December 1953

2 BERIA IS SHOT

The execution of Lavrenti Beria and his six associates has hardly shocked the world or even caused much surprise. The hangman hanged does not arouse sympathy. . . . Yet in some respects his trial was very surprising, even startling. To see just how surprising, it is enough to compare it with any of the great trials of 1936–38, in which the Bolshevik Old Guard was destroyed. . . .

In the first instance the atmosphere around the Beria affair has been much calmer than that which surrounded the affairs of Zinoviev, Kamenev, Bukharin, or Yagoda. No hysteria comparable to that of 1936–38 has been worked up. No piercing cry 'Shoot the mad dogs', a cry so memorable for its savagery, accompanied Beria to the dock. One had the impression that Beria's triumphant enemies were anxious to wind up this sordid affair quickly and without much ado and to pass on to other business. . . .

A somewhat closer look at the men in the dock is also revealing. By Beria's side we see Merkulov, former Minister of State Security, who was in charge of the mammoth forced labour camps during the 1940s; V. G. Dekanozov, B. Z. Kobulov, S. A. Goglidze, P. Y. Meshik, and L. E. Vlodzimirsky, all former heads of the political police in Georgia and the Ukraine and chiefs of departments at its Moscow headquarters. Not a single 'outsider' was added to them. The dramatic exclusiveness with which the limelight was focused on the bosses of the police was certainly not fortuitous. Nothing like it had ever happened before.

Beria's enemies intended to tell the Soviet people that in destroying Beria they were not just eliminating a rival but were destroying nothing less than arbitrary police rule. This was the *leitmotiv* of the whole performance. There was, of course, a ring of falsity about it: police rule is not abolished by means of phoney accusations and secret trials. But what is significant is again the relation of the trial to the climate of opinion, a climate hostile to police rule and compelling the ruling group to adapt itself to public opinion even now, after a certain reaction had set in in their midst against the quasi-liberal reforms of the first months of the post-Stalin era.

The haste with which the Beria affair was handled in its final phase may have been due to a sudden accentuation of rivalry among Beria's enemies. Signs of growing competition for power between Malenkov and Khrushchev have not been lacking; and both may have been anxious to get Beria finally out of the way before they come to grips with one another.

It would, however, be mistaken to view the whole development merely as the Party leaders' personal competition for Stalin's place. From the beginning, this competition has been merged with controversies over domestic and foreign policies; and in this connection the year 1953 stands out in the annals of the Soviet Union as a year during which Soviet policy fluctuated and changed with far more than average intensity. But even the Party leaders' personal rivalry for power is now complicated by the visibly growing political role of the army leaders. Significantly, the court which tried Beria was presided over by Marshal Koniev.

This is another quite unprecedented feature of the latest

trial; and it would take a lot of argument-stretching to explain it on grounds of judicial procedure. In 1937 Marshal Voroshilov conducted Tukhachevsky's trial; but what he presided over was a court martial: both the judges' bench and the dock were then crowded exclusively with Marshals and Generals. The court over which Marshal Koniev presided was predominantly and essentially civilian—only one other soldier, General Moskalenko, sat on it. Among its civilian members were the Party leaders Shvernik and Mikhailov. After Stalin's death, when Beria was at the height of his power, Shvernik ceased to be President of the Republic; there was therefore a touch of revenge in his presence among Beria's judges. Yet it was not these civilian second-rate Party leaders but the imposing figure of Marshal Koniev that dominated the court.

This was no regular judicial body but a court, especially appointed for this occasion by the Supreme Soviet. The appointments were intended as a political demonstration. As he looked up to the judges' bench, Beria saw on it the representatives of that coalition of interests that had defeated him: army leaders, stalwarts of Stalinism, and his own police in revolt against him.

26 December 1953

2
The Development of
Soviet Foreign Policy in 1954

The central issue of European politics after 1945 was the question
of Germany. The initial agreement at Potsdam gave way to the
conflicts of the cold war and the crisis of the Berlin airlift,
1948–49. Germany was then divided into two states: a German
Federal Republic supported by the West, and a German
Democratic Republic, supported by the Soviet Union. In June
1953, three months after the death of Stalin, there was a workers'
uprising in the German Democratic Republic which was sparked
off by an increase in work 'norms' and a decrease in wages.
Demonstrations in Leipzig on 16 June spread to Berlin and many
other cities by the 17th and the G.D.R. government, after some
hesitation, suppressed the demonstration with Soviet tanks. It was
not at first clear that this rising was related in a direct way to the
conflict within the Soviet Party leadership, but after some months
it became known that Beria had advocated a more relaxed policy
in Germany and that the June rising had contributed to his
downfall and arrest in the following month. The question
of Germany continued to preoccupy the leaders of East and
West and led to the Berlin Foreign Ministers Conference in
1954.

The Berlin conference of January–February 1954 was the first
conference to unite the foreign ministers of the Big Four for five
years. It had been preceded in the previous year by a more
conciliatory tone in Soviet statements on foreign policy and by an
emphasis on the possibility of a peaceful resolution of existing
problems. This optimistic atmosphere was dispelled by the Berlin
conference since, although the foreign ministers wished to settle
their differences peacefully, this did not enable them to agree
which of the possible alternative peaceful solutions they should
adopt.

The only thing they did agree on at the conference was to convene another conference at Geneva in April to discuss the Far East. They made no progress on the two central issues—Germany and Austria. Molotov proposed that a coalition government drawn equally from both German states be set up, and that Germany be neutralized under such a government. He did not accept the Western demand for free elections since, he pointed out, Hitler had come to power by such means. The Western foreign ministers, on the other hand, rejected Molotov's proposals on the grounds that there must be free elections prior to the establishment of any unified German government and because they refused to recognize the government of the German Democratic Republic as a partner to any solution. Confronted with this opposition, Molotov rejected any solution of the Austrian problem without a German settlement as well. He was particularly strong in his warnings about the rise of a new German militarism. The West German government had been a party to the agreement, signed in Bonn in May 1952, for the setting up of a European Army to form the European Defence Community. This project had not yet been ratified by the parliaments of the signatory governments, but it was seen by the Russians as a means of rearming West Germany and encouraging a resurgent German militarism.

The Geneva conference on the Far East met from April to July 1954 and discussed both Korea and Indo-China. No progress was made on Korea and the Armistice Agreement of July 1953 remained in force. On Indo-China a solution was facilitated by two events that took place during the conference: on 7 May the French base at Dien Bien Phu fell to the Vietminh, thus confirming the collapse of the French position in Vietnam; and in June the Laniel-Bidault government in Paris was replaced by that of Pierre Mendès-France, who was opposed to the E.D.C. plan and threatened to resign if he did not reach an agreement with the Vietminh by 20 July.

A settlement was agreed on in time whereby Vietnam was partitioned at the seventeenth parallel, with elections to be held within two years to reunify the country. The French remained in the Southern half, but their position was rapidly taken over by the Americans who had refused to participate at Geneva owing to the presence of a delegation from the People's Republic of

China. They would not sign the final agreement, although they made a vague promise to respect it.

Mendès-France's government remained in office, and on 30 August the E.D.C. Treaty was rejected by the French National Assembly; but the main purpose of this—to get West Germany into a military alliance with the West—was soon achieved in the London and Paris agreements.

1 SOVIET POLICY TOWARDS
GERMANY A YEAR AFTER STALIN

Since the Berlin Conference of the Foreign Ministers the commentators and propagandists of East and West, and the foreign ministers themselves, have been busy explaining the conference as 'neither-success-nor-failure'. The results of the conference are described as disappointing but not hopeless. The Soviet people have been told that the Western Powers have refused to consider Soviet proposals for the unification of Germany, the withdrawal of occupation troops, and the reduction of armaments; and that they have made agreement impossible by their insistence on rearming Western Germany. In the West the deadlock is ascribed primarily to the Russian opposition to free elections which would sweep away the Pieck-Ulbricht administration in the Soviet zone; and the motives of Soviet diplomacy seem as obscure and sinister as ever. Some commentators have seized, not without some *Schadenfreude*, on the results of the Berlin conference to repeat the assurance that there has been no change in Soviet policy since Stalin's death.

What is the truth of the matter? The view that there has been 'no change' can hardly be squared with the facts and, in the first instance, with the obvious fact of an international detente, temporary and transient perhaps, but not devoid of significance. By the time of Stalin's death, the Korean war was dragging on with no visible prospect of a cease-fire; and on all sectors of the cold-war front the conflict was growing in bitterness and intensity. The state of 'neither-war-nor-peace' which prevailed a year earlier was much nearer to war than to peace. That state still persists but it is certainly further from war and nearer to peace.

The truth is that there has been not one but several distinct and less distinct changes in Soviet foreign policy since Stalin's death. To be sure, these changes do not imply any revision of the 'fundamental', 'ideological' communist attitude of the Russian government towards the West. Malenkov, Molotov, and Khrushchev have not ceased to take it for granted that, historically, capitalism is doomed and communism destined to be victorious. This, however, seems more or less irrelevant to the evaluation of Soviet foreign policy after Stalin. Within the framework of the same 'fundamental' attitude Russia's rulers can pursue the most divergent policies; and it is on those policies, as well as on the policies of the West, and not on fundamental ideology that peace and war depend. Catholic and Protestant Powers used to fight devastating wars and then, without ever revising their theological notions, to have long spells of peace and co-operation. Even in the seventeenth century those who suggested that there was no chance of a political accommodation between Catholic and Protestant as long as the one or the other did not modify his beliefs were considered simpletons or hotheads. Can it be that the fanatics of the religious wars were sober and clearsighted men in comparison with the cold-war strategists?

A change in Soviet foreign policy is, of course, a change in 'tactics' and 'operational plans', not more. But it is the changes in tactics that to a large extent make contemporary history. Suppose that Stalin had decided not to back the communist upheaval in Czechoslovakia in 1948 and had resolved that Czechoslovakia could well wait for a communist regime until, say, 1968; or that he had installed in Soviet-occupied Austria an Austrian version of the Pieck-Ulbricht regime in 1949 or 1951. Some commentators may remark profoundly that these would have been merely tactical decisions; maybe, but it is on decisions of this sort that the international situation depends, and it is over decisions of this or even of a higher order that Soviet policy has fluctuated and vacillated since Stalin's death more than at any time in recent years.

It is a mistake to see Soviet foreign policy as static, fixed, and closed in itself. The behaviour of Soviet diplomacy is, of course, affected by controversies and alignments within the ruling group and by many domestic pressures and even more so by foreign ones. The changing balance of those pressures is reflected in the pattern of diplomatic moves. In a critical period that balance changes more swiftly and dramatically than in normal times. Soviet foreign policy since Stalin's death has at times been like a see-saw in full swing. It has changed position several times. True enough, at certain moments the see-saw occupies a position very much like the one that it occupied before Stalin died. But those who see only this and therefore assume that there has been no change have missed the real significance of the picture.

To this day the East German revolt of 16–17 June 1953 remains in Moscow's eyes the most important single event of the post-Stalin era, the event that marked the transition of post-Stalin diplomacy from one phase to another. Up to that date the Kremlin was seriously considering a military and political withdrawal from Eastern Germany, a withdrawal which would have left the Pieck-Ulbricht regime to its own fate, that is to collapse in ignominy. The Kremlin was then evidently inclined to assume that at this price a general and relatively lasting detente between East and West could be obtained. All Soviet moves made in Germany and Austria before the middle of June were designed to set the stage for the withdrawal. (Beria was later accused of having worked for the surrender of Eastern Germany to world capitalism; and this accusation, unlike some other charges levelled against him, was no mere invention.)

The direct consequence of 16 and 17 June was the abandonment by the Kremlin of the idea of a real withdrawal at least in the near future. Stalin's successors decided that for the time being they must hold on to all their positions on the Elbe and the Danube and show no sign of vacillation or weakness. The new 'line' was gradually evolved in Molotov's series of notes to the Western Powers sent out by him between 4 August and 26 November. These notes anticipated all that Molotov had to say at the Berlin conference in February.

This then is the grim paradox of the East German revolt: the East Germans hoped that their 'direct action' would speed up the collapse of the Pieck-Ulbricht regime, which in early June looked as if it had already been half dismantled. The result achieved was the exact opposite: the revolt compelled the Kremlin to prop up the Pieck-Ulbricht regime in the most spectacular and demonstrative manner.

Russia's rulers are accustomed to formulating political plans in terms of military strategy. We may therefore obtain a better insight into their reasoning if we, too, view the situation in East Germany after 17 June in such terms.

Retreat is the most dangerous of all possible military (and political) operations. If a retreating army is overwhelmed by unexpected enemy pressure, if its ranks lose confidence, and, what is much worse, if it finds that its avenues of retreat are cut, the retreat may assume a panicky character and turn into a rout. In such circumstances a commander cannot afford a retreat, desirable as it may be from other viewpoints; he orders his troops to dig in or to counter-attack.

The June revolt gave Russia's rulers the warning that a retreat from Germany was likely to turn into a rout. The 'enemy' (i.e. the Western Powers *and* the people of Eastern Germany—the Kremlin had no doubt where the latter's sympathy lay) was not allowing them to stage an *orderly* withdrawal. Moscow could well afford to dismantle its East German puppet regime, to readmit the banned Social Democratic Party in the Soviet zone, and to form a new, more broadly based government to take the place of Pieck and Grotewohl; and Russian representatives in Berlin confidentially foreshadowed such moves in talks with German non-communist politicians. But from the Russian viewpoint these moves would have been worth while only if they could be made to appear as Russia's own policy pursued under no external compulsion, and carried out by those non-communist Germans who, like the old ex-Chancellor Wirth, were willing to act in 'friendly agreement' with Moscow. This would have been that orderly withdrawal in which Russia would have suffered as little loss of face as possible and which would not have any adverse effect on her power position outside Germany.

After the June revolt any major political concession by Russia, let alone a withdrawal, would have been seen as a revelation of Russia's weakness. Poles and Czechs, Romanians and Bulgarians, and Russians and Ukrainians, too, would have drawn their conclusions. From Berlin the revolt might have spread like wildfire throughout the Soviet orbit. The Western Powers left Russia, Eastern Europe, and Eastern Germany in no doubt that this was what they were hoping for. American broadcasting stations more or less openly called on Eastern Europe to rise. The 'enemy' was cutting Russia's avenues of retreat. All thought of retreat had to be given up. The policy of appeasement in Eastern Germany was at an end. The Pieck and Ulbricht regime was saved. The order of the day was to dig in.

To dig in or to counter-attack? This was in all probability the question hotly debated in the inner councils of the Kremlin between June and November. The reaction against appeasement reached its peak in October and November. From the eloquent friendliness of the spring months Moscow relapsed into a mood of boorish sullenness and was not at all eager for negotiations with the West; Molotov even failed to acknowledge the invitation to a conference in Lugano the Western Powers had addressed to him. But this phase did not last long. In Berlin Molotov was all smiles. But his standing orders were still the same: no withdrawal, no surrender of a single position, no display of weakness.

Excessive fear of showing weakness is itself a sign of weakness. At times Molotov behaved like a man sitting on a ridge and refusing to budge for fear that his movement might disturb the snow and provoke an avalanche. (But has this not at times also been the attitude of the Western foreign ministers?)

Stalin's successors are still racking their brains for some method of putting Stalin's legacy in foreign affairs into order. A year after Stalin's death they are still engaged in the attempt to disentangle the enormous assets of that legacy from its dangerous liabilities. Nowhere are the liabilities as dangerous, the assets as questionable, and the disentanglement as difficult as in Eastern Germany.

The problem is still whether Russia can retreat from Eastern Germany without being routed in the process. Will the Western Powers make possible an orderly retreat, and on what terms? Or, since Russia cannot withdraw as long as the Western Powers stay in Germany, are all Powers condemned to cling to their present positions? . . . Despite their public statements it is difficult to believe that Stalin's successors are as alarmed at the threat of a revival of German militarism as Molotov pretended at the Berlin conference. The talk about this seems somewhat parochial and anachronistic. Soviet propagandists understandably play upon the memories of German invasions and of the terrors that accompanied them; and they stir the popular fear of repetition. But what the propagandists say is not necessarily what the rulers think: the latter are well able to gauge the historic change which has occurred in the relationship between Russia and Germany, the change which makes it impossible for German militarism to resume the role it played *vis-à-vis* Russia in two world wars.

In 1914–18 Germany, fighting on two fronts, delivered with only one hand the knock-out blow against Russia. In 1941–42 Hitler, having thrown the bulk of his forces against Russia, failed by a narrow margin to achieve a similar result. Russia's victory in 1945 and the developments of the first post-war decade have so profoundly altered the balance of power that Germany, even if unified and rearmed to the teeth, can hardly ever again constitute a major and independent threat to Russia.

One need not be a Marxist to hold that the military power of a nation is as strong as the economy that supports it. To Russia's rulers this is an axiom. In this connection the prodigious progress of Soviet industrialization since the Second World War is of the greatest consequence. . . . In any abstract, yet quite relevant, comparison based on present relations, the industrial and military potential of a unified and fully rearmed Germany would have to be put at merely one third of the Russian potential. . . .

Contrary to popular belief, the spectre of a rearmed Germany does not cause a single sleepless night to the men in the Kremlin, who know perfectly well how many sleepless nights that spectre must cause to Germany's Western European neighbours. (Germany has grown so much weaker only in relation to Russia, not in relation to Britain and France.)

Nor are Stalin's successors gravely perturbed by the threat of the European Defence Community which they see to be so slow in materializing and so strongly handicapped by internal rifts and by the relative strength of communism in Western Europe. A West German *Wehrmacht* and even a European army would from the Soviet viewpoint be only the spearhead of American military power. It is American military power, its bases built up around the Soviet bloc, and its presence in Europe that give rise to genuine fear in Moscow. At the Berlin conference Molotov proclaimed openly, although not without hesitation, that the elimination of American military power from Europe is the major objective of Soviet diplomacy. On this all shades of opinion within the Soviet ruling group agree. Controversy can centre only on the question of whether a conciliatory or a tough policy is more likely to achieve this objective. Immediately after Stalin's death the conciliators had the upper hand. The June events in East Germany defeated the conciliators and strengthened the opponents of appeasement; but policy has since then been shaped not by the extreme groups but by the 'trimmers' for whom Malenkov and Molotov seem to speak.

Paradoxically, a revived *Wehrmacht* may well be expected in Moscow to help in speeding up an American withdrawal from Europe. This might from the Russian viewpoint be the redeeming feature of Germany's rearmament by the West. It is Molotov's policy to obstruct and delay the revival of Germany's armed forces as long as possible, but after that to make the best of a new situation. Molotov and his colleagues see the 'European outlook' of the Adenauer regime as a sham and hold that the Bonn government is interested only in reconstituting Germany's armed forces behind the façade of E.D.C. Once those forces are reconstituted, Western Germany will cease to be the well-behaved, democratic, and European-minded adherent of the Atlantic bloc which she must act as long as she is disarmed and under Western occupation. Rearmed she will aspire to play an independent role. Only then, Moscow apparently hopes, will the real contradiction between Germany and the West come to the surface; and only then will it be possible for Western Germany to resume a policy of balancing between East and West and of bargaining with both. Once the bargaining begins, Germany may be even more eager to make deals with Russia than with the West, because she will be more afraid of Russia, and Russia may have more to offer in territorial adjustments, concessions, trade, etc. Thus it may be that only a Germany rearmed by the West can become the neutral buffer that Molotov wishes her to be. It would be too much to suggest that this is Moscow's firm expectation. But this is a consideration which is certainly always present in calculation of policy. . . .

5 March 1954

2 THE GENEVA CONFERENCE ON
THE FAR EAST

When Molotov made his report on the Geneva conference in
the inner councils of the Kremlin, he may have summed it up
as follows: 'We have given up, Comrades, many of the local
advantages we held in Indo-China, but we hope to have
gained one general advantage for the Soviet bloc: the armistice
in Indo-China will promote the international detente for which
we have been striving since Stalin's death.'

It is indeed in the context of broad international strategy
that the communist attitude over Indo-China ought to be seen.
The armistice signed in Geneva makes little or no sense from
the viewpoint of the Vietminh alone. It does not in any way
correspond to the local balance of strength which has been
much more favourable to the Vietminh than are the terms of
the armistice. True enough, Ho Chi Minh and his colleagues
have now ceased to be 'rebels' and have become an internationally recognized government; the troops of Southern Vietnam
are in retreat; and the French expeditionary force is about to
evacuate towns, harbours, strongpoints, and outposts. But what
the Vietminh obtain is, by common consent of all observers,
only part of the ripe fruit of their recent political and military
victories. If the struggle had continued, Ho Chi Minh's armies
might, in a few sweeping offensives, have conquered the whole
of Indo-China as Mao Tse-tung's armies conquered the whole
of China. Mao Tse-tung's victory of 1949 came as a surprise to
Moscow; but neither Moscow nor Peking had had any doubt
about Ho Chi Minh's ability to bring the whole of Indo-China
under his control. It must have taken them some effort to
persuade Ho Chi Minh to stop half-way, and some people in
Ho Chi Minh's entourage and in the rank and file of his armies
may well resent the Geneva 'betrayal'.

It will be remembered that at one point during the civil war
in China Stalin tried to curb Mao Tse-tung and to persuade
him that he should not march into Nanking and Canton. Mao
Tse-tung was strong and independent enough to ignore Stalin's
advice. Ho Chi Minh, however, could not pursue the war
against Molotov's and Chou En-lai's advice. He has had to

accept the demarcation line on the seventeenth parallel; and he has had to agree to a postponement of elections for two years, during which the popularity of his party may well decline from its present peak. He has had to withdraw from Laos and Cambodia and to recognize France's right to move her military forces into both these states, a right hitherto fiercely denounced. He has even had to guarantee solemnly the inviolability of French property and French interests throughout the area where his writ runs.

From any communist viewpoint these are major concessions. Why were they made? In Geneva neither Molotov nor Chou En-lai explained their motives. Yet their motives are not far to seek. They have made these concessions in expectation of greater diplomatic settlements elsewhere. Since Western diplomacy has disdainfully declined any sort of 'global bargaining' there was no talk or suggestion of this, even—so we are told—during the long, private conversations between ministers at Geneva. However, this does not alter the fact that global bargaining has been inherent in the situation, or at any rate in Molotov's view of the situation. He has been willing to observe the etiquette of non-bargaining, if Western diplomacy whimsically insists on it, but he has distinguished etiquette from the substance of things. Tacitly and implicitly he has been engaged in global bargaining all these months, bargaining space against time, and positions in Asia against positions in Europe.

This is apparent even from the terms of the Geneva agreements. Under these no South East Asia Treaty Organization, sponsored by the United States or by the United States and Britain, can cover Southern Vietnam, Laos, or Cambodia. No American military base may be established in any part of Indo-China, although the areas south of the seventeenth parallel and Laos remain a zone of French military influence. Indirectly France herself is committed to keep aloof from any American military initiative in that part of Asia. The fact that Indo-China remains barred to American military power is likely to affect the mood of some other South-East Asian nations. It is bound to confirm India in its attitude of neutrality.

The leaders of the Soviet bloc may well calculate that, if they succeed in the neutralization of South-East Asia, then the whole of the Middle East will also prefer to keep aloof from military entanglements. One of the repercussions of the cease-fire in Indo-China may be to weaken or even eventually to destroy the American-built military 'bridge' joining Pakistan with Turkey.

In Geneva the Soviet bloc has been sufficiently strong to be able, for the first time, to set up something like a neutral zone between itself and the military power of the United States. It now becomes the purpose of the Soviet bloc to interpose between itself and the Atlantic bloc a vast and more or less continuous buffer zone in both Asia and Europe. Molotov's successful essay in the neutralization of most of Indo-China is to be followed by analogous essays elsewhere; the other end of the buffer zone, which stretches from the Gulf of Tonking, should lie between the Oder and the Rhine.

The idea of 'peaceful coexistence between different systems' is now apparently being re-interpreted in Moscow and Peking; and it is giving rise to a diplomatic and political conception more specific than that which prevailed in Stalin's days. Peaceful coexistence is now held to require first that antagonistic regimes should in fact stop fighting each other arms in hand, and, second, that they should, if possible, be well insulated from one another. It is in these two points that the evolution of Soviet diplomacy can best be seen. In Geneva Soviet diplomacy has now put its signature under the second armistice —the first being the Korean—concluded in the relatively short time since Stalin's death: Moscow has considered the two armistice agreements as preliminaries to peaceful coexistence and it sees a continuous zone of neutral states, stretching across Asia and Europe, as an essential condition and guarantee of peaceful coexistence. Molotov acted in line with this conception when, on the day after the neutralization of much of Indo-China, he confronted the Western Powers with a renewed proposal for the neutralization of Germany.

The idea of a Eurasian buffer zone may be too neat and tidy for practical diplomacy and politics. It presupposes not only the suspension of armed fighting but a truce in class and ideological warfare throughout the buffer zone. And, what is just as important, a buffer country must have internal unity and must be integrated in order to be able to keep its balance between the two power blocs. The Geneva conference, however, has produced the opposite of this—a new partition. Vietnam has now joined the ranks of Germany, Austria, and Korea, the countries split or broken up by the conflicting pulls of antagonistic powers. True, the Geneva agreement provides for the holding of elections throughout Vietnam in 1956 and for consequent reunification. But after the experience of Korea and Germany the promise of reunification carries little conviction: it seems quite realistic to assume that Vietnam will remain partitioned long after 1956; and that once again *le provisoire* will prove the most lasting part of the settlement.

This then is the dangerous paradox confronting the Soviet bloc. Its diplomacy, apprehensive of the potentialities of war, tries to set up a Eurasian buffer zone only to discover that it is precisely inside that buffer area that lie the main storm centres of international politics. Korea, Germany, Austria, Indo-China as long as they are divided, provide an abundance of causes and pretexts for war and near-war. . . .

26 July 1954

3 A NEW COURSE IN MOSCOW: RUSSIA AND CHINA

Moscow is carrying out a significant revision of its policy towards China and towards the East European members of the Soviet bloc. A New Course, contrasting sharply with the practices of the Stalin era, has been initiated. Its purpose is to give Russia's allies the feeling that they are no longer bullied puppets, that Stalin's successors intend to respect their national pride and susceptibilities and will have nothing to do with any quasi-imperialist exploitation of their weakness. . . .

Red China has so far been the chief beneficiary of the new policy exemplified in the agreements concluded between Khrushchev and Mao Tse-tung on 12 October, when a large Soviet delegation, including several members of the Presidium of the Soviet Communist Party, attended the celebration in Peking of the fifth anniversary of the People's Republic of China.

Already the size and the character of the Soviet delegation was unprecedented: in Stalin's days it was unthinkable that so many members of the Politbureau should simultaneously pay a visit to a foreign country. More remarkable, of course, are the agreements signed. To begin with, Russia has agreed to evacuate the naval base of Port Arthur before the end of May 1955. Thus Stalin's successors are relinquishing the strategic trump card which Stalin had obtained at Yalta after hard bargaining and to the beating of all his chauvinistic Great Russian drums. Stalin had obtained that card at the expense of Chiang Kai-shek's regime; but even after Mao's advent he used it not only to defend Russia's and China's common military interests, but also to exercise pressure on China, to control Manchuria indirectly, and to blackmail Mao into obedience. To the Chinese the Russian occupation of Port Arthur was a standing insult; and so the withdrawal is naturally received as a gesture of 'socialist disinterestedness and generosity'.

However, the evacuation of Port Arthur is dictated by the change in the situation in the Far East as much as by the new mood in Moscow. Even Stalin, in his last years, was anxious not to offend Chinese sentiment and was quite willing to give up some of the Yalta acquisitions. He returned to China the Far Eastern (Manchurian) Railway. He withdrew from Manchuria. And as early as February 1950 he promised to evacuate Port Arthur. But having made the promise he was in no hurry to carry it out. Later, when the Korean war dragged on, it was Mao who requested that the Russians should delay evacuation because he saw in the Russian presence in Port Arthur a deterrent to the possible extension of the war to Manchuria. The cessation of hostilities in Korea has lifted the danger from Manchuria. Moscow has no desire to see hostilities renewed and it reckons with the continuation of the present state of affairs in Korea.

The evacuation of Port Arthur follows perhaps logically from the changed situation; but under Stalin the Russians might have acted illogically and stayed on. For once perhaps Soviet and Chinese propagandists tell the truth when they claim that the evacuation is a token of Russia's confidence in the main-tenance of peace in the Far East, in China's growing strength, and in the unperturbed future of the Russo-Chinese alliance.

Basing their policy on these assumptions the Russians have

taken a calculated strategic risk in the hope that the risk will be greatly outweighed by the moral advantages to be gained by their move. Throughout Asia Russia's action is going to be acclaimed: Asians know only very few instances, if any, in which a great Western Power has given up a first-rate strategic base on foreign territory other than under direct hostile pressure from another Power or under the immediate threat of a revolt in the occupied country. Throughout Asia Chinese and Soviet propagandists will contrast Russia's 'voluntary' evacuation of Port Arthur with Britain's 'enforced' withdrawal from the Suez Canal, and even more insistently, with the establishment of new American bases under the South East Asia Treaty Organization. Moscow has chosen this moment to emphasize that it sees the rivalry between East and West in terms of economic and political competition rather than of military action. From this point of view its spectacular abandonment of a great naval base may be a more profitable operation than the acquisition by the United States of a score of new bases. It helps to make the whole of China into a single solid base of communism. For all their 'materialism', Stalin's successors have shown in this case more understanding of the imponderable moral factors in the present world conflict than do some of their 'idealistic' antagonists in the West.

The withdrawal from Port Arthur implies also a re-orientation of both Chinese and Russian policies towards Japan. Until quite recently the Russo-Chinese alliance was justified officially as a re-insurance against the 'revival of Japanese aggression'. The reference to the threat from Japan was inscribed in the clauses of the pact of 1950; and Russia's moves in the Far East were as a rule justified by that reference. The declaration of 12 October, reasserting the Russo-Chinese alliance, for the first time omits to mention the threat from Japan. It is accompanied by a separate statement which expresses Russia's and China's sympathy with Japan and their regret that so many years after the war Japan is still 'a semi-occupied country'. From now on Japan is to be treated not as the enemy of yesterday, but as the victim of the United States, the victim of the enemy of today, and as a potential recruit to the Asian neutral camp. The evacuation of Port Arthur is intended to reassure Japan that Russia has buried the hatchet.

In the 1950 agreements the Russian promise of a withdrawal from Port Arthur was explicitly linked with the conclusion of a peace treaty between Russia, China, and Japan. The evacuation is now being carried out before the conclusion of such a treaty; and Moscow and Peking hardly expect Tokyo to conclude a peace treaty with them in the foreseeable future. They know that under the San Francisco Peace Treaty of 1951 Japan is barred from making a separate peace with her communist neighbours. But neither Moscow nor Peking attach much importance to the formal diplomatic aspect of affairs. They would be contented with the establishment of *de facto* relations, especially with the resumption of trade which should in itself strengthen the neutralist trend in Japan.

Moscow's departure from the practices of the Stalin era shows itself more startlingly in the disbandment of the Soviet-Chinese Joint Stock Companies which have exploited the gold mines, the petrol wells, and possibly also uranium deposits in Sinkiang. Moscow is also giving up its share in the mixed Companies which have controlled the whole of China's civilian aviation and some of her shipyards. Unlike the evacuation of Port Arthur, the disbandment of these Companies had not been promised or foreshadowed in any previous agreement. Stalin viewed the mixed Companies as more or less permanent features of the relations between Russia and China and the Eastern European countries. He was determined to use the Companies as instruments of pressure and intervention in the affairs of other communist countries. The control of civil aviation laid the whole of China open to the Soviet intelligence services, a point to which Stalin was known to attach extraordinary importance.

Malenkov's government has thrown away this trump, too, with barely suppressed contempt. It has also restored Chinese sovereignty in Sinkiang, where Stalin's agents have long worked to achieve economic penetration and where the mixed Companies had established a sort of Soviet-Chinese condominium. In Inner Mongolia, too, the old Russo-Chinese rivalry is now resolved in China's favour and it is possible that a new settlement is being prepared under which Inner and Outer Mongolia would be united in a single People's Republic. . . .

These agreements do not lead to any weakening of Chinese

dependence on Russia. On the contrary, they strengthen that dependence, but at the same time they give it a new aspect. The dependence is inherent in the balance of the economic strength of the two countries. . . . China still needs Russia's economic, military, and administrative assistance. What is new in the relations between the two countries is Moscow's readiness to grant that assistance in a dignified and considerate manner, without insult and injury to the recipient. This may make of the 'solidarity of Socialist states' something more than the empty and hypocritical phrase which it so often was in Stalin's lifetime.

24 October 1954

4 A NEW COURSE IN MOSCOW: CHANGES IN EASTERN EUROPE

Important as Moscow's new policy towards China is, it is the application of its underlying principles to Eastern Europe which is even more significant, because in Eastern Europe Moscow cannot be said to be seeking opportunistically to placate a great ally. Throughout Eastern Europe, too, the mixed Companies are being disbanded, and so the Soviet Union is relinquishing those 'commanding heights' from which it could control local economic life. The mixed Companies, it will be remembered, loomed large in the conflict between Stalin and Tito. The Yugoslav communists regarded them as tools of 'imperialist exploitation'. There can be no doubt that the setting up of such Companies in Eastern Germany, Romania, Bulgaria, and Hungary gave rise to similar resentment, even though the communists of those countries could not afford to voice it.

That Russia exploited her satellites through the mixed Companies is true only in part. It was mainly during the immediate post-war years, roughly up to 1950, when the Soviet economy was labouring under the after-effects of war and struggling to recover from devastation and ruin, that Moscow used the Companies to extract wealth from the satellite countries. Later, after Russia had recovered economically, a two-way traffic developed; and Eastern Europe began to benefit from Soviet investments and technological assistance. All the same, Moscow was entitled to take its share of the profits made by the Companies; and this enabled communist critics, for instance Djilas, the Yugoslav leader, to accuse Moscow of practising 'state capitalist' exploitation. With the disbandment of the mixed Companies this accusation falls to the ground.

It is only natural that at this stage Moscow should initiate the rehabilitation of Tito. It is some time now since the virulent campaign against Titoism was quietly called off throughout the Soviet bloc. More recently Bulgarian and Hungarian troops which had, since Tito's break with the Cominform, been massed on Yugoslavia's frontiers were withdrawn; this enabled the Yugoslav government to decree a partial demobilization and to cut armament expenditure.

The ideological cease-fire, ordered in Moscow, induced heart-searching in the Yugoslav Communist Party, the leaders of which even before had not seen eye to eye with one another on the prospects of their conflict with Russia. A group headed by Djilas reckoned with an indefinite prolongation and aggravation of the conflict, while Kardelj and his associates made allowance for changes in the Soviet regime which might make an ultimate reconciliation possible. Marshal Tito himself tried to keep the balance between the conflicting views until, some months ago, he disavowed Djilas and his theories, and cautiously threw his authority behind Kardelj's views.

However, until the last few weeks neither Moscow nor Belgrade was prepared to go beyond an ideological truce. . . . But now Moscow has decided to allay Tito's fears: of its own accord it has initiated his rehabilitation. The occasion chosen was the tenth anniversary of the Red Army's entry into Belgrade, which was celebrated in both Moscow and Belgrade on 20 October. On that day *Pravda* and other Soviet newspapers mentioned Tito's name without the customary abuse for the first time since 1948. Moreover, they underlined in a warm and dignified manner the heroic role which Tito and his partisans had played in the last war. Stalin consistently played down that role and shortly before the schism he rudely told the Yugoslavs that it was not they but the Soviet army which had liberated Yugoslavia from German occupation. The Yugoslav partisans —this was the new version of history produced in the letter of the Soviet Central Committee to the Yugoslav Central Committee on 4 May 1948—were incapable of effective action against Hitler's troops because of a 'severe crisis' in Tito's army. From then onwards Soviet writers repeated this version till the end of the Stalin era; and the version accorded all too well with the late Stalinist adulation and glorification of all things Russian.

Since 20 October the Soviet press has made amends for the insults Stalin heaped on Tito and his partisans. Its writers now almost lean over backwards to pay tribute to Tito. This is what *Pravda* writes now: 'We had to act in close co-operation with the National Liberation Army of allied Yugoslavia. We had to aid a country which had made a serious contribution to the general struggle of the peoples of Europe for their emancipation. . . . We knew how much courage and steadfastness Yugoslav partisan detachments had shown, in operating for several years in most difficult conditions, deep behind German and Italian lines. . . . The Yugoslav soldiers and partisans took a very active part in the battles, and they were with us everywhere . . . and not rarely it was they who secured the outcome of a battle. Indeed, this happened many times.' *Pravda* also explicitly acknowledges Tito's role as Commander-in-Chief. Thus the Stalinist myth about the 'severe crisis' which paralyzed Tito's armies and compelled the Soviet army to fight almost singlehandedly for Yugoslavia's liberation has been relegated to the lumber room, to which some other myths of the Stalin era are now confined. Stalin's successors are evidently ready for a full and explicit rehabilitation of Tito as a good communist. . . .

Behind the new turn in Soviet policy towards Chinese and Eastern European communism looms the greater issue of a change in the inner regime of the Communist Parties. Reluctantly and hesitantly Stalin's successors are abandoning the hallowed principle of the infallibility of communist leadership. If a dissenter like Tito was right against the Soviet Central Committee, then dissent is no longer a crime. The 'monolithic' outlook of the Communist Parties is thus called into question.

Since Stalin's death the Communist Parties have certainly known far less dictation from Moscow than they did in his days. The Russian Party now seems to exercise its influence primarily through the example which it sets to others. It favours in any case the substitution of 'collective leadership' for the Party regime controlled by a single leader. Collective leadership or government by committee implies free debate at first within that committee, and later on also in the lower grades of the Party.

The transition from the one regime to the other is, of course, causing friction and dissent. Here and there the single leader of the Stalin era attempts to defend his prerogatives and privileges. This seems to be the case with Rakosy in Hungary. Moscow is against the little Stalins of the satellite Parties; and the Hungarian Central Committee at its last session put Rakosy, still its First Secretary, in his place. In Poland Bierut seems to have easily reconciled himself to collective leadership. In the Czechoslovak Party the problem solved itself with the death of Gottwald, the single leader of the Stalin-era. In Romania the Party is still in the throes of a crisis: the fate of Anna Pauker is still in the balance; and purges continue, though they are less destructive than they were under Stalin.

What is retarding, obstructing, and confusing the new evolution of the East European Communist Parties is the fact that the present regimes of Eastern Europe are far less stable than the post-Stalin regime in the U.S.S.R. The peasant smallholder still dominates the rural life of Eastern Europe. The old bourgeois parties still have their potential or actual following. A social democratic tradition is still alive in the working class. Relaxation of discipline in the ruling Communist Parties may be taken as a sign of their weakness, may encourage opposition, and may lead to political convulsions. The communist rulers view with mixed feelings the infectious reformist ferment in Moscow. This accounts for the paradox that the Eastern European Communist Parties at times cling to Stalinist orthodoxy much more obstinately than does Stalin's own Party. On the other hand, the Stalinist tradition is less deeply embedded in their political mentality; and so, once they take courage, they may throw off its deadweight much more easily than can the Russian Party....

24 October 1954

3
The Fall of Malenkov

Malenkov's resignation from the post of Chairman of the Council
of Ministers came during the Supreme Soviet Session of 3–9
February 1955; his successor was Marshal Bulganin, whose place
as Minister of Defence was taken by Marshal Zhukov. On 24
January Mikoyan had resigned from the post of Minister of
Internal Trade, but although this was a result of his alliance with
Malenkov on economic matters, he returned to prominence in a
government re-shuffle on 28 February as Senior Deputy Prime
Minister. This meant that Malenkov had lost his closest ally, and
that the new leadership had strengthened its position.

Malenkov had pressed, since becoming Prime Minister, for an
increase in the production of consumer goods, a policy which he
announced to the Supreme Soviet in August 1953. In this speech
he emphasized that 'The government and Central Committee
consider it necessary . . . to raise the targets for the production of
goods for the masses very considerably'; but enthusiasm for these
new economic policies decreased in 1954 and on the day of
Mikoyan's resignation *Pravda* carried an article by Shepilov
praising heavy industry as 'the granite foundation of all branches
of the Soviet economy'. In his letter of resignation Malenkov said
that the Soviet Union needed 'a Chairman who possesses greater
experience in government matters' and blamed himself for
shortcomings in economic and agricultural policy; he praised the
new policy in agriculture which, he said, 'is based on the only
correct principle—the further development of heavy industry to
the maximum'.

Malenkov must have seen that no one would accept his plea of
inexperience for he finished his letter by saying 'It is to be
expected that various bourgeois sensation-mongers will resort to
slanderous inventions with regard to my statement. . . . But we
will ignore these slanders'.

1 THE ISSUES BEHIND
MALENKOV'S RESIGNATION

Malenkov's sudden resignation on 8 February from the post of the Soviet Prime Minister was the outcome of a dramatic struggle which had gone on in Moscow's ruling circles throughout 1954 and which concerned every major aspect of Soviet domestic and foreign policy. It is now possible on the basis of circumstantial evidence to trace the main phases of the struggle and to outline the broad alignments which formed themselves in the process and the crucial issues which were at stake.

Early last year the Presidium of the Central Committee, the government departments, and Gosplan (the State Planning Commission) began to formulate the principles on which the sixth Five Year Plan is to be based. The Plan will start to operate next year, and it will determine the development of the Soviet economy up to 1960. Its special importance lies, among other things, in the fact that it will aim for the first time at a comprehensive and close co-ordination of the Soviet economy with the economies of the entire Soviet bloc.

The crucial issues over which the struggle, which has led to Malenkov's downfall, was waged can be listed under the following headings: first, the question of the relative importance of heavy and light industries, or producer goods and consumer goods, in the new Plan; secondly, the scale of planned capital investment in power stations working on atomic energy; thirdly, the scope and character of the Soviet contribution towards the economic development of China and of Eastern Europe in 1956–60; and, last but not least, the size of the Soviet armaments expenditure during that period, with special reference to the armament of China.

As the debate over these issues proceeded, two distinct groups formed themselves within the Presidium. The group headed by Malenkov and Mikoyan saw the main objective of the new Five Year Plan as the achieving of a continuous and massive rise in Soviet standards of living, a rise which would result in approximately the doubling of consumption between 1955 and 1960. To attain this objective, light industry would have to be given priority in the allocation of capital equipment, manpower, and raw materials; and the general tempo of its expansion would have to be either quicker than, or at least equal to, the tempo of development in heavy industry throughout the coming five-year period.

The advocates of this policy, headed by Malenkov, argued that in view of the enormous success achieved by Russia during the first post-war decade in the reconstruction and expansion of her heavy industrial base, she could well afford such a programme. Indeed, they said, the mood in the country and considerations of social and political stability demanded a long respite from the forcible industrialization of the Stalin era. They pointed to the lack of balance between the various branches of the Soviet economy, to the long-lasting neglect of consumer industries, and more especially to the intolerable condition of Soviet housing.

The debate was indeed concentrated more on the housing problem than on consumer industries in general. In the last thirty years the urban population of the Soviet Union had increased by over fifty million, and by not fewer than seventeen million in the last five years alone. The new houses built had been barely enough to make good the war-time destruction. The overcrowding of the Soviet cities, towns, and industrial centres had become a social calamity, and was having a very adverse effect on the morale and industrial efficiency of the working class. Housing loomed therefore larger in the controversy than the output of clothing, footwear, etc., as large, indeed, as the shortage of meat and dairy produce. At least a decade of building on a gigantic scale would be needed to clear the slums left behind by Stalin's industrial revolution and to bring the housing conditions of the Soviet people nearer to the standards of any modern industrial nation. But a housing programme on the scale required would obviously be in heavy competition with the basic industries for materials and man-power.

From the beginning Bulganin and Kaganovich were apparently the chief opponents of this ambitious pro-consumer programme. Khrushchev apparently joined them only later, and not without hesitation. From the Presidium of the Central Committee the controversy spread to government departments, planning authorities, universities, the General Staff of the

Soviet Army, and the editorial offices of the most important papers. Although the broad public was kept in the dark, wider circles than it appeared were drawn into the debate: indeed, no controversy as wide as this had occurred in Russia for at least twenty-five years.

Bulganin and Kaganovich found powerful allies in the army and in Gosplan. The Malenkov-Mikoyan view, on the other hand, found widespread but less influential support in academic and journalistic circles, among the intelligentsia, among the heads of the light industries, and in Party cadres concerned closely with the nation's morale. It was apparently with the greatest surprise that Malenkov saw the economic planners arrayed against his policy—he must have expected Gosplan to lend strong support to his pro-consumer line. But the spokesmen of Gosplan argued that his programme was unrealistic, and that Russia's present industrial base could not yet support it, especially not the vast housing programme. On behalf of the Gosplan 'brains trust' S. Strumilin, the veteran chief of Gosplan, pointed out that as a rule capital goods industries must expand at the rate of at least eighteen per cent if the consumer industries are to expand by as much as ten per cent per year; otherwise the consumer industries will stagnate after a short time for lack of machinery. Heavy industry must therefore still be given top priority even if only to enable it to sustain a rather modest rise in the standard of living. It was imprudent and positively dangerous, so the Gosplan leaders concluded, to arouse exaggerated popular hopes: only during the first two or three years of the next Five Year Plan could consumer industries, including the building industry, expand by about twelve per cent annually—after that even that rate could not be maintained. Throughout that period the rate of expansion in heavy industry must be of the order of twenty per cent; and industrial construction must come before housing.

The Gosplan spokesmen also insisted that the coming Five Year Plan ought to initiate the conversion on a fairly large scale of Soviet industry from coal to atomic energy. This again required heavy capital investment. Gosplan, finally, waited for the Party leaders to make up their minds about whether and how much Russia should contribute to the industrialization of the People's Democracies. There, too, the question had to be resolved whether heavy or light industry should be favoured. The Malenkov group favoured light industry throughout the Soviet bloc, while its opponents were inclined to favour the development of the basic industries in Eastern Europe as well.

The debate was further complicated by conflicting predictions of the armament expenditure in the coming five-year period. The pro-consumer group hoped that Soviet diplomacy would, by means of its 'peace offensives', bring about a decline in international tension and a stop or a slowing down in the armament race. The opponents of the Malenkov group dismissed this view as wishful thinking.

The army leaders were from the beginning alarmed by the Prime Minister's 'consumptionist' bias. They saw in it a threat to the Soviet military potential and almost certainly argued that it was dangerous to tie up a high proportion of the country's resources and manpower in light industry. If the threat of war arose suddenly, heavy industry could be switched over to the production of munitions almost overnight; the reconversion of light industries, on the other hand, would be difficult and slow. The army was, therefore, on principle interested in seeing as much labour and materials as possible concentrated in the basic industries. The Marshals joined hands with the leaders of Gosplan in an otherwise somewhat unnatural alliance against the Prime Minister and his supporters. The bloc of Gosplan and army finally brought over Khrushchev to its side.

International developments continuously and closely influenced the course of the controversy. The rejection of E.D.C. by the French parliament last summer strengthened the Malenkov group for a while, and Khrushchev vacillated. But early in the autumn the Presidium was no longer in the mood of exultation in which it was caught immediately after the rejection of E.D.C. Molotov evidently reported that the NATO powers were after all likely to obtain France's agreement to Germany's inclusion in NATO. By the beginning of October the Presidium had already adopted draft directives for the Five Year Plan. These provided only for a modest growth of consumer industries, and this only in the first two or three years of the coming five-year period.

By the beginning of October, too, the Presidium had already prepared a tentative scheme for the Soviet counter-moves to the inclusion of Western Germany in NATO. The scheme provided for a massive rise in armament expenditure (the ten per cent increase in the 1955 defence budget announced just before Malenkov's resignation is only a first instalment). The scheme also provided for the setting up of a joint command for all the armed forces of the Soviet bloc, a counterpart to SHAPE. The Presidium had also resolved to propose to Mao Tse-tung that he should decree universal military service in China.

The implications of this last proposal were staggering. China had so far refrained from introducing conscription because her industrial weakness would not allow her to arm her conscripts. The training of, say, a five-year age-group could in a few years place at the disposal of the Supreme Command of the Soviet bloc a reserve of twenty million soldiers. (Molotov apparently had this counter-*coup* to the armament of Western Germany in mind when he said at the last session of the Supreme Soviet that the 'Western imperialists' would adopt a different language *vis-à-vis* Russia once they saw what were the Soviet counter-measures.) But in order to obtain so vast a strategic reserve the Soviet Union would have to build China's armament industries and also to supply much of the armament from its own stocks.

It was with this scheme that Khrushchev, Bulganin, and other Soviet leaders went to Peking last October to obtain Mao Tse-tung's consent. (The factions in Moscow had, of course, vied with each other for Mao Tse-tung's support.) Mao Tse-tung consented to work on the basis of the new military-industrial scheme. Thus a decisive blow was struck at the hopes for a rapid expansion of Soviet consumer industries.

The defeat of the Malenkov group was sealed when the French parliament ratified the London and Paris agreements at the close of last year. Malenkov's resignation was a foregone conclusion. The chief opponent of the consumptionist policy, Marshal Bulganin, backed by Khrushchev, army leaders, Gosplan, and by all those who viewed with suspicion the 'liberal' trend of the Malenkov regime, stepped forward as candidate for the Premiership. And, significantly, on the day after Malenkov's resignation Peking decreed universal conscription. The intensified building up of Soviet heavy industry, increased armament expenditure, the new Chinese army, and Supreme Soviet Command over all the armed forces from the China Sea to the Elbe—these are the new 'positions of strength' from which Molotov expects to negotiate with the West.

10 February 1955

2 THE RISE OF THE MILITARY

The appointment of Marshal Zhukov to the post of the Soviet Minister of Defence has emphasized the growth of the military influence in the Soviet government. The Marshal is not only Minister of Defence—he has also been introduced into the inner Cabinet as one of the Vice-Premiers. Thus, three Marshals now stand at the head of the administration: Voroshilov as President, Bulganin as Premier, and Zhukov.

Never before in the history of the Soviet Union was the military element so strongly represented in the government. To keep the military influence within very narrow limits was a matter of deliberate policy. The leaders of the Bolshevik Party had always had the precedents of the French Revolution in their minds and had given much thought to the idea that in Russia, too, a Bonaparte might one day 'climb to power on the back of the Revolution'. Both Stalin and Trotsky, for all their bitter disagreements, agreed on this; and each (from his own angle) kept an anxious eye on the danger of the 'potential Bonaparte'. Stalin himself eventually donned the Generalissimo's uniform and acted as a half-phoney Bonaparte in order to keep out any authentic candidate to the role. He sent the three most popular Marshals of the pre-war period, Tukhachevsky, Bluecher, and Yegorov, to their death; and then he relegated to obscurity the victorious Marshals of the Second World War and exiled Zhukov, whose name became a legend among the Russian people, to the melancholy backwater of Odessa.

Are Stalin's heirs then no longer obsessed with the fear that the phantom of a Russian Bonaparte may materialize and turn against them? It is difficult to believe that they are not; but evidently they could not help yielding so much ground to the military. Since March 1953, amid all the uncertainties of the struggle for the succession to Stalin, while the triumvirate was breaking down in ignominy, the Marshals have gained in status, prestige, and influence. They represent an element of

stable authority. For the time being they wield the only instrument of power capable of dealing effectively with any internal
disorder, should disorder arise. The other instrument, the
security police, has been discredited, disorganized, and shattered, first by the exploding of the 'doctors' plot', then by
Beria's disgrace, and finally by the extensive purging of Beria's
followers. The prerogatives of the security police have been
drastically curtailed and its self-confidence and striking power
have been broken. Nobody now represents the political police
in the Presidium of the Party, while in Stalin's days the chief of
the police, as long as he was its chief, was one of the first members
of the Politbureau. The head of the Security Committee, which
was formed after Beria's downfall, is an obscure and subordinate
official who has only now been promoted to the rank of junior
minister. Stalin's regime was predominantly, but not entirely,
a police state. What replaces it is not yet a military dictatorship.
There is still the rule by the Party, but that rule contains an
unmistakable and growing ingredient of a military dictatorship.
The Marshals, aware of their strong position, are claiming a say
in the conduct of affairs; and the Party leaders cannot ignore
the claim.

However, Soviet military leaders do not form a single group
united in outlook and aspirations. For obvious historical reasons the Soviet officers' corps is even now more heterogeneous
than the officers' corps of any other country. Its members are
divided over issues of strategy and policy and by differences in
background and tradition, not to speak of clashes of personal
ambition. These cleavages have in recent years been epitomized
in the antagonism between two Marshals: Vassilevsky and
Zhukov. The rivalry of these two soldiers was close under the
surface in the latest governmental crisis in Moscow. It is indeed
a striking outcome of that crisis that the rise of Zhukov is
accompanied by a quiet eclipse of Vassilevsky. Vassilevsky is
now Zhukov's subordinate—he presumably still holds the
office of Vice-Minister of Defence—while for the last ten years
he was Zhukov's superior.

The antagonism between the two Marshals goes back at
least to the time of the Stalingrad battle in 1942. Ever since then
it has been reflected in all of Moscow's military arrangements
and shifts of power. The personal rivalry has been tied up with

conflicting claims to credit for victories, to honour and glory. But apart from this, the two Marshals also represent two different outlooks in the Soviet officers' corps, two different political mentalities, and two different shades of the attitude of the soldiers towards Party leaders. The rise or the eclipse of the one Marshal or the other has therefore as a rule had some broader significance, and the rise of the one has invariably been accompanied by the eclipse of the other.

Both are the supreme leaders of the Soviet officers' corps, but while Vassilevsky has been its most powerful Chief of Staff, Zhukov is its greatest combat general. Vassilevsky's domain is overall planning and logistics. He has kept aloof from other aspects of army life. Zhukov, on the other hand, has come to be looked upon as the very embodiment of the army, of its endurance, courage, and popular spirit, in a word of all those qualities which Tolstoy in *War and Peace* attributed to Kutuzov, and which Russians still like to attribute to their military heroes.

Vassilevsky came to the Red Army as a 'specialist', not as a communist. In the early years of the Soviet regime many professional officers served the Soviet government from a feeling that, whatever their political reservations, they owed allegiance to the Bolshevik government as to the only effective government of Russia. In the minds of those soldiers Russian nationalism prevailed over dislike of communism. The most eminent of them was Marshal Shaposhnikov, a General Staff Officer in Tsarist days. Vassilevsky was Shaposhnikov's disciple and follower, and it was indeed Shaposhnikov that he succeeded as Chief of Staff. It is characteristic of Vassilevsky that he refused to join the Communist Party until 1938; and when, after the Tukhachevsky purge, at last at the age of 43, he joined the Party he did so in order to demonstrate his loyalty to the government in view of approaching war.

During the Second World War he was one of the chief inspirers of the vehement nationalism of those years and of the glorification of the old Tsarist military traditions, legends, and heroes. In the post-war years he stood for a most rigorous political regime inside Russia and for keeping Russia and the Soviet bloc hermetically isolated from the West. He feared that contact with the West would have a disintegrating effect on popular morale. He threw the whole weight of his influence behind the reactionary campaigns waged during the close of the Stalin era against 'rootless cosmopolitanism', against 'kowtowing before the West', against the Jews, etc. It is almost certain that he lent a hand in concocting the 'doctors' plot'. When the accusation of the doctors was being prepared, Vassilevsky was singled out to be presented to public opinion as the conspirators' chief target. And, curiously enough, Zhukov was not even mentioned among the military leaders whom the conspirators allegedly planned to assassinate. Vassilevsky enjoyed Stalin's confidence; he was Minister of Defence in the dark years of 1950–52, and until the moment of Stalin's death.

Zhukov's background is very different. Of peasant origin, a workman in his youth, he volunteered for the Red Army early in the civil war. He joined the Communist Party in 1919, when Bolshevik fortunes were at their lowest ebb and the White Armies were almost within reach of Moscow and Petrograd. Mentally formed in the Leninist period, he adapted himself to Stalin's regime but apparently preserved much of his early communist conviction, some internationalist sentiment, and an informal kindness and even warm-heartedness in personal relations. As Commander and as head of the Soviet Military Administration in Germany he resented the interference of the security police with the army and chafed at Stalin's suspicious control over his own doings in Berlin. That control was so clumsy and so obvious to Western Commanders that it made Zhukov's proud face blush. He could not conceal his humiliated embarrassment from General Eisenhower, with whom he established something like a friendly relationship, but before whom he also defended his communist conviction with dignity. For his disregard of some of the instructions from Moscow, for the informality of his behaviour and, above all, for his dangerous popularity Zhukov had to pay the penalty. Only after five years spent in his Odessa retirement was he allowed by Stalin to reappear in public. But at the nineteenth Party Congress in October 1952, Stalin prepared for him the last humiliation: at that Congress Vassilevsky was elected a full member of the Central Committee of the Party, while Zhukov, the authentic veteran communist, was elected only a candidate member.

Zhukov seems by all accounts to be a more sympathetic

character than Vassilevsky. Whether President Eisenhower will find him 'easy to get along with' is another question. The memories of the 'soldierly friendship' of the two allied Commanders hardly carry much weight in the shaping of foreign policy. They will certainly carry little weight with Molotov who remains in charge of diplomacy. But Zhukov's rise does indicate that the Party leaders, while yielding to the army's pressure for more toughness in both foreign and domestic policies, are nevertheless anxious to keep at bay the more extreme, xenophobe, and politically ambitious elements of the officers' corps, the elements who presumably follow Vassilevsky's lead.

The present alignment is, to all intents and purposes, an alliance between the 'tough' Party leaders and the moderate, Party-minded soldiers. But even the moderate soldiers have evidently turned against Malenkov's 'soft' policy; and Zhukov, too, seems to fear that 'Soviet softness is mistaken for weakness by the West'.

11 February 1955

5 THE ROLES OF KHRUSHCHEV AND BULGANIN

Nearly two years after Stalin's death the problem of the succession to Stalin is further from a solution than ever. The battle for the succession is now on. . . . Where does Khrushchev stand in this struggle?

He has undoubtedly led the stalwarts of Stalinism in the attack against Malenkov and those who have come to symbolize in Russia's eyes a break with Stalinist orthodoxy. Every step in Khrushchev's rise has been accompanied by an attempt to galvanize the Stalin cult and to restore Stalin's political methods. Even his ascendancy looks like a deliberate repetition of Stalin's rise to power from the obscure inner recesses of the General Secretariat of the Party.

Yet it is doubtful whether Khrushchev is really going to fill the place left vacant by Stalin. The Party and the country have heard recently too many emphatic warnings against the single-leader regime. The principle of collective leadership has just been proclaimed with too much resounding solemnity; and the reaction against Stalin's method of government has been too strong and genuine and popular to be openly flouted now.

Nor have Khrushchev's frequent public appearances in recent months done much to build up his prestige in Party cadres. True, he is by all accounts an administrator of considerable drive and energy—this is the feature he has in common with Stalin. But he obviously lacks Stalin's cool-headed, taciturn, calculating reserve. Expansive, talkative, pushful, he seems too crude and at times almost too naive for the delicate and dangerous job of Stalin's sole successor. In his mental make-up he seems to belong to the Russia of twenty to twenty-five years ago, the Russia which was only embarking upon planned industrialization, not to the Russia of today with her vast and complicated modern industrial equipment and atomic piles. His recent speeches have indeed borne no relation to the real problems of this economy—they have resembled the irrelevant lucubrations of the little plumber that he was, risen to be boss of a large, complicated, modern concern, hoping to manage its affairs by the primitive methods to which he was accustomed. This is most decidedly not the man which post-Stalinist Russia is in need of. If anybody should plead incompetence as a reason for resignation, then it is surely—Khrushchev. . . .

However, it is not Khrushchev who has taken Malenkov's place as Soviet Premier. His ambition to concentrate in his hands all the power that Stalin wielded, if indeed he cherishes that ambition, is not yet fulfilled. He remains only the Secretary of the Central Committee of the Party and thus holds only one of the offices held by Stalin in the last twelve years of his life. The fact that he has not been allowed to take control of both Party and government indicates that he, too, has still to contend with powerful opponents.

It is difficult to treat the appointment of Marshal Bulganin to the post of Prime Minister as anything more than a stopgap. It should be emphasized that this is the first time in the history of the Soviet Union that a Marshal has been appointed head of the Soviet government. When Stalin became Premier in 1941 he was only the Party's General Secretary, and even later, as Generalissimo, he was first and foremost the Party leader. As the head of government he symbolized, during the last war, the unity of Party and army. With Bulganin as Prime Minister and Khrushchev as Party Secretary there appears something like the beginning of a division of influence between the Party and the army. In any case, the weight of military influence on Russia's affairs is visibly growing. It is quite possible, and even probable, that the army has in fact stood between Khrushchev and the office of Prime Minister.

Bulganin himself is not the authentic representative of the officers' corps. He represents the Party *vis-à-vis* the army—he is the Party's supervisor over the officers' corps—and he puts the army's viewpoint before the Party leaders. His appointment shows that the Party has found it necessary to meet the ambitions of the army leaders half way; but it is not prepared to go any further. The new Premier is in the army, but not of it. But behind his back stand the real leaders of the officers' corps, Marshals Vassilevsky, Govorov, Zhukov, and others, the real candidates to the still vacant post of a Soviet Bonaparte. Should international tension mount even further, should grave domestic trouble develop in the Soviet Union, threatening to overwhelm the present obviously ineffective Directory, a further shift in power may occur, as a result of which the reins of government would be placed in the hands of one of the authentic military leaders. . . .

8 February 1955

4

The Foreign Policy
of Malenkov's Successors

Following the ideological detente between Russia and Yugoslavia that developed in 1954 (see chapter 2), relations were further improved by the visit of an important Soviet delegation to Belgrade in May of the following year; it was led by Khrushchev and included Bulganin, Mikoyan, and Shepilov. During the visit, which lasted from 26 May to 3 June, Khrushchev demonstrated his desire for renewed Russo-Yugoslav friendship, and blamed Beria for having been responsible for bad relations in the past. Normal relations *at governmental level* were re-established at the close of the visit, but it was not until Tito's return visit to Moscow in June 1956 that relations between the two *Parties* were normalized as well.

Following his conciliatory trip to Yugoslavia, Khrushchev went to Geneva in July for the first Big Four summit meeting since Potsdam. His Western counterparts—Eisenhower, Eden, and Edgar Faure—appear to have expected Khrushchev to make important concessions in foreign policy misled by the belief, current at the time, that Russia was on the edge of economic collapse. At the conference, which opened on 18 July, Eisenhower chose to raise three issues: Germany, 'international communism', and Eastern Europe. His allies followed suit and, since Khrushchev was not prepared to debate either of the two latter topics, discussion centred on Germany. Khrushchev, accepting the impossibility of a quick reunification, wanted the Western Powers to recognize the existence of two German governments, but the Western Powers insisted on the holding of elections. The pattern of the Berlin Foreign Ministers' Conference (see chapter 2) was repeated and the summit broke up on 23 July, its only achievement being the decision to convene another Foreign Ministers' conference in Geneva on 27 October. This conference met from 27 October to 16 November, but no progress was made.

1 THE RETREAT FROM MONOLITHISM: KHRUSHCHEV IN BELGRADE

The visit of the Soviet leaders to Belgrade has aroused world-wide attention because of its possible implications for Soviet foreign policy. It is generally assumed that after the signing of the peace treaty with Austria Moscow is now eager to encourage, with an eye on Germany, those governments which may be inclined to favour the formation of a neutral buffer zone in Europe.

This seems indeed to be the purpose of the Soviet pilgrimage to Belgrade; but it is not perhaps its sole or even its main objective. If the Soviet leaders were interested only in gaining a diplomatic advantage, a visit by the Soviet Prime Minister alone would have been more than enough. The fact that the first Secretary of the Party, Khrushchev, will be among Marshal Tito's guests and that he will head the Soviet delegation indicates that Moscow would like above all to settle the 'ideological' and political differences between the Soviet and the Yugoslav Communist Parties. Khrushchev certainly intends to speak to Tito, the head of the Party, rather than Tito, the head of the State.

The Soviet mission has been described as a Canossa. This is Canossa in reverse, however: it is not the heretic who goes to beg pardon from the Pope, but the Muscovite Pope who goes to apologize to the heretic; and he does so without being sure that the heretic is willing to accept the apology. At least since last October Moscow has gone out of its way to demonstrate its desire to rehabilitate Tito as a good communist. His revolutionary merits as leader of the partisans, merits denied in Stalin's days, have been publicly and generously recalled by the chiefs of the Party and the army, indeed by almost every personality that matters in Moscow, with the exception of Molotov whose signature had figured next to Stalin's under the act of the 1948 excommunication. Khrushchev himself has ostentatiously drunk the health of *Comrade* (not of 'Mr.' or 'Marshal') Tito.

Marshal Tito, however, has accepted all this meed of praise rather gingerly. He has paid a few reserved compliments to the 'courage of Stalin's successors', and has been wary of further military entanglements with the West. But he has been equally wary of any spectacular *rapprochement* with the East. He has not in his turn drunk to the health of *Comrade* Khrushchev. And he has now emphatically stated that he will negotiate with his Soviet guests only about the affairs of their respective governments, not about the relationship between their respective Parties.

What then, after this snub, still impels the Secretary of the Soviet Communist Party to pay this unprecedented homage to Tito?

The answer may be found only in that slow, confused, yet unmistakable break-down of Stalinist orthodoxy, which has been going on in the U.S.S.R., despite all the shifts in the ruling groups and despite Khrushchev's own embarrassed attempts to call a halt to the process. The Belgrade visit indeed immediately seems to throw more light on Russia's internal situation than on her foreign policy. There is evidently a sense of guilt and shame abroad in Moscow, even in the highest ruling circles, for Stalin's worst blunders and follies; and there is a desire to make good some of these. Khrushchev and Marshal Bulganin may have overthrown Malenkov with the intention of bringing the Party back to its old Stalinist ways. But the recoil against Stalinism is still strong enough to send both of them off to Belgrade.

Willy-nilly (and perhaps even unawares) Khrushchev is now dealing a new blow at the monolithic outlook of his own Party. When *Pravda* recently wrote about the close affinity between the Soviet and the Yugoslav social systems, saying that both were based on public ownership and the political predominance of workers and toiling peasants, and when it underlined that this 'basic' affinity was not diminished by still existing 'substantial differences of views', *Pravda* was in fact injecting a huge dose of 'heresy' into the minds of its own readers. The Stalinist canon of the 'monolithic' Party consisted precisely in this that no 'substantial differences of views' could be allowed to develop among communists, because only one view, the official one, represented the real interest of socialism, whereas the heretical view inevitably led to the restoration of capitalism. In accordance with this canon *Pravda* and the whole Soviet press until recently depicted Titoist Yugoslavia as a country in which capitalism had been or was being restored—without this the 1948 excommunication would not have been 'ideologically' justified.

There is some evidence to show that the story about the restoration of capitalism was accepted at its face value not only by the uninformed Soviet public but even in Party circles which might have been expected to know better. *Pravda* has now not only exposed the humbug; it has gone further and declared that where there are disagreements among communists, the 'heretical' view does not necessarily amount to a betrayal of communism or socialism. Yet if this is true of differences of views between two Parties, may it not also be true of disagreements inside one Communist Party? This question must have occurred to some of *Pravda*'s readers who may have wondered whether *Pravda*'s words were not an indirect and implicit legalization of inner controversy in the Soviet Party as well.

That this is not a conclusion drawn over-hastily from a few vague sentences in *Pravda* is shown by other developments in the Soviet bloc, which are, from the inner communist angle, perhaps even more significant than Khrushchev's visit to Belgrade, although they have attracted little attention outside the Soviet bloc. A rehabilitation more strange and startling than that of Tito has just taken place in Poland. Those familiar with the history of the old Comintern remember that in the late 1930s, in the period of the great purges, Stalin disbanded the Communist Party of Poland as one which was 'riddled with spies, Pilsudskists, Trotskyists,' etc. The Polish Party had always worked underground and had been mercilessly persecuted. By the time it was disbanded at least 7,000 of its members crowded the Polish prisons. Most of its leaders, virtually its whole Central Committee, had sought refuge in Moscow. During the Yezhov terror nearly all of them were imprisoned there and executed as traitors and spies. Among them were men and women who had fought for thirty and even forty years, without a break, in Poland's underground movement. The best known was Adolf Warski, Rosa Luxemburg's close associate, who had represented the Polish Social-Democratic Party in the Second International before 1914 and who later led the Communist

Parliamentary group in the Warsaw Diet. He was, with Kostrzewa—another victim of this purge and a woman of great intellect and heroic character—the leader of the Party's 'right wing'. Both Warski and Kostrzewa had indeed stood close to Bukharin and Rykov, at least in their political views. But Warski's chief opponent and rival, Julian Lenski-Leszczynski, who had for many years represented the Polish Party at the Executive of the Comintern and had been known for his Stalinist zeal—it was he who expelled the writer of this article from the Party—was also executed. (So was, incidentally, another eminent communist propagandist, and a close friend of mine, Jan Hempel, of whom the Polish President Bierut was a devoted disciple.)

All these victims of the Stalinist terror, all these traitors, spies, Trotskyists, and Bukharinists, have now been suddenly rehabilitated. The act was carried out in a rather odd fashion. The Party newspapers have published long historical accounts of the Polish communist movement, extolling the 'heroic' roles which the men executed in Moscow had played as 'leaders and inspirers of the Polish working class'. *Trybuna Ludu,* the organ of the Central Committee, has filled its columns with the pictures of Stalin's victims. Not a word has been said, however, about the circumstances in which they found their death.

In undertaking this rehabilitation Bierut and his associates have hardly acted only on their own initiative. They have evidently had Moscow's blessing for the act. The Polish like the Yugoslav rehabilitation is only a part—only the beginning of a much wider historical revision of Stalin's great purges, a revision which it may take years to accomplish, but which is inseparable from the breaking up of Stalinist orthodoxy.

Another, a more subtle but perhaps even more significant indication of 'ideological' ferment may be found in the new style of the homages which are now paid in Moscow to the memory of Lenin. In recent weeks the Soviet press has brought out a spate of memoirs about Lenin. The memoirs, written by the few survivors of the Old Bolshevik Guard, differ in many respects from almost everything that appeared during the Stalin era. They are more realistic, closer to historical truth, and they no longer portray Lenin as the demi-god who has begotten that other demi-god Stalin. To be sure, Lenin continues to be idealized as the paragon of virtue, but one of his virtues is now thrown into particularly sharp relief: his respect for 'inner Party democracy'.

As a rule the memoir writers emphasize that Lenin never tried to impose himself upon the Party, that he was tolerant of dissent and controversy in its ranks, and that he submitted to the will of the majority of the Party, even when he disagreed with it—briefly, that he led the Party in a democratic not in an autocratic manner. The purpose of these writings is not merely to re-establish historical truth, as the writers see it, but to point a significant moral for the present. The moral seems to be: the Party has had enough of autocracy and of monolithic orthodoxy; and it expects Stalin's successors to give it back its freedom of opinion, of dissent, and of controversy.

It is, of course, an open question whether the Party will in fact regain that freedom. Attempts to preserve and restore its monolithic outlook are, and certainly will be, made; and the struggle over this may be expected to last a long time, during which the pendulum will swing this way and that. But the present mood in Moscow of a continuing reaction against Stalinism forms an essential part of the background to the visit of the Soviet leaders to Belgrade.

23 May 1955

2 STATUS QUO IN GERMANY

The Geneva conference of Heads of States has shed a sharp light on the evolution of Soviet foreign policy since Stalin's death: it has thrown into especial relief the changes which have taken place since then in the Soviet approach to the German problem. More than ever it is now clear that this issue has been at the centre of the controversy which has rent the Soviet ruling group, a major cause of the two dramatic governmental crises of 1953 and 1955; and that, conversely, every shift in the ruling group has entailed a change in Moscow's German policy.

The brief but intricate story of the post-Stalin era falls into three chapters. In the first, which lasted from March till the middle of June 1953, the Soviet Union was ruled by Malenkov and Beria; in the second, from July 1953, power was exercised by the coalition of Malenkov and Khrushchev, which in February 1955 gave place to the Khrushchev-Bulganin combination. It is striking that the transition from one chapter to another was never preceded by any startling event in Soviet domestic affairs which offers a clue to the subsequent governmental crisis. But at the end of each chapter a most dramatic development took place in German affairs. The Malenkov-Beria coalition collapsed in the days of the June rising in Eastern Germany. The Malenkov-Khrushchev combination broke up immediately after the ratification of the Paris and London agreements and Germany's inclusion in NATO. In each case the impact of German developments shook Moscow, replaced one political alignment by another, and led to a revision of Soviet foreign and domestic policies.

After Stalin's death his successors set out to bring into order the legacy of the Stalin era. They sought to preserve the assets and to reduce the liabilities Stalin had bequeathed to them. It was in the months of the Malenkov-Beria coalition that most of the conciliatory moves of Soviet foreign policy, beginning with the Korean armistice, were initiated. The Malenkov-Beria government saw in the German situation, as Stalin had left it, the greatest single liability of Soviet diplomacy, its dangerous Gordian knot. Malenkov and Beria viewed Germany's division and the presence of the armed forces of East and West on German soil as the chief obstacles to a rationalization of Soviet foreign policy and the chief source of international tension. They contemplated nothing less than a withdrawal from Germany and the virtual abandonment of the East German communist regime, hoping that they would be able to persuade the Western Powers to agree to a withdrawal of their forces too.

The accusation which was later levelled against Beria that he intended to 'surrender Eastern Germany to world capitalism' was thus not quite groundless; only Beria, far from being an 'agent of imperialism' and guilty of conspiracy and treason, had advocated this 'surrender' as part of a definite political and diplomatic conception for which he pleaded in the normal way with his colleagues of the Party Presidium. This conception was reflected in the Soviet documents of the time and it was emphatically formulated in the famous Reply to President Eisenhower which appeared in *Pravda* on 25 April 1953. The Reply,

which was Beria's and Malenkov's explicit appeal to the West,
stated categorically that 'a peace treaty with Germany giving
the German people the possibility of a reunion in one State . . .
should be concluded as early as possible; and following closely
upon this the occupation troops should be withdrawn . . .'

When this statement is compared with the attitude taken up
by Bulganin and Khrushchev at Geneva, the change and the
contrast are self-evident. In April 1953 Moscow gave top
priority to Germany's unification; only after unification were
foreign troops to be withdrawn; and the fact that two antagonistic states with 'differing social and political systems' had
existed in Germany for nearly eight years was not seen as an
insuperable obstacle to early unification. In Geneva the Soviet
leaders based their policy firmly on Germany's continued
division, which had, in their view, been rendered inevitable not
only by Western Germany's adherence to NATO but also by
the existence of the two antagonistic German regimes. Malenkov and Beria were prepared to try and reverse Stalin's policies
in Germany and to dismantle the Pieck and Ulbricht government, believing that this would secure a stable peace. Khrushchev and Bulganin appear to have ruled out any such reversal:
they stand firm by the communist government of Eastern
Germany.

It may be assumed, although this cannot be proven of course,
that if the Western Powers had attempted to negotiate with
Russia in the spring or early summer of 1953, when Sir Winston
Churchill first urged them to do so, they would have found the
Soviet leaders much more ready to make important concessions
of substance on Germany than they have found them at Geneva.
But at that time most Western statesmen were convinced that
'nothing had changed in Russia', viewed the Russian scene with
incredulity, and were not inclined to act at once. Then the
rising of 16–17 June suddenly brought to light the risks and
dangers to Russia which were inherent in the Beria-Malenkov
policy. The opinion gained ground in Moscow's ruling group
that an orderly retreat from Germany was almost impossible
and that, if attempted, it was likely to turn into a rout and to
shake the communist regimes in Eastern Europe.

What now followed was a phase of transition characterized by
indecision and ambiguity. Under Malenkov and Khrushchev

the emphasis of Soviet diplomacy was no longer on Germany's early reunion, but it had not yet shifted to continued division. In the long series of Notes which Molotov addressed to the Western Powers in the second half of 1953 and during the Berlin conference early in 1954 at no point did he argue from Germany's continued division. Half-heartedly he still pleaded for unification and even advanced fairly specific schemes for the setting up of an all-German government. Throughout 1954, while the Western campaign for Germany's rearmament was not concluded, Soviet policy was in a state of suspense. Moscow encouraged the French opposition to E.D.C. and then sought to obstruct the passage of the London and Paris agreements. The failure of these efforts ended the state of suspense; after Malenkov's fall Molotov relegated his schemes for an all-German government to the archives.

Whatever one may think about the hopes raised by the Geneva conference, on the German issue the attitude of the Soviet government is now more clearly defined than it was before; and it is much stiffer. Amid smiles and friendly handshakes (which came after the renunciation by Moscow of the Anglo-Soviet and Franco-Soviet alliances!) Khrushchev and Bulganin carried out the threat that they would not seriously negotiate over Germany's unification as long as the Federal Republic was part of NATO. From Geneva the two Soviet leaders went straight to Eastern Germany to demonstrate that they backed to the hilt the Pieck-Ulbricht regime. (In June 1953 Beria went to Berlin in order to set the stage for the dismantling of that regime.)

This is not to say that the Geneva conference was a mere hoax or that the present Soviet rulers are not in earnest when they express the desire for a detente. But the limitations of the detente they envisage should be clearly realized. Malenkov and Beria believed that a change in the German *status quo* was the most essential prerequisite for a detente. Bulganin and Khrushchev seek to achieve the detente on the basis and within the framework of the *status quo*. The former aimed at what they believed would lead to a thorough and radical disengagement of the armed forces of East and West, while the latter aim at a partial disengagement only.

Behind all the trappings of Geneva and the paraphernalia of

the Soviet collective security pact (designed to last into the next millennium) there is a genuine Soviet desire to call a halt to the arms race and, if possible, to bring about an all-round, substantial reduction of armaments.

Parallel with the change in the Soviet approach to Germany a significant modification has occurred in Soviet strategic thinking. In 1953 Russia was not yet confident of her ability to match the United States in the production of nuclear weapons and trans-continental bombers. Soviet strategic thought still moved mainly along the lines of conventional warfare. Russia clung obstinately to her superiority in conventional weapons. From the point of view of traditional strategy, no military disengagement between East and West was possible as long as Germany was divided and Eastern and Western armies were garrisoned on German soil. Since then, however, Soviet strategic thought has advanced in step with Soviet nuclear power. The atomic stalemate between East and West has become a fact. The maintenance of superiority in conventional forces is no longer essential to Russia.

This creates the possibility of a detente based on a universal reduction of armaments. But the new strategic outlook affects Germany in a rather unexpected way. In terms of transcontinental atomic strategy, no thorough military disengagement of East and West is possible at all. Even the evacuation and the neutralization of a unified Germany cannot bring it about. Transcontinental airforces are not disengageable. Thus, from the Soviet viewpoint, a decisive incentive for ending Germany's partition has vanished. Russia's security can no longer be enhanced, at least in the view which seems recently to have prevailed in Moscow, by any German settlement agreed with the Western Powers. But Russia's—and the world's —insecurity may be lessened by a reduction of armaments. This is why Bulganin and Khrushchev are more conciliatory over disarmament than were their predecessors and why they argue that collective security and disarmament should be given priority over the German problem and be tackled independently of it.

In all these reasonings Germany is still treated as the mere 'object of history' she was during the first post-war decade. If it is at all possible to speak now of continued division, this is largely because no strong popular movement for unification has so far emerged in Germany to force the hands of the victors of 1945, a fact by which future historians will certainly be puzzled. Yet in their long-term plans Soviet policy makers are undoubtedly making allowance for the emergence of such a movement and they foresee the moment when the *status quo* will become untenable.

1 August 1955

5
The Twentieth Congress

The Twentieth Congress of the Communist Party of the Soviet
Union was held from 14 February to 25 February 1956 and was,
according to Mikoyan, the most important Party Congress since
the death of Lenin. Its consequences were enormous: the results of
Khrushchev's denunciation of Stalin were felt throughout Russia
and Eastern Europe; and the first serious disagreements between
Russia and China arose over the theses on revolution and relations
with the capitalist world that Khrushchev propounded to the
delegates.

Khrushchev made two speeches: one on 14 February, and
another secret speech on 25 February. The denunciation of
Stalin came in this second speech the existence of which was not
immediately known, although it became public knowledge by the
first days of March. (For a detailed analysis of this speech see the
essay in *Ironies of History* entitled 'Khrushchev on Stalin'.)[1] The
first two sections of this chapter were written before the existence
of the speech was known; the third section refocuses the analysis
in the light of subsequent revelations.

In his public speech as Secretary of the Party Khrushchev
attacked the cult of the personality without mentioning Stalin by
name, and asked delegates to cease the practice of applauding
Party leaders as they came into the congress hall. In his treatment
of foreign affairs, he said that the foreign policy of the Soviet
Union was based on the Leninist principle of peaceful coexistence,
and that, owing to the increased strength of the socialist camp,
war was no longer inevitable; it was also possible for revolutions
to be carried out by non-violent means and thus there were
several alternative ways of reaching socialism. In their subsequent
dispute the Chinese traced their disagreements with Russia to
these statements by Khrushchev on foreign affairs, and they were
quick to state their own position on these issues of socialist

[1] Isaac Deutscher, *Ironies of History*, 1966.

strategy in two articles that stressed the importance of revolutionary struggle: 'On the Historical Experiences of the Dictatorship of the Proletariat', published on 5 April, and 'More on the Historical Experiences of the Dictatorship of the Proletariat', published on 19 December.

Mikoyan spoke after Khrushchev's first speech and his statement was notable for being more outspoken in criticizing Stalin. He stressed that the Party had at last re-established a Leninist form of leadership and he specifically attacked Stalin for making ill-informed and dogmatic assertions about economic collapse in the West. Mikoyan also criticized the official Party history, the *Short Course on the History of the All-Union Communist Party (bolsheviks)*, which had been produced in 1938 by Stalin and contained many distortions and slanders against former communists; he called for the rehabilitation of those slandered in it and for the re-writing of Party history.

The conference went into secret session for Khrushchev's second speech, but the contents were distributed to local branches in the Soviet Union and to foreign Communist Parties as well. The only text that was ever published was the one produced by the State Department on 4 June.

The conference was followed by a series of rehabilitations in Russia and Eastern Europe. These included the Russian generals executed in 1937—Marshals Tukhachevsky, Bluecher, and Yegorov—and Eastern European leaders executed as 'Titoists' in the late 1940s like László Rajk, the Hungarian resistance leader, and Traicho Kostov, the leader of the Bulgarian Party.

These rehabilitations, and the fact that Khrushchev in his secret speech blamed Stalin for the breach with Yugoslavia, facilitated a further improvement in Russo-Yugoslav relations and the visit of Tito to Moscow on 2 June. He stayed in the Soviet Union for three weeks. The day before his arrival, Molotov resigned from the post of Foreign Minister and was replaced by Dimitri Shepilov. Shepilov, regarded as a protégé of Khrushchev, had been editor of *Pravda* since 1952 and since 1954 Chairman of the Foreign Affairs Commission of the Supreme Soviet. He had visited Cairo in July 1955 to negotiate the delivery of Soviet arms, an event that was one of the factors leading to the Suez crisis.

However neither Russo-Yugoslav friendship, nor Shepilov, survived the events of the autumn of 1956. Although Tito and

Khrushchev exchanged visits again in September, Tito made a public criticism of Soviet policy in Hungary on 11 November and this was followed by a deterioration in Russo-Yugoslav relations. Shepilov was dismissed from the post of Foreign Minister in February 1957 and following his alliance with Malenkov and Molotov in the Anti-Party Group he was expelled from the Presidium.

1 THE TWENTIETH CONGRESS OF
   THE SOVIET COMMUNIST PARTY

The Twentieth Congress of the Soviet Communist Party was from beginning to end a repudiation of Stalin's autocracy and the idea of the single leader. This alone makes of it an event of extraordinary importance. There was something paradoxical that it should have been Khrushchev who presided over this spectacle, for it was in Malenkov's heyday that the Stalin cult was in fact undermined. Khrushchev's rise was accompanied by vague attempts to restore Stalinist orthodoxy and by moves which appeared to be designed to put Khrushchev into Stalin's vacant post. These moves have apparently come to nothing. If Khrushchev did indeed aspire to become the Party's sole leader, then the collective leadership has so far kept him in his place. He spoke to the congress with the voice of the Central Committee, but not as the Central Committee's master. And if it had been his intention to stem the tide of anti-Stalinism, then that tide has proved stronger than he expected and has carried him with it some way.

The break with Stalinism is now apparent in almost every field of Soviet domestic policy, not merely in the denunciation of the leader-cult. It is a deep and radical break, especially in social policy.

For a quarter of a century Stalin indefatigably fostered social inequality. He furiously and incessantly fought the 'egalitarian heresy' and enforced a system of salaries and wages under which those who earned much could easily earn more and more, while those who earned little had few chances of improving their lot. He was the ruthless guardian of the privileges of the bureaucracy, the managerial groups, and the élite of skilled workers. Consequently, when Khrushchev announced at the congress that the Central Committee proposed to raise the wages and pensions of the lower paid workers and to cut some of the high salaries and pensions, he proclaimed a truly sensational reversal of Stalin's social policy. To the mass of the Soviet people this was probably more startling and welcome than was the renunciation of the leader-cult. The same is true of the abolition of all school fees for secondary and higher education. For the first time in more than thirty years the rulers of the Soviet Union have now practically attacked social inequality; and in this most Soviet citizens certainly see an effective guarantee of a progressive democratization of their regime.

Nothing was perhaps more characteristic of the new climate of opinion than what Khrushchev said at the congress about the degradation of the political police and the contempt with which this once-dreaded institution was now surrounded. Khrushchev even found it necessary to warn his audience that they should not carry their hostility towards the security services too far! Voroshilov, the President of the U.S.S.R., announced that the work on the new Criminal Code, the promulgation of which was promised in 1953 but repeatedly delayed, was at last completed, that the whole judiciary had been reorganized to ensure 'the rule of the law', and that a new Labour Code would now be prepared. Together with Stalin's permanent purges and permanent terror, his Draconian labour discipline was thus receding into the past.

At the same time something which was unthinkable only a short time ago has happened: most of the ill-famed concentration camps and forced labour camps have been closed without much ado. Many of their inmates have been given back complete freedom and rehabilitated. Those not rehabilitated have been allowed to live and work as free men in prescribed areas of settlement. Thus the regime appears to have freed itself at last from the most prodigious of its abuses and to have thrown off its heaviest load of shame.

All these measures have done much to consolidate the post-Stalin regime and to give it a greater measure of popularity and stability than even the Party leaders expected. No wonder that they addressed the congress in a mood of genuine confidence and unconcealed relief. The congress responded in the same mood.

Yet the oppressive weight of the Stalin era is still felt, and the regime is still far from being the proletarian democracy it claims to be. The proceedings of the congress itself testify to that. The congress adopted its resolutions by unanimous vote, in accordance with the Stalinist custom, which has nothing to do with the Leninist practice now allegedly revived. No *open* controversy or *direct* clash of opinion disturbed the smooth flow of the 'monolithic' debates. Not one of a hundred or so speakers dared to criticize Khrushchev or any other leader on any single point.

The change in the inner Party regime consists in the fact that major decisions of policy are now taken not by Khrushchev alone and not even by the eleven members of the Presidium, but by the Central Committee which has about 125 members (or 250 if alternate members are included). Inside that body free debate has been restored; and differences of opinion are resolved by majority vote. Under Lenin, differences in the Central Committee were not, as a rule, kept secret from the Party; and the rank and file freely expressed their own views. This is not the case at present. The Central Committee does not air its differences publicly or in the hearing of the whole Party. Only at its higher levels does the Party appear now to be managed more or less in the Leninist fashion; but it is still by and large in the Stalinist manner, though less harshly, that the lower ranks are ruled.

This can be only a transitional state of affairs. In the long run the Party cannot remain 'half-free half-slave'. The higher ranks will either have to share their newly won freedom with the lower ranks; or they themselves must lose it to a new dictator. In demonstrating hostility towards the 'un-Marxist leader-cult' the congress was anxious to bar the road to a new dictator, whoever he might be.

I have said that the congress witnessed no open and direct controversy. I should now add that one definite and fundamental controversy did develop at the congress, but it was conducted obliquely, in hints and by implication so that only the initiated could follow it. The chief antagonists in that controversy were Khrushchev and Mikoyan.

Their speeches reflected two different, and in part sharply conflicting, trends of opinion. The question over which they were divided was this: how much of the Stalinist orthodoxy should the Party throw overboard and how much should it preserve? On the answer depend, up to a point, the methods of government, the Party regime, and, last but not least, the country's spiritual climate. The question has its critical implications. It may be dangerous for the ruling group to try and preserve too much of Stalinism; but it may be equally dangerous

to repudiate too much of it, or to do so too abruptly. The issue
is further complicated by the fact that all the present leaders
have been Stalin's accomplices to some degree or other.

Khrushchev's attitude in this matter is one of great caution,
not to say timidity. He has ceased to glorify Stalin. He *alludes*
to Stalin's vices and arbitrariness; and he does this all the more
sincerely because he himself suffered from them in Stalin's last
years: Khrushchev's career and perhaps even life hung then by
a thread. But Khrushchev has not so far gone beyond allusions
although these are clear enough for anyone to grasp their
meaning. He is desperately avoiding an explicit repudiation of
his dead master. When he castigates the leader-cult, he never
mentions Stalin's name. He is afraid of the emotional reaction
against Stalinism which runs high in the Party and in the
nation; and he does not wish to encourage that reaction by
debunking the dictator's memory.

He has offered the country a scapegoat for all of Stalin's
misdeeds. That scapegoat is Beria. Yet too many people in the
Soviet Union remember that Beria became chief of the
political police only towards the end of 1938, and that the
great purges, the mass deportations, and the worst outbursts of
terror had occurred earlier. Still Khrushchev clings to Beria's
corpse as if to a protective shield.

He is afraid of 'too much' liberalism, 'too much' egalitarianism, and 'too many Utopian illusions'. Tough and practical
administrator that he is, he looks askance at the Party intellectuals who pose too many embarrassing questions and are too
anxious to know or to tell the whole truth about the Stalin era.
To Khrushchev's mind they threaten to awake too many
sleeping dogs at once, the sleeping dogs of Trotskyism, Buk-
harinism, bourgeois nationalism, etc., all the heresies which the
Party canon has condemned and which he, Khrushchev, has
no wish to exonerate.

Khrushchev's strongest ally is Kaganovich, who represents
the same frame of mind and is even less inclined to renounce
the Stalinist canon. They both yield to the new spirit of the
time only reluctantly, step by step, fighting Stalinism's rearguard battle all the time.

Mikoyan has emerged as the mouthpiece of militant anti-
Stalinism. He has been the first and so far the only leader to

repudiate Stalin explicitly. He has been the first to say that Stalin's theoretical pronouncements (which at the previous congress Mikoyan himself had no choice but to hail as the revelations of genius) were so much trash. It is not on Beria that Mikoyan heaps abuse. Instead he told the congress that the evil against which the Party was now fighting had taken root long before they knew Beria, in the early years of the Stalin era—perhaps even at its very beginning.

While Khrushchev inveighed against Trotskyists and Bukharinists and other 'enemies of the people', Mikoyan protested against slandering the leaders of the Revolution and of the Red Army as enemies of the people. He mentioned as an example Antonov-Ovseenko, who was one of the chief leaders of the Bolshevik insurrection of October 1917—he led the Red Guards in the storming of the Winter Palace, the seat of Kerensky's government whom he arrested, and was one of the first three Commissars of War before Trotsky was placed at the head of the Red Army. He was Trotsky's devoted friend and one of the chiefs of the Trotskyist Opposition in the 1920s. Later he gave up the struggle and surrendered to Stalin only to perish in the great purges. I knew Antonov-Ovseenko personally, and I can say that he retained to the end the highest respect and affection for Trotsky.

Mikoyan, to leave no doubt as to what he meant when he spoke up in defence of this man, roundly denounced the whole 'school of law' and the judiciary established since Lenin's death, the 'school of law' and the judiciary which were headed by Vyshinsky, the Chief Prosecutor in the purge trials of 1936–38. His speech amounted, therefore, to a demand for a revision of those trials and virtually for a rehabilitation of the defendants, Trotsky, Zinoviev, Kamenev, Bukharin, Radek, Rakovsky, and others.

Moreover, when Mikoyan urged the congress to wage a 'merciless struggle against *bureaucratic centralism* and for a full reinstatement of Lenin's *democratic centralism*', he consciously borrowed these terms, as well as many other ideas and formulae, from none other than Trotsky, who coined them. And it was in an almost characteristically Trotskyist manner that Mikoyan hinted at Lenin's testament, that lost document, unknown to the new Soviet generation, in which Lenin had advised the Party 'to remove Stalin' from the post of General Secretary.

Mikoyan's speech is a remarkable political and human document if only because he himself had been an ardent Stalinist at least since 1922, long before Khrushchev and Kaganovich joined the Stalinist faction. But while Khrushchev and Kaganovich owed their careers entirely to Stalin, he had risen in the Party in Lenin's days, and his mind had been formed in Lenin's school. His speech was something of an old Leninist's recantation of the part he had played in helping Stalin to his ascendancy. It was not a recantation in the familiar Stalinist style, but a genuine, restrained and only implicit confession of grim and grave errors committed during a lifetime. It was, however, also a confession of communist faith and of a desire to undo some of the still rampant evils of Stalinism.

The Khrushchev-Mikoyan duet has disclosed to the world the Party's divided mind, or the divided mind at least of the ruling group. It has also revealed something about the differences of opinion and the alignments inside the Central Committee. There can be little doubt that one of the consequences of the duet will be to project these differences and alignments from the Central Committee to the lower ranks of the Party and to draw the latter into the controversy. . . .

That Mikoyan was permitted to state his views from the platform of the congress is in itself an important innovation which sets a precedent. Again, this is no evidence of any real reinstatement of Leninist 'inner Party democracy'. In Lenin's days it was customary, when there was disagreement in the Central Committee over an important issue, for the majority to express its view in the official report to the congress, while a spokesman for the minority came out with a frankly controversial 'counter-report'. Mikoyan, it may be surmised, may have intended to come out with such a counter-report, but the Central Committee refused to permit at this stage an open clash between two members of the 'collective leadership'. A compromise was reached, under which Mikoyan was allowed to state his views in a positive form without making it explicit where, on what points, he dissented from Khrushchev. He was accorded the freedom of expression, but not the freedom of polemics.

The effect was some confusion at the congress. While many delegates certainly understood well what Mikoyan was driving at and how far-reaching were the implications of what he said, the less informed missed the nuances and believed that Mikoyan merely toed the Khrushchev line. When Mikoyan finished, the congress gave him an ovation such as it accorded no other leader, except Khrushchev and perhaps Bulganin. But while Khrushchev and Bulganin received the homages due to their office and rank, Mikoyan was applauded only for what he had said and for the manner in which he had said it, even if some who applauded him did not grasp the full import of his words.

Mikoyan's triumph suddenly brought to light the strength of the anti-Stalinist feeling in the Party. It gave rise to intense speculation, probably inside Russia as well as outside, about the forthcoming rehabilitation of Stalin's enemies, including Trotsky. All this was hardly welcome to Khrushchev and to the majority of the Central Committee. And here came the next great surprise: neither Khrushchev nor any one of his associates rose to disavow Mikoyan in congress. Both sides scrupulously observed to the end the rule, agreed upon in the Central Committee, that they should not engage in direct controversy. Only indirectly, without mentioning Mikoyan's name, did *Pravda* remind the Party that he did not represent the official view. Some days after he had been hailed by the congress, *Pravda* published an editorial which began with the emphatic statement that Trotskyists and Bukharinists were still considered 'enemies of the people', as Khrushchev had just described them. Notice was thus given that this crucial canon of Stalinist orthodoxy was still valid.

For how long will it remain valid? That is the question. The fact that Khrushchev refrained from attacking Mikoyan in public is a sign of the time. In similar situations Stalin, when he still struggled for power, never hesitated to disregard any gentleman's agreement reached in the Central Committee and to hit Trotsky, Zinoviev, and Bukharin below the belt. Khrushchev, whatever he may do in the future, has so far treated Mikoyan with fairness and even loyalty, although he would have found it quite easy to arraign Mikoyan, on the strength of his speech, as a Trotskyist and enemy of the people. Mikoyan was then elected to the Commission which framed the final resolution on Khrushchev's report; and he, like Malenkov, has retained his seat on the Presidium. Moreover, the final resolution is worded so as to give some satisfaction to those who share Mikoyan's views. It calls upon the new Central Committee to 'keep up the struggle against the remnants of the leader-cult'. It was only Mikoyan who had sought to impress upon the Congress the full weight of those sinister 'remnants' while the tenor of Khrushchev's speech suggested that by now not even a vestige of the leader-cult was left.

The congress thus ended on a note of compromise. Its final resolution contains no explicit disparagement of Stalin, and this should soothe the epigones of Stalinism. But it also authorizes a further revision and cleansing of the Party's record, which is what the anti-Stalinists desire. Such a resolution, designed to please everybody, can hardly prevent the opposing views from clashing after the congress. Far from closing the conflict, it carries the controversy into a new phase.

Who stands behind each of the antagonists? Broadly speaking the groups which enjoyed privileges under Stalin are certain to defend their 'acquired rights'; and their action assumes the form of an 'ideological' defence of residual Stalinist orthodoxy. Radical workers, the advanced intelligentsia, and the 'Leninists' in the Party all desire, from different motives, to rid themselves of the remaining fetters of that orthodoxy. Khrushchev and the practical administrators behind him try to strike a balance between the conflicting interests and aspirations and to avoid the sweeping 'ideological revisions' which may rend the Party and complicate the business of government.

The leaders have so far been wary of injecting bitterness into the controversy. It remains to be seen whether they will persist in this attitude. Economic progress, rising standards of living, and a degree of popular contentment in the country make it possible for the ruling group to settle its inner differences in a milder and more loyal manner than that in which differences were settled in Stalin's days. But the ideological revisions cannot be arrested half-way. The Party and the country feel that they have behind them a great yet dark and mysterious chapter of history. They desire to unravel it, to understand it, and to draw lessons from it. No nation can go through experiences such as the Soviet Union has lived through in the last thirty years without feeling the need for a great idea or a generalizing theory to illuminate those experiences. The post-Stalinist generation of communists wants to know whence it comes before it can be sure whither it goes. This explains the impatience with the falsified and lifeless Stalinist 'histories' of the Revolution and the cry for historical truth which resounded at the congress. That cry expresses not a Platonic interest in a dead past, but the search in the past for a key to the future.

The anti-Stalinist trend in the Soviet Union is a matter of vital interest to Communist Parties in other countries. It is, paradoxically, in some of those parties that Stalinism now finds its most stubborn defenders. Behind the scenes, the foreign communist leaders who were present at the congress as guests of honour were drawn into the controversy; and some indication of the attitudes they had taken could be found even in their ceremonial greetings to the congress.

The Soviet leaders, even the most pro-Stalinist ones, refrained from making a single laudatory remark about Stalin: in fact Mao Tse-tung and Thorez were, it seems, the only ones to bring in notes of adulation for Stalin, notes which smacked of the year 1952 and sounded strangely out of place now. The attitude of the French communist leader was perhaps not surprising: rushing to the rescue of Stalinist orthodoxy, he defended his own interest as the autocratic leader of the French Communist Party, an interest jeopardized by the new requirements of collective leadership.

Mao Tse-tung's attitude is more puzzling, because his own political record is, from the Stalinist viewpoint, by no means irreproachable. Has perhaps Mao's preoccupation with the industrialization of his own country and the collectivization of Chinese farming converted him at this late hour to full Stalinist orthodoxy? That orthodoxy certainly fits a primitive country in the throes of upheaval and in need of harsh discipline better than it fits present-day Russia. In any case, Mao's intervention must have greatly strengthened the hands of the pro-Stalinist elements in the Soviet Party. Most other foreign communist leaders appear to be sitting on the fence. Only Togliatti, the leader of the Italian Party, and Bierut, the leader of the Polish Party, seem to be definitely in favour of the break with Stalinism.

Three years after Stalin's death the Soviet Union is happier, stronger, and more self-confident than it was in the dictator's lifetime. But it is also, ideologically and politically, in a state of momentous, and perhaps salutary, ferment. This much can be forecast with certainty: the next congress of the Soviet Communist Party, whatever it may bring, will be at least as different from the congress now concluded, as this has been from the congress of 1952, that last and final orgy of the Stalin cult.

26 February 1956

2 FOREIGN AFFAIRS AT THE TWENTIETH CONGRESS

In foreign affairs the Twentieth Congress of the Soviet Communist Party has not brought to light any evolution as startling as that which it revealed in Soviet internal affairs. In the conduct of diplomacy the change from the Stalin era has been in manner rather than in matter; but it is not unimportant. Stalin's foreign policy alternated over the years between extremes of conciliation and recklessness. He was at times, in the 1920s and 1930s, almost abjectly meek in his dealings with foreign powers; at other times he was preposterously blunt and provocative. His successors avoid these extremes. Their policy is set on a far steadier course. It is less clumsy, less devious and secretive, more self-confident, flexible, straightforward, and sensitive to public opinion.

In a curious aside the now semi-retired Molotov confided to the congress that barely ten years ago the Party leaders could only in their boldest dreams imagine a situation as advantageous for the Soviet Union as the one in which they are now placed. This was no mere boast. In a very real sense, the Soviet Union is now playing from strength—strength derived from its own economic progress, from the consolidation of communist rule in China and even in Eastern Europe, from the possession of a vast and massive assortment of atomic, hydrogen, and conventional arms, and (last but not least) from the anti-colonialist ferment in Asia and Africa. All these elements of strength had been maturing during the last years of the Stalin era. But some of them have come to fruition only since then and have only recently made themselves fully felt in the conduct of foreign affairs.

Thus, at present, Moscow's foreign policy shows no sign of the hesitation and wavering which it showed soon after Stalin's death and throughout most of the Malenkov period, when Moscow appeared to be half-inclined to consider an overall settlement with the West on the basis of a joint evacuation of Germany and seemed only to be waiting for encouragement from the West. At that time almost every one of Molotov's diplomatic notes to the Western Powers called insistently for an early evacuation of Germany. Of that nothing more is heard. 'What we have we hold'—as Churchill once said—is now the implicit maxim of Soviet diplomacy.

This certainly applies to the major bulwarks and bastions of communist power, though not to such dubious acquisitions of the Stalin era as the Soviet naval bases in Finland and Manchuria and the Joint Stock Companies which Russia set up in the Balkan countries and in China. These have been given up with little real loss and with much moral gain; and at the congress Mikoyan had no inhibition in describing Stalin's efforts to secure these acquisitions as grievous errors. With the balance more or less cleared of such liabilities, the broad purpose of Soviet diplomacy is now to preserve the international *status quo*.

In a sense Stalin's successors are doing what Stalin did in the 1920s, when he, too, based his policy on the international *status quo* of that time. But the congress was naturally much more aware of the differences than of the resemblance. Thirty years ago the *status quo* meant the isolation of a weak and backward Soviet Union in the face of immensely superior non-communist powers. It was then still possible for Trotsky and Zinoviev to argue that, by reconciling itself with the *status quo*, communism was weakening its own chances and playing into its enemies' hands. The question whether Bolshevism should bank primarily on 'socialist construction' at home or on the early spread of revolution abroad presented a real dilemma then, because of the extreme weakness and precariousness of Soviet 'socialist construction' and of the apparently great strength of communism abroad, especially in Germany and China.

No such acute dilemma is troubling Moscow at present. The main strength of communism, actual and potential, now lies within the Soviet bloc, not without. The old controversy has become irrelevant to the new facts. Stalin's 'socialism in a single country' is a mere memory of the past; and Trotsky's prophecy that the Soviet Union depended for its survival on the spread of revolution has in some respects been fulfilled and in others become outdated.

Yet never perhaps since the 1920s have professions of faith in the eventual triumph of world communism over capitalism resounded from Moscow with as much inherent strength of conviction as they do now. There is a quasi-Trotskyist under-tone in those professions. In the middle 1920s the Soviet Party and the Comintern assumed, despite Trotsky's criticisms, that Western capitalism had achieved a measure of stabilization. No such assumption is made about the present state of the Western economy, in spite of boom-like conditions, continued full em-ployment, and feats of bourgeois progress which are no longer crudely denied. Moscow is convinced that the long and 'arti-ficially sustained' prosperity of the West is bound to end, sooner or later, in a collapse as disastrous as the slump of 1929.

How are these forecasts and professions of faith in world communism related to the defence of the diplomatic *status quo* and to the much over-worked slogan of peaceful coexistence? The answer is found not in the abstract logic of the Soviet attitude but in a specific, and in part tacitly assumed, concep-tion of the international class struggle. That the 'tide of history' carries mankind as a whole, through whatever stages and cross-currents, towards communism, is an old Bolshevik, indeed an old Marxist, axiom. That the 'tide' is moving faster than the Soviet leaders expected it to move ten or twenty years ago, and that it is doing its work all the better the fewer their attempts to force its pace, is the lesson they have learned, or re-learned, from the upheavals and conflicts of the last decade—in Germany and Korea not less than in China and Indo-China.

But the communist leaders have had to face anew the fact that the process of international revolution has not been con-tinuous. It has so far developed in two distinctly separate cycles or 'waves'.

From the first wave of revolution, that of 1917–20, Bolshevik Russia emerged victorious but bled white and isolated. From the second there has emerged the Chinese revolution, compared with which the Eastern European revolutions, carried out in the shadow of the Red Army, in 1944–48, have been of minor importance. This second wave has now nearly spent its force. That the third wave will come communists take for granted; but when—nobody can say. The interval, whether short or long, requires adjustments in communist policy and a *modus vivendi* with the capitalist world. The first two waves of revolution came in the wake of world war. It is therefore a matter of some interest to communist theory and policy whether the third wave, too, can have its origin only in a cataclysm of war. The congress has answered this question in the negative, because—so Khrushchev argues—the general balance of strength between East and West, the atomic stalemate in the first instance, militates strongly against the likelihood of a third world war, even though the attitude of the United States is partly unpredictable. This is the meaning of the 'thesis' about the avoidability of armed conflict.

The message of the Twentieth Congress, not altogether novel, is that the third wave of revolution need not be let loose, as the first two waves were, by the destructive furies of war—it may be generated by the constructive achievements of the Soviet bloc, especially of the Soviet Union. These achievements, however, require time for their materialization, a long 'respite' from the most acute forms of international class struggle, forms of struggle which may lead to world war. Both camps, the Western and the Eastern, may hope to benefit from a 'respite'. Both have therefore (this is the Soviet reasoning) a common interest in preserving the 'respite' and prolonging it indefinitely. Soviet policy invokes this common interest; and it does so all the more insistently because, whatever the variations of Soviet pronouncements on this subject, in the age of hydrogen weapons a clash of arms threatens both camps with annihilation.

The Soviet leaders have certainly a clear idea as to how they intend to use the respite. Having broken the Western, or rather the American, monopoly of atomic and hydrogen weapons, they plan to use the time at their disposal for breaking another, equally decisive, monopoly the West has enjoyed so far—the monopoly of a high standard of living. They argue that it is up to the West to defend this, its advantage, with all its economic might; and that it is legitimate for the Soviet Union to challenge the West on this ground. Such is the meaning of 'peaceful competition' in peaceful coexistence.

The new Five Year Plan, endorsed by the congress, is seen in Moscow as a milestone in the struggle to break the West's most vital monopoly. But the struggle must last another ten to twenty years. If and when it is concluded, the Soviet leaders expect that the attraction of communism, which will offer the masses high standards of living and education and will no longer have to force itself on unwilling subjects by means of terror, will be so overwhelming that the bourgeois order will not be able to resist effectively.

The third wave of revolution may then not carry with it all the blood that the first two waves carried; and the roads by which other nations approach socialism will prove much easier and smoother than the pioneers' thorny roads trodden by the Russians and the Chinese. Even now, Khrushchev pointed out, the roads (he insisted on the plural) are already easier for the People's Democracies: unlike the Soviet Union they need not give strict priority to heavy industry: they can afford a less strenuous economic policy. (After Malenkov's downfall the song 'Heavy Industry First and Foremost' was sung all over Eastern Europe. Khrushchev plainly discouraged this aping of the Russian fashion.)

The thesis about the 'different roads to socialism' is also designed to serve another more immediate and opportunistic purpose. When Moscow's leaders expatiate vaguely on the admissibility of a parliamentary road to socialism, a road unsullied by civil war, they intend to reassure Nehru and the Congress of India and similar neutral governments and parties in Asia. The Communist Party of India is already adopting a conciliatory attitude towards Nehru. The lure of the parliamentary road is also meant to overcome the misgivings of Western Socialist Parties about united fronts with the communists, the misgivings especially of the French Socialists and Radicals.

This policy gives a moderate and 'rightist' twist to communist tactics. It obliges the Communist Parties to exert themselves more than hitherto in the search for parliamentary alliances, to refrain from revolutionary ventures, and to behave with a good deal of bourgeois respectability. This seems to be the price Khrushchev is prepared to pay, or rather to make the Communist Parties pay, for peaceful coexistence.

Not unlike Stalin in the 1920s and 1930s, he sees that in coming years the decisive element of the international class struggle will be not the action of the French, Italian, or Indian communists, but 'socialist construction' within the communist realm. The Twentieth Congress looked forward not to the seizure of new positions of power for communism, but to the consolidation and the building up of the power which communism has already won.

29 February 1956

3 THE U.S.S.R. AFTER THE TWENTIETH CONGRESS

The Soviet Union and Eastern Europe are being shaken by a political fever which is not likely to subside soon. The Twentieth Congress of the Soviet Communist Party has set in motion new processes and new forces which are working towards a further transformation of the post-Stalinist regime.

The most important new development of recent weeks consists in the fact that the Communist Party as a whole has begun to discuss its affairs. It has begun to do so only after the Twentieth Congress; and it is doing so for the first time in nearly thirty years. Until the middle of February, when the congress was convened, only the top leaders had argued among themselves, within closed circles. Since the end of February the debate has been carried down to every cell and branch of the Party, where the rank and file wonder over the meaning of the break with Stalinism. Millions of members are involved in the argument. Further millions of non-Party men are drawn into it. And in Poland, Czechoslovakia, Hungary, and other communist countries the ferment has reached an even higher pitch of intensity.

The last impulse to this momentous debate came from Khrushchev when at the now-famous secret session he attacked Stalin's political record. Yet it looks as if he had not at first intended to make the attack; and as if he had not expected his own words to stir up so much commotion. He opened the congress with a rather shy report in which he did not even once criticize Stalin explicitly. Mikoyan alone of all the Party leaders demanded frankly that Stalin's whole record should be subjected to critical review. On the other hand, Kaganovich warned the congress against excess of anti-Stalinist zeal. Khrushchev at first placed himself prudently half-way between Mikoyan and Kaganovich. It was only just before the close of the congress, at one of its last sessions, that he came out with his bombshell.

Had Khrushchev intended beforehand to launch his attack, he would have done so at an early stage of the proceedings, when pronouncements of great importance are usually made to set the tone of the debates. In the event, it was not Khrushchev who set the tone of the debates—it was rather the debates which set the tone of Khrushchev's closing speech.

What happened between Khrushchev's first and second speech, between the opening and the close of the congress, to bring about this change? The proceedings of the congress were evidently more turbulent than one could judge from reports in the Soviet press. Khrushchev's inaugural address left the congress lukewarm and disappointed. Mikoyan's more outspoken remarks on the Stalin era evoked a much stronger response. The debates brought into the open the force of the anti-Stalinist emotion which ran through the Party. Only when this had been revealed did Khrushchev adjust himself. Then anxious to demonstrate that he was as good an anti-Stalinist as Mikoyan or anyone else, he delivered a diatribe against Stalin which was more violent than on sober reflection he might have liked it to be. The words he spoke in secret session leaked out almost at once and burst upon the country with shattering effect.

Whatever the truth of the matter, his closing speech has created a new situation. It has given fresh impetus to anti-Stalinist currents of thought and emotion. It has, incidentally, also provoked the epigones of Stalinism to come out in defence of their fallen idol. The pro-Stalin demonstration of the Tiflis students was an event rich in historic irony. Was it not a quirk of fortune that the first free street-demonstration which any Soviet city had seen for decades, that the first spontaneous expression of dissent and opposition should have taken the form of a homage paid to the man who had mercilessly suppressed all dissent and opposition? The young Georgians may resent the desecration of Stalin as a blow to their patriotic pride—they have no inkling of the fact that their famous countryman was also Georgia's relentless Russifier.

This paradoxical pietism for Stalin, however, is not likely to be widespread. Nor is it likely to become a serious political factor. There is hardly any sign of it among the working classes —not even among Georgian workers who did not, it seems, join the students in their demonstration, or down tools to defend Stalin's memory. It is the reaction against Stalinism, not the attachment to Stalinism, which counts at present.

What makes the situation look incongruous is that it is the old leaders of the Stalinist faction who are in revolt against Stalin's ghost. Willy-nilly one thinks of another revolt which took place in Rome well over four hundred years ago, when Cardinals eager to reform the Church from the corrupt condition in which the Borgia Popes had left it, denounced the memory of those Popes whom they themselves had served. Cardinal Gaspar Contarini, one of the famous reformers of the Church, wrote then to Alexander Farnese, Pope Paul III, in terms strikingly similar to those in which the 'cult of the individual' is now denounced in Moscow: 'Can that be called a Government whose rule is the will of one man by nature prone to evil? . . . A Pope ought to know that those over whom he exercises power are free men.' When other Prelates feared that discredit thrown on the memory of Popes would confuse the faithful and benefit Protestantism, the Cardinal retorted: 'How? Shall we trouble ourselves so much about the reputation of two or three Popes and not rather try to restore what has been defaced, and to secure a good name for ourselves?'

'To restore what has been defaced and to secure a good name for ourselves'—this concise formula expresses well the purpose of Moscow's Party leaders today. But how to define what exactly has been 'defaced' and what should be 'restored'? Only three months ago it was still the fashion in Moscow to

swear by Marx-Lenin-Engels-Stalin; and although it was admitted that the end—but only the end—of the Stalin era was
marred by grievous abuses of power, Beria, not Stalin, was
blamed for these. This was still the tenor of Khrushchev's
inaugural address. Within the fortnight during which the
Twentieth Congress was in session came the change in the
canon: Stalin's name was definitely deleted from the Apostolic
succession; and he himself came to be blamed for abuses of
power. What followed was an iconoclastic outburst, one of the
greatest in all history. This is not surprising: iconolatry always
leads to iconoclasm.

The emotional outburst need not perhaps greatly worry
Stalin's successors. The debunking of Stalin may even serve
them as a safety valve for pent-up discontents. Yesterday's
idol may be conveniently turned into the scapegoat of today—
and what a gigantic scapegoat he is! What is politically much
more serious is the critical scrutiny of the Stalin era which is
going on at various levels of the Party and which aims at
discovering the facts and fixing the responsibilities. To that
scrutiny no halt can be called. It delves deeper and deeper into
the record. It ranges over it irreverently, backward and forward. It threatens to leave no fragment and no aspect of the
Stalin era intact. And it may turn from Stalin himself to his
disciples, accomplices, and successors.

Anti-Stalinist revisionism works with the momentum of a
chain reaction. The Party leaders could not achieve, for instance, the final reconciliation with Tito without rehabilitating
Rajk and Kostov, who had been executed as 'Titoist traitors'.
They cannot rehabilitate Rajk and Kostov without rehabilitating Slansky and Clementis as well. They cannot declare null
and void all the Czech, Hungarian, Bulgarian, and other trials
and 'confessions' without declaring null and void the models
on which these were based, the Russian purge trials of the
1930s. They must rehabilitate the victims of those trials, too,
the 'traitors' and 'enemies of the people': Trotsky, Zinoviev,
Kamenev, Bukharin, Rykov, Tomsky, Rakovsky, Radek, and
many others, not to speak of Marshal Tukhachevsky and the
eminent generals who perished with him.

The problem for Khrushchev and his colleagues is whether
by doing this they will 'secure a good name' for themselves or,

on the contrary, disgrace themselves. An issue of staggering dimensions is involved—the judicial murder not merely of a handful of leaders, but of hundreds of thousands of Party members who were executed or have perished in concentration camps. The families and friends of the victims are now clamouring for posthumous justice.

In his inaugural address to the congress Khrushchev still described the mass of those victims, Trotskyists and Bukharinists, as 'enemies of the people'. It was not until the purge trials that Vyshinsky, the Prosecutor General, attached that label to Trotsky, Zinoviev, Bukharin, and their followers— before that they were as a rule attacked for their various 'deviations from Leninism' but not denounced as 'enemies of the people'. Khrushchev had in fact come to the congress ready to restore honour only to members of the Stalinist faction itself who had perished by Stalin's whim, not to anti-Stalinists. But the tide of anti-Stalinism has been moving fast. According to circumstantial evidence only a few weeks, or even days after the congress it had already been decided in Moscow to proceed with a revision of all the purge trials of 1936–38 and to rehabilitate the defendants. It is now virtually certain that the memory of Trotsky, Zinoviev, Bukharin, and their comrades will be cleared of the crimes imputed to them: terrorism, sabotage, espionage, and high treason.

The question which is still unresolved is in what form and to what degree the rehabilitation is to be carried out. This is going to be the most delicate and, morally, the most risky of all the revisions of the post-Stalin era. And it will pose at least as many problems as it will solve.

7 April 1956

4 STALIN AND THE SOVIET LEADERSHIP

In an article which echoed Khrushchev's secret speech *Pravda* has already declared that Stalin was guilty of 'gross violations of the law'. Some communist leaders (for instance J. Morawski, Secretary of the Polish Party) speak more bluntly about the

'crimes' which in his 'morbid suspiciousness and revengefulness'
Stalin committed.

The question of constitutional responsibility for those crimes,
which rests not only with Stalin, may thus arise; and when the
Soviet leaders talk so much about the 'rule of law', the 'inviolability of constitutional rights', etc., this aspect of the
matter may not perhaps be negligible. Two men, in the first
instance, bore the burden of constitutional responsibility for the
great purge trials: Kalinin, former Head of State, who is dead;
and Molotov, Prime Minister from 1930 to 1941, who is alive.
Molotov's place, it might be argued, should be in the dock. He
is nominally answerable for the 'violations of the law' which
took place during his tenure of office. The actual responsibility
rests, of course, with all members of the Politbureau of those
years: Kaganovich, Shvérnik, Voroshilov, Mikoyan, and
Khrushchev. (Khrushchev, however, was not appointed to the
Politbureau until 1938 when the trials were coming to an end.)

Stalin's successors plead *force majeure*. They say that all
resistance to Stalin was useless. Even as Prime Minister Molotov
would have paid with his head if he had clashed with Stalin.
He might even argue that he did at the outset oppose the purge
trials, and that he desisted only when Stalin threatened to place
him, too, among the purged. In 1936 it was widely believed in
opposition circles that this was indeed how Molotov had
behaved. Khrushchev has invoked the same argument in his
self-defence when he related to Eastern European communists
how he, Malenkov, and Bulganin interceded with Stalin in
1949 in order to save Voznessensky, their Politbureau colleague
and chief Soviet Planner, from Stalin's wrath. Voznessensky had
mysteriously vanished after Stalin had assailed him at the
Politbureau as an 'enemy agent'. Khrushchev, Malenkov, and
Bulganin allegedly pleaded with Stalin that Voznessensky was
innocent. 'Do you wish to inform me', Stalin replied coolly,
'that you, too, are enemy agents? Voznessensky was executed
this very morning.' Khrushchev is reported to have concluded
the story by saying that for some time afterwards he felt ill at
ease at the Kremlin and expected to be arrested any moment.

Such revelations and pleadings may shelve the issue of constitutional responsibility but they cannot dispel misgivings in
the minds of millions of communists. What Stalin's successors

are now anxious to establish is their political rather than their legal alibi. Can they establish it? In the Party cells their revelations were received with the utmost stupefaction. Rank and file communists are expected to show absolute devotion to communism, frankness towards their Party, and a readiness to sacrifice themselves and to lay down their lives for it. They cannot but ask now whether their leaders have lived up to these standards, and whether it was not the leaders' duty to go down fighting against Stalin's crimes rather than condone them. No doubt, the Party cells are relieved to see that an end has been made to the hypocrisy which surrounded Stalin's terror and that the terror has been exposed in all its nakedness. But if Stalin's successors deserve credit for revealing the truth, the truth does not reflect much credit on them. Had there existed anything like a genuine independent Party opinion, the cry would by now have gone up for a radical change in the leadership. Had any organized opposition existed in the ranks, it would by now have declared that there must be no room for Stalin's accomplices in the Central Committee and in the Presidium.

However, the essence of Stalinism lay precisely in the fact that it did not allow any independent opinion to form itself or any opposition to crystallize. The cry for a change in the Party leadership is therefore not likely to go up soon. There is probably nobody there to raise it. Moreover, Stalin destroyed the men who were able to form an alternative leadership; and his regime did not allow potential leaders from the young generation to come to the fore. Consequently, in the near future leadership can be provided only by that Stalinist élite which forms the present ruling group. No matter in what light Khrushchev, Bulganin, Malenkov, and their team may have shown themselves, they are not likely to have shaken their dominant position in the Party and the state. On the contrary, their revelations enable them to rid their government of the liabilities of the Stalinist legacy. (The situation may be different in the People's Democracies in Eastern Europe where remnants of the anti-communist parties may perhaps be in a position to benefit from the disarray in communist ranks. In the Soviet Union not even a trace is left of the old pre-revolutionary parties.)

How far do Stalin's successors intend to go, and how far can they go, in dissociating themselves from their own past? Even while they are making ready to denounce the purge trials they still declare that Stalin was right to stand against the Oppositions up to the time of the purges. He was right, they say, in advocating 'socialism in one country' against Trotsky, and in furthering industrialization and collectivization against Bukharin. When precisely, at what moment, did Stalin then go wrong? Party ideologues discuss this question with the fervour with which some theologians once argued over the exact moment at which man's fall had occurred. The fall occurred, Khrushchev replies, at the moment when Stalin, having defeated the Oppositions, freed himself of all democratic control and 'placed himself above the Party'. Up to that time (that is up to the year 1934 or perhaps 1932), Khrushchev claims, Stalinism preserved its innocence; and it is that innocent Stalinism, unstained by the blood of the Old Bolshevik Guard, that he seeks to recapture and reinstate. This answer is not likely to satisfy searching minds for long, and many searching minds are at work on these issues in the Soviet Union. Even at the Twentieth Congress Mikoyan suggested that the 'fall' may have begun much earlier, at Lenin's death in 1924, or shortly thereafter. And at cells in the Soviet Party and in foreign Communist Parties members have already posed further embarrassing questions which have raised *Pravda*'s ire.

When communists are told that 'Stalin placed himself above the Party', they ask how it happened that he succeeded in that. How could one man impose his will upon a Party which prides itself on holding the doctrine that masses and social classes, not 'great individuals', make history? Where was the Party and where was the working class when Stalin subjected them to autocratic rule? Were they taken by surprise? Many a communist reflects over one of Marx's famous *obiter dicta*: 'It is no excuse to say that a nation is taken by surprise' (which he wrote when he was probing into the origin of France's Second Empire). 'Neither a nation nor a woman is forgiven for the unguarded moment in which she allows a chance comer to seize the opportunity of overpowering her. Such turns of speech do not solve the riddle; they merely thrust the problem a stage further back.'

The conclusion which inevitably occurs to many a communist is that there must have been something wrong with their Party even before Stalin 'placed himself above it'. What was it? And had not both Trotsky and Bukharin, each in his own way, warned the Party that this was Stalin's ambition? Were the leaders of those 'anti-Leninist Oppositions' as wrong as Khrushchev still says they were?

The inquest on the Old Bolshevik Guard goes on; and these are the lines upon which it proceeds. The archives are being thrown open in Moscow and elsewhere; and those who conduct the inquest find in them plenty of new ammunition. *Pravda* fires back and thunders that it will not allow old 'deviations' to be resuscitated. But *Pravda* now 'allows' many things to happen which it did not dream of allowing barely a few months ago. It will 'allow' many more.

The original protagonists of the strange dispute, Stalin, Trotsky, Zinoviev, Bukharin, and their immediate disciples, are all dead. Yet it looks as if they are back at the contest posthumously, and as if a new generation is to fight their battles again. This is not just a case of *le mort saisit le vif*, of the dead gripping the living. The inquest on the past is essential to the clearing of the moral climate of post-Stalinist Russia. And its results have a bearing on practical policy. In some respects the events of the last twenty years have settled, transcended, and rendered outdated the old inner Party controversies. But in other respects these controversies are still relevant to the issues which occupy the Soviet Union today.

Those, for instance, who are distinctly inclined to favour the peasant interest are likely to embrace some sort of an up-to-date version of the Bukharinist doctrine—Bukharin once led the pro-*muzhik* school of thought in the Bolshevik Party. Those eager above all to fight inequality and to further a 'proletarian democracy' may draw inspiration from the ideas of Trotsky and Zinoviev. The orientation of communist policy in foreign affairs, the extent to which that policy acquires an active internationalist character or remains coloured by the nationalism of the Stalin era, is also bound up with old alignments. Finally, even a partial rehabilitation of the old oppositions saps that monolithic outlook which Stalin gave to the Party and may pave the way for a different conception of the communist regime, one which admits a certain diversity and contest of ideas, views, and policies.

The inquest on the Stalin era, involved and obscure as it may be at times, is therefore of vital importance for the Soviet Union and the world at large.

7 April 1956

5 MOLOTOV RESIGNS

Molotov's exit from the Soviet Ministry of Foreign Affairs is an event in Soviet domestic affairs as well as in diplomacy. It marks the progress of the break with Stalinism which has been taking place for some time now; and it foreshadows the approach of a new phase of de-Stalinization. All those elements in the Soviet Communist Party and in Communist Parties outside Russia who have viewed this trend with misgivings or hostility and have sought to obstruct it, have until now looked to Molotov for support, if not for leadership. They are greatly weakened and disappointed by his departure, and must expect new disappointments in the near future.

Molotov's 'resignation' was timed to coincide with Marshal Tito's arrival in the Soviet Union. Stalin's successors have welcomed the Yugoslav leader by, metaphorically, putting his enemy's head on a platter before him. It would, indeed, have been a grotesque spectacle for Molotov, who together with Stalin pronounced the anathema of 1948, to assist, as Foreign Minister, at Tito's triumphal entry into Moscow. . . .

In foreign affairs the change of ministers does not foreshadow any distinct change of policy. It is already some time now since Molotov was removed from the effective direction of his department and made to suffer humiliation after humiliation. Not he but Bulganin and Khrushchev received important foreign visitors, went on missions abroad, and dealt with current diplomatic business. In the Central Committee Molotov was under strong attack from none other than Shepilov, the new Foreign Minister. Thus the change of ministers puts a seal on a change of policy already accomplished.

Western diplomacy will find in Shepilov a man very different in temper from Molotov—it would indeed be difficult to find two more contrasting characters. Molotov was the perfect bureaucrat of the Stalin era, orthodox, shrewd yet dull-minded, suspicious, secretive, and impassive. Shepilov is one of those younger Party intellectuals who somehow managed to preserve a certain independence of mind even in the ritualistic atmosphere of the Stalin era. He is quick-minded, sharp-witted, and full of verve. He also appears to be much better educated as a Marxist theorist and an economist than his predecessor.

Molotov was almost a symbol of the isolationism of the Stalin era, with its obtuseness and lack of sensitivity to the outside world; and this was even reflected in his ignorance of any foreign language. The new Minister brings to his job a far greater knowledge of world affairs acquired from, among other things, wide reading in foreign languages. Molotov's habits of thought were formed at a time when Western Europe still was, or seemed to be, *the* centre of world policy; and old Bolshevik though he is, he belonged essentially to the nineteenth-century diplomatic school whose horizon rarely transcended Europe. He felt completely out of his depth whenever he stepped into the 'Anglo-Saxon world'; and in his diplomatic conceptions he made little or no allowance for the rising nations of Asia and Africa. Shepilov is much more a man of this century. The Anglo-Saxon world has loomed very large on his horizon: he appears to have studied English and American history; and in his diplomatic calculations he gives much weight to the affairs not only of Asia and Africa but even of Latin America.

It was on these points that Shepilov has attacked Molotov, holding that Molotov pursued his diplomatic action on too narrow a basis, as a game between Great Powers only, and that he neglected the opportunities open to Russia in the vast, 'uncommitted' areas of the world. Molotov, indeed, viewed suspiciously the nations that remained neutral in the cold war; and he treated the governments of India, Burma, Indonesia, Egypt, etc. as mere stooges of Western imperialism. Against this, Shepilov insisted on the need for Soviet diplomacy to encourage neutralism and to treat India, Burma, Indonesia, and the Arab states with the consideration and respect due to independent states. He castigated Molotov's tactical rigidity and lack of initiative. He carried the day within the Central Committee: his was to some extent the initiative for Khrushchev's and Bulganin's visit to India; he undertook to test his line in Egypt, which he did with notable success; and he had the satisfaction of being able to listen to Molotov's 'self-criticism' at the Twentieth Congress.

Shepilov may be expected to conduct foreign policy *fortiter in re, mediocriter in modo*. He will, to quote Theodore Roosevelt's dictum, carry a big stick and speak softly, unlike Molotov who had a preference for speaking rudely. But the contrast between the two ministers is probably less a matter of personalities than of the different situations in which each has had to work. Molotov's outlook fitted a time when the Soviet Union acted from weakness, inferiority, and fear—first the fear of Europe at large, then fear of the Third Reich, and finally fear of the American atomic monopoly. Soviet diplomacy then relied on the defences of the weak: secrecy, stone-walling, bluff, and surprise. Molotov carried a rather short stick during most of the time when he spoke so rudely; but he found soft speech rather uncongenial even after the Soviet stick had become much bigger.

By just how much the stick had grown was indicated by Shepilov when, at the recent Party Congress, he pointed out that before the Second World War communism was in control of only seven per cent of the world's industrial output, but that it now controlled not less than thirty per cent, and was rapidly increasing its share. These two figures stand for two different eras of Soviet diplomacy; and the different eras require different men.

It should perhaps be added that in one crucial respect the old Foreign Minister probably represented a more conciliatory attitude towards the West than that which his successor is likely to take. Molotov was still vaguely inclined to consider a settlement with the West on the basis of Germany's unification. This seems now to be ruled out in Moscow. Shepilov will indeed speak softly, avoid provocation, and make the most of Russia's 'unilateral disarmament'; but he enters the stage with an awareness of the new power which backs his diplomacy, and with a quite new sense of confidence.

3 June 1956

6
Crisis in the Soviet Bloc

Khrushchev's denunciation of Stalin and the rehabilitation of Titoists had a catalytic effect in Eastern Europe, both on the upper echelons of the Party and on the masses. Riots at the industrial centre of Poznan in Poland on 28 June 1956 were the first open sign of a new popular mood. The riots were caused mainly by economic pressures but, in addition to purely economic demands, the workers also voiced hostility to the Soviet Union. Although the Polish government used troops to suppress the riot and blamed the disturbances on 'imperialist saboteurs', the authorities responded by dismissing the Ministers of Engineering and of the Motor Industry, by refunding taxes that had been 'unjustly collected' from the Poznan workers, and by other economic and political reforms. In Hungary the main pressure for reform came from the Petöfi circle, a club of Budapest intellectuals, and in July the old Stalinist Rakosy was replaced as Secretary of the Party by Ernö Gerö.

These gradual liberalizations formed a prelude to the explosions of October. In Poland popular pressure built up during the summer and early autumn, and it centred specifically on the person of Marshal Rokossovsky, the Minister of Defence. The Polish leaders were split, and the Central Committee of the Party met on 19 October to discuss the situation. The arrival of Khrushchev and the other Soviet leaders on the same day ensured that the Russians would agree to whatever conclusion was reached. On 21 October it was announced that Marshal Rokossovsky had left the Presidium, and that Ochab had been replaced as Party Secretary by Gomulka, a popular leader who had spent the period from 1951 to April 1956 in prison as a Titoist. Marshal Rokossovsky resigned as Minister of Defence in November. (For a full discussion of the dismissal of Rokossovsky see the essay entitled 'Warsaw's Verdict on Rokossovsky' in *Ironies of History*.)

This victory of the Polish reform movement had an important

impact on the situation in Budapest where public pressure had already started to mount following a ceremonial reburial of László Rajk on 6 October and the re-admission to the Party of Imre Nagy, who had been Prime Minister from 1953 to 1955. A violent demonstration by students and workers in Budapest on 23 October in favour of Nagy led to his replacing Hegedüs as Prime Minister that night and the new government called in Russian troops to restore order. It now appears that Gerö, not Nagy, called in the Soviet troops but this was, and is, unclear. The Soviet troops withdrew gradually and it seemed at first as if a repetition of the Polish change was to take place; but at the end of October Nagy announced the formation of a National Government and withdrew Hungary from the Warsaw Pact. On 4 November Soviet troops intervened for the second time, and after some weeks of fighting complete control was re-established. Nagy fled to the Yugoslav Embassy for asylum, and a new government under Kadar was created.

The events in East Europe coincided with the attack on Egypt by Israeli, British, and French forces on 31 October following the nationalization of the Suez Canal in July. The Soviet Union gave full diplomatic support to Egypt and threatened to fire rockets at London; but, following international pressure, the attacking forces withdrew. An immediate consequence of Russia's new prestige in the Middle East was an increase in American interest in the area. In a special address to Congress in January 1957 Eisenhower spoke of the 'greater responsibility' that now devolved on the U.S. in this area, a 'responsibility' which the U.S. was to demonstrate in the crises of 1957 and 1958 (see chapters 8 and 9). Shepilov denounced this Eisenhower Doctrine at the meeting of the Supreme Soviet in February but he was then dismissed from the post of Foreign Minister and replaced by Gromyko. The October crises also had economic consequences, and important changes were made at two plenary sessions of the Central Committee of the Party in December and February; it was at the former session that Saburov was replaced by Pervukhin as head of the *Gosekomkomissiya*.

1 THE POLISH AND HUNGARIAN REVOLTS

Never since the 1812–13 insurrection of the European peoples against Napoleon—an insurrection that combined the features of revolution with those of counter-revolution—has Europe seen as confused and desperate a popular revolt as that which has shaken Poland and Hungary and sent its tremors through the rest of Eastern Europe.

The background of the October events was very much the same in Poland and Hungary. In both countries the explosion of the Stalin myth and the disintegration of the Stalinist police terror had put into motion vast popular forces impatient with the slowness and half-heartedness of official de-Stalinization and pressing for an immediate and radical break with the Stalin era. Both in Poland and in Hungary the movement grew from modest beginnings and gained scope and momentum until it assumed a nation-wide scale. In both countries the offended dignity of peoples reduced to the roles of Russian satellites had powerfully asserted itself, claiming its rights. Yet the Poles and Hungarians struggled for political freedoms as well as for national emancipation, and they rose against the Stalinist police state through which Russia had dominated them. Last but not least, they revolted against an economic policy that had sacrificed their consumer interests to industrialization and armaments and had plunged them into intolerable misery.

The upsurge of nationalist emotion, the yearning for political freedom, and despair at the economic plight in both countries were common to workers, intelligentsia, students, civil servants, army officers, and the still numerous survivors of the old bourgeoisie. In both countries all social divisions were for a time completely overshadowed by the single and all-embracing antagonism of the peoples at large to a handful of Stalinist die-hards clinging to power. Even the die-hards were politically disarmed, and none other than Khrushchev had disarmed them. After his speech at the Twentieth Party Congress they stood naked before the peoples as the high priests of a dethroned idol and a desecrated church. They themselves were fitfully engaged in smashing the idol and desecrating the church—that is, in preaching de-Stalinization. By preaching it they supplied to the popular movement surging from below the slogans, the banners, and the moral weapons of insurrection.

De-Stalinization gave a legal cloak to the popular revolt in its initial phases and concealed the diverse currents and cross-currents of the revolt. Communists and anti-communists, Leninists and Catholics, socialists and conservatives all spoke in the same idiom—the idiom of de-Stalinization. For a time all seemed united in the enthusiasm for a new leader—Wladyslaw Gomulka in Poland and Imre Nagy in Hungary, both national communists and martyrs of the Stalin era whose names had become symbols of opposition to Russian domination and to the Stalinist police state.

Yet within this outwardly harmonious anti-Stalinist movement there were from the beginning two separate currents in actual or potential conflict with one another, and a tense and only partly open struggle went on between communists and anti-communists. It should not be imagined that the line of division ran only between members and non-members of the Communist Party. It cut across the Party itself, which in the last twelve years had absorbed the most diverse elements, some who would normally, given their freedom of choice, have followed a Social Democratic lead, and others who would have joined right-wing clericalist and nationalist parties.

As long as the Communist Party was the Stalinist monolith, these differences mattered little; they had no opportunity of expression. But now the Party was no longer the old monolith, and so the tug of war between communism and anti-communism—conscious or only instinctive—began to develop in its own midst. Outside the Party, anti-communism had behind it a numerous and influential Catholic clergy, the sentiments of vast sections of the peasantry and of the intelligentsia, and the hopes cherished by the remnants of the urban bourgeoisie. The new anti-Stalinism appealed to non-Party men as well, to workers, intellectuals, and members of the bureaucracy.

There were, however, also vital differences between Hungary and Poland—differences that were to determine the vastly different results of the struggle in the two countries. In Poland, anti-Stalinist communism was incomparably stronger than in Hungary even in the heyday of Stalinism. Polish communists, especially the older ones, had never at heart forgiven Stalin the blow and insult he inflicted on them in 1938, when he disbanded the whole of the Polish Communist Party, denouncing it as 'a nest of Trotskyist *agents provocateurs*' and ordering the execution of all its leaders who had fled to Moscow from Marshal Pilsudski's prisons and concentration camps. Even in the years 1950–53 the communist leaders of Warsaw used all their cunning to cheat Stalin and avoid staging trials in the style of Rajk in Hungary and Slansky in Czechoslovakia, and it was thanks to this that Gomulka lived on to fight another day. (Among the papers of Boleslaw Bierut, the Stalinist Polish leader who died early this year, were found documents in which he urged his subordinates to ignore Stalin's insistent demands for Polish purge trials.)

No wonder that Polish communist activists received de-Stalinization with relief and joy as a most congenial job, while Matyas Rakosy and his men did their utmost to curb and delay de-Stalinization in their country. The Polish communist cadres remained on the whole sensitive to popular moods and kept in touch with them, while the Hungarians were cut off from the masses and were blind and deaf to the ground-swell of political emotion in their country.

To the Polish communists the Poznan riots last summer came as a timely and salutary warning. Poznan made them aware of the gulf that had opened between their own ruling group and the working class. It made them realize that unless they, the communists themselves, broke rapidly and radically with the Stalin era, Poland's de-Stalinization might be carried out against them by anti-communists. Hence the Polish Party did not use Poznan as a pretext for tightening screws. On the contrary, it pressed democratization and worked to narrow the gulf between the rulers and the ruled.

By far the most important Polish development since Poznan has been the rise of a strong movement for 'industrial de-Stalinization' among the workers in the factories. This essentially communist movement, which was to play a decisive role in October, found its main base in the factories of Warsaw, especially in the suburb of Zheran, and in the mines and steel mills of Silesia and Dombrowa. The spirit animating this movement was closely akin to that which animated the Bolshevik masses of Petrograd and Moscow in the early days of the Russian Revolution.

The Polish workers were quick to translate the intelligentsia's call for de-Stalinization and democratization into specific industrial demands of their own. For them, democratization has meant first of all 'the workers' direct control over industry' and the abolition of an over-centralized economic dictatorship by bureaucracy that had ridden roughshod over the workers' needs and rights. The Party leaders at first viewed with some apprehension this movement and its potential challenge to national economic planning, but the movement had an irresistible force and they made their peace with it. It created something like a ready-made proletarian class basis for de-Stalinization.

Up to the Poznan riots the intelligentsia led the movement for de-Stalinization. Afterwards, however, the workers came to the fore, and the whole weight of the movement shifted from university halls, literary circles, and editorial offices to industrial workshops. These became the scene of something like a genuine revolution from below, developing just at the time when that 'revolution from above' which Stalin had imposed on Poland was on the point of exhaustion and perhaps collapse. In this lay the strength of Polish communism during the October crisis. The workers came to feel for the first time that the promise of communism might after all be fulfilled, that they might become masters in their factories, and that the words 'a workers' state' might cease to be empty. They were and still are inclined to credit the new Gomulka leadership with the intention of carrying out this programme and so are prepared to back that leadership against anti-commun it assaults.

Gomulka seems to be aware that the best chance of his survival in independence from Russia, and of the survival of Polish communism in general, lies in that newly emerged native strength of the Polish working class. Twice when in danger he has already appealed to that strength: first on 19 October, when he threatened Khrushchev, Molotov, Mikoyan, and Kaganovich, on their arrival in Warsaw, that he would arm the workers of Warsaw against any Soviet inspired military coup; and then on 22 October, when he sent the same workers

—not the army or even the police—to disperse anti-communist student demonstrations in the capital.

In this way, Gomulka managed for the time being to avert the threat of Soviet intervention and to check anti-communism. The fact that he acted resolutely when threatened with Soviet intervention helped greatly to consolidate his position. For the first time since its inception, Polish communism freed itself from the odium of being a Russian puppet condemned to remain forever in irreconcilable conflict with Polish national aspirations. Until then, the Poles had looked and could look only to anti-communists to assert what they regarded as their national interest and national dignity. Now, for the first time in its long, checkered, and tragic career, Polish communism had assumed the role of the exponent of the national longing for independence.

Faced with this situation, Moscow had to acknowledge Gomulka's ascendancy and to recognize that it was preferable from its own viewpoint that the heretical communism of Gomulka rather than anti-communism should find itself at the head of Poland's national resurgence. When Khrushchev arrived in Warsaw on 19 October, he was not in fact motivated by any special hostility toward Gomulka—it was indeed far easier for him to come to terms with Gomulka than it had been to make apologies to Tito. What brought Khrushchev and his colleagues to Warsaw was, it seems, the fear that anti-communist forces might gain the upper hand in the upheaval and that Gomulka, playing unwittingly the part of a 'Kerensky in reverse', might pave the way for a counter-revolution. The fear was not altogether groundless. At any rate, some Polish anti-communists certainly viewed the situation similarly, for they too looked upon Gomulka as upon a Kerensky in reverse.

It was, however, Imre Nagy who was cast for that part, although he was not destined to act it to the end. Like Gomulka, Nagy was at first acclaimed by communists and anti-communists alike and carried back to power on a wave of national enthusiasm. But in that wave the anti-communist current from the beginning was much more powerful than the communist one. The Hungarian Party now had to pay the heaviest price for its rigid addiction to Stalinist orthodoxy. No large and important section of its membership had intimately and in good time identified itself with the popular revulsion against the Rakosy era. Ernö Gerö, whose name still symbolized that era to the popular mind, remained at the Party's head even after the rehabilitation of Lászlo Rajk and his grimly provocative re-burial. Only on the night of 23–4 October, after the storm had broken over its head, did the Communist Party recall Nagy to the leadership. By this time Budapest was already the scene of civil war, and the weakness and the sense of isolation of Hungarian communism showed itself in its panicky call for Soviet armed help after the first shots had been fired.

The alignment of social and political forces in Hungary on the eve of civil war was also very different from that which had taken shape in Poland. No agitation for workers' control over industry and no communist 'revolution from below' comparable to the Polish one had developed so as to enable the communist regime to gain fresh strength and find a 'proletarian class basis'. Students and army officers took the initiative; the workers followed the intelligentsia's lead.

Such, at any rate, appears to have been the situation in Budapest. In the provinces, two distinct centres of insurrection sprang into being, at Miskolc in the north-east and at Györ in the west. In both cities, communists and anti-communists were active, and in both cities they soon came to blows with one another. At Miskolc, the insurgents appealed to the country in the Marxist-Leninist idiom, and it was in the name of proletarian internationalism that they demanded the withdrawal of Soviet troops and the restoration of Hungary's sovereignty.

The real headquarters of the rising in the provinces was at Györ, where after an interval during which Attila Szigeti, a communist, led the insurgents, the anti-communists—among whom the clergy were prominent—gained the upper hand. It was no longer de-Stalinization that was the battle cry at Györ; it was 'Down with Communism!'

The split in the rebel camp came to a head when the communist insurgents, responding to the appeal of Nagy—their man—were ready to lay down their arms and demanded that their comrades in arms do the same. By this time, a religious peasantry had risen and thrown its weight behind the anti-communists. This was apparently one of the decisive differences between Poland and Hungary: in Poland the peasantry had remained passive through all the phases of the crisis from the Poznan riots to the October upheaval.

In vain did Nagy's spokesmen now broadcast the desperate appeal: 'We beg you, stop the slaughter. You have won. All your demands have been accepted'. The anti-communist insurgents did not agree that they had won, and as the insurrection was spreading over the countryside they played for ever higher stakes. Together with the call 'Down with Communism!' went up their cry for the immediate withdrawal of all Soviet troops. This demand was as sure to arouse the passions of a nation driven to frenzy by Soviet armed intervention as it was unlikely to be accepted.

The ascendancy of anti-communism found its spectacular climax with Cardinal Mindszenty's triumphal entry into Budapest to the accompaniment of the bells of all the churches of the city broadcast for the whole world to hear. The Cardinal became the spiritual head of the insurrection. A word of his now carried more weight than Nagy's appeals. If in the classical revolutions the political initiative shifts rapidly from Right to Left, here it shifted even more rapidly from Left to Right. Parties suppressed years ago sprang back into being, among them the formidable Smallholders' Party. The Communist Party disintegrated. Its newspaper *Nepszabadszag* ceased to appear. Its insurgent members perished at Russian hands or at the hands of Hungarian anti-communists. Its erstwhile leader, Gerö, was killed. Its powerless Premier hoped to avert the catastrophe by bowing to the storm and accepting every anti-communist demand, until on 30 October he proclaimed the end of the single-party system and agreed to preside over a government in which the communists did not have a majority. This spelled the end of the communist regime, and Nagy drew the only logical conclusion from the fact when, on 1 November, he proclaimed Hungary's neutrality and denounced the Warsaw Pact. He was now indeed 'Kerensky in reverse'.

The events in Poland and Hungary undoubtedly led to a grave political crisis in Moscow, by far the gravest since Stalin's death. That the Soviet ruling group was divided could be seen even during the Polish crisis, when the leaders of the three main factions came to Warsaw: Molotov and Kaganovich, the Stalinist diehards; Mikoyan, the 'liberal'; and Khrushchev, the middle-of-the-roader. Khrushchev's first inclination was to side with the die-hards and to use force or at least to threaten it.

Only when the threat failed and it turned out that the Polish upheaval did not after all imperil the communist regime did Khrushchev reconcile himself to the new situation. The 'liberals' in Moscow had won the day. But the Hungarian rising at once aggravated the division. Mikoyan, in Budapest, assisted by Gomulka's envoy on the spot and by Tito's appeals from across the frontier, negotiated for the withdrawal of Soviet troops, while the government in Moscow was preparing the declaration of 30 October, in which it virtually committed itself to the withdrawal and openly confessed its errors in treating other countries as satellites. But Zhukov and Shepilov publicly stated on 29 October that Soviet troops would not be withdrawn before the Hungarian revolt was suppressed. Were perhaps the chief of the Soviet armed forces and the Minister of Foreign Affairs airing their differences with other Party leaders?

The Soviet army, it may be assumed, could have acted with greater vigour and determination at the beginning of the rising, between 24 and 27 October, if it had not been hampered by divided counsels in Moscow and contradictory orders. When the army feigned a withdrawal from Budapest on 30 October, it probably did so under pressure from the 'liberals' in the Presidium who hoped that this would enable Nagy to establish a national communist regime that would, like Gomulka's regime, still remain aligned with the Soviet bloc. This hope was dashed two or three days later, when the disintegration of Hungarian communism became evident and Nagy denounced the Warsaw Pact.

The 'liberals' in Moscow had suffered a signal defeat. The die-hards of Stalinism and the army dictated policy, and they dictated renewed and more massive intervention. Probably no one in Moscow had the desire or the courage to defend Nagy, whose government was seen as due to be presently replaced by an openly anti-communist regime—failing Soviet intervention. It was no longer Hungary but the whole of Russia's position in Eastern Europe, in Germany, and in the world at large that was at stake. The collapse of communism in Hungary was sure to increase a hundredfold the anti-communist pressures everywhere. The Presidium was therefore probably unanimous in sanctioning the new Soviet intervention in Hungary...

15 November 1956

2 THE CAUSES OF THE CRISIS IN EASTERN EUROPE

The Hungarian tragedy is a direct consequence of the changes that have come about in Russia since the death of Stalin, and it will certainly have a profound influence on the development of the situation within the Soviet Union. When Khrushchev demolished the Stalin myth at the Twentieth Congress, he did not imagine that a short time afterwards Hungarian rebels would have pulled down Stalin's statue in the heart of Budapest and smashed it to pieces.

Unwittingly, Khrushchev became the inspirer of the Hungarian revolt which turned into a revolt against communism and against the Soviet army. There is a close connection between these two events: between the ideological destruction of the Stalin myth carried out by Khrushchev and the revolt against Stalinism in Hungary. Stalin's successors have tried to rationalize and liberalize the system of government they inherited. They have dismantled Stalin's massive machine of terror; they have broken the back of the political police; and they have done away with the horror of the purges and of the Stalinist concentration camps. They have also lessened the rigours of the industrial discipline to which the workers were subjected, and have tried to satisfy to some extent the popular longing for equality, a desire violently suffocated by Stalin. They have allowed a more liberal intellectual climate to develop and have, to some extent, lifted the iron curtain.

This, briefly, is the record of de-Stalinization. It is an achievement that is not completely satisfactory; nor could it have been: the legacy of Stalinism has continued to weigh heavily on the new epoch. Nevertheless, the Soviet Union has begun to be very different from the totalitarian society described by George Orwell in *Nineteen Eighty-four*. We have seen that it is a society liable to change, evolution, and reforms. At the present moment when the Hungarian events have been so vividly impressed on everyone's minds, many people are asking if de-Stalinization has in fact been a reality. Some people have got the impression that it has just been one enormous deception. I must say straightway that this is not my opinion at all. On the contrary, the Hungarian tragedy has been possible only because de-Stalinization was something profoundly real. This makes the tragedy still greater and also makes it a tragedy for Russia no less than for Hungary.

In the Soviet Union de-Stalinization has developed so far as a gradual reform, regulated from above and controlled by the authorities in all its phases. It has never got out of control. Among the Soviet masses there has been no spontaneous movement on a nation-wide scale that has arisen from below with the aim of forcing concessions from the government, or threatening the regime and the social order. In the first place, the social order of the Soviet Union, forty years after the October Revolution, is based on foundations that are by now sufficiently secure. In addition, after thirty years of totalitarian control, the Soviet people are not yet capable of creating any independent movement at the base. So far, the Soviet masses have been content to watch the destruction of Stalinist orthodoxy carried out by its former guardians and priests.

The situation is very different in the rest of Eastern Europe where the communist regime is not even ten years old. The regime's foundations have not been consolidated. The masses have not lost the capacity for spontaneous political action. From the moment the Stalinist political police in the various countries were deprived of their omnipotence and ceased to inspire terror, an anti-Stalinist mass movement began to grow from below. The movement was inspired by a few simple ideas and a few vivid sentiments: down with Soviet domination; away with all traces of the Stalinist regime; down with the privileges and powers of the bureaucracy; down with the new inequality. In Poland as in Hungary de-Stalinization was no longer the reform carefully controlled from above and directed in all its stages. On the contrary, it was an explosive anti-Stalinist movement by the masses who aimed at seizing power from the hands of those who held it.

A serious conflict thus developed between the logic of de-

Stalinization in Russia and its logic in the rest of Europe. How could and how can the Soviet leaders deal with this problem? There are two solutions open to them. The first is to allow Eastern Europe to continue de-Stalinization in its own way; and in this case they must accept the risk of one part of Eastern Europe, or the whole of it, leaving the Soviet orbit, and of the satellite states disappearing. Alternatively, the Soviet leaders can try to co-ordinate the development of de-Stalinization in Russia and Eastern Europe. Since there is no force, not even Soviet tanks, that could stop it in Eastern Europe, the Soviet leaders must accelerate the process in Russia and give it a more radical emphasis than they have given it so far. In theory there is also a third possibility: they could also try to renounce de-Stalinization completely.

There is another problem of great importance to consider: more than ten years ago Stalin exported the Soviet revolution to Poland and Hungary at bayonet-point and he imposed it on people who did not want to have anything to do with it. After this, he used police terror to keep this revolution alive. Now that police terror is finished, or has ceased to be so frightening, people are asking two questions: can a revolution imposed by force from outside ever be accepted by the local population and obtain their sincere support? Must this revolution necessarily collapse as soon as the conqueror withdraws his bayonets?

There is probably more than one answer to these questions. The latest developments, in fact, have given two different answers to them. Poland revolted against Russia but remained communist; it expelled the bayonets but it preserved the revolution. Moreover in Poland something like a proletarian revolution from below has developed, a revolution that has taken over the communist regime in order to liberate it from Stalinist influence and to transform it. In Hungary conditions were different. Here, too, the anti-Stalinist insurrection was at first inspired by communism and tried to regenerate the revolution, not to reject it. But then the revolution passed from the hands of the communists into those of their adversaries. What began as an attempt to reform the communist revolution developed later—to a large extent as a result of provocation by Hungarian and Soviet Stalinists—into a struggle between communism and anti-communism. Hungary in effect rejected the

Russian revolution together with the Russian bayonets that brought it. But this Hungarian counter-revolution was not, as most counter-revolutions are, the work of an isolated and hated propertied class defending its own power against the people; on the contrary it was the work of an entire nation in revolt. One can say that the Hungarian people, driven to desperation and to a state of heroic frenzy, tried to wind the clock back while Moscow tried once more with its bayonets to re-wind the communist revolution in Hungary, although the clock had already broken.

It is perhaps not out of place to remember that about thirty years ago Trotsky warned the Communist Party against the monstrosity of communism being imposed by force of arms on a foreign people. 'Anyone who wants to carry the revolution abroad at bayonet-point', said Trotsky, 'would do better to hang a stone round his neck and be cast into the sea'. Stalin did not heed this warning and he bequeathed the stone to his successors. We now see it hanging round Khrushchev's neck.

The revolutions in Hungary and Poland have shaken the Soviet Union. However, I do not believe it is possible to re-establish Stalinism. Two attempts have already been made to do so: the first after the Berlin revolt of June 1953, at the time of Beria's fall; and then at the beginning of 1955 when Malenkov was forced to resign. Both attempts failed and succeeded only in stimulating de-Stalinization; the shocks of Hungary and of Poland can only provoke, perhaps with some delay, an intensified decay of Stalinism. Poland and Hungary have shown that a reluctant and in part hypocritical de-Stalinization, which has given too little too late—in short, a de-Stalinization *à la Khrushchev*—is no longer enough.

This is a retranslation of an article that appeared in L'Espresso *on 25 November 1956.*

3 SHEPILOV'S EXIT

The storms over Hungary and Egypt produced a governmental crisis in Moscow. This was to be expected. Both in Hungary and Egypt Soviet policy underwent severe tests, the results of which could not be regarded as satisfactory in Moscow. Yet neither at the Supreme Soviet, which held its session in the first half of February, nor at the two sessions of the Central Committee in December and February were these tests made the subject of public scrutiny. The Supreme Soviet upheld the pretence of a unanimous approval of Shepilov's foreign policy. The Central Committee carried the pretence to the point of not placing matters of foreign policy on its published agenda for either of its two sessions. Yet at both its sessions the situation in Hungary and in the Middle East was, without the slightest doubt, at the centre of an animated and probably sharp controversy. Behind the scenes of the Supreme Soviet, too, rival groups indulged in recrimination and jockeying for position. However, the leaders have obviously been anxious to conceal and also to reduce the intensity of their controversies; and they have dealt with the governmental crisis in instalments. The first instalment was the dismissal, in December, of Saburov from the direction of economic affairs. The second was the removal of Shepilov from the Ministry of Foreign Affairs only three days after the Supreme Soviet had 'unanimously approved' his foreign policy report.

Taken together these changes in the economic and diplomatic leadership amount to a major governmental upheaval. The upheaval is not yet over. Further changes are likely to follow later in the year. In Warsaw and Budapest there is much talk about a forthcoming reshuffle in which Voroshilov, Bulganin, Khrushchev, and Malenkov are to be involved.

What is the nature of this governmental crisis? Outside Russia the abrupt end to Shepilov's brief diplomatic career has naturally aroused the greatest interest. That the end was abrupt is clear from the circumstances which preceded it. In a country where every successive Foreign Minister has hitherto enjoyed a very long tenure of office, Shepilov held the post only about eight months. On assuming it last summer he relinquished his post as Secretary of the Central Committee. The announcement about this was not made until December, which indicates that at that time his removal from the Foreign Ministry and return to the Secretaryship of the Central Committee were not yet envisaged. The decision was evidently taken only in the last few weeks, if not days, before the event. What could have caused it?

Shepilov has not been dismissed as a result of the events in Hungary and of the tension in Eastern Europe. He was not personally or directly responsible for Soviet policy in Eastern Europe, which has long since ceased to belong to the sphere of diplomacy proper. It is the Party's first Secretary, Khrushchev, and not the Foreign Minister, who is directly in charge of Russia's relations with other communist governments. Shepilov was dismissed because he was held responsible for the deterioration in the relations between Russia and the West in so far as that deterioration was caused by Soviet policy towards Egypt.

Moscow's *rapprochement* with Nasser's government was Shepilov's specific and, in a sense, personal contribution to Soviet foreign policy. At the Twentieth Congress he came forward as a critic of Molotov's diplomacy which he openly reproached with neglecting the 'uncommitted areas', especially the Middle East. Even before he became Foreign Minister Shepilov had paid a visit to Cairo and prepared the ground for the *rapprochement*. And no sooner had he become Foreign Minister than he went again to Cairo—this was his first trip abroad in his new capacity. He was in fact the initiator of the Soviet diplomatic offensive in the Middle East. Consequently, by dismissing him the Soviet leaders have acknowledged that this offensive has ended in a fiasco. Shepilov may be regarded as a casualty of the Eisenhower Doctrine.

Shepilov took office at the height of the detente, when it seemed that at last Russia's overtures to the West were beginning to meet with a serious response from both the United States and Western Europe. He was to have been the diplomat of the detente; and he had some reason to view the prospects hopefully. But he made a fatal miscalculation. He was convinced that the U.S.S.R. could pursue its diplomatic and economic offensive in the Middle East without thereby compromising or impairing the detente. He evidently believed that that offensive, by strengthening Russia's bargaining position, would, on the contrary, help to consolidate the detente. To this view he stuck throughout the Suez crisis. After the Anglo-French invasion of the Suez, when at a crucial moment the U.S.S.R. and the U.S.A. acted almost in unison at the United Nations, appearances seemed to justify Shepilov's confidence. The two Powers appeared to behave like joint umpires in the

Suez conflict; and Shepilov may have believed that the United States had in fact agreed to recognize Russia as a co-equal partner in the Middle East. In this mood of confidence he and/ or his Prime Minister badly overplayed their hand when they announced that Russia would send volunteers to fight the British and French aggressors in Egypt. They did not reckon with the shock this was bound to produce in the U.S.A. and with the reaction to it.

Shepilov seemed to have reckoned with only two possibilities in Egypt: one was the continuance of Anglo-French predominance; and the other was a policy of 'open doors' in the Middle East, which would have automatically favoured both the United States and Russia and, equally automatically, reduced British and French influence there. He did not foresee that the Soviet initiative in Egypt might lead to a head-on collision between the U.S.S.R. and the U.S.A. With the proclamation of the Eisenhower Doctrine this collision has become a fact. As Moscow sees it, the Eisenhower Doctrine is designed to keep Russia out of the Middle East and to establish exclusive American predominance in place of the lapsed Anglo-French supremacy. Hence the tone of frustration in which Shepilov, addressing the Supreme Soviet, denounced the Eisenhower Doctrine as a policy of 'closed doors' in the Middle East. From the Soviet viewpoint, American predominance in that area would represent a far greater danger than did the old Anglo-French predominance. Shepilov is blamed for having provoked or precipitated that greater danger.

He has been ousted by the old hands of the Soviet Foreign Office, who were trained under Molotov and are now led by Gromyko, the new Foreign Minister. The career diplomats all along resented the intrusion in their domain of Shepilov, the 'temperamental amateur' and the blundering intellectual outsider. They have never been as sanguine as he was about the detente; and they were, and are, less inclined to work on the assumption of a progressive improvement in Russia's relations with the West. They also viewed with apprehension Shepilov's improvisations in Egypt, holding that if the policy of detente was to be pursued, it could be pursued only on the basis of the existing balance of power. Shepilov's pro-Nasser policy threatened to upset that balance in Russia's favour, to provoke counter-action and thereby to disrupt the detente. This reasoning underlay Molotov's apparent *désinteressement* in the Middle East for which Shepilov had attacked him. Molotov, and presumably Gromyko, have held that Russia had little or nothing to gain in the Middle East. They saw an advantage in the relative aloofness of the U.S.A. from that area thanks to which the Middle East remained outside the frameworks of NATO and SEATO—in fact a gap between the European and the Far Eastern chains of U.S. strategic bases. Britain had tried to fill that gap by means of the Baghdad Pact, but this was an ineffective stop-gap; and Soviet diplomacy has been less afraid of a British-led grouping of nations than of American military expansion in the Middle East.

Gromyko's assignment is to try and clear up the mess in the Middle East and to 'save the detente', if that is possible. He will pursue no line of his own. He stands much lower than Shepilov in the Party hierarchy; and he can only be an executant of decisions taken higher up. But with him Soviet diplomatic routine comes back into its own. Gromyko will at first try to 'save the detente' by quietly winding up his predecessor's Middle Eastern enterprises, if the detente can be saved in this way. He will, in other words, try to restore up to a point the *status quo* which existed before the Suez crisis. If, however, this cannot be restored, as it almost certainly cannot, and if the detente cannot be 'saved', then Gromyko is the right man to be placed at the head of Soviet diplomacy for a new spell of cold war.

No 'temperamental amateur' or 'blundering intellectual', he is a cold war veteran, second only to Molotov in inexhaustible capacity for patient manoeuvering, for tireless obstructiveness, and for all those interminable contests of mud-slinging and pettifogging which belong to the cold war. It may be, of course, that this characterization is unjust to Gromyko. During the Stalin era all Soviet public figures had to behave in the same manner; and only now are some of them beginning to shed their puppet-like qualities and to acquire and show characters of their own. Perhaps the familiar Gromyko postures of the past concealed an unknown character somewhat more attractive than that hitherto associated with the name of the new Foreign Minister. But unless and until Gromyko has revealed himself as such a new personality, one is entitled to think that Soviet diplomacy, after the short spell during which it was led by a volatile mind, is now once again being led, as it was in Molotov's days, by a 'Stone Bottom'.[1]

17 February 1957

4 MALENKOV RETURNS TO THE ATTACK

The change in the Ministry of Foreign Affairs was only incidental to the main controversy caused in Moscow by the crisis in Eastern Europe. That controversy has centred on de-Stalinization and economic policy. Adherents and opponents of de-Stalinization were, and are, at loggerheads once again; and for the first time since Malenkov's dismissal from the premiership two years ago, the Malenkov group felt strong enough to return to the attack and to criticize the new Five Year Plan from their pro-consumer viewpoint. Over both issues the Khrushchev-Bulganin leadership came under fire from different sides; and over both it had to yield some ground.

After the Hungarian uprising the initiative momentarily passed to the opponents of de-Stalinization. Shortly before the session of the Supreme Soviet Khrushchev, yielding to their pressure, made an attempt to rehabilitate something of Stalinist orthodoxy. 'Stalin was a great Marxist' and 'We are all Stalinists'—these, his *obiter dicta*, were meant to rebuff heretics in Poland and Yugoslavia but also to appease Stalinist conservatives at home. One might have expected the Central Committee or the Supreme Soviet to elaborate on Khrushchev's latest texts. Nothing of the sort has happened, however. The Party leaders have not used the recent sessions for any new pronouncements flavouring of a partial rehabilitation of Stalin. It is evidently too late for them to try and put their broken idol together again. Instead the Supreme Soviet has voted for several legislative measures which carry de-Stalinization a stage further. Thus, the Chechens, Ingushes, Kalmyks, and other minor

[1] A Russian phrase implying dogged tenacity and the ability to out-sit opponents at a discussion.

nationalities and tribes who had, on Stalin's orders, been charged with treason and deported to Siberia towards the end of the last war, are to be resettled in their native lands. At the Twentieth Congress Khrushchev denounced these deportations as acts of Stalin's cruel barbarism. By rehabilitating these nationalities and voting for their repatriation, the Supreme Soviet staged a striking demonstration against Stalinism. Once again public attention has been focused on the injustices and crimes of the Stalin era, and this cannot but stimulate the critical rethinking of policies and principles which is going on in the Soviet Union.

The administrative reforms passed by the Supreme Soviet go in the same direction. They drastically reduce Moscow's jurisdiction over the non-Russian Republics. These reforms are inspired by Lenin's 'Notes on the Nationalities' first published after the Twentieth Congress, the 'Notes' where Lenin expressed his anger at the 'chauvinist Great Russian' spirit in which Stalin was depriving non-Russian nationalities of their rights as far back as the early 1920s. The administrative reforms go fairly deep. They affect the judiciary and the working of the economy; and they invest a fairly large measure of autonomy in the non-Russian Republics. All these measures follow logically from the decisions adopted at the Twentieth Congress. Their implementation now, after and despite the Hungarian shock, shows once again that the momentum of de-Stalinization within the Soviet Union itself is quite irrepressible.

Soviet citizens are certain to see another important symptom of de-Stalinization in the debates over the 'errors' committed in the drafting of the present Five Year Plan. This is the first time that the Soviet government has in fact admitted that a Plan is wrongly conceived and requires correction.

The admitted 'errors' of the Five Year Plan consist briefly in this: the Plan, it is said, was not based on a realistic assessment of available resources; it included over-ambitious schemes for capital investment, threatening to freeze too much capital in too many long-term construction projects; and it did not make sufficient provision for solving the housing problem by allocating adequate resources for this purpose.

Saburov, until December the head of the State Economic Commission, has been made to pay the price of these 'mistakes'.

Yet the critics did not aim at him alone. They aimed somewhat higher—at Bulganin; for it was the Prime Minister who introduced and recommended the Five Year Plan, with all its 'erroneous' features, to the Twentieth Congress. Since Bulganin is primarily an economic administrator and not just a 'pure politician', he cannot be held to be blameless in this matter. For the time being Saburov alone has been brought to book, although not in the old Stalinist fashion. However, with his dismissal from the *Gosekomkomissiya*, the coalition which two years ago defeated Malenkov's pro-consumer policy has approached dissolution. In that coalition Saburov played an important part. (Incidentally, Shepilov, too, who was then Editor of *Pravda*, was a most vocal critic of Malenkov's pro-consumer bias; and so his dismissal from the Foreign Office may also have domestic implications.)

This then has so far been the visible effect on the Soviet Government of the East European tensions. The Polish and Hungarian upheavals were brought about, at least in part, by the fact that the governments of those countries, following Moscow's example, had overstretched their economic resources and had tied them up, to the consumers' detriment, in too many heavy industrial schemes, while the U.S.S.R. was not in a position to relieve their economic plight at a moment which became politically critical. This has now induced the Malenkov group, after it had lain low for nearly two years, to return to the attack.

The attack, it seems, is still on; and its final results must still be awaited. The Supreme Soviet was not presented at its February session with any revised and corrected version of the entire Five Year Plan, although the need for such a revision had been admitted. It had before it the corrected Plan only for the year 1957. The corrections were in the nature of a compromise between the opposing views. The principle of priority for heavy industry was upheld. (In truth that principle can hardly ever be disavowed entirely and in earnest, for in the economy of any great industrial power heavy industry of necessity enjoys a certain priority.) But some of this year's targets have been reduced, although not drastically. The chief 'correction' consists in the attempt to avoid the freezing of resources in too many new and long-term construction jobs and in the concentration on the completion of industrial projects which are already under construction. This need not necessarily slow down for good the tempo in heavy industry but it may free resources for the building of more houses. The importance of this problem is illustrated by a recent disclosure that nearly two-thirds of all Soviet capital investment go at present into long-term construction projects. (In the 1930s the proportion was nearly nine-tenths!) Less than thirty per cent of capital investment goes into the equipment of industry, both heavy and light, with the actual 'working' machines and tools. Under these circumstances the competition between industrial building and housing is extremely severe; and even a mild reduction in new industrial building may help to relieve the present disastrous housing shortage.

This year's revised Plan provides for the building of nearly thirty per cent more houses than were erected last year. An expansion at this rate would be an impressive feat in any country under normal circumstances. But it is quite inadequate in the U.S.S.R., where the housing shortage, which is of a gravity unimaginable to people in the West, may become the source of explosive political discontent. It was over housing that two years ago the Malenkov group fought its losing battle against the coalition of Khrushchev-Bulganin-Saburov-Shepilov; and it is over housing again that this coalition is breaking down while the Malenkov group is regaining influence.

However, Malenkov's pro-consumer policy had as its premiss the detente in foreign affairs and a massive reduction in arms expenditure. Without the detente and partial disarmament the pro-consumer policy and its advocates must be suspended in a vacuum. That is why the success of the Malenkov group has so far been rather modest despite the fact that the Khrushchev-Bulganin-Shepilov-Saburov team has been weakened and discredited and despite the growing ferment within the Soviet Union itself. The decisive question now is whether Soviet diplomacy under Gromyko will succeed in 'saving the detente' or whether it will have to revert to the cold war.

17 February 1957

7
Mao and the Hundred Flowers Campaign

The period of the Hundred Flowers Campaign was in sharp contrast to subsequent developments in China, and the explanation for this dramatic change is given in chapter 9. The slogan 'Let a Hundred Flowers Blossom' was first raised in 1955 and it received its full amplification in a speech in May 1956 by Lu Ting-yi, the head of the Communist Party's Propaganda Department, entitled 'Let a Hundred Flowers Blossom, Let a Hundred Schools of Thought Contend'. The aim of this policy was to allow an increased measure of freedom in political and cultural life, and in particular to allow the intellectuals and non-communist parties greater freedom of discussion. The crisis in East Europe may have raised some doubts in the minds of the Chinese leaders about the wisdom of this policy, and about the resilience of correct ideas once they were removed from the 'hot-house', but the liberalization policy received further endorsement by Mao in his speech to the State Conference in February 1957 entitled 'On the Correct Handling of Contradictions Among the People'. In this speech Mao also announced a 'Rectification Campaign' against the 'three evils'— bureaucratism, sectarianism, and subjectivism. It is curious that this speech was not published till June, by which time the policies it advocated had been abandoned and a new 'anti-rightist' campaign had begun. The causes and consequences of this latter change were most obvious on the home front: the intellectuals had not proved their loyalty to the fundamentals of Marxism, and it was they who felt the change most severely; the ideological struggle at the universities was stepped up and many intellectuals were sent to reform their consciousness through manual labour. But the deeper meaning of this change in terms of foreign policy also became clear with time.

MAO AND THE HUNDRED FLOWERS

Mao Tse-tung's address 'On the Correct Handling of Contradictions among the People' represents by far the most radical repudiation of Stalinism that has come out of any communist country so far. It is certainly more thoroughgoing than was Khrushchev's 'secret' speech at the Twentieth Congress. Khrushchev, despite the vehemence of his tone and his macabre exposures, did not go beyond a purely negative repudiation of the cult of Stalin's person and the denunciation of Stalin's 'errors' and 'abuses of power'—he did not criticize the basic economic and political conceptions of Stalinism. On the contrary, he argued from the supposedly sane and rational Stalinism of the 1920s and early 1930s against the excesses and the insanity of the latter-day orthodoxy. Mao Tse-tung has subjected Stalin's entire management of the economy and method of government to a critique.

With a mandarin's discretion and tact he has made this critique only by implication and concentrated on developing a positive alternative to Stalinism. He is evidently anxious not to give undue offence to Stalin's successors in Moscow; and he wishes to spare the communist movement another shock of the kind that Khrushchev inflicted on it. This does not make his pronouncement any the less portentous.

Mao is attempting in effect to redefine the whole concept of proletarian dictatorship and to restore to it the meaning which Marxists generally gave to it before the onset of the Stalin era. From the doctrinal point of view his ideas are therefore far from original; but this does not lessen their immense political importance. In the U.S.S.R. socialism, the totalitarian state, and the monolithic Party had become identified to such an extent that communists brought up in the Stalinist school of thought could not even imagine the one without the other. Against this Mao argues that socialism can and indeed must dissociate itself from the totalitarian state, which is essentially alien to it, and that the Communist Party to be united and effective in action need not be 'monolithic' in thought.

This is what Khrushchev and his colleagues will not admit even now, after all they have done to reform and 'liberalize' post-Stalin Russia. The 'people's democratic dictatorship' (which is the Chinese euphemism for 'proletarian dictatorship'), Mao argues, should suppress only the 'reactionary classes' and the confirmed counter-revolutionaries; but it must not deny democratic freedoms to workers and peasants and even to the 'national bourgeoisie': 'dictatorship does not apply in the ranks of the people'.

Mao's appeal 'let a hundred flowers blossom; and let a hundred schools of thought contend' has already been much discussed; and sheer repetition has turned the evocative image into a cliché and a slogan. However, Mao restores to it some freshness when he argues against those who ask anxiously how to tell the flowers from the weeds and how to distinguish which of the hundred schools of thought contribute to the growth of socialism and which obstruct it. Mao replies that communists must be tolerant and take risks. They must even let the weeds grow, for in politics and in spiritual life the distinction between weed and flower is not at all clear.

As if paraphrasing a great English agnostic, Mao reminds his followers that it is the customary fate of new truth to begin as heresy; and, citing Marxism and communism as examples, he pleads that the Party should allow any heresy, as distinct from the obviously counter-revolutionary attitude, the chance and the time to prove itself; and that it should, in any case, beware lest the Marxist truth itself ends in superstition. (Here Mao argues exactly as Trotsky did nearly thirty-five years earlier!)

He does not proclaim 'socialist realism', which is officially still sacrosanct in Moscow, as the artistic creed of the communist writer and painter—he does not even mention it. 'Different forms and styles in art can develop freely . . . it is harmful to the growth of art and science if administrative measures are used to impose one particular style or school of thought and to ban another'. Moreover, in philosophy and even in politics Marxism should not claim a monopoly for itself, according to Mao. Even after its revolutionary victory it must still defend its ascendancy in open conflict with other ideologies; and it cannot do so unless it allows those ideologies freedom of expression:

As a scientific truth Marxism fears no criticism. If it did and could be defeated in argument, it would be worthless . . . Marxism can only develop through struggle; and this is true not only of the past and present—it will necessarily remain so in the future as well.

What is correct always develops in the course of struggle with what is wrong. The true, the good, and the beautiful always exist in contrast to the false, the evil, and the ugly and grow in struggle with the latter. . . . Such struggles will never end.

Mao remains as convinced as ever that Marxism 'formulates correctly the laws of historic development'; but precisely because of this, he holds, it cannot and does not claim to be above those laws. It needs diversity of thought like men air to breathe; and it needs resistance and opposition to flourish. It can gain nothing from hot-house cultivation: 'Plants raised in hot-houses are not likely to be robust' Mao says with an eye undoubtedly on the state of Marxism at the end of the Stalin era in Hungary and the rest of Eastern Europe, and perhaps also in China and Russia. The Stalinist fetish of the 'monolith' is thus torn to shreds.

How does Mao apply these principles to the more difficult regions of economics and politics? Here, too, he acknowledges as legitimate a diversity of social interest and the conflict of these interests within the framework of a socialist regime. In somewhat scholastical style, in rudimentary Hegelian terms mixed with truisms borrowed from Lao Tsu, he speaks about the various categories of 'contradictions' and lists three of these: first, the 'antagonistic', that is irreconcilable conflicts of interests; secondly, the 'non-antagonistic' which lend themselves naturally to conciliation and peaceful accommodation; and thirdly, the intermediate type of conflict which prudent communist policy can mitigate and resolve peacefully, but which a blundering policy may aggravate and make potentially explosive.

Only the struggle between revolution and unmistakable counter-revolution, says Mao, is irreconcilable; and he goes on to proclaim that the era of this struggle is definitely closed for China. Ordinary class struggle will continue; but it should be conducted in an evolutionary and reformist manner, not in violent, revolutionary forms. The working class, the peasantry, the bureaucracy, and the 'national bourgeoisie' have divergent and even conflicting interests; but their conflicting claims can and should be settled through mutual compromise in the process of socialist construction.

In effect, Mao proclaims China's New Economic Policy. Or,

as China has not gone through a period of war communism, it would be more accurate to say that he proclaims that the Chinese N.E.P. is established 'seriously and for long', as Lenin once said of Russia's N.E.P. The basic ideas of Mao's N.E.P. are indeed the same as Lenin's, although there are important new features in the application. The main principle is that the 'construction of socialism' should proceed within the framework of a mixed economy, in which the 'socialist sector' should expand by transforming, again 'peacefully', and gradually absorbing the private sector, not by destroying or suppressing it violently, as was done in Russia.

One may read into Mao's words a retrospective repudiation of the Stalinist abolition of the N.E.P., forcible collectivization, and 'liquidation of the kulaks as a class', which now appear to him as colossal errors through which Stalin needlessly aggravated the conflicts between socialism, the N.E.P. bourgeoisie, and the peasantry, and turned them into bloody convulsions and war *à outrance*. Whether this is or is not what Mao now thinks of Stalin's 'Second Revolution' of 1929–32, he leaves us with no doubt that he envisages no such second revolution for China, where it would be an unmitigated calamity.

Although Mao preaches the 'inevitability of gradualness' in communist policy, his variety of N.E.P. is incomparably more leftish than that which was in operation in Russia under Stalin's and Bukharin's direction from 1924 to 1929. He does not destroy or expropriate the Chinese N.E.P. bourgeoisie; he buys up its property cautiously yet relentlessly, in a manner not very different from that in which the large capitalist concern absorbs small family businesses. At present the state is already a major shareholder in all 'capitalist' enterprises. The private owner receives interest on his capital, or a share in profits, in addition to the salary he gets as a state employee. The bourgeoisie is thus spared the shock of sudden unsettlement and social degradation and is given time to adjust itself to new conditions, while the state benefits by using the bourgeoisie's managerial experience and skill, which were largely wasted in Russia.

Similarly, the collectivization of farming is progressing by slow degrees and subtle transitions; and confiscation of property and the use of coercion are avoided. The present co-operatives, which already embrace the bulk of the peasantry, are based mainly on the pooling of labour—the pooling of land, implements, and cattle is planned to take place at later stages; and the process is to be drawn out over many years. In this way the Chinese communists hope gradually to form in the peasantry the habits of collectivist work and to condition its mind for new economic forms.

Stalin, it will be remembered, switched from one extreme, that of appeasing and pampering the kulaks, to the opposite extreme of 'liquidating' them. Mao now seems anxious to avoid either of these extremes. The outcome of the Chinese collectivization cannot yet be taken for granted, and is not so taken by Mao himself; but, by avoiding the 'rightist' errors of the Russian N.E.P., Mao's Party may be in a better position than Stalin's Party was to avoid a cataclysmic collision with the peasantry. In any case, the Leninist idea of a transition to socialism through N.E.P. is being given its first practical and gigantic test in China; in Lenin's own country it was never applied.

Mao has made his most striking departure from Stalinism in labour policy. Bluntly and without hedging, he declared that the workers have the right to strike, and that incitement to strike must not be punished in any way. If workers have grievances and down tools, the fault lies with the bureaucracy; and in so far as strikes help to keep the bureaucracy in its place they may even be welcome. Here, too, Mao's reasoning links up with Lenin's, who expressed the same view more subtly when he said that 'the workers are bound in duty to defend their state, but they should also defend themselves against their state'.

If workers, peasants, and other social groups are to be free to exercise their pressures upon the state, it follows that the state must in its economic policy give greater weight to consumer interests than it has given hitherto. Mao says, in effect, that China need not rely as much as Russia did on forced saving to provide her with the sinews of investment; and that a better balance must be maintained between light and heavy industry. If, as a result, industrialization does not proceed at breakneck speed, it will develop on a sounder basis, with less waste and suffering for the people. Mao also spurns the edifying lie on which Stalinism lived and he insists with great emphasis that there is no paradise around the corner and that it will take China 'many decades' before she catches up with the advanced countries.

When Russian communists introduced N.E.P., the act was described as an attempt to steer the revolution 'down a steep hill, with brakes on'. This description may be applied with even better reason to what is going on in the communist world at present. De-Stalinization is indeed, for all communist countries, a descent with brakes on; but while some Communist Parties have to go down very steep hills, others move on gentler slopes.

Mao's is a relatively mild slope; and he has so far handled his brakes skilfully and with a more even temper than Khrushchev, who has rushed down one or two stretches of his very steep hill with no brakes on.

Communist China has not been an 'isolated and besieged fortress' as Bolshevik Russia was for three decades. Soviet assistance has smoothed China's progress. Consequently, only seven years after the revolution the Chinese economy, which started from a lower level than the Russian, appears to have achieved an advance comparable to that which Russia only achieved after eleven or twelve years of Bolshevik rule. China's standard of living, inevitably low, is nevertheless well above the pre-revolutionary level, whereas for very many years after the Revolution the Russian people were poorer and lived harder than before. In part this was due to a major difference in the fortunes of the two regimes. The Bolsheviks *first* seized power and *then* had to fight civil wars and foreign intervention. The Chinese communists, on the other hand, fought their civil war *before* they seized power; and so once they took office they were more or less free to turn to constructive economic tasks.

This difference has had important political consequences. Any nation driven by misery and despair to make a revolution looks forward hopefully and impatiently to the fruits of revolution; and it judges its new rulers according to whether these fruits are forthcoming or not. They cannot be forthcoming if civil war develops after the revolution. In 1924–25, seven years after they had seized power, the Bolsheviks still faced the nation they ruled empty-handed; while the Chinese communists can

already take pride in having improved the people's lot. Consequently, China has experienced little of the social and political
tension, of the disillusionment of the masses and their estrangement from communist rulers which were characteristic of
post-revolutionary Russia and to which the Bolshevik leaders
reacted with an obsession with the Revolution's and their own
insecurity, with an acute distrust of the people and a determination to suppress all opposition and to set up a totalitarian state.

Mao and his colleagues seem to be more or less free from
such obsession and distrust. Their system of government, for
all the terror that has gone into its making, has never had the
massive mechanical and nightmarish oppressiveness of Stalinism. Their Party has not been shaken and torn by any internal
conflict as dramatic and bitter as the struggle between Stalin
and Trotsky which was at its height seven years after the
Revolution and resulted in the Party's mental paralysis and
moral degradation. (The Chinese Party, on the other hand, has
never enjoyed the inner Party democracy which was characteristic of early Bolshevism.)

Thus for a variety of reasons the Chinese have not moved in
the totalitarian direction even half the way the Russians have
gone. This makes it easier for them now to withdraw, to change
direction, and to move towards a non-totalitarian communist
regime. This is not to say that they are ready to withdraw all the
way. They are beset by the dilemma which is inherent in any
single-party system: if various social interests are to be allowed
scope for exercising pressure, and if diversity of opinion is to
be tolerated and even encouraged, will this not result in the
breakdown of the single-party system (in which most communists still see a condition of the revolution's survival) and in
the emergence of several parties?

It is curious to note how Mao wrestled with this dilemma.
He first referred to some people in China who have already,
under the influence of the remote Hungarian rising, asked 'for
the adoption of the two-party system of the West, where one
party is in office and the other out of office'. He rejected this
demand quite categorically. Yet the Chinese communist regime
is not nominally a single-party system, for it has allowed
various non-communist parties to lead a shadowy existence.
And so Mao went on to argue that the middle classes should be

allowed political expression and that 'the democratic parties of the bourgeoisie and petty-bourgeoisie should be allowed to exist' side by side with the Communist Party 'for a long time to come', and even to 'supervise' the Communist Party as the latter 'supervises' them. The bourgeois parties should exist, express their views, even 'supervise', but under no circumstances must they behave like an opposition striving for office.

It would probably be wrong to say that all this is sheer hypocrisy and make-believe, and that Mao is merely interested in using puppet-parties as a façade. What he really wants—and this is true of Gomulka as well—is a half-way house between the single-party system and a multiparty set up, a half-way house in which the non-communist parties should act as real and even vigorous pressure groups but not as the alternative government. The trouble, from the communist angle, is that such parties, half-real and half-puppet-like, tend to assume flesh and blood and even to become pretenders to power at moments of crisis, if the Communist Party is apparently losing or even only loosening its grip. Both Mao and Gomulka have already found themselves compelled to address stern warnings to their non-communist or bourgeois parties.

It is doubtful whether any of these parties will ever become a real threat to Mao, but they may become dangerous to Gomulka. However, for the time being both Mao and Gomulka appear to be convinced that they must face the risk of a limited break with the single-party system for the sake of that diversity of opinion, without which the Communist Parties would be condemned to ossification and impotence.

Let us now try to foreshadow briefly the impact which Mao's pronouncement is likely to have on the U.S.S.R. and other communist countries. Mao's statement has come at a most inopportune moment to those elements in Moscow which since the Hungarian revolt have exerted themselves to curb and to reverse in part the process of de-Stalinization. *Pravda* has nevertheless had no choice but to publish Mao's address in full. It is now avidly read, scrutinized, and pondered by many millions of Soviet citizens who draw from it their conclusions.

There is not a shadow of doubt that Mao's words are giving a new and powerful impulse to de-Stalinization. He has come to the rescue of the intellectual opposition in Russia, especially the writers and historians who are now under strong attack for the heresies they have voiced. They will turn his words into their battle-cry, the words about the flowers and the weeds and about the harm of hot-house protection for Marxism and the advantages of tolerating heresy.

More important than the repercussions in intellectual circles will be the impression which Mao makes on the Soviet working class. For nearly thirty-five years Soviet workers have been told that to strike under a socialist regime is a counter-revolutionary crime. Masses of workers have spent many years in concentration camps not even for striking but for ordinary absenteeism and even less serious offences. Now Mao tells the Russians that the worker has a right to strike, that if he downs tools not he but the bureaucrat must be blamed, that strikes may even be a useful check on those in power, and that strike agitation should go unpunished. All this is politically explosive for Russia. Why should we, Soviet workers will ask, be deprived forty years after the Revolution of the rights which the Chinese enjoy after seven years? Are we now coolies? Nor are the workers likely to miss Mao's incidental remarks directed against wide discrepancies in wages and salaries or the quasi-egalitarian tenor of his strictures on the bureaucracy.

After decades of suppression an egalitarian mood has been reasserting itself recently and gaining strength among the Soviet working class. It will now feed on Mao's views; and as the ferment of ideas spreads from intellectual circles to the workers, this renascent opposition to inequality will come to the fore.

Mao's speech will probably not stun and confuse minds in the communist world as Khrushchev's secret speech did; but it is certain to contribute considerably to the winding up of what is still left of Stalinist orthodoxy and methods of government.

22 June 1957

8
Khrushchev Gains the Ascendancy

It was clear from speeches he made in December 1956 and in the following February that Khrushchev was envisaging a decentralization of Soviet industry, and at the end of March he announced a series of proposals that included the abolition of many industrial ministries and the setting up of regional planning bodies. Throughout April there was public debate on the precise nature of these reforms and over 500,000 meetings were held. In May the Supreme Soviet met and enacted Khrushchev's proposals in a modified form: twenty-five industrial ministries were abolished and ninety-two Regional Economic Councils— *sovnarkhozy*—were set up. The *Gosekomkomissiya*, the short-term planning organization established in 1955, was abolished, and only Gosplan, the long-term planning body, remained. Gosplan was put under the direction of a little-known official, I. I. Kuzmin.

A significant aspect of the April debate was that none of the prominent Soviet leaders participated in it: Malenkov, Molotov, Bulganin, Mikoyan, Voroshilov, Kaganovich, and Saburov were all silent; and all but Mikoyan were later to be accused by Khrushchev of membership in the 'Anti-Party Group'. The defeat of this group came at a Central Committee meeting in June, and on 3 July it was announced that Molotov, Malenkov, and Kaganovich had been dismissed from the Presidium and the Central Committee of the Party; that Shepilov had been dismissed from his post of Secretary of the Central Committee, and that Saburov had been dismissed from the Presidium. They were accused of having formed an Anti-Party Group, of resisting the decisions of the Twentieth Congress, of opposing the reorganization of industry, of opposing peaceful coexistence, and of trying to resist the re-establishment of socialist legality.

Molotov in particular was accused of 'narrow-mindedness' in foreign affairs, of resisting the Russo-Yugoslav *rapprochement* and of denying the possibility of different roads to socialism. Molotov, Malenkov, and Kaganovich were all said to be 'shackled by old ideas and methods' and of having 'a pedantic and inert approach to Marxism-Leninism'.

Malenkov had been made Minister of Electric Power Stations on losing the premiership in 1955; he was now sent to manage a power station at Ust-Kamenogorsk in Kazakhstan, 2,000 miles from Moscow. Molotov lost his post of Minister of State Control and was sent as Soviet Ambassador to Outer Mongolia. Shepilov was sent to manage an economics institute in Kirghizia and Kaganovich to run a factory in the Urals. In November 1958 *Tass* announced that Bulganin had also been a member of the Anti-Party Group, and at the Twenty-second Congress of the Party Voroshilov admitted his complicity as well.

On 6 July Khrushchev was in Leningrad where he delivered a vigorous attack on Malenkov, and on Shepilov whom he accused of having joined the Group after it started and of having 'proved to be the most shameless, double-dealing individual'. He then left for Czechoslovakia and during his absence Marshal Zhukov also made a speech in Leningrad that was censored by *Pravda*. This was the first open sign of a conflict between the Marshal and Khrushchev, but his dismissal came during the Syrian-Turkish crisis of October. Russia had armed Syria and the Turks had massed forces on their border with Syria; in the first two weeks of October it was widely believed in Syria that Turkey was about to invade, yet the U.S.A. and Turkey blamed Russia for having provoked the crisis. Between 8 and 26 October Zhukov was on a visit to Yugoslavia and Albania and on the day of his return it was announced that he had been dismissed from the Ministry of Defence and replaced by Marshal Malinovsky. In November he was expelled from the Central Committee and Presidium of the Party and accused of violating Leninism, of resisting Party influence in the army, of building up his own cult of the personality, and of being 'a politically unsteady person and disposed to adventurism'.

The dismissal of Zhukov represented a further consolidation of Khrushchev's power; and in March 1958 the Supreme Soviet gave formal recognition to this new position by making Bulganin

Director of the State Bank and appointing Khrushchev as Prime
Minister in his stead. But the reshuffle following the defeat of the
Anti-Party Group had also involved the promotion of those
'dark horses' who, Deutscher noted, would finally threaten
Khrushchev: in July 1957 Leonid Brezhnev was appointed to the
Presidium of the Party and Alexei Kosygin became a Candidate
Member of it.

1 KHRUSHCHEV'S ECONOMIC
REFORM

What can the world learn from the mass of technical detail with which Khrushchev introduced to the Supreme Soviet in May his scheme for the overhaul of the whole of Soviet industry? The provisions of the scheme must appear somewhat abstruse to the Western public unaccustomed as it is to think in terms of a nationally owned economy which is planned from a single centre as the Soviet economy has been. Yet the Supreme Soviet's decision to adopt Khrushchev's scheme, with a few modifications, is a momentous event. It is likely to have the most far-reaching consequences for Russia and, therefore, in some measure for the world at large. Khrushchev has set in motion a chain of developments no less important, though less spectacular, than that which last year he started with his exposure of Stalin at the Twentieth Congress.

This is another great break with the Stalin era. With one mighty blow Khrushchev is trying to sweep away the whole administrative structure of Soviet industry as it has grown up, taken shape, and become fixed in the course of nearly thirty years. In this endeavour Khrushchev has lacked neither courage nor sweep of initiative. It remains to be seen whether his foresight and capacity for organization will prove equally great. Will he remain in control of the great change he has initiated? Or will he once again have to shrink in fear from the consequences of his deed as he has had to shrink from the consequences of his attack on the Stalin myth?

The scale of this new reform should be noted first. Involved in it are no fewer than 200,000 functioning industrial concerns and about 100,000 establishments still under construction. Between them these concerns employ a good half of Russia's adult working population.

Obviously, no government undertakes so vast a reform unless it has weighty and urgent reasons for doing so. That the Soviet government has had reasons for sharp dissatisfaction with the work of its economic agencies is evident. Last February Bulganin, the Prime Minister, admitted to the Supreme Soviet that the current Five Year Plan had not been based on a realistic assessment of resources, that it had led to the waste and freezing of much capital, and that it was in need of a thorough revision. The government has so far not yet been able to produce the revised Plan. Within recent months it has repeatedly re-organized the planning agencies, first splitting them up into two separate bodies, one designed for long-term and the other for short-term planning; and then merging them back into a single Gosplan. The two chief planners have been dismissed: Saburov in December and Pervukhin in May. They have been re-placed by I. I. Kuzmin, a relatively unknown economist who has been appointed head of Gosplan and first deputy Vice-Premier, although he has not even been a member of the Presidium and has held a subordinate place in the Party hierarchy.

But discontent in the Soviet ruling group with the economic-administrative set-up inherited from the Stalin era can be traced much further back. When Malenkov took power, on 6 March 1953, he abolished many ministries within a few hours of Stalin's death. By 15 March 1953 he had cut down their number from forty-five to fourteen. Later, at the time of Malen-kov's eclipse, the ministries proliferated again. In a way, therefore, Khrushchev has now picked up the idea with which Malenkov first came forward.

Khrushchev's scheme, however, is wider than Malenkov's. The latter tried merely to simplify the existing economic administration. Khrushchev is changing the whole structure from top to bottom. Hitherto Soviet industry has been organ-ized almost exclusively along vertical lines. Thus, a Coal Ministry in Moscow controlled all the coal mines of the country —the Ministry formed the board of a single monopolistic trust. All the steel mills came similarly under a single ministry. . . . The underlying principle of Khrushchev's reform is, in contrast to Stalin's principle, that of horizontal organization. The whole of the Soviet Union is now being divided into ninety-two regions, each with an Economic Council or *sovnarkhoz* of its own. All state-owned concerns in any given area (with the exception of smaller factories run by the municipalities) come under the management of the Regional Council. The coal producer, the steel maker, the engineer, and the textile manu-facturer on the spot will at last be able to deal directly with one another, or, if need be, through their Regional Council.

Most of the economic ministries in Moscow have been abolished. Even those that are left—the ministries in charge of defence industry—are divested of the functions of management. . . . Under the new dispensation the role of Gosplan, the supreme planning authority, assumes new weight.

Gosplan is to co-ordinate the work of the ninety-two Economic Councils and to ensure that the right proportions are maintained in the production of the various regions and branches of industry. Since Gosplan must continue to plan vertically, for entire national industries, it will absorb some of the personnel and of the functions of the ministries which are now disbanded. But Gosplan is to plan, not to administer; to guide, not to enforce.

The method of planning is to be radically reformed. Until now—this practice too has been in force for nearly thirty years—Gosplan fixed the overall quinquennial and annual targets for every industry. These were broken down into smaller targets for the various sections of the industry, down to the basic productive unit. Gosplan's target was the law. The manager of a factory or of a mine could not in practice declare that any target was unattainable, even if it was. He could not refuse to accept the target for fulfilment. The whole process of planning proceeded from above.

This practice is now to be abandoned. Planning from below is to take its place. The basic units of production are first to declare how much they expect to be able to produce within a year- or a five-year-period. On this basis the Regional Councils are to fix their targets; and only then is Gosplan to integrate the ninety-two regional plans into a single national Plan. If the reform is carried out in letter and spirit, the Plan should, for the first time in Soviet history, represent not the imposition by the government of its policy upon the nation, but the national sum total of a multitude of genuine acts of social initiative. . . .

In launching his scheme Khrushchev has banked on two factors: first, on the bureaucracy's inability to obstruct and sabotage the reform; and, secondly, on the people's 'mature outlook' on economic affairs.

At first sight the whole reform looks like a fantastic duel between the Party's General Secretary and the entire body of a powerful bureaucracy. None of Khrushchev's colleagues in the Presidium has uttered a single word in public to support him on this occasion. By its silence the Presidium has demonstrated its reserve and indicated that Khrushchev 'is going it alone', although he must, in fact, have obtained the approval of at least a slight majority in the Central Committee. (This seems to be the second time that he is in such a situation, for he had behind him only a slight majority of the Central Committee when he came out with his secret speech about Stalin at the Twentieth Congress.)

It appears all the more puzzling that the leaders of the Soviet managerial groups should allow themselves to be so ruthlessly shorn of power, prerogatives, and privileges. What has happened to them? Whence their meekness?

It would be incorrect to suggest that Moscow's bureaucracy has put up no resistance at all. Nearly six weeks elapsed between 30 March, when Khrushchev first launched his scheme in public, and 7 May, when he presented it to the Supreme Soviet. During these weeks the leaders of the industrial trusts directed a most vehement fire against the scheme; and echoes of the barrage reverberated even in the Soviet press. (This is the first time that more than a semblance of public debate over an important issue of national policy has been allowed to develop; but the main struggle was still fought out behind the scenes.)

As a result, Khrushchev has been compelled to retreat on one sector, the one comprising ministries in charge of the defence industry. In March he held his axe over those ministries too. In May he came to the Supreme Soviet to plead in a somewhat chastened mood that the ministries be allowed to survive. This incident throws a significant light on the alignment within the ruling group: it shows that only the military were strong enough to stand up to Khrushchev. But even his retreat on this sector underlines the strength of his position, for he has not gone back all the way—he has merely struck a compromise with his opponents. The ministries in question are not to be disbanded; but they are not to remain in operational command of their industries either. The armament plants, too, are to pass under the effective management of the Regional Councils; and the ministries are to act only as planning and co-ordinating authorities.

Khrushchev has foreshadowed a continuation of the attack·

on the bureaucracy. He revealed that since Stalin's death no fewer than 900,000 'bureaucrats' had lost their jobs; and he gave advance notice of further reductions. He ridiculed the vast staffs of 'industrial comptrollers' spawning on the productive labour of Soviet workers. There were, he said, at present at least 400,000 such useless creatures on industry's payrolls; and most of them would be sacked. As to the managerial groups entrenched in Moscow and the other capital cities, well, they would have to scatter to all the corners of the Soviet Union; this seems necessary indeed if his scheme is to be realized. If Khrushchev succeeds in all this, he will have carried out a trust-busting operation the like of which the world has never seen. But can he succeed?

So far Moscow's bureaucracy has displayed confusion and disarray, while Khrushchev has shown himself determined not to give it time to recover. He is waging his *Blitzkrieg* against it. He will not, he says, allow the reform to be killed by procrastination: the whole work connected with the overhaul should be seen through by the end of June!

Where does Khrushchev draw the strength for his drive from? Whom, what forces, has he contrived to rally against the powerful managerial groups? It is tempting to suggest, as some commentators have done, that he is backed by the Party machine which hopes to gain at the expense of the industrial bureaucracy. But it is difficult to see what benefit the Party machine can possibly derive from Khrushchev's operation. If anything, it too stands to lose, because as long as Moscow exercised control over all industry, it was in a large measure the Party machine in Moscow which exercised that control or participated in its exercise.

The alignment, however, is not as simple as an image showing Khrushchev as the St. George slaying the dragon of bureaucracy might suggest. He has, in fact, succeeded in dividing the bureaucracy itself. He has set the provincial managers against the bigwigs in Moscow. The provincial managers are not, by any means, a negligible force. As industrialization has spread from the centre outwards, their numbers, achievements, and aspirations have grown. But, bullied and downtrodden by Moscow, they have suffered frustration and have long nursed their grievances in silence. Khrushchev has set himself up as the mouthpiece of that frustration, which he himself probably experienced during his years in the Ukraine.

Yet the legions of provincial managers provide him with only part of his backing. He also appeals to the mass of the workers, and most specifically to the foremen, against the managerial oligarchies at large. He made no bones about this when he addressed the Supreme Soviet. He referred to the demands for wider prerogatives which factory managers had raised. He cold-shouldered such demands and went on to say: '...we ought rather to raise the status of those who should in the first instance be responsible for the quality of production, the status of the foreman, and of the shop manager. The worker, the foreman, and the shop manager are our best comptrollers.' These—the worker, the foreman, and the junior manager—are the forces Khrushchev has deployed against the industrial oligarchies.

In the last instance, his initiative reflects a nation-wide revulsion against bureaucracy. It reflects the tide of popular hostility that has so far half-paralysed the leaders of the managerial groups and made it difficult, if not impossible, for them to rally to the defence of their positions. The overgrown bureaucracy, jealous of its power and greedy for privilege, arrogant and heartless, could still claim to serve a vital national interest in the early phases of industrialization and of the planned economy. It is now a costly and useless anachronism. It is seen by the nation as an impediment to further progress; and it feels it. The sense of its own uselessness and absurdity has shaken the bureaucracy's self-confidence and militancy.

Forty years after the October Revolution, questions concerning the meaning of social control over the economy have come once again to occupy Russian minds intensely. The slogan of 'the worker's control over the factory' has penetrated into the Soviet Union from Yugoslavia and Poland, where that control is supposed to be exercised by Workers' Councils. This, incidentally, was a Leninist slogan in 1917; but it has since been forgotten in Russia and has returned by a round-about way from abroad.

The Workers' Councils and their direct control over production have found no favour with Khrushchev or any of his colleagues. When he last visited Yugoslavia and the Titoists showed him with pride their Workers' Councils, Khrushchev replied: 'If we were to introduce such Councils in our factories, our whole industry would collapse overnight.' And in truth, it may be relatively easy for Workers' Councils to manage a shoe factory, a textile mill, or a copper mine; but it is much more difficult to imagine such a Council running complex engineering works or an atomic plant—unless the workers have achieved a level of education and social responsibility immensely superior to anything so far achieved by workers anywhere.

But if the idea of the workers' 'direct control over production' remains taboo in public debate, another idea, somewhat akin to it, has cropped up. In his address to the Supreme Soviet Khrushchev dealt with demands 'raised by some comrades' that the elective Soviets, not the provincial governments, should appoint the Regional Economic Councils and control them. The vesting of economic powers in the Soviets—this, too, was originally a Leninist idea—might give back to the Soviets part of the political prominence they once enjoyed.

Khrushchev has rejected this demand too; but he did so rather gingerly. 'This', he said, 'would not be expedient *for the time being*'. He was aware that he was on delicate ground and that the demand that elective Soviets should assume control over industry might in due time become a battle cry of 'Soviet democracy'.

Khrushchev has thus to fight on two fronts: against those who claim for the mass of the people a far higher degree of control over the state and the economy than he is prepared to concede; and against the bureaucracy which may still seek to obstruct his reform. For the time being, the 'front against the bureaucracy' is for him the more important and the more dangerous. He himself has given the *caveat*: 'This reform', he said, 'will not by itself kill bureaucracy'; and he has called for continued vigilance and a continuous crusade. He has amended the constitution and written the abolition of the ministries into it. It remains to be seen whether and when these ministries vanish in reality. . . .

13 May 1957

2 THE ANTI-PARTY GROUP

The showdown between Khrushchev and his opponents, which has led to the expulsion of Molotov, Kaganovich, and Malenkov from the Central Committee, developed out of a situation in which Khrushchev was threatened with nothing less than the loss of power. In the weeks preceding the crisis he clearly found himself in a minority at meetings of the Presidium.

Of the eleven members of the Presidium at least six regularly cast their votes against him. The six were: Molotov, Kaganovich, Malenkov, Pervukhin, Saburov, and Suslov. Voroshilov vacillated; and even Bulganin's attitude was uncertain. The majority of the Presidium appeared to be on the point of deposing Khrushchev from his post as the Party's First Secretary. This compelled Khrushchev to appeal from the Presidium to the Central Committee, as he was, according to the Party statutes, entitled to do.

The anti-Khrushchev opposition was not a uniform group. Ever since Stalin's death the alignment within the Presidium has been fluid. Yet some points about it have been quite unmistakable. Molotov and Kaganovich have been the official leaders of the Stalinist die-hards, and have fought a prolonged and stubborn rearguard battle against all the reformist changes in Soviet policy, domestic and foreign.

Malenkov represented at first a different attitude. He favoured a pro-consumer line in economic policy and detente in foreign policy; but he was opposed to drastic de-Stalinization in the political field. Shepilov differed in foreign policy from both Molotov and Khrushchev; but he was opposed to Malenkov on economic policy. Pervukhin, Saburov, and Suslov backed the Stalinist die-hards. As the struggle went on the various groups, in spite of their different viewpoints, became more and more united in opposition to Khrushchev.

After the Hungarian rising last October the Stalinist die-hards were in an aggressive mood and confident that they could regain power. It was only by a very slight majority, consisting of one or two votes, that Khrushchev had been permitted to make his secret speech about Stalin in February 1956; and his position within the Presidium was even weaker when he initiated the overhaul of the entire Soviet industry last May. In recent weeks the conflict was brought to a head over three major issues.

The industrial bureaucracy of Moscow and a section of the Party machine were in revolt against Khrushchev's decentralization of economic management. Molotov, Kaganovich, Pervukhin, Saburov, and probably Malenkov, led this revolt.

The next great controversy concerned Moscow's attitude towards Mao Tse-tung, especially after the publication of Mao's speech, with its strongly anti-bureaucratic accents, its encouragement of greater freedom of expression, and its liberal attitude even towards workers' strikes. All this was dynamite for Russia. The Stalinist die-hards refused to swallow Mao's speech; and they adopted towards him an attitude so hostile that if it had become official it would have led to a momentous breach between the U.S.S.R. and China.

Finally, Molotov and his associates were strongly critical of Khrushchev's proposals made in his televised interview with the Columbia Broadcasting System for a withdrawal of American and Soviet troops from Europe.

It must have been in near panic that the Central Committee met on 22 June. Men of the Molotov-Kaganovich faction had been canvassing influential Party members, talking about Khrushchev's 'treason', hinting at his forthcoming dismissal, and inciting the heads of Moscow's industrial trusts to resist his trust-busting operation.

However, at the Central Committee, the membership of which is much younger than that of the Presidium, the anti-Stalinist elements have been stronger than in the Presidium. Khrushchev counted on their support; and his calculation was correct.

Yet Khrushchev's claim that the Central Committee has backed him unanimously may be dismissed as sheer fantasy. The Central Committee, too, is divided; and the anti-Khrushchev factions are represented on it in strength. What determined the outcome of the session and the apparent meekness of the Central Committee was the attitude of the military elements, especially Marshal Zhukov's personal intervention. For some time past Marshal Zhukov had already acted as virtual umpire *vis à vis* the opposed factions; and he now threw his decisive weight behind Khrushchev.

How strong has Khrushchev then emerged from the contest?

The new Presidium, its membership enlarged from eleven to fifteen, is by no means uniformly pro-Khrushchev. Khrushchev's own group consists of seven or eight members, not enough to give him a stable and comfortable majority. The Stalinist die-hards, among whom Shvernik and Suslov must be counted, have retained a few seats; and they are likely to enjoy from time to time Voroshilov's support. Mikoyan maintains an independent attitude which is not without reserve towards Khrushchev. So does Bulganin. Marshal Zhukov is a newcomer to the Presidium; but from the moment of his appearance there he seems as if cast for the arbiter's role.

Having eliminated his most influential opponents of the old Stalinist guard, Khrushchev cannot relish his dependence on the army. He is therefore making a determined attempt to bolster up his own position by an appeal to the country. He has denounced Molotov and Kaganovich for what they are: 'narrow-minded and conservative' Stalinists seeking to obstruct the country's progress; and he has tried, but with a somewhat trembling hand, to tar Malenkov and Shepilov with the same brush.

At the same time he has come forward as advocate of further de-Stalinization and 'democratization', as champion of the people against the bureaucracy, as well-wisher of the peasants (to whom he promises further and substantial economic relief), as fighter for the rights of the non-Russian nationalities, and, last but not least, as the man who stands for a conciliatory foreign policy which would allow the U.S.S.R. to ease the burden of armaments and enable it to take care at last of its standard of living.

10 July 1957

3 KHRUSHCHEV, MALENKOV, AND THE STALINIST PAST

Immediately after the expulsion of Molotov, Malenkov, and Kaganovich from the Central Committee Khrushchev went to Leningrad to explain there in person the motives for the expulsion. To all the accusations contained in the Central

Committee's announcement he added new and significant charges directed exclusively against Malenkov. Malenkov, he stated, was responsible for staging the so-called Leningrad Case in 1949 and also for the execution, in 1951, of Voznessensky, member of the Politbureau and chief of the State Planning Commission. These charges have brought a new element into the political situation in the Soviet Union.

It is difficult to say whether or to what extent Khrushchev's new allegations are based on facts. The bloody tangle of the Leningrad Case, with its secret purges and counter-purges, can hardly be unravelled by anyone without access to the archives of the Soviet political police. As to Malenkov's alleged responsibility for Voznessensky's fate, Khrushchev's latest version conflicts with an earlier account he himself gave to Eastern European communists. In that earlier version he related that he, Malenkov, and Bulganin had jointly tried to save Voznessensky's life. . . .[1] Evidently one of Khrushchev's own accounts of Malenkov's role in this matter must be false.

Whichever is the false version, it must be asked what has induced Khrushchev to level against Malenkov this additional accusation, about which the communiqué of the Central Committee was silent? Why did he single out Malenkov rather than Molotov and Kaganovich as the special target for attack? Both Molotov and Kaganovich were involved in staging a very long series of purges throughout the Stalin era. Molotov was the Soviet Prime Minister during the great trials of the 1930s; and so he may be held to bear the strictly constitutional responsibility for the judicial murders of those years. Why then does Khrushchev spare Molotov and Kaganovich the kind of accusation with which he has chosen to burden Malenkov?

Evidently the charges against Malenkov contained in the Central Committee's announcement have not been enough to carry conviction with the Soviet people and to justify his expulsion in their eyes. The politically-minded Soviet public can readily accept as true all that is now said against Molotov and Kaganovich. It has known them as foremost Stalinist leaders, second to Stalin only, since the 1920s. It has watched them since Stalin's death and guessed from their taciturn and reserved behaviour their real attitude towards de-Stalinization;

[1] See chapter 5, page 74.

and it finds it only too plausible that they should have obstructed the new reformist trend of Soviet policy. There is, indeed, nothing in the charges levelled against Molotov and Kaganovich that flavours of crude invention or slander. And ordinary Soviet people probably rejoice at their fall as they rejoiced at Beria's fall; they see in it a promise of better times.

This, however, has not been, and could not have been, the country's reaction to Malenkov's disgrace. Malenkov has owed his, by all accounts great, popularity to the fact that it was he who initiated the era of reform on the very day of Stalin's death. It was primarily with his name that the process of de-Stalinization had been associated up to the time of the Twentieth Congress in February 1956. It was he who tried to give to Soviet economic policy a new pro-consumer bias and was therefore attacked and overthrown by those who held that heavy industry must continue to enjoy absolute priority. It was Malenkov also who initiated the detente in foreign affairs and insisted that atomic warfare threatened with destruction mankind as a whole (and not merely capitalism, as Molotov and Khrushchev have argued). In short, the Soviet public has, rightly or wrongly, seen Malenkov as *the* antagonist of the Stalinist old guard. It must therefore have received with utter incredulity the claim that he has been a Stalinist die-hard plotting with Molotov and Kaganovich; and it must have viewed with suspicion Khrushchev's motives for the showdown with Malenkov.

Khrushchev has thus found himself compelled to try and prove to the country that Malenkov has not in fact been the kind of man that the country has taken him to be: he had to make a special effort to destroy Malenkov's popularity. There is no surer way of destroying a man's popularity in Russia today than to expose his association with any of the blood purges of the Stalin era. And so Khrushchev has unearthed the victims of the Leningrad purge and has laid them and Voznessensky's corpse at Malenkov's door. In so doing he may have succeeded in achieving his purpose. People may still wonder whether Malenkov had indeed made common cause with Molotov and Kaganovich, but their sympathy for him must have cooled off.

However, Khrushchev has probably achieved more than he

intended. He intended to defeat his rivals and to deprive them
of all influence, but not to stage a purge in the old Stalinist
style. Now the logic of his deed drives him to do precisely this.
He cannot lay the corpses of Voznessensky and others at
Malenkov's door without staging a trial with Malenkov in the
dock. He cannot easily put Malenkov in the dock without
placing Molotov and Kaganovich by his side. Nor can he put
Molotov on trial without going over Molotov's record, including the chapter of the Great Purges.

Yet Khrushchev has his own good reasons for shrinking from
this course of action. He has set out to destroy Stalin's old
guard; yet he himself is one of it. Of all the charges he is
bringing against Molotov, Kaganovich, and Malenkov there is
not a single one that could not be turned against him as well.
They, he says, have obstructed de-Stalinization. But has he not
done the same? Has he not just told us: 'We are all Stalinists'?
They, he claims, have obstructed the detente in international
affairs. But can the same charge not be made against Khrushchev on the grounds of some of his more militant pronouncements on foreign policy? They, he asserts, have been in the way
of an improvement of the standard of living of the Soviet
people. But has Khrushchev not been the foremost champion of
the school of thought that holds that 'heavy industry must come
first'? Their hands are stained with the blood of innocent
Party members; but are Khrushchev's not?

Of course, they are; otherwise he could not have reached the
top of the Stalinist hierarchy and survived there. In his secret
speech at the Twentieth Congress he related the grim circumstances under which Kossior, the Stalinist boss of the
Ukraine, had been purged in the 1930s. What he did not say
was that he himself took Kossior's place at the head of the
Ukrainian organization. However, in the Soviet Union people
in their forties remember this; and they know that he could not
have taken Kossior's place if he had not enjoyed Stalin's complete confidence and if he had not been one of the most zealous
purgers. There are presumably still enough men alive, in the
Ukraine and in Moscow, who have been victims of Khrushchev's purges and who would readily testify against him on this
count.

Thus, it was a most risky undertaking for Khrushchev to

raise the issue of his erstwhile colleagues' responsibility for the purges; and until this July he refused to raise it. But now he has made a new departure; and he cannot know where this may lead him. . . . The Stalinist guard is no longer in a position to exercise power; and its chief destroyer comes from its own midst. At the same time, however, the country is paying the ultimate penalty of totalitarianism; for while the Stalinist ruling group is disintegrating no coherent opposition group exists that would be able to come forward to form an alternative government. Khrushchev's ascendancy is highly precarious and may well be shortlived.

A repetition of the Stalinist purges amid an intense and widespread revulsion against Stalinism can only convulse the country and stir up popular revolt. But any *early* popular revolt is likely to be leaderless and therefore to be doomed. There are still the dark horses around Khrushchev: Marshal Zhukov on the one hand; and on the other, the younger men who have been brought up by the Stalinist old guard but who have not belonged to it, and who have now taken their places in the new Presidium and in the Central Committee. It is from among these dark horses that the political initiative is likely to come in the next few years.

7 July 1957

4 BONAPARTISM IN THE SOVIET UNION

The expulsion of Marshal Zhukov from the Presidium and the Central Committee of the Soviet Communist Party concludes the latest crisis in Moscow. For the first time since the October Revolution the Party leadership has now openly admitted that its supremacy was threatened by the Bonapartist ambitions of a famous general. It has levelled three charges against Marshal Zhukov: he allegedly aimed at removing from the Party's control the armed forces; he fostered a cult of his own personality, claiming for himself all the credit and glory for Russia's victory in the last war; and he stood for an 'adventurous' foreign policy, that is for a policy which threatened to involve Russia in armed conflict with the West.

The first two charges are largely true; but by themselves they would not be likely to discredit the Marshal. On the contrary, his striving to free the armed forces from an all too rigorous Party control could only evoke widespread sympathy in the officer corps. The accusation that he indulged in self-glorification was perhaps more likely to harm the Marshal's reputation in view of the intense revulsion of the Soviet people against any personality cult. On the other hand, his exceptional record as a military leader cannot easily be effaced. He *is* the victor of Moscow, Leningrad, and Stalingrad, and the conqueror of Berlin. No general since Napoleon I has been covered in anything like Zhukov's martial glory. No one did more than Khrushchev himself to remind the world of it, when at the Twentieth Congress he described how Stalin, envious of the Marshal's fame, had cast the man and his military record into the shade. Now Khrushchev appears to be treating the Marshal no better than Stalin had treated him, perhaps worse. Many people in Russia must reflect that if Khrushchev is right against Zhukov, then he was wrong against Stalin at the Twentieth Congress; and if he was right against Stalin, then he is wrong against Zhukov. And the charge about the personality cult is double-edged, for people must be wondering whether Khrushchev may not be trying to foist on them his own personality.

It was precisely because Khrushchev was not sure of the effect of these charges, that he threw in the third accusation, according to which the Marshal's policy constituted a virtual threat to peace. This is the only count in the indictment which may set the pacifist Soviet masses against Zhukov. How much truth there is in it is another question, however. Any military dictator would be likely to pursue a more bellicose foreign policy than that which the civilian Party leaders can contemplate. Yet, the characterization of Zhukov's attitude consists of a mixture of fact and fiction. He was certainly the prime mover of the Soviet intervention in Hungary last year. He has been opposed to proposals for a withdrawal of Soviet and American troops from Europe, proposals with which Khrushchev has been toying. But other Marshals, such as Vassilevsky, and more recently Vershinin, the Supreme Commander of the

Soviet Air Force, have shown a much more aggressive frame of mind than Zhukov. Nor was Zhukov responsible for the recent tension over Syria and Turkey, which developed during his absence from Russia and was exacerbated precisely by Khrushchev's utterances. On this issue Zhukov appears to have been opposed to Khrushchev and to have attacked him at the latest session of the Central Committee. To deprive the Marshal of his arguments Khrushchev went straight from the Central Committee to the Turkish Embassy in Moscow to make peace gestures and to announce that the tension over Syria had subsided. As Stalin had done so often, Khrushchev paraded in the clothes of his defeated opponent.

Has the Party leadership then succeeded in dispelling the 'Bonapartist threat' for good? It is too early to answer with a definite Yes. Khrushchev has so far gained his success, because the political climate in Russia does not, or does not yet, favour a military *coup*. Discussing the chances of such a *coup* in my book *Russia After Stalin*, I wrote shortly after Stalin's death in April 1953: 'A Bonaparte can reach out for power and have his eighteenth *Brumaire* only in a country ruled by an ineffective Directory, where disorder is rampant, discontent rife, and the Directory is in frantic search of a good "sword". No army can set itself up as an independent political force against a government enjoying popular confidence.'[1] Disorder is clearly not rampant in Russia at present; and discontent, although there is no lack of it, has not been acute. In any case, it has been mitigated by popular reforms, a rise in the standards of living, continuing evidence of Russia's tremendous industrial and educational advance, and a general sense of national achievement and pride. The Soviet 'Directory' or collective leadership has not been 'in frantic search of a good sword'. Marshal Zhukov's bid for power has therefore been premature. However, should the domestic situation suddenly deteriorate, and should the social and political tensions become accentuated— a possibility which cannot be ruled out—then the military might once again defy the Party leadership; and the challenge may be more effective than it was in recent months.

The view I expressed on this in *Russia After Stalin* still holds good:

[1] *Russia After Stalin*, London, 1953, p. 163.

The Russian Revolution has been the only one among the modern revolutions which has so far not led to a military dictatorship. But the ghost of Bonaparte has haunted it for three decades; and both Trotsky and Stalin, each in his own way, wrestled with the ghost. [In Stalin's days] the trend towards Bonapartism . . . remained only latent, in part because Russia was too weak to breed a Bonaparte. A Bonaparte cuts no figure if he cannot conquer a continent. The Soviet generals of the past were incapable of such a feat—Russia's industrial military strength was altogether inadequate for that. At the close of the Stalin era this may no longer be true. Nobody can say whether a real general, whom the uniform of a Bonaparte would fit much better than it fitted Stalin, may not appear in the Red Square one day.[1]

The ghost of Bonaparte will probably continue to haunt Moscow. Zhukov has, after all, not been 'liquidated'. He has emerged triumphantly from one disgrace; he may yet re-emerge from another. His popularity is still far greater than Khrushchev's. Millions of soldiers and thousands of officers who fought under him in the last war still look up to him as to the national hero. The mass of the peasantry is strongly susceptible to the magic of a 'military saviour', though the urban workers may be less impressed by it. (Only the other day I watched how that magic works even in quite unexpected quarters, when a former high official of the Communist International, who had spent twenty-two years—from 1934 to 1956—in Soviet concentration camps and prisons, sought to persuade me of the advantages of military dictatorship to present-day Russia.)

Marshal Zhukov's position may be similar to that of General de Gaulle's in France. In the late 1940s General de Gaulle was the claimant to power. He then had to withdraw into the wilderness. Still, at moments of acute political instability many of the French turn their eyes to him; and a violent social convulsion may yet bring him to power. Similarly, many Russians will still turn their eyes to Zhukov; and political turmoil or a warlike emergency may yet bring him back to the fore.

The trend towards military dictatorship has been inherent in more than one society unable to govern itself in a democratic manner. As long as the Soviet peoples have not learned to govern themselves, this trend will remain under the surface of

[1] p. 157.

monolithic party politics; and it is a matter of only secondary importance whether Zhukov or any other Marshal acts as its exponent. . . .

If Russia's spectacular industrial advance—exemplified by the *sputniks*—is continued, and if it is accompanied by marked improvement in the economic conditions of the masses and wider social progress, then the present strains and stresses are likely to diminish and the political conflicts to grow milder until the precedents of the Stalin era, those of autocracy and recurrent purges, cease to be relevant to the new situation. Then the rivalries of the Soviet rulers may come to be seen as merely the belated reflexes of people bred and conditioned by Stalinism, but belonging to a closed epoch. And then a new era would follow, in which the peoples of the U.S.S.R., confident in the vitality of their social institutions and needing no Tsar or tyrant, would reassert their dignity and rights and become masters of their own destiny.

3 November 1957

5 KHRUSHCHEV BECOMES PRIME MINISTER

Khrushchev's assumption of the office of Prime Minister gives rise to questions about his standing and the real extent of his power. Has he, at last, five years after Stalin's death, 'stepped into Stalin's shoes'? Has he become the new autocrat? Is this the end of 'collective leadership' in Moscow?

On the face of it, his new office adds little or nothing to Khrushchev's power. Stalin, throughout most of his career, exercised absolute dictatorship from the Party's General Secretariat, without even being a member of the government—he became Prime Minister only on the eve of world war. Real power still resided in the Party's Secretariat and Presidium, whose will any Soviet Prime Minister has to carry out, and by whose will he is appointed or removed, as the fortunes of Malenkov and Bulganin have shown. Khrushchev has taken the formal lead of the Council of Ministers not so much in order to strengthen his position internally as to regularize his standing in relation to other Heads of State, in preparation for a summit meeting—or for any important moves in the international field which he may contemplate independently of a summit meeting.

Yet the change in the Soviet Premiership also undoubtedly has a bearing on domestic affairs. Khrushchev appears now to be on top of all, or nearly all, his adversaries. To the long list of casualties in the struggle for power Bulganin's name is now added—he has had to pay for the ambiguous attitude he took last summer during the showdown between Khrushchev and the Anti-Party Group of Molotov, Kaganovich, and Malenkov. To judge just how solid Khrushchev's position is, however, the circumstances of the struggle, and the methods by which he has won it, have to be carefully considered. He has so far vanquished under the slogan of a 'return to socialist democracy'. He has owed every one of his successes to the blows he has struck at the Stalinist system of government. He destroyed or helped to destroy Beria as the symbol of the police state with its insane terror, purges, and concentration camps. He has discredited Molotov and Kaganovich and expelled them from the seats of power as the leaders of the Stalinist die-hards. He has been able to dispose of Malenkov by associating him, not quite truthfully, with Molotov and Kaganovich, and by stressing Malenkov's co-responsibility for the Stalinist purges (to which he himself had also lent a hand). Finally, he has also won against Zhukov by mobilizing the Party cadres against the not altogether imaginary danger of a military dictatorship.

Thus at every step in his climb Khrushchev has stirred the Soviet people's distrust of any pretender to dictatorship; and has appealed to the popular craving for freedom and emphatically promised to satisfy it. No doubt there has been a great deal of demogoguery in all this. All the same, Khrushchev is now to some extent the prisoner of his own promises and slogans. He has won at a price which makes it extremely difficult for him to use power in a tyrannical and autocratic manner.

He has also had to make very real, if limited, concessions to the social aspirations of the Soviet people. He has had to satisfy in some measure the egalitarian yearnings of the workers, to improve the lot of the lowest paid among them, to relieve them all of the industrial terror of the Stalin era, and to give them some say in the factories and workshops. He has had to meet half way the demands of the peasants, to relieve them of the burden of taxation, to pay them higher prices for farm produce, and to allow them far greater freedom in the management of the collective farms. At present he is transferring, on surprisingly easy terms, the property of the state-owned Machine Tractor Stations to these farms. He has also had to dismantle the over-centralized bureaucratic machine of industrial control and bestow a high degree of economic autonomy on the provinces.

Frightened by the political ferment provoked by his own revelations about Stalin's misrule, Khrushchev recently tried to turn the screws of political control. All the same, the Soviet Union today is in every respect a much freer country than it was five years ago; and it can hardly be robbed again of its newly won, very limited, but very real, freedoms. The popular pressure for a 'socialist democracy' that has wrested so many concessions from the ruling group persists; and the new Prime Minister, even if he has defeated all his rivals, has to reckon with it. He himself represents all the contradictions of the present period of transition, during which the Soviet Union has been breaking with the habits and traditions of the Stalin era while still bearing many marks of Stalinism. Khrushchev is, so to say, half a Stalin. His background being what it is, he can hardly be less than that; but he cannot be more either.

We need only compare Khrushchev's present position, five years after Stalin's departure, with Stalin's position five years after Lenin's death to see the difference. By 1929 Stalin had already established his tyrannical rule. He had already banished Trotsky not merely from Moscow but from Russia, and deported thousands of Trotsky's followers to Siberia. From month to month the terror was gaining in momentum and insanity. His relentless and hysterical campaigns against all oppositions, right and left, raged without a moment's break. Stalin was already a demi-god. Khrushchev's campaigns against his adversaries have so far had little of the venom, vehemence, and ferocity of Stalin's drives against Trotsky, Zinoviev, and Bukharin. Malenkov, Zhukov, and Molotov are still as if waiting in the wings. Attempts at fostering a Khrushchev cult are being made; but they are very timid indeed in comparison with even the earliest beginnings of the Stalin cult. The phoney

elections and votes, the pretences of unanimity, and the monolithic outlook of the Party are still what they were in Stalin's
days. But they now form a mere façade behind which a new
public opinion with diverse cross-currents is forming itself.
And there are few signs of any real recrudescence of the old
terror.

Khrushchev's powers thus appear to be limited by the new
political climate in the country, even if they are not checked by
envious rivals in the Presidium. Apart perhaps from Zhukov,
his old rivals, though they may be staying in the wings, have
little chance of a comeback. Their weakness *vis-à-vis* Khrushchev lies precisely in their belonging to the old climate and the
old era, and, for the most part also, to the old generation.

Men of a new generation and outlook are coming to the fore.
From among them are likely to come Khrushchev's potential
rivals and successors. They have been quite unknown until
recently; and so little or nothing can be said about them. Most
of them have been promoted by Khrushchev. This, however,
does not necessarily make of them his creatures or stooges. He
has recently brought a few of them from the Secretariat to the
Party's Presidium to fill the places vacated there by the
Stalinist old guard. But already he is sharing his power with
them to an extent to which Stalin never shared his.

In this connection the new relationship between the Presidium and the Secretariat deserves attention. The fact that
these two bodies have recently been so overhauled as to become
almost identical in composition has been generally interpreted
as indicating the growth and consolidation of Khrushchev's
power. In the light of the historic relationship between these
two bodies, however, the opposite conclusion would seem to be
far more justified. Stalin built up and secured his autocratic
dictatorship precisely by keeping the Politbureau (the Presidium's predecessor) and the Secretariat strictly separated
from one another. He alone was the link between them. In
theory the Politbureau was the Party's supreme authority; but
in practice the Secretariat wielded the fullness of power. Stalin
never allowed other members of the Politbureau to gain any
foothold in the Secretariat or any share of control over it—this
was his exclusive domain. As a rule he also kept the men of the
Secretariat away from the Politbureau. Stalin's adversaries

made repeated attempts to bring the Politbureau and the Secretariat closer together. All these attempts failed, because Stalin was bent on keeping the Politbureau, which was in name the policy-making body, deprived of the machinery needed for the implementation of any policy.

The present close connection between the Presidium and the Secretariat has changed all this. The chiefs of the Secretariat have been promoted to the rank of policy-makers; but as policy-makers they maintain control over the Party machine. Khrushchev shares with them the responsibility for policy decisions as well as the power to carry out decisions. They may not be Khrushchev's actual rivals as yet—for that they are too fresh to their offices. But this arrangement may well limit his powers much more effectively than any old style rivalry within the Presidium could do.

Khrushchev has reached his pinnacle as almost the last representative of the Stalinist old guard. That guard as a whole has been removed from power. For how long the men of the new generation will recognize him, the survivor of the Stalin guard, as their leader remains to be seen. He can lead them only if he yields to them and follows them. Should he try to establish himself against them as the new autocrat and demi-god and to rule by means of a Stalinist terror, they will probably know how to deal with him. He has done something to immunize Russia against the 'cult of the individual'; and he has to bear the consequences.

28 March 1958

9
Khrushchev on the Defensive

The first four sections of this chapter were written together in June 1958 under the title 'What is Going on in the Soviet Bloc?', and represented a unifying analysis of what appeared at the time as disconnected events. The immediate occasion for the analysis was the announcement, on 17 June, that Imre Nagy and his Defence Minister Pal Maleter had been tried and executed. This announcement coincided with a meeting of the Soviet Central Committee at which it was decided to abolish the compulsory delivery of agricultural produce by collective farms and to institute a system of planned state purchases. This was the second part of Khrushchev's agricultural reform: it had already been announced in February that the state-run Machine Tractor Stations were to be closed and the equipment handed over to the individual farms. The Machine Tractor Stations had been established under the First Five Year Plan (1928–32) and their abolition was justified on the grounds that collective farms were now large enough to make efficient use of their own machinery.

This year had also seen a series of diplomatic initiatives: in January Bulganin had sent a letter to nineteen heads of state proposing a summit conference, and in March the Soviet Union had unilaterally ceased testing all nuclear weapons. But Russia's relations with the West reached a new crisis-point in July when American troops were sent into the Lebanon and British troops into Jordan at the 'request' of the governments of those countries. Lebanon had been politically disturbed since the spring and the overthrow of the Hashemite regime in Iraq on 14 July led the Lebanese and Jordanian regimes to ask for Western help against internal and, so they claimed, external opposition forces.

Khrushchev's immediate reaction to these events was to renew the call for a summit conference and he accepted a proposal of Macmillan's that there should be such a meeting at the Security Council of the United Nations. But at the end of the month

Khrushchev flew to Peking; on his return he withdrew his support for a summit at the U.N. The Security Council, he claimed, was 'a kind of committee dominated by the member-countries of NATO, the Baghdad Pact and SEATO'.

This abrupt about-turn clearly indicated the force of Chinese objections. Mao had attacked the Russian interpretation of peaceful coexistence at the meeting of the twelve ruling Communist Parties held in Moscow in November 1957; and at the Eighth Congress of the Chinese Communist Party in the following May a new policy, the Great Leap Forward, was announced. In the summer and autumn a campaign to set up agricultural communes was launched to further the Great Leap Forward in agricultural production. As Khrushchev indicated in an interview with Senator Humphrey later that year, he was sceptical of this new Chinese economic initiative. In spite of this he had to take note of Chinese militancy in foreign affairs: they forced him to cancel the summit, and stepped up their own campaign against the off-shore islands of Quemoy and Matsu that the Kuomintang still held. It seemed for a time in the autumn of 1958 as if they were about to launch the long-heralded liberation of Taiwan. At this stage, both Russia and China had to present a united front in their foreign affairs; the time was not yet ripe for their differences in interest to become differences in policy.

1 THE EXECUTION OF IMRE NAGY

The trial and execution of Nagy, Maleter, and their friends was preceded by a long and bitter controversy of which Moscow and Peking were the main centres. The Hungarians had little or no say in the matter. Janos Kadar, the present communist leader of Hungary, endorsed the decision with a trembling hand. No one, not even Tito or Gomulka, could be more frightened of it than he was. No one can be more haunted by Nagy's and Maleter's ghosts than he will be; and no one needed this bloody business less.

Nagy and his followers represented no real or immediate threat to the present Hungarian regime. To be sure, in the eyes of many Hungarians Nagy was, and is now more than ever, the hero and the symbol of the October insurrection of 1956. But he possessed no solid organization capable of effective political action. What is more important, no political organization could possibly induce the Hungarians to revolt once again in the foreseeable future. No people defeated in a bloody insurrection rises again and takes up arms as long as the memory of its last defeat weighs upon its mind; and another generation will have to grow up before that memory is effaced. The Soviet armoured divisions that quelled the 1956 rising are still on Hungarian soil, just as those that suppressed the Berlin revolt of June 1953 are still on the soil of Eastern Germany. Nagy's execution took place on the fifth anniversary of the Berlin rising; and during these five years East Germany has, despite much ferment among the intelligentsia, seen no revival of any effective mass movement against Ulbricht's government. The present rulers of Budapest, according to all evidence, were not afraid of any mass movement hostile to them or of Nagy's comeback.

They had many reasons, on the other hand, to be afraid of a great purge. Less than two years had passed since Hungarian communism suffered the odium of the purge of László Rajk, denounced as a traitor and a spy. The whole of Hungary still remembered Rajk's spectacular rehabilitation and the dramatic pilgrimage of immense multitudes to his grave. In a country which has lived through such a shock it was dangerous for the rulers to stage another false trial, to produce another national martyr, and to invite the people to make a mental pilgrimage to the new martyr's grave.

Kadar had even more specific reasons to shrink from this trial. To justify Nagy's execution, its prompters had to produce an elaborate legend of Nagy's deep-laid 'counter-revolutionary plot'. This legend inevitably ensnared Kadar himself.

The legend was and is, of course, a perverse mixture of truth and falsehood. In October 1956 Nagy found himself at the head of a movement which at the outset aimed merely at reforming the communist regime, but which ended in an attempt to overthrow it. Nagy had not 'planned' this movement as his indictment claims. The revolt unfolded as a spontaneous and nation-wide reaction first against Rakosy's misrule and then against Soviet armed intervention. The real inspirer of that reaction was Khrushchev: his Twentieth Congress speech about Stalin was the spark that ignited it.

Nagy was not the leader of the movement—he lacked the qualities for that—he was led by it. At every stage events overtook him and forced his hand. He was unable to resist popular pressure as it grew more and more anti-communist; and, overwhelmed by it, he proclaimed the end of the communist regime and Hungary's withdrawal from the Warsaw Pact. Eventually the anti-communist mood rose to such a pitch that the insurgent crowds shouted: 'Death to Nagy!'; and it was with these shouts, as well as the thunder of Soviet guns, ringing in his ears, that Nagy took refuge in the Yugoslav Embassy. Twenty months later, the cry 'Death to Nagy!', raised originally by Hungarian anti-communists, resounded from communist quarters.

The circumstances in which Nagy fled to the Yugoslav Embassy have, for curious reasons, remained obscure to this day. I would like to relate here a conversation about this I had with Moshe Pijade, the late Yugoslav leader, a short time after the event. When I mentioned that Nagy had sought asylum from Russian vengeance, Pijade gave me an ironical look and remarked: 'Do you believe in this story? Nagy did nothing of the sort. When he came to our Embassy he was afraid not of the Russians but of Hungarian counter-revolutionaries and fascists, who were gaining control of the movement towards the end of the rising.' In fact Nagy was afraid of both the Russians and the Hungarian right-wing. Whatever the truth, his tragedy was that he was surpassed by events. He was the victim of the October rising as much as its hero; but he was not its architect.

Throughout the rising, almost to its end, Kadar was at Nagy's side as his close associate and comrade. On 30 October 1956, a week after the insurrection had started, Kadar declared over the Budapest radio: 'I am in full accord with my friend Imre Nagy'. As the new leader of the Communist Party he was minister in Nagy's coalition government formed on 2 November. (That government has now been denounced as 'illegal'; and its formation was one of the main counts in Nagy's indictment.) Only after that government had constituted itself did Nagy and Kadar part company, and Kadar made for the Soviet headquarters whence he emerged as the new Prime Minister.

Kadar could not be unaware that Nagy's execution might shake his own position. Nothing would be easier than to level against him the accusations under which Nagy had been sentenced to death. If it came to Kadar's trial, there would not even be any need to produce a new indictment. It would be enough to take Nagy's indictment, or nine-tenths of its text, and to substitute Kadar's name for Nagy's.

Before Nagy was handed over to the hangman, Kadar therefore sought to insure his own position. He had to beg and bargain for his life; and the evidence of this could be found in the official announcement about Nagy's trial. Speaking of Nagy's 'illegal' government the announcement said: 'That government was already constituted in such a way that the reactionary forces had the upper hand in it, although Imre Nagy, in order to deceive the masses, *included in it also persons devoted to socialism.*' This sentence was to serve Kadar as a safe conduct. Kadar knows, however, that its reliability is dubious, to say the least. What is the worth of a communist leader, it may now be asked, who so conspicuously lacked vigilance as to participate in a counter-revolutionary government? And what would be easier than to say at a later stage that Kadar had joined that government not because he had been deceived by Nagy, but because he had been his accomplice?

Kadar struggled on to disentangle himself from the net. While Nagy's trial was drawing to a close and its outcome was a foregone conclusion, Kadar made a desperate appeal to Moscow to stop the new chain of purges before it was too late.

Surprisingly, he made part of that appeal in public. Four days before the announcement of the execution *Nepszabadszag*, Kadar's organ, published a curious article on Titoism. Ostensibly Kadar joined in the denunciation of the Yugoslavs; but he did it in an extremely mild manner (far more mildly even than did Gomulka's *Trybuna Ludu*), as if he were only going through a ritual motion. *Nepszabadszag* made not a hint about Tito's 'treachery'. On the contrary, it described Tito and the Titoists as 'comrades with a heroic record'; and it insisted that 'despite mistakes' those comrades were 'engaged in building socialism'. Alone in the whole communist press, the paper even excused Yugoslavia's staying out of the Soviet bloc by saying that this was due to the 'wrongs done to Yugoslavia by all of us' during the Stalin era, wrongs which the Yugoslavs could not easily forget. (Nagy's chief 'crime' was his attempt to detach Hungary from the Soviet bloc!)

Even more surprisingly, Kadar's paper indicated that it held Peking rather than Moscow responsible for the harsh and quasi-Stalinist forms of the drive against 'revisionism'; it contrasted explicitly the sharpness of the Chinese attacks on Tito with *Pravda*'s 'calm and restraint'. (Incidentally, *Nepszabadszag* compared Nagy to Djilas; but as Djilas had so far received much milder treatment at Tito's hands, the comparison sounded like a reflection on Nagy's trial.)

Finally, *Nepszabadszag* emphatically and repeatedly warned all Party members against a relapse into the sinister Cominform methods of the years 1949–53, the years of the Rajk and Slansky trials: 'In dealing with our differences of view all members of our Party should beware of back-sliding into the Cominform line of 1949. We desire to continue our discussion with the Communist Union of Yugoslavia in a spirit of good comradeship.'

This was Kadar's appeal directed not only, in fact not so much, to Hungarian communists as to the communist leaders in Moscow—an appeal all the more desperate because it was made to the accompaniment of the salvos of the execution squad.

And—here is a startling sequel to the story—on 16 June, the day of the announcement about Nagy's trial, *Pravda* reprinted the long *Nepszabadszag* article just as it had reprinted statements coming from other Communist Parties. None of these other statements, however, had contained anything like this explicit plea for moderation, conciliation, and against the repetition of the follies of the Stalin era. It looked as if an influential group in the Soviet leadership had been anxious to give resonance to Kadar's plea—and as if the struggle in Moscow itself and a tug-of-war between Moscow and Peking had still been unresolved. . . .

24 June 1958

2 MAO ABANDONS THE HUNDRED FLOWERS CAMPAIGN

Before the Hungarian rising and for some time afterwards Mao acted as the champion of de-Stalinization. His assumption of this role had been something of a surprise since as late as February 1956, at the Twentieth Congress of the Soviet Communist Party, he had tried to save the Stalin cult from the shattering blows which Mikoyan and Khrushchev were inflicting on it. However, in October of the same year Mao lent his support to Gomulka and he warned Moscow against armed intervention in Poland. He then proclaimed a new era in Chinese communist policy and held out the promise of freedom of thought and expression: 'Let a hundred flowers blossom; and let a hundred schools of thought contend'. . .

It came therefore as a shock to some of the leaders of the Communist Parties, who assembled last November in Moscow for the fortieth anniversary of the Bolshevik Revolution, to hear Mao call for an end to de-Stalinization and urge all Communist Parties to launch a full-scale attack on 'revisionism'. During his stay in Moscow Mao was not even on speaking terms with Gomulka and the Yugoslav communist leaders. Khrushchev, somewhat embarrassed, tried to act as a go-between and to soften the sharpness of Mao's attacks on the 'revisionists'. But Mao would not abate his hostility.

His word carried great weight. In the international communist hierarchy he alone at present enjoys the immense prestige of the leader of a great and victorious revolution and of an original theorist and ideologue. The more sophisticated men of the hierarchy regard Khrushchev merely as a narrow-minded, if able and dynamic, administrator, and they receive his crude pronouncements on matters of theory and ideology with more or less discreet irony.

'What has caused the change in Mao's attitude?', the baffled Poles and Yugoslavs asked in Moscow. No doubt Mao saw the Hungarian upheaval as a grave warning. This, however, was not decisive. For several months after, the rising call 'Let a hundred flowers blossom' still resounded from Peking; and Mao still spoke as the most radical de-Stalinizer. He changed sides primarily from considerations of domestic policy. In Moscow it was said that in his own Politbureau he had had to contend with an opposition which, led by Liu Shao-chi and Chu Teh, held that he had gone too far in de-Stalinization—much further than was safe for Chinese communism. The opposition, it was claimed, had gained considerable ground in the higher reaches of the Chinese Party; and in the end Mao himself recognized that the result of his 'hundred flowers' policy was disappointing and himself turned against those who wished to continue it.

Whether this is true or not, Mao's deeper motives must be sought in China's internal situation. When Mao initiated the 'hundred flowers' line, he was confident that the mass of the Chinese people were genuinely contented with his government, that there existed an overall harmony between rulers and ruled, and that, consequently, the newly proclaimed freedom of expression and criticism, far from harming the regime would strengthen it.

Not all of these assumptions were groundless. The great mass of the Chinese people had since the revolution improved their living conditions strikingly and had benefited from the spread of social hygiene, educational facilities, and from the chances of advancement offered by an expanding economy. But popular satisfaction at improved living conditions is not necessarily the same as harmony between rulers and ruled. Mao, it appears, mistook the one for the other. He was convinced that, since the Communist Party had such great achievements to its credit, the mass of the people favoured its collectivist policies. He evidently underrated the craving for private property felt by the vast majority of the Chinese. The benefits which the 1949 revolution brought to China have not killed that craving. They have, on the contrary, intensified it.

Of 600 million Chinese 500 millions are peasants. As smallholders they at first benefited from Mao's land reforms. However, in the last few years collectivization has come to the villages. True, Mao's collectivization has been far more flexible and far milder than Stalin's. He has carried it out by relatively slow stages, designed to accustom the peasantry gradually to the new organization of farming. The country has nevertheless been in the throes of a profound and unprecedented upheaval which, by its scale alone, dwarfs even Stalin's collectivization.

It is hardly possible as yet to gauge the effect of such an upheaval on 500 million human beings and to make any definite generalizations about it. One can only say that so far the Chinese peasantry does not seem to have put up that desperate and bloody resistance to collectivization that the Russian peasantry put up a generation earlier. But it would be very surprising indeed—and it would be most surprising to the Marxist—if the peasants accepted the end of the smallholding in meek submissiveness. There can be no doubt that the Chinese countryside is now the scene of many conflicts between government and farmers, amounting to a great clash between collectivism and individualism, especially since Mao, like Stalin, set out to collectivize farming without the technical resources (machinery, fertilizers, etc.) required for the job. The resulting tension between town and country must at times endanger the supply of food to the urban population and threaten to upset plans for industrialization.

In the town Mao has tried to transform the 'patriotic bourgeoisie', which had once supported him and which he had once treated very gently, into state employees. He has done this mainly by buying up their property, not by dispossessing them in the manner in which Stalin dispossessed the Russian N.E.P.-men. The application of this anodyne method seems to have spared China some of the worst convulsions which Stalin's Russia suffered in the early 1930s. The Chinese merchants and small entrepreneurs, seeing no other way out, allowed them-

selves to be bought up and transformed virtually into government employees. They even pretended to be pleased with the
change in their status and to be 'enthusiastically re-educated
for socialism'.

Incredible as this may seem, Mao and some of his colleagues
believed in this make-believe. They were convinced that the
bourgeoisie had indeed given up the hope of a return to any
form of private economy. As long as 'monolithic' discipline
prevailed, the real aspirations and thoughts of the peasantry
and the bourgeoisie remained hidden. But no sooner had Mao
proclaimed the new era of free expression than the suppressed
craving for private property welled up and burst out.

An important section of the intelligentsia, having its roots in
the peasantry and in the bourgeoisie, became the mouthpieces
of these classes and directly or indirectly voiced their grievances.
They also voiced their own intellectual resentments, protesting
against the canons of Maoist orthodoxy—Party control over
science, literature, art, and so on. Many of the intelligentsia had
joined the Communist Party during the phase of the so-called
bourgeois revolution when Mao fought, under the anti-
imperialist banner, for China's independence and unification
and carried through his first land reforms. With these aims the
great majority of the intelligentsia were indeed in enthusiastic
agreement. But they baulked at the transition to the collectivist
phase of the revolution; and once they were encouraged by
Mao himself to express their innermost thoughts and feelings,
they did so. The workers also spoke up, demanding higher
wages and more consumer goods—more, in any case, than the
government's investment plans could allow.

Thus for the first time for years Mao saw the true face of the
nation; and it frightened him. He had expected the 'hundred
flowers' all to blossom out in various shades of red, or perhaps
pink—instead, they came out in a great variety of colours
among which white was quite conspicuous.

The 'rightist' mood, so widespread in the nation, also found
its reflection within the Communist Party (not to speak of the
various surviving puppet parties which early last year suddenly
appeared to shed their puppet character and show signs of an
independent existence). Within the Communist Party there
began to emerge a trend reminiscent of the Bukharinist school

of thought which had, in Russia in the 1920s, stood up for the property-loving *muzhik* and called for a neo-N.E.P.

Mao thus found himself in a paradoxical situation. Having made a bold attempt to exorcize Stalin's spirit, he was now confronted by the ghost of Bukharin; and this appeared to him far more menacing than Stalin, whether alive or dead. He saw collectivization suddenly imperilled, the bourgeoisie straining to regain lost ground, and the intelligentsia in revolt. This led to the conclusion that Stalin had, after all, not been as wrong-headed as Khrushchev portrayed him at the Twentieth Congress; and that, in any case, communist China was still 'too backward and poor' and not yet consolidated strongly enough to indulge in further de-Stalinization.

He was confirmed in this conclusion by difficulties in the industrial field. Too much capital had been frozen in gigantic long-term construction projects which were hampered by scarcity of raw materials. There were acute shortages of consumer goods. Disgruntled workers were all too ready to avail themselves of the right to strike which Mao had just solemnly guaranteed them. The trade unions tended to assume independence and to clash with the government. It became clear to Mao that without the reimposition of very severe discipline China could not industrialize and collectivize as rapidly as he wished. So in the end he yielded to those of his own Politbureau colleagues who had viewed his 'hundred flowers' policy with apprehension. He decided to restore the 'monolithic' outlook of his own Party and to throw his weight against de-Stalinizers and 'revisionists' in the international communist movement.

Since the November conference of the communist leaders in Moscow Mao has thus acted as the chief inspirer of a broad alliance of die-hard Stalinists and the so-called 'de-Stalinizers of the left' against the 'anti-Stalinists of the right'. He has apparently acted from the conviction that de-Stalinization can at present only strengthen the right-wing of the communist movement, and through it the non-communist right, and that consequently much of the de-Stalinization should be reversed until such time as the resumption of the process becomes less dangerous to communism than it is now—whenever that may be.

On this issue the needs of the Chinese Communist Party

evidently clash with those of the Soviet Party. The U.S.S.R. is industrially and culturally the most advanced member of the Soviet bloc; China is the most backward. To advance still further the Soviet Union needs to overcome the constraining legacy of the Stalin era, while China can hardly advance as rapidly as its rulers would like it to do, especially in industrialization, without re-adopting some of the Stalinist methods.

Mao has, nevertheless, been able to obtain influential backing in Moscow and to make Khrushchev himself toe his line. And his success on this front is largely due to the fact that he could threaten to align himself against the Soviet leader with the Stalinist die-hards in Moscow.

20 June 1958

3 KHRUSHCHEV'S DOMESTIC OPPOSITION

Despite his seemingly unrivalled leadership in the Presidium, Khrushchev has been under more or less continuous attack over his domestic and foreign policies. It was to divert this attack from himself that he agreed to give the cue for Nagy's execution trying thus to disarm part of the Stalinist opposition at home, with which he had had to contend since the Twentieth Congress and whose disfavour he finally earned when he brought about the disgrace of Molotov and Kaganovich.

The Molotov-Kaganovich faction has not laid down arms. It seems that it has, on the contrary, been very active in recent months. Since the beginning of this year Molotov and Kaganovich have paid frequent visits to Moscow, probably to instruct their followers and to direct the inner Party attack against Khrushchev. (They have, in any case, not yet been expelled from the Party, but only from the Central Committee.)

Their attack, it appears, was more dangerous to Khrushchev and Khrushchev's own position is weaker than at first seemed the case. No doubt, he is very popular in the country among the farmers, and in town among the 'backward workers', though he appeals far less to the more educated elements in the nation —the intelligentsia and the advanced workers. But the environ-

ment in which he has met with definite and even determined
resistance is that of the industrial bureaucracy; and in a country
where politics is inseparable from the management of socialized
industry as a single concern, the managers, administrators, and
technicians play a far greater role than they do in any other
country.

Khrushchev antagonized the economic bureaucracy last year
when he broke up the central industrial ministries in Moscow,
formed about a hundred Regional Economic Councils (the
Sovnarkhozy), and, decentralizing the whole industrial structure,
put these Councils in charge of economic management within
more or less autonomous areas. From the beginning many
officials of the disbanded central ministries have obstructed the
reform, refused to take up appointments with the provincial
Councils, and, in defiance of orders, stayed on in Moscow.
Consequently many of the Regional Councils have remained
understaffed till this day. This is in fact a silent sit-down strike
of Moscow's once all-powerful, and still very influential,
'managerial class'. These 'strikers' form, in all probability, the
core of Molotov's, Kaganovich's, and in part also of Malenkov's
political following. They are an important centre of opposition.

Khrushchev at first relied on the support of the provincial
economic bureaucracy against the Muscovites. To some extent
he still retains that support; but it, too, has been giving him
serious trouble. Under the new dispensation, the harmonious
working of the Soviet industrial machine depends primarily on
the willingness of ninety-two Regional Councils to co-ordinate
their activities and secure a regular inter-regional exchange of
goods. According to all the evidence, this exchange has been
breaking down quite often, and co-operation between the
Regional Councils has been anything but smooth. Local
initiative, which had so long been subject to over-rigorous
control from the centre, is now asserting itself with a vengeance,
and is ready to sacrifice national interest to local, particular,
and sectional demands. Thus a threat has arisen to the coherence
of the national economy.

This threat grew grave enough to make Khrushchev issue a
decree providing for a whole range of penalties, including
prison, for managers of Regional Councils who fail to meet
their obligations towards other regions in keeping them sup-

plied with raw materials, semi-manufactured, and manufactured goods. This is the first punitive decree of this kind
published since the Stalin era; and it is directed against 'top
people'. Clearly, Khrushchev's position at the head of government and Party depends very largely on whether he is able to
bring these industrial managers to heel.

Simultaneously, he has been carrying out a series of momentous reforms in agriculture. He has resolved to disband the
state-owned Machine Tractor Stations and to sell their
machinery to the collective farms. The importance of this step
consists in the fact that it deprives the government of its hitherto
most potent instrument of direct control over farming, that it
transforms the collective farms into co-operatives owning their
means of production, and that it takes an enormous mass of
farm machinery out of the 'planned sector' of the economy and
throws it into the market.

This degree of reform would still leave farming in a highly
unsettled and abnormal condition, as farmers would be allowed
to trade in their means of production but not in their produce—
in tractors but not in grain. Realizing this, Khrushchev sponsored the great reform of 18 June. For the first time for at
least thirty years the farmers have now been freed from all
obligation to make compulsory deliveries of food to the government. Henceforth the entire exchange of goods between town
and country is to be conducted on a commercial basis; and in
preparation for this the government has raised the prices of
farm produce. The supply of food for the urban population is
thus to be secured by price mechanism and economic incentives
instead of by administrative pressure.

This great change in the relations between government and
peasantry—a revival of N.E.P. on a far higher level of economic
development—should at last help Soviet farming to overcome
its backwardness, to raise efficiency, to solve the Soviet Union's
own food problems, and to make the U.S.S.R. the granary of
the communist world. However, this change comes as a great
shock. A large part of the economy is in flux. The transition is
bound to cause difficulties, especially if this or next year's
harvests do not come up to expectation. The peasantry may
rejoice in the reform and eventually produce huge masses of
food to put on the market; but there are bound to be partial or

temporary breakdowns and irregularities in the food trade and in the flow of supplies to urban areas.

These then are the two major domestic issues with which Khrushchev has had to grapple: the resistance of the industrial managers and their threat to disorganize the workings of the national economy; and the uncertainties of the new outlook in farming. As long as he has not found a definite solution to either of these problems, and as long as his opponents continue to exercise influence, he is in a position of political weakness.

The Molotov-Kaganovich faction attacks both these reforms as the fruit of 'revisionism'. Decentralization of industry, it says, is 'Titoist' or worse; and the abolition of compulsory food deliveries represents a 'rightist' policy. Molotov's and Kaganovich's followers (who are also still entrenched at various levels of the Party hierarchy) have attacked Khrushchev for 'revisionism' in other fields of Party policy as well, notably for his dealings with Tito and Gomulka. Since Mao too has set his face against these aspects of 'revisionism', there was clearly ground enough here for the line-up between the Chinese Party and the Stalinist die-hards in Moscow. To forestall this Khrushchev made an important 'ideological' concession to Mao and to a section of the Stalinists at home: he agreed to the launching of a full-scale attack on 'revisionism' and then to the executions in Budapest. . . .

23 June 1958

4 THE COLLAPSE OF KHRUSHCHEV'S DIPLOMACY

The renewed breach between Moscow and Belgrade and the Nagy affair have marked a critical turn in Khrushchev's foreign as well as in his domestic policy. To put it more precisely, they have been the outward signs of a change which goes much deeper and which affects every aspect of relations between East and West.

The crucial event here was, of course, the development by the Soviet Union, ahead of the United States, of the transcontinental missile. This feat altered the world's strategic balance. Before it had been accomplished the Soviet Union could oppose only its strictly circumscribed and essentially Eastern European military establishment, powerful yet severely limited in range, to the far-flung American network of naval and land bases. The transcontinental missile allowed the Soviet Union to outflank the American system of bases by way of outer space and to create a direct potential threat to the vital centres of American power. Khrushchev and his advisers assumed that having achieved this, and having demonstrated the achievement to an incredulous West by launching the first Sputnik, they could use the new strategic balance, the new 'equilibrium of deterrents', for an international bargain on a grand scale.

The bargain, as Khrushchev saw it, was to be concluded within the framework of the international *status quo*, with Eastern Europe integrated into the Soviet bloc, Germany left divided, and the Middle East opened to an 'orderly' penetration by all powers. The essence of the bargain was to consist in the trading of outer space, the element in which Russia had freshly acquired superiority, for naval and land bases, the element in which the United States and NATO had long enjoyed the advantage. Khrushchev hoped to induce the United States to give up its power to strike Russia from nearby bases, especially those in Europe, in exchange for Russia's sacrifice of her power to attack the United States directly from outer space. This implied the establishment of joint control over the use of outer space, a ban on the atomic armament of Germany, and a gradual thinning out of NATO bases.

The Soviet unilateral cessation of atomic tests was to have served as an overture to the trading of strategic advantages—and it might possibly have been followed up by a unilateral cessation of nuclear armament. (A few months ago Khrushchev assured a neutral ambassador in Moscow that he was strongly inclined to call a unilateral halt to Soviet production of nuclear bombs.) The Rapacki Plan for a European zone free of nuclear weapons was seen in Moscow as a crucial element of the scheme. Finally, the scheme was to be buttressed by proposals for large-scale trade between the U.S.S.R., the U.S.A., and other Western countries. As the first news of the growth of mass unemployment in the United States reached Moscow, Khrushchev assumed that the trade proposals would prove attractive to American business, and that they might be used in particular to speed up the development of the Soviet chemical industries —a belated echo of this belief can still, be found in his message to President Eisenhower of 2 June.

This, briefly, was the programme with which Moscow had set out to prepare the summit meeting, hoping that it would take place some time this summer. In January President Eisenhower agreed to start preparations for the meeting; and this was interpreted in Moscow as a sign that things were beginning to move in the desired direction. Khrushchev and his entourage beamed confidence.

Since then Khrushchev's confidence appears to have received shattering blows—from Washington on the one hand, and from critics at home on the other. His critics argued from the outset that his doctrine of the detente was unrealistic and that even if his scheme were technically workable, which they apparently doubted, Washington would under no circumstances accept it. The scheme, they said, would detach Western Europe from the U.S.A. and tilt the balance of strength in favour of the Soviet bloc to an extent to which the United States could not possibly agree. It was therefore useless, so the critics concluded, to spread illusions about the possibility of a bargain and the prospects of a summit meeting. This had, *inter alia*, been Molotov's attitude and led to his elimination from the Central Committee; but even after he had gone, his view was upheld by members of the Presidium and military strategists.

Subsequent reactions from Washington have tended to confirm the predictions of Khrushchev's critics. The unilateral cessation of nuclear tests has failed to evoke the response from the West for which Khrushchev had hoped. Even its propagandist reverberations have turned out to be feeble to a degree which could not but disappoint the Soviet Premier. The Rapacki Plan has been rejected by the Western Powers without discussion. The atomic armament of Western Germany is in progress. The United States government is clearly not in a mood to trade its superiority in naval and land bases against Soviet superiority in outer space. Thus the crux of the Khrushchev plan has fallen to the ground: a fact that has been apparent in the whole course of the negotiations over the summit meeting.

Not since the end of 1954 (that is since the inclusion of Germany in NATO, which preceded Malenkov's 'resignation' from the Premiership) has Soviet diplomacy suffered a comparable setback. Even if Khrushchev has at present no effective rival for leadership, his position is by no means impregnable, and his diplomatic fiasco has weakened it. To strengthen his hand he has apparently resolved to align himself with at least some of those who have been among his critics.

The attitudes of these critics embrace a whole range of different shades; but they have centred on an interpretation of 'peaceful coexistence'. The essence of the criticism is that Khrushchev—in advocating 'peaceful coexistence of the two systems'—has placed, in quasi-'revisionist' fashion, too much emphasis on its 'peacefulness' and too little on its 'necessarily antagonistic' character. We and NATO—so the argument runs —may not throw bombs at one another, but enemies we are and enemies we remain; and it is a dangerous illusion to hope for a real detente or to bank on mutual concessions, on the trading of strategic advantages, or even on partial disarmament. Those who make this criticism of the Khrushchev line do not necessarily prejudge the length of time for which 'coexistence' can remain both 'antagonistic' and 'peaceful'; they see it as the task of Soviet diplomacy to prolong that time.

Another school of critics argues that the spell of peaceful coexistence is bound to be shorter than is commonly believed; and that, to quote an authoritative source, Soviet diplomacy 'works against a deadline'. The present equilibrium of deterrents, they say, cannot last much longer. International tension cannot mount much higher than it has already risen. If it does not lead to real peace—and there are no signs that it will— then it must burst into war, because neither the West nor the East can stay on the brink indefinitely. This view has recently found far more emphatic expression in Russia than it did a year or even some months ago. It would be surprising if at least a few men in the Soviet ruling group were not to draw extreme conclusions from it and advocate preventive war, although there is, naturally, no evidence of this in the press. But certain assumptions which might logically lead to the advocacy of preventive war are now—and this is a novelty—almost as freely discussed in Russia (in specialized periodicals) as they have been in the West.

Two major points debated in this context may be mentioned here: first, the idea that for the first time in military history the advantage of the surprise attack may be strategically decisive, an idea which is, on the whole, new to Russian strategic thinking traditionally sceptical of all forms of *Blitzkrieg* and confident in the advantages of defence; and, secondly, the assumption that the United States 'has failed to develop a reliable defence system'.

It is impossible to say just how strong are these divergent currents of thought and what their outcome is likely to be. But it seems fairly certain that among Moscow's policy-makers the tide of opinion has turned against Khrushchev. Nor can there be much doubt that Mao Tse-tung has also thrown his weight against what had hitherto been the Khrushchev line. Although Mao's word may carry little weight with Moscow's military thinkers, it carries a great deal with the political strategists.

Even during the November conference of the communist leaders, one is told, Mao made no bones about his dislike of the *detentisme* associated with Khrushchev. If one of Khrushchev's chief counts against Molotov was that he obstructed summit diplomacy, then Mao appeared in the Soviet capital as if to vindicate Molotov's attitude. Mao, too, apparently considers summit diplomacy to be more or less worthless. He was apprehensive of Soviet concessions to the West, of a softening of Soviet morale, and of a dispersal of Soviet economic resources in politically and strategically uncoordinated ventures. He spoke as the virtual head of those who stood for 'tough' diplomacy; and, although he did not speak directly as a warmonger, he saw no reason why the horror of nuclear warfare should eat too deeply into communist minds or weaken their determination to face the capitalist world, if need be arms in hand. He is quoted as saying that, if two world wars had brought victories of communism in their wake, the third would do the same: 'And even after the Americans have discharged their H-bombs, there will still be at least 300 million people in communist China, far more proportionately than there would be in the capitalist countries; and they will go on building socialism.'

All these pressures, Russian and Chinese, seem for the time

being to have forced Khrushchev into a retreat on the diplomatic and ideological fronts. Here, too, he has been anxious to
forestall, or to upset, a line-up of his Soviet critics with the
Chinese. The encouragement which he gave to such 'revisionist'
policies as 'the parliamentary road to socialism' and 'the
nationally different roads to socialism' made sense to him as a
means to the international detente and within the context of
the detente. Without this, the nations of the Soviet bloc may
once again find themselves in the grip of a semi-Stalinist or
quasi-Stalinist isolationism and monolithic discipline. The shots
fired at Nagy and his comrades were meant as a demonstration
of 'vigilance'.

24 June 1958

5 CHINA'S PRESSURE ON
MOSCOW

The events of this summer have brought to light, with somewhat
artificial sharpness, the fact that Soviet foreign policy is no
longer made in Moscow alone, that Peking plays an essential
part in formulating it, and that Mao Tse-tung may have a
decisive say at crucial moments. For some time past this had
been obvious to close students of Russo-Chinese relations, but
now this conclusion is generally drawn from the conference
which Khrushchev and Mao held in Peking between 31 July
and 3 August; and, for a change, this conclusion is not only
generally accepted—it is also frequently overstated.

The circumstances of the Mao-Khrushchev meeting were
indeed unusual. This was the first time that the Soviet leader
had been to China since he had become Prime Minister. He
undertook the visit at a moment of particularly intense diplomatic activity, temporarily interrupting his copious corre-
spondence with Western statesmen about the summit meeting
which had already been so long delayed and which allegedly
brooked no further delay. On his arrival in Peking Khrushchev
was not greeted by any of the usual demonstrations of friendship
and solidarity. The vast multitudes, that had only a few days
earlier demonstrated in the streets against American and

British intervention in the Middle East, did not come out to welcome with flowers and smiles the 'great champion of the colonial and semi-colonial peoples against Western imperialism'. Evidently Khrushchev had no time to waste on crowds, flowers, and flowery speeches. For three full days he and Mao, and their Ministers of Defence and advisers, held council behind closed doors. They had important issues to thrash out and differences to settle; and when Khrushchev emerged from the council chamber he announced that for the time being he would have no East-West summit meeting. It looked, in effect, as if that meeting had been replaced by the summit conference of the two communist powers.

What were the issues discussed in Peking? The official communiqué mentioned summit diplomacy, the crisis in the Middle East, and the 'danger of revisionism'. These are interconnected topics, involving the Soviet and the Chinese approach to all the major issues of war and peace. It had been known at least since the conference of the Communist Parties held in Moscow last November that on two of these points, summit diplomacy and revisionism, Mao's views were not exactly the same as Khrushchev's. . . . Mao's line of reasoning, as far as it can be reconstructed, was approximately as follows.

It is foolish and dangerous, he argued, to stake too much on any genuine detente between East and West. No number of summit meetings can achieve it. Hostility and tension between communism and capitalism are bound to persist. 'Coexistence' and 'peaceful competition' between the two systems virtually means the continuation of cold war, in one form or another. The idea that it may be possible by some act of wise statesmanship to put an end to the cold war is 'pure revisionism', as unrealistic as would be the belief that it is possible to 'put an end' to class struggle at large.

If Stalin's successors, whether Malenkov or Khrushchev, had any illusions about the possibility of a real detente, Mao further intimated, Washington's attitude should have opened their eyes: 'The leaders of American capitalism have had no use for any summit diplomacy or detente.' To the extent that Khrushchev had, at the Twentieth Congress, fostered such illusions he bore some responsibility for the spread of revisionism and for Tito's behaviour—Tito's ambition to keep Yugoslavia 'outside the two power blocs' was dictated primarily by his belief in an eventual accommodation between the power blocs. To some extent, therefore, Mao held that Molotov's criticisms of Khrushchev's diplomacy were justified.

It did not follow, however, according to Mao, that communist diplomacy and propaganda should remain as rigid as they were under Molotov. They should display far greater initiative in placing the odium for the cold war on the West, in deriving from every situation as much profit for the Soviet bloc as possible, and in preventing the cold war from turning hot. But fear of war should not be, as it had tended to become, the dominant motive of Soviet and communist policy. Soviet diplomacy, like its American counterpart, must not be afraid of going to the brink of war, if need be. Communist morale must not be allowed to soften, relax, or fall into pacifist daydreaming—it must be shaken up and hardened by means of an all-out attack on revisionism.

From the beginning of this dissension Khrushchev has tried to take up a central position between Mao and the 'revisionists' and to patch up the differences. Last autumn and during the subsequent months, partly under the pressure of events and partly as a result of complex developments in Soviet domestic policy, which caused Khrushchev to fear a line-up between Mao and Russian Stalinists or neo-Stalinists, he accepted Mao's demand for an open attack on the revisionists. The new conflict with Yugoslavia and Nagy's execution followed. At this price Khrushchev still hoped to save his summit diplomacy. He had been encouraged in this hope by President Eisenhower's apparent agreement, expressed in January, to hold a summit conference. As the months passed without bringing the summit meeting any nearer, Khrushchev's position became more and more embarrassing; and the pressure on him to abandon summit diplomacy, and all that it implied, grew in force.

He was, it seems, on the point of abandoning it when the Americans landed in Lebanon and the British in Jordan. For a few days there was genuine alarm in Moscow. Khrushchev and his advisers viewed the landings as operations designed to obtain bridgeheads for an immediate Western attack on Iraq and possibly on the United Arab Republic. In this situation Khrushchev resolved to do two things at once: to go to the brink of war and to make a dramatic effort to save his summit diplomacy. On 19 July he proposed an urgent summit meeting to be held at three days' notice; and he accompanied the proposal by the announcement that important Soviet military manoeuvres were opening on the U.S.S.R.'s Middle Eastern frontiers and by the statement that 'the guns are already beginning to fire'.

His purpose was, on the one hand, to deter a British-American attack on Iraq and on the United Arab Republic and, on the other, to use the acute crisis to induce the Western Powers to consider at last, at a summit conference, his schemes for 'neutralization' of the Middle East and partial disarmament. He apparently succeeded in his first purpose (or so at least it is thought in Moscow) and failed in the second. The British and the Americans committed themselves to refrain from hostilities against the new regime in Iraq and the U.A.R.; but they still refused to hold a summit conference on Khrushchev's terms. This was the final failure of his summit diplomacy; but he could use the apparent or real success of his 'deterrents' to veil the failure.

The Middle Eastern crisis, however, had also revealed something like a crisis in Soviet-Chinese relations. When in July Khrushchev himself went 'to the brink', it seemed for a moment as if the Chinese were either not aware where the brink was or that they were pushing him to go beyond it. Even outsiders could see how much in those critical days Moscow and Peking were at cross-purposes. There was a striking discrepancy between the anti-Western demonstrations which took place in Moscow and those that were staged in Peking. In Moscow the demonstrations were a relatively minor, though significant, incident; in Peking they were played up and made into a great national event. Only a few thousands of Muscovites came to shout 'Hands off the Lebanon and Jordan!' in front of the British and American embassies. No leading political personality addressed the demonstrators. In Peking over a million people were marched out, and gigantic meetings were reported from all over the country. Top Party leaders and Arab envoys addressed the crowds in Peking; and the language they used was far more vehement than anything that was being said in Moscow. The cry for an early liberation of Taiwan went up again; and while the Russians dwelt anxiously on the 'catastrophic' consequences of Western policy, the Chinese Foreign Minister said, in answer to journalists' questions, that the Western intervention in the Middle East had served a good purpose, for it had let loose a wave of anti-imperialist emotion throughout the world.

To sum up, while Khrushchev was still concerned mainly with averting a head-on collision between East and West, the Chinese leaders appeared to be more interested in the advantages that the Soviet camp could, in their view, derive from such a collision, which they consider to be ultimately almost inevitable.

It was the revelation of this discrepancy between Moscow's and Peking's reactions to the events in the Middle East that sent a gravely disturbed Khrushchev on his journey to China. Having gone 'to the brink', the Soviet Prime Minister evidently felt disconcerted by the noisy Chinese back-seat driving. He knew that on some future occasion he might have to go to the brink once again; and he was afraid of having to do so and running the risk of dangerous prodding from his Chinese allies. There was, briefly, pressing need for some co-ordination of Moscow's and Peking's policies and reactions. During the three days of Mao's and Khrushchev's conference there was hard bargaining, and there were mutual concessions. Mao certainly did not simply dictate policy to Khrushchev. He had to give as much as he took. While Khrushchev called off the planned summit meeting over the Middle East, Mao acknowledged publicly the merits of summit diplomacy in general and recognized in advance that Khrushchev would be acting correctly if he sought another summit meeting on some future occasion. In their joint communiqué the accents of bellicosity and the emphasis on peaceful Russo-Chinese intentions were finely balanced in such a way as to reconcile the conflicting moods and attitudes. Even on the subsidiary point of revisionism the Chinese did not have it all their own way: revisionism was defined as 'the chief danger within the communist movement'. In other words, Titoism was recognized as a current *within* communism and not, as the Chinese had tended to treat it, as an external force hostile to communism. During his three days in Peking Khrushchev made his 'ideological' adjustments to

Mao, but at the same time gave Mao an emphatic 'lesson in statesmanship'. The outcome was thus a token of co-ordination and a compromise, which is not, however, likely to prove very stable.

14 August 1958

10
From the Twentieth to the Twenty-first Congress

The Twenty-first Congress of the Communist Party of the Soviet Union was held in Moscow from 27 January to 5 February 1959. It was called a year in advance of the statutory time to discuss the new Seven Year Plan. The Plan, to run from 1959 to 1965, replaced the sixth Five Year Plan (1956–60) and had been approved by the Central Committee in the previous November. It envisaged an 80 per cent rise in industrial production, a 70 per cent rise in agricultural production and a 40 per cent rise in real wages. In his address to the delegates Khrushchev voiced the aim of overtaking the United States in per capita output by 1970, by which time the transition from socialism to communism would have been achieved. He stressed that economic competition was the main arena for the rivalry of the socialist and capitalist camps, and the congress itself was officially named 'The Congress of the Builders of Communism'.

The congress was not noted for any major political revelations; the Anti-Party Group was frequently attacked, but only two of its junior members, Pervukhin and Saburov, appeared before the delegates to make a self-criticism of their role in the events of 1957.

1 FROM THE TWENTIETH TO THE TWENTY-FIRST CONGRESS

The Twenty-first Congress of the Soviet Communist Party has assembled in Moscow almost three years after Khrushchev's secret speech at the Twentieth Congress. For the Soviet Union and the other communist-ruled countries these have been eventful years, crowded with reforms, counter-reforms, inner Party struggles, turmoil, and confusion. Khrushchev's secret speech was, of course, the formative event of the period: it has reverberated through all subsequent developments and it will still echo in the proceedings of the forthcoming congress. Whatever the formal agenda of this assembly—officially it has been convened only to endorse the new Seven Year Plan—the essential question before it is whether or not communism is to follow the signposts set up three years ago. How much of the Stalinist orthodoxy is still valid and how much is discarded? And what is the order of the day: de-Stalinization or re-Stalinization?

That these questions should have given rise to controversy and splits was inevitable. It is now officially admitted that, despite the pretence of unanimity maintained at the Twentieth Congress, the Party leaders were then deeply divided over all major issues, as they had in truth been even earlier. It was only while the Twentieth Congress was in session that the Central Committee authorized Khrushchev to make his revelations about Stalin; and only a small majority of the Committee voted for this momentous decision. Nearly half the members, led by Molotov and Kaganovich, fought desperately right up to the last moment to save the idol and the dogmas of Stalinism. What was at stake was the entire system of government and Party leadership, not merely Stalin's good or bad name and ideological canons. None of the major administrative, economic, and social changes that have since then been introduced in the Soviet Union could even have been contemplated as long as the Party was shackled by the Stalinist orthodoxy. Khrushchev's secret speech was the prelude to the long series of reforms which has filled the interval between the two congresses.

The story of the interval, however, is full of contradictions and paradoxes. It falls into, at least, three major chapters: the first brought to a close by the Polish and Hungarian upheavals in October and November 1956; the second ending with the expulsion from the Central Committee of Molotov, Malenkov, and Kaganovich in June 1957. And the third and last chapter could well be divided into several sub-sections; its story is one of the greatest complexity and confusion.

In the first period the movement for de-Stalinization developed almost openly and assumed great explosive force. It met deep and widely felt needs; it evoked a powerful popular response; and it aroused boundless hopes. The range of the movement, however, was relatively limited, at least as far as the Soviet Union is concerned. It was primarily political in character. Its emphasis was on inner Party reform, collective leadership, and freedom of inner Party criticism—in a word, on the replacement of Stalinist 'bureaucratic centralism'. These were also the months of the 'thaw' in literature and in the arts and of an intense ferment of ideas in academic circles. From month to month de-Stalinization made startling conquests in vital but narrowly circumscribed fields. The intelligentsia led the movement, while the bureaucracy was divided against itself; but the mass of the working class, not to speak of the peasantry, remained on the whole inarticulate. Therein lay the weakness of the movement. Yet its momentum was strong enough to force Molotov, Kaganovich, and their adherents into a deep retreat. They could only watch events in alarm and warn the Central Committee that it was losing control of the situation.

The Hungarian rising gave the Stalinist die-hards the opportunity of rallying and going over to the offensive. They denounced Khrushchev as the unwitting inspirer of the rising and prompter of revisionism, who had jeopardized communist rule in Eastern Europe and exposed the Soviet Union itself to dangerous shocks. The perils of which they spoke were real enough; and so all the leaders, de-Stalinizers as well as Stalinists, were seized with panic. For eight months Molotov and Kaganovich pressed home the attack and succeeded in regaining much of the ground they had lost. Khrushchev was compelled to call a halt to the debunking of the Stalin era, to declare war on revisionism, and to try to discipline the restive intelligentsia. But it was impossible to undo the effects of the Twentieth Congress or to make people forget his disclosures about Stalinist misrule. There was too much pent-up discontent and disillusionment in all social classes. The workers began to react against the privileges of the bureaucracy, against social inequality, and against the old severe industrial discipline. The peasants refused to increase agricultural production, which was disastrously low, and threatened to impede industrial progress.

The Party leadership had reason to fear that the disgruntled intelligentsia (whose ranks had been politically strengthened by the release from concentration camps and the rehabilitation of old heretics and 'enemies of the people') might appeal to the workers and peasants and set in motion a genuine popular opposition. Something had to be done to dispel popular discontent—at the very least a new wages policy and a new approach to collective farming were needed.

Thus, even if only to be able to call an effective halt to political and ideological de-Stalinization, Khrushchev had to carry de-Stalinization into the fields of economic and social policy. Moreover, the Hungarian and Polish upheavals had put a severe strain on the Soviet economy. It had become necessary to prop up the shaky communist governments of Eastern Europe economically and to step up the output of consumer goods in the Soviet Union as well as in the other communist countries. But it was well nigh impossible to achieve this—and at the same time both to maintain a rapid rate of development in heavy industry and force the pace in the nuclear arms race —under the old over-centralized and rigidly bureaucratic system of economic administration.

Khrushchev set out to break up that system and to replace it by the Regional Economic Councils, to enhance the status of the Trade Unions, and to accord new rights to factory councils and factory committees; by means of local initiative and responsibility he hoped to increase the efficiency of the entire industrial machine. Acting on the same principle, he released the collective farms from bureaucratic tutelage, transferred to them the property of the Machine Tractor Stations, abolished compulsory food deliveries, and offered the farmers all sorts of material incentives.

The Stalinist die-hards put up a stubborn resistance to this series of reforms. They relied on the backing of Moscow's powerful industrial bureaucracy and on the caution and fear which had, since the Hungarian rising, taken hold of large sections of the Party machine. In June 1957 Molotov and Kaganovich were on the point of bringing their counter-offensive to a successful conclusion. Strengthened by the adherence of Malenkov and Shepilov, de-Stalinizers of the previous period, and by Bulganin's hesitations, they obtained a majority within the Presidium of the Central Committee and carried a motion deposing Khrushchev from the post of the Party's First Secretary. This was to have put an end to the 'Time of Troubles' and 'risky experiments'.

At this point, however, Khrushchev appealed from the Presidium to the Central Committee. If the records of that session of the Committee were to be published, the effect, at least in the Soviet Union, might be almost as shocking as was that of Khrushchev's secret speech. The debates were stormy. The antagonists charged one another with working for the ruin of the Soviet Union and communism; and each side dragged out quite a few skeletons from the family cupboards. At one point, for instance, while dwelling on his adversaries' responsibility for the great purges of the 1930s—the topic invariably recurring in all secret debates since Stalin's death—Khrushchev pointed at Molotov and Kaganovich and exclaimed: 'Your hands are stained with the blood of our Party leaders and of innumerable innocent Bolsheviks!' 'So are yours!', Molotov and Kaganovich shouted back at him. 'Yes, so are mine', Khrushchev replied, 'I admit this. But during the purges I was merely carrying out your orders. I was not then a member of Politbureau and I bear no responsibility for its decisions. You were.'

Thus, Khrushchev went on playing on the revulsion against Stalinism; and this was strong enough to assure his success. The Central Committee expelled Molotov, Kaganovich, and Malenkov from its midst (but not from the Party) and it confirmed Khrushchev in his office. Essentially, the vote reflected the majority's conviction that it was impossible for the Party to go on ruling the country as before and that the reforms advocated by Khrushchev were sound and overdue. The new and modern economy and structure of society could no longer be reconciled with the old administrative and political superstructure.

It was no accident that in June Marshal Zhukov threw his weight behind Khrushchev. Perhaps more strongly than any other group, the officers' corps had resented the Stalinist purges; and it was convinced of the urgency of economic and administrative reform. Zhukov himself undoubtedly entertained Bonapartist ambitions—in the months which followed the June session he spoke the language of a Soviet de Gaulle. The following November it was his turn to be expelled from the Central Committee. He found no Guy Mollet among the Party leaders; and Voroshilov was no President Coty. The Central Committee declared that it had not discarded the Stalin cult in order to embrace a Zhukov cult and to submit to the rule of the sabre.

Yet, how paradoxical is the outcome of all these disputes and showdowns! On the one hand, his triumph over his adversaries has enabled Khrushchev to go ahead with his reforms, every one of which takes the Soviet Union further and further away from the Stalinist system of government. On the other, his triumph appears to have driven the Party, politically, a long way back towards Stalinism. By eliminating his adversaries, Khrushchev appears to have destroyed the post-Stalinist 'collective leadership' and to have become the Party's sole master. The 'dialectically contradictory' and ambiguous outcome of all the recent struggles showed itself strikingly in the December sessions of the Central Committee and of the Supreme Soviet, which were convened in preparation for the congress. An immense amount of new legislation was placed before these two bodies. Nearly all of it has been designed to demonstrate that the break with Stalinism is continuing, is deepening, and is spreading to ever new spheres of Soviet life. The new Seven Year Plan does not aim only at approaching the level of American industry. Its special feature is the new emphasis on the need for the 'harmonious' development of producer and consumer industries; and this has necessitated some slowing down in the rate of overall development. The Plan makes important concessions to consumer interests. It also marks a further departure from Stalin's anti-egalitarian policy: it provides for a steady narrowing of the gap between high and low incomes; and for a shortening of working hours in industry and the gradual introduction, within the coming decade, of a working week of thirty to thirty-five hours.

In apparent contrast to this egalitarian trend is Khrushchev's school reform, also passed in December, which partly curtails universal secondary education. The truth is that the Soviet educational system has, in its unparalleled growth, run ahead of the social system as a whole and has outrun the nation's resources. Every year millions of young people, their secondary education completed, knock at the doors of the universities and are turned away. The universities, where expansion cannot possibly keep pace with expansion in secondary education, have been unable to accommodate so many candidates; and the rush of the young to the universities has threatened to starve industry of manpower. Khrushchev is now chasing the mass of Soviet youth from the university gate to the factory bench; and he is anxious to stop the rush to the universities at an earlier stage—at the secondary school. But he has met with widespread, and more than usually articulate, opposition; and he has had to compromise. He has increased this year's budgetary grants for education by as much as fifty per cent, declared that the retrenchment in secondary education is only temporary or denied that there has been any retrenchment; and he has had to dwell on the egalitarian character of the polytechnical school where theoretical education is to be combined with productive labour.

The principle of de-Stalinization, however, has been most strongly in evidence in the new Criminal Code, which its sponsor introduced to the Supreme Soviet as an act of legislation designed to 'liquidate the shameful heritage of the past'. The Code had been under debate for many years; and it is the result of conflicting viewpoints. It does not go as far as the most liberal of Soviet jurists had expected, but it does go a very long way towards transforming a police state into a state 'ruled by the law'. The Code deprives the political police of the powers to sentence, imprison, and deport citizens. No one is to be sentenced otherwise than by a normal court in open trial. Penalties are reduced. Guilt by association, the 'category' of the 'enemy of the people', the co-responsibility of the defendant's relatives, the penalty of the deprivation of citizenship, and many similar features of the old Code are abolished. No defendant may be charged with 'terrorism' unless there is *prima facie* evidence of an actual attempt at political assassination.

Under such a Code it would have been impossible for Stalin

ever to produce his *univers concentrationnaire*, to stage any of his great purges and the Moscow trials, or even to deport Trotsky to Alma Ata and Constantinople. As if to stress the meaning of the Code General Serov, the grim old policeman, has been replaced, as chief of State Security, by the ex-Comsomol leader Shelepin. Yet—and here was the greatest paradox—the ghosts of the great purges seemed to be crowding back into the Central Committee's conference hall in December 1958: Bulganin made his confession of guilt, denouncing Molotov, Malenkov, and Kaganovich, and extolling Khrushchev's merits; the Central Committee rejected this 'confession' as hypocritical and inadequate; and Rudenko, Vyshinsky's successor as State Prosecutor, spoke about the *'crimes* of the Anti-Party Group'. The spectacle was evidently staged in order to bring pressure to bear on Molotov and his associates and to make them appear before the Twenty-first Congress in sackcloth and ashes, with confessions similar to those that Stalin's adversaries were once forced to make. For a moment it looked as if the Party were back if not in 1936, the year of the Zinoviev trial, then at least in 1930–34, the years when the stage was being set for the great purges.

But the clock was not and could not be turned back by a quarter of a century. At the Central Committee Rudenko may have spoken in Vyshinsky's voice, demanding the heads of the leader's enemies; but Khrushchev himself would not or dared not make that demand. A few weeks later, in January 1959, while the Twenty-first Congress was in session, this issue was at the centre of an intense struggle behind the scenes; the noises off could be heard in full congress, even in speeches made from the rostrum. Spiridonov, the leader of the Leningrad organization, insisted that Malenkov, Molotov, and Kaganovich should appear before the congress, 'lay down their arms', and recant. Mikoyan, however, ridiculed those anxious to see a repetition of such Stalinist practices and urged the congress to consider the controversy with the Anti-Party Group as closed. In effect, Molotov and his friends refused to humiliate themselves and did not 'lay down arms'; and the congress did not give Khrushchev a free hand for a showdown in the Stalinist style. The majority evidently responded to Mikoyan's appeal and preferred to wind up this inner Party feud with a little vituperation against the opposition but without any of the old bloodthirsty threats. This was the year 1959, after all. It was only three years since Khrushchev had denounced the Stalinist witch-hunts, 'confessions', and terror; and the denunciation was still ringing in the ears of the Twenty-first Congress.

17 January 1959

11
Khrushchev's Diplomatic Initiatives

In spite of recurrent diplomatic discussions, the German situation remained unsolved and unchanged under Stalin's successors. The Berlin Foreign Ministers' Conference of 1954 and the Geneva Summit of 1955 had achieved nothing. In 1957 a new initiative was taken by the Polish Foreign Minister, Adam Rapacki, who proposed the setting up of a nuclear-free zone in Central Europe, to include both Germanies, Poland, and Czechoslovakia. Although the three socialist states accepted this plan, it was rejected by the West; and in November 1958 Khrushchev launched a new, more militant diplomatic offensive on the German issue. In a speech on 10 November he said that Russia intended to hand over all Soviet responsibilities in Berlin to the government of the German Democratic Republic, and he proposed that the three Western Allies should quit West Berlin, which would then be turned into a 'free city'.

Western rights in Berlin were now the main issue in discussions on the German problem: they were discussed by Macmillan when he visited Moscow in February 1959, and at the Geneva Foreign Ministers' Conference that began in May. But even these latter discussions failed to produce any agreement on West Berlin or the status of the East German government.

In September Khrushchev went to the United States with his family on an official visit; although this achieved nothing substantial, it did generate an atmosphere of international optimism, the 'Camp David spirit'. The Chinese did not like Khrushchev's fraternization with the Americans and immediately after his return to Moscow Khrushchev set off for Peking. Russia had adopted a neutral position in the Sino-Indian border dispute of August and September: on 9 September a *Tass* statement said that 'One cannot fail to express regret at the fact that the incident on the Sino-Indian frontier took place'. In their subsequent polemics the Chinese cited this *Tass* statement as the beginning of open criticism by one Party of another, and in the same text (published in February 1963) they also gave their view of Khrushchev's initiatives at this time. They were in violation of the Moscow Declaration of November 1957 and, the statement continued, 'After the Camp David talks, the heads of certain comrades were turned and they became more and more intemperate in their public attacks on the foreign and domestic policies of the Chinese Communist Party'. This attitude of the Chinese was muted, though clear, at the time. The night he arrived Khrushchev delivered a hectoring oration to them on the need for peaceful coexistence. This only aroused their hostility; and a few days later he left without a communiqué being issued.

The Camp David spirit lasted for some months. The Russians reacted sympathetically to Eisenhower's world tour late in 1959; and in January 1960 it was announced that 1,200,000 men, a third of the Soviet Army, were to be demobilized. All seemed to be set fair for the summit conference scheduled for Paris in the middle of May, but on 5 May Khrushchev told the Supreme Soviet that an American U-2 reconnaissance plane had been shot down over Sverdlovsk. Given his many statements about the excellence of Eisenhower's personality, Khrushchev tried to exonerate him by saying, two days later, 'I am quite willing to grant that the President knew nothing about the plane having been sent into the Soviet Union'. On 11 May, however, Eisenhower accepted full responsibility for reconnaissance flights over the Soviet Union: they were, he said, 'a distasteful but vital necessity'.

On his arrival in Paris Khrushchev refused to begin summit discussions until Eisenhower had stopped all U-2 flights, had apologized, and had punished those responsible for the incident. Eisenhower ordered a temporary suspension of the flights but rejected Khrushchev's other demands; the summit was deadlocked before it began, and on 18 May Khrushchev made a vituperative attack on Eisenhower. The Camp David spirit had evaporated, and Khrushchev exhibited maximum hostility to Eisenhower in the following months; in June he said that Eisenhower could have a job in the Soviet Union looking after a kindergarten since that at least would prevent him from doing any harm.

The collapse of the summit was directly related to Khrushchev's troubles at home. In January two Presidium members, Belyaev and Kirichenko, were demoted; and in May they were expelled from the Presidium altogether. At the same time four members of the Central Committee Secretariat were expelled, and Voroshilov was pushed out of the Presidency and replaced by Leonid Brezhnev. There had been an agricultural crisis in 1959, and this, together with disputes over military demobilization, the results of Khrushchev's economic reforms, and the vicissitudes of foreign policy, all contributed to making Khrushchev's position unstable. By rearranging the leading personnel and by adopting a more aggressive line in foreign affairs he was able this time to overcome the opposition; but it was these same issues—foreign, economic, and personal—that were ultimately to bring him down.

1 THE SOVIET PERSPECTIVE IN GERMANY

During the six months that have elapsed since Khrushchev made the demand for a change in the status of West Berlin, his diplomacy has displayed much initiative and a great deal of confusion. Initiative has brought rewards. It has sent the British Prime Minister on an unprecedented diplomatic errand to Moscow; it has caused reluctant Western governments to accept the prospect of a summit meeting or even of a series of such meetings; and it has helped to reveal, if not produce, discord in the Western camp.

But the signs of Soviet confusion have been no less evident. At the start of the Berlin crisis last November Khrushchev denied that the Western Powers had any right to stay on in Berlin; he appeared to be confronting them with the demand for an early withdrawal and with an ultimatum. Since then he has reacknowledged explicitly and solemnly the right of the Western Powers to maintain their positions in Berlin. As the Foreign Ministers assemble in Geneva, the Soviet purpose thus appears to be more modest than it was six months ago. Moscow claims that it wishes merely to change the legal and diplomatic basis of the Western presence in the German capital: the Western Powers should stay on in Berlin on the basis of new rights which ought to be defined through negotiations, not by the right of conquest dating back to 1945.

This then is the main item of Gromyko's Geneva brief. He is not to parley about larger issues such as the unification of Germany or disengagement. Instead, he is to propose that the former belligerents conclude a peace treaty with the two German governments. As the Western Powers are not prepared to agree to this, the re-definition of the legal basis for their continued presence in Berlin remains the only real object of negotiations. Even some of Khrushchev's closest associates may now be wondering whether it was worth while raising so much dust over this question.

Underlying the confusion there is a deeper conflict between Soviet political strategy *vis-à-vis* Germany and Soviet tactics. Strategically, Moscow is playing from strength; tactically, it is playing from weakness. Its policy-makers are convinced that in the long run the rapid industrial and technological ascendancy of the Soviet Union is bound to have its effect on Germany and eventually to draw the whole of Germany into the Soviet orbit. In the short run, however, Germany remains the most important European bulwark of the West; and even East Germany, because of the mood of its people, is a potential stronghold of anti-communism. For all its strength, Soviet policy has been helpless against this fact.

The contrast between strategic strength and tactical weakness has its source in the legacy of the Stalin era in Germany. Though Khrushchev will not openly admit it, he knows full well that it was Stalin's Potsdam policy, with its emphasis on reparations, territorial annexation, and nationalist Russian revenge on the defeated Reich, that produced the present, long-lasting slump of communism in Germany, weakened the economy and lowered the standard of living of East Germany, and utterly discredited the Ulbricht regime. As long as the consequences and the memory of this Stalinist legacy are not effaced, Soviet policy *vis-à-vis* Germany is bound to be torn between a sense of power and a sense of weakness.

The latest Soviet initiative over Berlin illustrates this state of affairs. What has prompted Khrushchev and his policy-makers to press for a revision of the status of Berlin is precisely their confident awareness of the great shift in Russia's favour that has recently taken place in the international balance of power. They see the division of Berlin as the remnant of a now closed era, an era during which the outlook in Germany was determined on the one hand by the predominance of the Russian land power in Europe and, on the other, by the American monopoly of atomic power. With the lapse of that monopoly, and with Russia's present lead in the development of missiles, Soviet policy is tempted to do away with the Berlin 'anachronism', especially since the position of the Western Powers in Berlin is particularly exposed and vulnerable to Soviet pressure.

However, when, in November, Khrushchev set out to probe the exposed Western outpost, he soon found out, for the nth time, that in Berlin the Soviet position is no less vulnerable. To both East and West Berlin is the chink in their armour. But while the weakness of the Western Powers is of a military nature, Russia's weakness is mainly political; the stubborn opposition of the local population to any change that might increase Russian influence on the spot. Since East and West now conduct their contest by political, not by military, means, Khrushchev has had to acknowledge the precariousness of his position and climb down.

The mixture of strength and weakness also determines Khrushchev's attitude towards disengagement. On strictly strategic grounds, he could well afford to withdraw Soviet troops from East Germany—nothing indeed would suit him better than to be able to do so. He could even afford to carry out a unilateral withdrawal for he knows that, whether Soviet troops stand on the Elbe, on the Polish, or on the Soviet frontier, the NATO powers cannot, with the present balance of military strength, risk a move across the Elbe; under certain circumstances a unilateral Soviet withdrawal might even compel them, too, to withdraw. Yet Khrushchev is, in fact, almost as much afraid of disengagement as are most NATO leaders. But while the latter fear that disengagement might lead to the disintegration of NATO, Khrushchev's fear is that it might be followed by an anti-communist upheaval, of which the Berlin rising of 1953 and the Budapest rising of 1956 gave him a foretaste. He has to keep Soviet military power, or at least to preserve his freedom to use that power, in East Germany and Eastern Europe in order to protect not Russia's security directly, but the security of the governments of Ulbricht, Kadar, and Gomulka.

As Moscow sees it, the great question on which the prospects of its diplomacy hang is how and how soon the legacy of the Stalin era in Eastern Europe can be lived down—and most especially in East Germany. It would be a mistake to overlook or belittle the efforts the Soviet Government is making to overcome the liabilities of that legacy. Soviet economic policy towards East Germany is no longer governed by the Stalinist spirit of ruthless Russian egoism—not for nothing has the doctrine of 'socialism in one country' been replaced by that of 'international division of labour within the socialist camp'. East Germany is already benefiting from the change. It is no longer treated, as it was in Stalin's days, as both a defeated enemy and an exploitable satellite. It derives definite advantages from economic exchanges with the Soviet Union. Its trade with the countries of the Soviet bloc has grown considerably: its engineering industries play an important part in the industrialization of China and other under-developed, communist-ruled countries. The standard of living of the East German people has been rising steadily, even though it is still well below that of the West Germans.

All this has probably been enough to soften the acute popular discontent, which exploded in Berlin in 1953, but not enough to create contentment. Moscow expects, however, that East Germany will continue to make progress and will achieve full employment and prosperity for its people, while conditions in the Federal Republic may become stagnant or even deteriorate into a slump and mass unemployment. As Khrushchev puts it: in the 1950s the German people were impressed by the 'economic miracle' of West German capitalism; in the 1960s they will see the 'economic miracle' of East German socialism, which will radically alter the political climate in the whole of Germany. But even by Khrushchev's most optimistic calculations, it must take quite a few years before this happens.

Khrushchev and his advisers are aware that the problem is not merely an economic one. Since his visits to East Germany, the Soviet leader has had few illusions about the Ulbricht regime. Some of his advisers are well aware of the distrust and hatred with which it is surrounded. But on this point Khrushchev is extremely cautious and is avoiding any 'risky experiments'. Any hint about the desirability of a change in the East German communist leadership has been met with the argument that the experience with Rakosy was enough for him and that he was not going to 'turn Ulbricht into another Rakosy'; in other words he will not make him into a scapegoat for all that has happened in East Germany and thereby encourage the anti-communist opposition there. He is trying, on the contrary, to build up Ulbricht's prestige, in the belief that the opportunity for a relaxation of the East German regime will come later when, helped by economic progress, East German communism has recovered from its moral slump. It is also assumed in Moscow that new political trends at work in Bonn may favour East Germany. Some Soviet political observers at least interpret Adenauer's assumption of the Presidency of the Federal Republic as a move towards a new authoritarianism modelled on General de Gaulle's Presidential government; and they believe that this will deprive the Federal Republic of the moral-political advantages and the popular appeal as a parliamentary democracy it has hitherto enjoyed.

As all these changes, economic and political, which are expected to strengthen Russia's hand in Germany, must take time—a long time—Soviet diplomacy is at present determined to postpone any general German settlement. Khrushchev expects that in eight or ten years, but not before then, Russia's economic and political ascendancy will alter the international balance of power to such an extent that she will be able to withdraw her forces safely from Germany and that an all-German confederation, possibly even under a Social Democratic government, would be drawn into the Soviet orbit. This was the meaning of the appeal which Khrushchev made to the Germans from Leipzig earlier this year, begging them to bear patiently with the continued division of Germany. The time when the Soviet Union will be ready to press for a general German settlement will, in his view, be around 1965—perhaps even later, between 1965 and 1970 after the completion of the present Seven Year Plan, when the Soviet Union will be able to play new trump cards in its foreign policy.

5 Mäy 1959

2 KHRUSHCHEV GOES TO WASHINGTON

... Khrushchev's addiction to personal diplomacy and his fervent advocacy of summit and super-summit meetings are somewhat puzzling. Does he really believe these meetings to be so important? Does he expect them to produce the beneficial effect on the international situation of which his propagandists never tire of talking? The question is psychological rather than political. Khrushchev seems in fact to be harking back to the great precedents of Teheran, Yalta, and Potsdam. If Stalin, closeted with Roosevelt and Churchill, could plan great military campaigns, draw new frontiers, shift populations, and give the world a new shape, why should he, Khrushchev, not be able to make history in the same way and by the same method? Having first smashed Stalin's idol, and then tried to rescue what was left of it, he is now trying to appropriate for himself something of Stalin's 'grandeur' and 'magic' in the international field. He would like to have *his* Teheran, or *his* Yalta.

It may be argued that these precedents are now irrelevant and that Khrushchev's diplomatic thinking is bogged down in an anachronism. The Teheran and Yalta method had its uses for allies fighting a common war, when important decisions had to be made swiftly and in complete secrecy, because time and secrecy are of the essence of war. At Teheran the Big Three laid final plans for the invasion of Europe from the West; at Yalta they attempted to solve the Polish problem while Soviet armies were already on Polish soil, they settled Russia's entry into the Pacific war, made plans for the joint occupation of Germany, etc. The issues which have troubled East-West diplomacy since the war are different in character; they neither can nor need be solved by the *fiat* of a few heads of states with comparable swiftness and secrecy. The most important diplomatic decisions taken in Moscow since the war—the decisions to call off the Berlin blockade, to evacuate Austria, and to bring about a cease-fire in Korea—were all taken without recourse to summit diplomacy. Nor do Russia's war-time allies now act in the power vacuum in which they acted while the Third Reich was collapsing. They have now to consider the views and the interests of Adenauer and de Gaulle, and the Soviet Premier himself can hardly ignore Mao.

Some of these arguments against summit diplomacy were made, I believe, by Molotov before his downfall, and also by Mao Tse-tung. In his polemics against the former Khrushchev suggested that Molotov was opposed to summit diplomacy because he stuck to the old, and now obsolete, Leninist view about the inevitability of war between capitalist and communist powers. It is hard to establish whether this precisely was Molotov's argument—if not Molotov then others among Khrushchev's opponents might well have criticized summit diplomacy even if they did not believe war to be 'inevitable'. Whatever the truth, Khrushchev has established a link between the 'struggle for peace' and his style of personal diplomacy.

Thus it is in part the logic of his polemics against Molotov that compels him now—and not only him—to treat his American journey as something in the nature of a test. He has to prove himself as a fighter for peace and to prove the worth of his 'personal contacts'.

He has, of course, wider and more important considerations. It is now almost a truism that the easing of international tension is an essential condition for the success of the Khrushchevite domestic policy which aims simultaneously at the further building up of Russia's economic strength and at a more rapid improvement of the popular standard of living. If it is too much even for Khrushchev to believe that he can end the cold war, he is still anxious to soothe it and to avoid the repetition of situations in which going to the brink of war is part and parcel of the cold war technique. The cold war has been waged primarily in the field of propaganda; and it is in that field that its intensity can be most effectively reduced. So, even if his American journey were to result in no specific agreement, Khrushchev and his supporters would be satisfied with its results if he can make of it a propagandist *tour de force*.

This is not to say that the Soviet premier is out to score merely a propagandist success. He hopes to negotiate in earnest and considers the moment to be propitious. He believes that what has begun in Washington is a delayed mental reaction to the Soviet Sputnik, and that the U.S.A. has come to realize that the period of its strategic superiority over Russia is definitely at an end. He even seems to detect a new sense of strategic inferiority in recent pronouncements by various American statesmen. This is the interpretation he puts on some of the things said, or slips of the tongue committed, by Nixon during his visit to Moscow. Khrushchev intends to try and cash in on this new American mood. He is taking with him something that may be described as the maximum programme for his talks with the President and something like a minimum programme; between the two there is, of course, room for intermediate tactical variants. The maximum programme envisages an overall agreement providing tacitly for what would in fact be a Russo-American world condominium, based on a clear-cut division of spheres of influence between NATO and the Soviet bloc. Up to a point this condominium has been a fact of world politics; but the

U.S.A. and the U.S.S.R. have so far exercised it in mutual hostility. Khrushchev will explore whether they could not possibly exercise it in mutual agreement.

This would be, from his point of view, the most satisfactory way of preserving the international *status quo*, that avowed objective of his diplomacy. True, recently he still gave his American interlocutors to understand that what he was after was the consolidation of the *status quo* in Europe, but not in Asia and Africa, where Soviet influence had been on the ascendant. He may be travelling to the States with second thoughts on this, Soviet influence in Africa and Asia having since suffered a few severe setbacks. Arab nationalism has proved to be a highly unreliable ally—it is already half-ally half-enemy. Similarly, and more importantly, Nehru's new attitude to communism may foreshadow India's abandonment of neutrality in favour of a closer connection with the West. (Official Moscow opinion is convinced that the trouble on the Indian-Chinese frontier has been of Nehru's, not of Mao's making: far from suspecting Mao of creating tension there in order to obstruct any Russo-American *rapprochement*, it treats the frontier incidents as a by-product of Indian domestic policy and part of an all-Indian anti-communist campaign which Nehru has launched in connection with his disbandment of the communist government of Kerala.) Thus Khrushchev may now be much more inclined than he was until recently to favour the preservation of the *status quo* in Asia and Africa.

However, now, as before, it is in Europe, notably in Berlin, that the chief difficulty lies. According to Khrushchev, the consolidation of the European *status quo* requires a clear-cut boundary between East and West, a boundary behind which the communist governments of Eastern Europe would feel more secure than they feel now. That the Western enclave in Berlin is to them a source of insecurity need not be doubted; and so Khrushchev is calling for its elimination. But here the dialectics of the Berlin issue are playing a trick on him: seeking to preserve the European *status quo* he calls for the Western withdrawal from Berlin; but precisely such a withdrawal would upset the *status quo*, as the Western Powers realize only too clearly. In other words, it is enough to seek to consolidate the *status quo* in order to disrupt it. All that the Soviet leader can do about it in Washington is to try and persuade the President to favour a gradual, long drawn out and decently camouflaged withdrawal, whose impact on German and European opinion might be softened or rendered imperceptible by being so drawn out.

If it were possible to square the Berlin circle, the other items in Khrushchev's maximum programme might be easier to tackle. These are: a general reduction of armaments—conventional and nuclear—under fair conditions of control and inspection, a degree of co-operation and sharing of information in those fields of nuclear and missile technology where Russia has an advance over the United States, Russo-American trade, and some sort of a standstill in propagandist warfare. The Soviet leader, however, can hardly have many illusions about the immediate feasibility of such an overall deal.

His minimum programme is simply to keep his diplomatic pot boiling, to increase the personal contacts, to keep open the prospects of further meetings of heads of states, and to mark time. Although any one of these meetings may achieve little or nothing, their cumulative effect should be to lower the tension between East and West. From this point of view it does not even matter much whether or when Eisenhower goes to Moscow. After his 1956 trip to London Khrushchev waited three years for a British Prime Minister to return the visit. Nor does it greatly matter when a summit meeting takes place, as long as the prospect is kept open. The main purpose of Khrushchevite diplomacy is not so much to score any specific gains as to gain time—to gain another three, five, or possibly ten years, until new factors, resulting from the continuous growth of Russia's economic, military, cultural, and ideological potential, come into play and affect the international outlook deeply and dramatically.

Quite apart from these grave strategic and tactical considerations, Khrushchev's temperament and idiosyncracies will, no doubt, make themselves felt and give his American journey quite a few amusing, all-too-human twists. His ebullient temperament is by now familiar; but it is rarely remembered that throughout the Stalin era the present Soviet leader had to keep his temper under severe control, to conceal his thoughts, to avoid contacts with strangers, and to remain, even as high

dignitary, virtually imprisoned in his country. He is now reacting against these long lasting restraints, as if he craved to make
good in his old age all that he missed for the best part of his
life. He travels endlessly, receives endless queues of visitors,
talks endlessly, and overflows with his own verbosity and vitality.
In this he is undoubtedly representative of the Russian popular
temper, for the whole of Russia is reacting against the Stalin
era with a craving, unstilled as yet, for contacts with the world
and for self-expression.

As the President's guest, Khrushchev is at long last able to
cross America from coast to coast, to talk and chat and indulge
in goodness knows how much back-slapping; and, as he is
travelling with his wife, children, and son-in-law, he will no
doubt exhibit to millions of Americans not merely his political
personality, but his private and family virtues as well. And
millions of Americans will make the world-shaking discovery
that 'the Russians are human'. What a wonderful experience
for Khrushchev!

Back in Russia, people will watch the progress of their Prime
Minister and wish him well. They want peace, they are tired of
international tension, and they enjoy the contrast between the
morbidly silent, secretive, and Kremlin-immured demi-god
who ruled them ten years ago and the homely, talkative fellow
who rules them now—the contrast between an Ivan the Terrible and Nikita the Cheerful. But quite a few thoughtful or
sophisticated Muscovites, Leningraders, and others will probably reflect with sad irony on the condition of the world after
thirteen or fourteen years of cold war, when one great nation
needs to discover about another that it is 'human' and when
that world's hopes hang on a political travelling circus in which
heads of governments are the chief performers.

3 September 1959

3 RUSSIA AND THE INTERNATIONAL COMMUNIST MOVEMENT

'We too like Ike', chanted the Italian communists when President Eisenhower arrived in Rome early in December. Their leader, Palmiro Togliatti, told them to forget their old slogan 'Yankee, go home!' and to turn out *en masse* to welcome the President along his route. This incident highlighted, somewhat ironically, Khrushchev's efforts to align all Communist Parties behind his summit diplomacy. The Italian communists accomplished their change of front just after the long-prepared conference of seventeen West European Communist Parties had taken place in Rome, the first such conference to be held since the dissolution of the Cominform; and so it was with the blessing of that conference that Togliatti instructed his Party to 'like Ike'.

In Asia and Africa as well as in Europe the Communist Parties have had to adjust themselves to the consequences of Khrushchev's American journey and the abatement of the cold war. Moscow has made it clear to them that henceforth 'peaceful coexistence' must be treated as something more than a propagandist shibboleth; and that its requirements must govern the conduct of every Communist Party. It is true that even Khrushchev seems a little afraid that in an atmosphere of detente the Communist Parties might get too soft; and so he has reminded them that peaceful coexistence, no matter what compromises and conciliatory policies it may entail, must cause no break in the communist 'struggle against bourgeois ideology'. The reminder was needed partly as a face-saving device and partly to shield Khrushchev's policy from criticisms within the communist camp itself.

The fact is that—under Khrushchev as under Stalin—Communist Parties are called upon to subordinate their policies to the requirements of Soviet diplomacy. If in 1956, in the aftermath of the Twentieth Congress, some communist leaders outside the communist bloc hoped that de-Stalinization would allow them to frame their own policies without constant reference to Moscow's foreign policy, they must now be somewhat disappointed. No one had expressed that hope more sanguinely than Togliatti who proclaimed that the time when the Communist Parties took their cue from Moscow was over and that a new era, the 'era of polycentrism', had now opened. There was therefore a touch of the grotesque in the eagerness with which he once again saw to it that his Party's policy should so spectacularly suit Moscow's diplomatic convenience.

'We are fighting for the preservation of the international *status quo*', is the cue that now comes from Moscow; and so communists everywhere must stand for the *status quo*. They have been told that they must not 'provoke' the Western governments and the Western bourgeoisie, or indulge in, or even threaten, any action that might possibly upset the *status quo*. They must not be guilty of 'ultra-left extremism', for that plays into the hands of those Western reactionaries who seek to continue the cold war and to obstruct President Eisenhower's benevolent policy. In a word, communists must now be sensible, moderate, well-mannered.

These instructions, brought to Paris by Maurice Thorez, the leader of the French Party, after his recent stay in Moscow, and endorsed by the conference of the seventeen Parties, are not likely to come as a shock to Western European communism. Having for years been either on the defensive or reduced to political impotence, the Western European Communist Parties have had no chance to upset the *status quo* anyhow. Whatever the Party line, the Italian communist leaders were not preparing to seize power in the near future; and the French have been only too glad and pleasantly surprised to see that de Gaulle has so far allowed them to carry on as a tolerated opposition. Yet there has been some heartache among communists in Paris who seem to 'like Ike' somewhat less than their Roman comrades do.

It is in other parts of the world, in the Middle East for instance, where the *status quo* is far more fragile and liable to be overthrown by the communists that the impact of Khrushchev's policy on the Communist Parties has been far more dramatic. This is especially true of Iraq, where conditions are still highly unstable and where the communists could well upset the whole precarious balance of the Middle East. The Baghdad revolution of July 1958 gave them great opportunities. They were at the head of the insurgent crowds that rose against the monarchy and brought General Kassem to power. In the following months, between July 1958 and May-June 1959, their influence grew by leaps and bounds. They led the trade unions; they captured the student organization; and they entrenched themselves in the armed forces. They demanded their share of power, and when Kassem refused to offer them seats in his government it looked as if they were preparing to carry the revolution a stage further and to overthrow Kassem. *Ittihad Ash-Sha'ab*, the communist paper of Baghdad, openly accused the General of treason to the revolution and communist speakers at turbulent mass meetings echoed the accusation. Most Western observers on the spot agreed that Kassem could hardly hold his ground against an all-out communist offensive. His own following was small, and he refused to try and rally the anti-communist forces which were intimidated and disorganized and for whose support Nasser made a bid when he attacked Kassem as a 'communist stooge'.

Then, in the summer, the communist offensive was suddenly called off—on urgent demands from Moscow. In Moscow reports about the rising revolutionary temperature of Iraq had caused alarm. Khrushchev refused to countenance a communist upheaval in Baghdad, afraid that this would provoke renewed Western intervention in the Eastern Mediterranean, set the Middle East aflame, and wreck his policy of peaceful coexistence. He was already reckoning with the prospect of his visit to Washington and was anxious to produce evidence of Soviet 'goodwill' in the Middle East.

A bill of indictment against the Iraqi communist leaders was drawn up in Moscow and the Iraqi Party was ordered not merely to make its peace with Kassem, but to surrender to him unconditionally with only a minimum of face-saving. These were the main counts in the indictment: the Central Committee of the Communist Party of Iraq was wrong in turning against Kassem and denouncing him as a traitor. It was a mistake on its part to raise a loud clamour for communist participation in Kassem's government and to call for turbulent mass demonstrations in support of that demand; the Party had overplayed its hand in forming the so-called National Front and allowing its own ranks to become swamped by ultra-left extremists who joined the Party in the months of its ascendancy after the revolution; the Party was 'dizzy with success' and it tolerated and even encouraged mob violence in the streets of Baghdad and elsewhere and thereby it played into the hands of the counter-revolution. In conclusion, Moscow 'advised' the Central Committee to demote those of its leaders who were guilty of these 'deviations', to purge the ranks and expel the ultra-left extremists, to come out openly with a *mea culpa*, to dissociate itself from 'mob violence and mob hysteria' and to acknowledge General Kassem as the 'national revolutionary leader'.

These instructions have been carried out to the letter; and the Iraqi Central Committee has published a cringing recantation in *Ittihad Ash-Sha'ab*, which Moscow's *Kommunist* has eagerly publicized. Since the far-off days in the middle 1920s, when Stalin ordered the Chinese communists to serve as the 'Kuomintang's coolies', no Communist Party has been exposed to quite so abject a humiliation.

At the same time Khrushchev has also called a halt to the incipient communist campaign against Nasser in which the latter was accused of selling out to Western imperialism. Khrushchev silenced these accusations partly in order 'not to drive Nasser further into Western arms' and partly in order to demonstrate to the West that Moscow had no intention of obstructing the improvement in relations between Egypt and the Western Powers.

The repercussions of this policy have also made themselves felt in North Africa. Moscow has never given more than tepid verbal support to the struggle of the Algerian insurgents; but since de Gaulle invited Khrushchev to France the lukewarmness has become a good deal chillier. Moscow has openly endorsed de Gaulle's scheme for an Algerian settlement. The French communists at first denounced the scheme as a fraud, only to be told by Thorez, after his return from Moscow, that this was wrong, that they must accept de Gaulle's scheme, and merely insist on its proper implementation. Such an attitude differs little, if at all, from that adopted by the 'Gaullist left', and it is no mean embarrassment for French communists to become almost indistinguishable from the latter. For the moment Thorez seems to be out of step even with his own Politbureau, while the Politbureau has trouble with the rank and file who feel that the moral credit that Moscow has given de Gaulle has enhanced his authority and strengthened his hand *vis-à-vis* the Communist Party even in domestic affairs.

In the Far East, too, Khrushchev has demonstratively assumed the role of guardian of the *status quo*. This is the meaning of his refusal to take sides in the frontier dispute between India and China and of his 'impartial appeal' to both for an amicable settlement of the conflict. This gesture of Soviet neutrality in a conflict between a communist government and a bourgeois one must have shocked not only Peking, but even some people in Moscow who hold that the frontier dispute has been artificially concocted not by Mao but by the Congress of India for domestic reasons, as part of a drive against the Indian Communist Party designed to justify the disbandment of the Communist government of Kerala and to discredit Indian communism. Khrushchev has evidently refused to endorse this view and has deliberately to some extent strengthened Nehru's position *vis-à-vis* both the Chinese and the Indian communists. Uncommitted opinion in Asia is bound to conclude that if even the Soviet leader refuses to declare his solidarity with Mao on this occasion, then Mao must be in the wrong. Khrushchev has not spared Mao this embarrassment in his determination to demonstrate once again that he 'means business' when he speaks of the preservation of the *status quo*—in the interest of the *status quo* he is even prepared to curb his great and sensitive ally.

Finally, official Moscow has watched with the utmost discretion President Eisenhower's triumphant progress through the countries of the Middle East and India. If the President had gone on such a tour under different circumstances or, say, a year earlier, Moscow would have denounced it as an attempt to bring the former colonial and semi-colonial countries under 'the domination of American imperialism' and to align them militarily with SEATO and NATO. Even now Moscow is uneasy about the implications of the journey and there are many suspicious minds there to whom it appears that Eisenhower has egged on Nehru to exacerbate the conflict with China and has virtually drawn India into the system of Western alliances. So far, however, no official voice in Moscow has been allowed to vent the suspicion and no unfriendly remark has been permitted to disturb in public the atmosphere of goodwill that is wanted in the months and weeks preceding the summit meeting.

The international communist movement appears to have accepted the new zigzag in the Party line without demur. But this 'unanimity' is not unruffled, for not all communist leaders are as eager to accept the consequences of Khrushchev's summitry as Togliatti has been. The French, we have seen, have their misgivings. They are hoping to make propaganda capital out of Khrushchev's visit to France, but they know that de Gaulle is likely to make far greater capital from it. In any case, when Khrushchev seeks to befriend de Gaulle, French communism finds the edge of its own anti-Gaullism uncomfortably blunted. Worse still, one of the incidental results of the new Party line is to hold up to ridicule the campaign against revisionism and Titoism, a campaign in which the French communist leaders have participated with great zeal. One of their chief charges against Tito has been his 'hob-nobbing with the West'. Yet the Yugoslavs have never come out with the cry: 'We too like Ike'; and compared with the crudities of the Khrushchevite 'friendship with the West', Tito's attitude must now appear to many communists as one of dignified reserve and discretion. The Yugoslavs themselves are not at all eager to make much of this difference, because, on the whole, they approve the latest trend in Soviet policy and have no intention of interfering with the French and Italian Communist Parties as these adjust their tactics to that trend. But the Yugoslavs feel that the anti-revisionist campaign has suffered a setback and that in due course this should have repercussions in Eastern Europe.

Much more important than these ripples of agitation in European communism is Peking's disapproval of Khrushchev's 'rightist' tactics. Peking's motives for disapproving are mixed. There is still too much revolutionary fervour in communist China for its rulers to be able to swallow easily Khrushchev's diplomatic opportunism; and Mao has no reason to be enthusiastic about summit meetings from which his government is excluded. He has more than once intimated to Khrushchev that he will not consider as binding on himself any East-West settlement to which he has not been a party. Khrushchev appears to pay little heed to the warning; and he has certainly done less than he might have done to associate China and other members of the Soviet bloc with his diplomacy. While the ministers of the Western Powers assembled in Paris for their pre-summit meetings and President Eisenhower and the Secretary of State went to great lengths to reconcile divergencies and dissensions within NATO, Mao and other communist leaders must have reflected on the fact that Khrushchev had not even bothered to call them together to thrash out with them his line of conduct at the summit. True enough, since his return from Washington Khrushchev has paid visits to various communist capitals, and to Peking in the first instance. But he has evidently preferred such 'bilateral contacts' to a full-scale pre-summit conference of communist governments—perhaps because such a conference might provide too resonant a sounding board for their discords.

The Chinese not only resent the rebuke implied in Khrushchev's declaration of Soviet neutrality over their border conflict with India. They are, generally speaking, not inclined to accept 'the preservation of the *status quo*' as the present objective of communist policy. They do not agree that the Communist Parties should act, if only temporarily, as the guardians of the *status quo*. Unlike the Russians, the Chinese have recognized the Algerian rebel government and demonstrated thereby that they are going much further than the Russians in backing anti-imperialist movements in colonial countries. Being themselves the outlaws of Western diplomacy, they had no inhibition in recognizing another 'outlaw' government. Nor do they approve the Moscow-ordered retreat of the Iraqi Communist Party and its virtual surrender to General Kassem: this is too reminiscent of the policies of submission to the Kuomintang and to Chiang Kai-shek that Stalin once imposed on them. And so the Maoists have more than once suggested, though they have not shouted this view from their rooftops, that in pursuing his summit diplomacy, Khrushchev has been needlessly sacrificing revolution in Asia and has come close to 'betraying proletarian internationalism'.

It was in reply to such voices that Khrushchev, in one of his recent speeches, suddenly declared that those communists who doubted the correctness of his policy and wanted to obstruct the detente were behaving in a Trotskyist manner; for it was

Trotsky, he alleged, who had held that there could be 'neither
war nor peace' between communist and capitalist countries.
Historically, the reference to Trotsky was neither here nor there.
Trotsky had never held that there should be neither war nor
peace between the communist and the capitalist countries. He
used the famous phrase in exceptional circumstances, in February 1918 at Brest Litovsk, during his peace negotiations with
Germany: after the Germans had dictated their terms, which
included contributions and annexations of Russian territory,
Trotsky refused to accept these terms and broke off the negotiations, declaring that there would be neither peace nor war. But
soon thereafter he himself voted for the Brest Litovsk peace; and
presently he became with Lenin, and even before Lenin, the
earliest advocate of 'peaceful coexistence'. Khrushchev was, of
course, concerned not with the subtleties of historical truth, but
with his current inner Party controversy. He invoked the
anathema on Trotskyism as a warning to his own critics. Even
in post-Stalinist communism Trotskyism has remained the
heresy of heresies; and Khrushchev would not have hinted that
some of his critics might be contaminated with Trotskyism if
the inner Party controversy had not become fairly acute.

The argument in the communist camp has centred on two
issues. Firstly, is peaceful coexistence not a mirage? Or, to put
it in the terms in which the argument is conducted, can the
conflict between capitalism and communism be resolved peacefully? Can capitalism fail to resort to war if and when it finds
that peaceful competition spells ruin for it? Secondly, what
price should communism be prepared to pay for peaceful coexistence? Should it agree to self-containment? And should it
agree to contain revolution in colonial and semi-colonial countries?

Khrushchev's answer is that, contrary to the traditional
Marxist and Leninist assumptions, capitalism may well refrain
from war, even if it finds itself to be the loser in peaceful
competition because in the nuclear age, and in view of the
growing Soviet military superiority, capitalism cannot even
hope to improve its chances through war. This being so, there
is no reason why the communist bloc should not accept a policy
of self-containment until such time as the Soviet Union has
overtaken the United States industrially and its higher standards

of living and of social efficiency and organization make the appeal of communism irresistible to peoples outside the Soviet bloc. In the meantime, no communist upheaval, say, in Iraq, and no frontier dispute between India and China should be allowed to disturb the peaceful progress of the Soviet Union and of the entire Soviet bloc, the progress which a detente can only speed up and make easier. To those who reproach him with subordinating the fate of revolution in Asia to his diplomacy, Khrushchev replies: 'Would you rather see us subordinate the progress and the security of the Soviet Union and of its allies to the supposed interests of communism in Baghdad?'

Peking continues to doubt the reality of the detente and to hold that 'Western imperialism' is not disposed to accept the prospect of 'peaceful coexistence and competition'. At the same time the Maoists speak much more emphatically than the Russians do about 'the invincible might of the countries of socialism' and about the 'irresistible wind from the East'. What they argue in effect is that if, as Khrushchev claims, the Western Powers are so overawed by the destructiveness of nuclear weapons and by Soviet military superiority as to accept peaceful coexistence—even if this were to bring them defeat—then this is one more reason why Moscow should not curb revolutionary movements abroad. Would Soviet progress and security really be endangered, Peking asks, if the communists of Iraq were to take a more aggressive line and even seize power? And how far is Khrushchev prepared to go in containing revolution? The Maoists view India as the next great battlefield of the class struggle; and recent developments in India, with which they are more closely concerned than the Russians, give them no ground for satisfaction. They contrast the meekness with which their Indian comrades have allowed Nehru to destroy the communist base in Kerala with the determination and stubbornness with which Mao and his men defended their Yenan base against Chiang Kai-shek for so many years. They see the surrender of their Indian comrades as part of Moscow's design to appease Nehru in the interest of peaceful coexistence—as part of the same design for the sake of which Khrushchev flaunted his neutrality in the boundary conflict.

In all these differences there is the basis of a grave controversy in which one may see reproduced, in a new context, some of the *motifs* of the Trotsky-Stalin controversy of the 1920s. . . . Both Khrushchev and Mao will do all they can to keep the Soviet bloc in being. But within the bloc resentments and tensions are mounting which may strain its unity, may affect Khrushchev's policy, and may in their turn be affected by the success or the failure of Khrushchev's diplomatic initiatives.

15 December 1959

4 THE U-2 INCIDENT

At the meeting of the Supreme Soviet, held in the first week of May, domestic developments were overshadowed by foreign policy and by Khrushchev's disclosures about the shooting down of an American reconnaissance plane near Sverdlovsk. No doubt the story of the American escapade into Soviet air space helped to divert the Soviet's and the public's attention from internal discords. It also emphasized the stiffening in the Soviet attitude on the eve of the summit meeting in Paris, a stiffening which might be regarded as part of the normal bargaining process in East-West diplomacy.

Yet there was more to that stiffening than just that. Khrushchev was genuinely disappointed with the evolution of American policy since his visit to the United States. He might well have wondered whether the famous 'Camp David spirit' had evaporated or whether the Americans were playing the same game that he, Khrushchev, was playing and had 'stiffened' merely for the bargaining process. The American intrusion into Soviet air space just before the summit suggested that the Camp David spirit, so loudly advertised as Khrushchev's personal success in foreign policy, had indeed been even less than a phantom.

Khrushchev's entourage had a ready theory to account for the instability and the ambiguity of American summit policy; and Khrushchev undoubtedly accepted that theory. Behind the divergent views of the State Department and the Pentagon and President Eisenhower's 'vacillations', Khrushchev's experts saw a more fundamental conflict of American interests—a clash between two big industrial and banking concerns, the Rockefeller concern on the one hand, and the Morgan concern on the other. The Morgan concern, so the theory ran, favoured detente, partial disarmament, and agreement with the Soviet Union; while the Rockefeller group, with its interest in the continuation of the arms race, was bent on keeping up the international tension and obstructing summit diplomacy. Khrushchev's visit to the States, it was said, took the adherents of the Rockefeller group by surprise and put them on the defence, but they then rallied and, in unison with the Pentagon and assisted by men like Dean Acheson, they went over to the offensive, regained lost ground, and forced Eisenhower to yield to their pressure. The American incursions into Soviet air space were inspired by this group. Khrushchev concluded that only by bringing the matter into the open and making of it an international scandal could he weaken the Rockefeller group and the Pentagon, save what could be saved of the 'Camp David spirit', and regain the diplomatic initiative.

However, Khrushchev was out to kill several birds with one rocket. If, on the eve of his visit to the States, a Soviet missile hitting the moon indirectly demonstrated the power of the new Soviet offensive weapons, then, on the eve of the summit meeting in Paris, the Soviet rocket that brought down the American plane was to reveal the progress and the power of Soviet anti-nuclear defences. Even if the ordinary public in the West were not to realize this, it was thought in Moscow that the Pentagon would surely see that the Soviet Union now possessed both a radar warning system able to detect and watch with the utmost precision a small jet plane in the stratosphere, and also missile forces able to bring down such a plane at a chosen place and chosen moment with a single rocket. What this implied, and was intended to convey, was that Russian defences could cope in the same way with any attacking nuclear weapon and explode it over wasteland or industrially unimportant areas. In case of nuclear war this would not save the Soviet Union from the hazard of radiation, but it might save its cities, towns, urban population, and industrial apparatus from destruction. In other words, before the summit in Paris Khrushchev intended to produce evidence that the U.S.S.R. was ahead of the U.S.A. not only in nuclear offensive power but also in anti-nuclear defence.

This claim, if true, would indicate a further momentous

shift in the international balance of power. It would not only render the concept of 'massive retaliation' utterly meaningless; it would also mean that the Western deterrent no longer deters, because the Russians can defend Moscow, Leningrad, Kiev, and Sverdlovsk from NATO's nuclear attack, while the United States is not in a position to prevent Soviet rockets falling on Chicago, New York, and Washington.

The demonstration of the defensive power of Soviet rocketry was also useful for Khrushchev domestically. It has helped him in his argument against those who have opposed his whittling down of conventional forces and have held that he has allowed himself to be carried away by enthusiasm for rocketry. The rocket that was sent to bring down the American pilot was also to administer a shock to conservative military thinking at home. It produced a fitting accompaniment to the eclipse of some of the glorious marshals of the last war and the setting up of a new Strategic Rocket Command.

Finally the incident also served to strengthen Khrushchev's position *vis-à-vis* Peking. The controversy between Peking and Moscow had become very acute in April: so much so that during Mikoyan's visit to Iraq Chinese representatives there almost openly displayed their hostility to Soviet policy. Moscow also expressed misgivings about the presence of an Algerian 'governmental delegation' in Peking. The controversy reached its climax during the celebration of the ninetieth anniversary of Lenin's birth, which was turned into a dispute over the principles of communist foreign policy. The image of Lenin presented in Peking was the exact opposite of the image presented in Moscow. Moscow glorified Lenin as the ardent peacemaker and far-sighted promoter of peaceful coexistence. The propagandists referred to an article, never quoted before, by Krupskaya, Lenin's widow, who related that Lenin once said that a day would come when a weapon of such devastating force would be invented as to make war impossible. That day, Moscow's propagandists concluded, had now come.

Peking presented quite a different Lenin: Lenin the class warrior, who always made the distinction between just and unjust wars, who did not believe in any lasting accommodation between imperialism and socialism, and who insisted that war was inevitable as long as imperialism was alive. Peking claimed that only revisionists and traducers of Leninism could portray Lenin as a simple-minded pacifist, while Moscow argued that only incurable dogmatists could go on dwelling on Lenin's statements about the inevitability of imperialist wars. Only dogmatists, it was further said, could ignore nuclear technology as a factor of peace which compelled even the stupidest imperialists to reckon with the fact that war would be their suicide.

Khrushchev's attack on American policy and the use he made of the incident with the American pilot must have gone some way towards clearing him from the taint of appeasement in Peking's eyes. And so he was able to strengthen his hands *vis-à-vis* both his partners at the summit meeting and his allies and critics within the Soviet bloc.

8 May 1960

5 THE COLLAPSE OF THE SUMMIT

Not since Trotsky broke off the Brest Litovsk peace negotiations in February 1918 has the world witnessed a diplomatic spectacle like the collapse of the summit conference in Paris. Yet, while Trotsky withdrew from Brest only after protracted negotiations and after the Germans had dictated to Russia unacceptable peace terms (such as the annexation by Germany of large parts of the former Russian Empire), Khrushchev turned his back on the summit conference before it had even opened; and he did so without any comparable justification. Nor can one compare Khrushchev's crude, *muzhik*-like vituperation or his recurrent stories about the bad village cat with Trotsky's grand eloquence and majestic thunder at Brest Litovsk.

Yet, it was Trotsky's cry: 'Neither war nor peace' that Khrushchev seemed somehow to echo in his own uncouth accents. The irony of it was that only a short time earlier he had castigated those (unnamed) communists who did not believe in his summit diplomacy and in 'peaceful coexistence' as crypto-Trotskyists enamoured of the 'neither-war-nor-peace' formula. But this was in those far off days when he invoked the Camp

David Spirit in almost every speech, and when he dwelt on the virtues which set President Eisenhower apart from all other imperialists, and when even communists in Europe greeted the President wherever he arrived with the chant: 'We too like Ike'.

It is perhaps in those Khrushchevite eulogies for the American President there lies part of the reason for Khrushchev's anger in Paris. It was almost the anger of the disillusioned lover. It may be difficult for people in the West to realize how much of his prestige and standing the Soviet leader had staked on his 'friendship' with the American President. For about a year he worked hard to build up something like an Eisenhower legend, and to gain for it acceptance within the Soviet bloc. This was the legend of the 'honest soldier and man of peace' who was at loggerheads with the Pentagon and the 'Rockefeller-led imperialists and war mongers'—the myth of an Eisenhower in whom the United States had at last found the true successor to the Roosevelt of Teheran and Yalta. If that Roosevelt was a saint in Stalin's calendar, the Eisenhower of Camp David was almost Khrushchev's saint.

Throughout this period Khrushchev had to contend with communist critics who maintained that it was 'the height of naivety' on his part 'to give Eisenhower so much credit'. Day in day out Peking's propagandists insisted that 'Eisenhower was no better than any other imperialist'. Underlying this difference over the person of the President was, of course, the controversy over the chances of the detente, policy in Berlin and in the Middle East, prospects of disarmament, and the uses or the uselessness of summit diplomacy. The 'Camp David spirit' and 'Eisenhower's goodwill' were the crucial arguments with which Khrushchev defended his policy.

It was therefore a shattering blow to Khrushchev when, after the shooting down of the U-2, Eisenhower himself came forward and, so to speak, destroyed the legend. On 7 May Khrushchev, addressing the Supreme Soviet, still made a desperate attempt to save, in communist eyes, his favourite Eisenhower image. He told the Supreme Soviet that he was sure that Eisenhower did not know about the American spy flights over the Soviet Union. Khrushchev's communist critics gnashed their teeth: 'Why should Comrade Khrushchev go out of his way to whitewash Eisenhower?' He, however, expected the President to play into his hands, to say that he had indeed known nothing of the U-2 affair, and so to save his own and Khrushchev's face, and, of course, the chances of the summit. When the President refused to take the hint and assumed full responsibility for the U-2 flights and then allowed his State Secretary to declare that these flights would continue, Khrushchev was dismayed. Not only was this a bad omen for the summit, but in addition he was made to look a fool in the eyes of the whole communist world. Mao Tse-tung was quick to make the most of it and to rebuke Khrushchev with a public and ironical: 'I told you so'. Eisenhower had indeed resolved the controversy between Khrushchev and Mao—the controversy over Eisenhower himself—in Mao's favour.

When, on the eve of his departure for Paris, Khrushchev faced the Presidium he found himself in a situation which may have been almost as difficult as that of June 1957, when a Molotov-led Presidium was on the point of deposing him. There was probably no threat of deposition this time; but the Presidium had had more than enough of the Khrushchevite Camp David Spirit and of all that went with it. What the Presidium decided is not known. It may have authorized Khrushchev to go to Paris only in order to smash up the summit. What is more probable is that at first it was in favour of holding the summit conference, and of Khrushchev adopting a very tough line in anticipation of eventual failure. The Presidium was certainly in constant session before and after Khrushchev's departure, and it may have reversed its earlier decision at the last minute. This would explain in part the suddenness of Khrushchev's somersault in Paris. No doubt the news of an American alert of armed forces on the eve of the summit, news that reached Khrushchev in Paris, also played its part.

Yet, there remain quite a few obscure points in the summit story which historians will probe. For instance: was it really Khrushchev's deliberate purpose to break up the summit before it had begun, or did he merely manoeuvre himself into a position in which he had to take the odium for the break? There are reasons to think that Khrushchev was surprised when the three Western heads of state announced, on the evening of Tuesday 17 May, that there would be no summit conference.

The evening before, it is said, Khrushchev had agreed with de Gaulle that the next day would be a 'day of reflection', during which no meeting would be held. And so on Tuesday morning he went out with Marshal Malinovsky to inspect the 1914–18 battlefields on the Marne. Did he think that he would not be needed in Paris on that day? He had hardly arrived on the Marne battlefield when he received de Gaulle's message asking him to meet the Western heads of state the same afternoon. What had happened to the 'day of reflection'?

Khrushchev rushed back to Paris, and the tragicomic series of telephone exchanges between the Elysée and the Soviet Embassy began. Khrushchev declared that he was willing to come to the Elysée to meet his partners, including the American President, for informal talks about the U-2 affair, but that he would not take part in a formal summit meeting before that affair was cleared up, on his terms. By that time President Eisenhower had already made public the statement that the U-2 flights over the U.S.S.R. were 'suspended'; and it may have looked to Khrushchev that in another informal meeting the ground could, after all, be prepared for the opening of the summit. By now, however, the Western Big Three no longer wanted any informal talks—it was to be either the summit or nothing. Up to the last minute Khrushchev behaved as if he did not quite know what to do; and it was the Western heads of state that resolved the dilemma for him when they said that, as he had not appeared at the Elysée, there would be no summit meeting. Both sides evidently felt that after all that had happened there was no chance of any agreement on the vital issues that figured on the agenda.

This became especially clear after Khrushchev had called off Eisenhower's visit to the Soviet Union, a decision which again reflected Khrushchev's resentment, not only at the President's handling of the U-2 affair, but also at his handling of the proposed visit. When Khrushchev journeyed to the United States last autumn, he did his best to play up his own visit, to give it quite exceptional importance, and to present it as an epoch-making event. Eisenhower did his utmost—or so it certainly appeared to Khrushchev—to belittle the importance of his return visit. Moscow was to be only one of the stops on his tour; from the Soviet Union he was to proceed to Japan and even to South Korea, where he was to meet Syngman Rhee, of all people. These snubs, the shifts in American policy that had taken place (or appeared to have taken place) since the Camp David talks, and the U-2 affair had a cumulative effect that the belatedly announced American decision to suspend the espionage flights failed to undo. If Khrushchev had contented himself with the mere announcement of the suspension, his position in Moscow and within the Soviet bloc might have been gravely weakened.

Just how precarious is—or was—his position? He has certainly had his critics in the party hierarchy in Moscow, among the crypto-Molotovites and the crypto-Malenkovites (not to speak of the critics in Peking); but he has no effective rival in the Presidium. Nor does the indubitable discontent in the military officers' corps, provoked by the reduction of the conventional forces, constitute a great threat to him. Since the demotion of Marshal Zhukov, the influence of the officers' corps has shrunk; and the rather colourless and docile Marshal Malinovsky is the last person to act as Khrushchev's political mentor. However, discontent in the conventional forces may be used against Khrushchev by his critics in the Presidium or in the Central Committee. And although he has no effective rival, and the return of Molotov or Malenkov is unlikely, he is not the autocrat that Stalin was. Matters of policy now appear to be resolved by the vote of the Presidium or the Central Committee; and Khrushchev must adapt himself to the prevailing mood.

He is playing a fairly complex game. He gives way to his critics, and then, having lessened their pressure, he tries to pursue his own policy again. This is what he has done several times in the past few years and what he also did on his way from Paris when he stopped in Berlin to tell Ulbricht that there must be no foolhardy or rash adventures in Berlin in the next few months.

21 May 1960

12
The Deterioration of Sino-Soviet Relations

In April 1960, a month before the Paris summit, the communist world celebrated the ninetieth anniversary of the birth of Lenin. The Chinese published a long theoretical work, 'Long Live Leninism!', in which they repeated their hostility to imperialism and their belief that after a nuclear war the peoples of the world would build socialism 'on the debris of a dead imperialism'. The Chinese emphasized Lenin's theses on capitalist bellicosity, while the Russians stressed his policy of peaceful coexistence. They were fortunate that the ninetieth anniversary of Lenin's birth was also the fortieth anniversary of his work on 'Left-wing Communism— An Infantile Disorder', a text which they felt was singularly applicable to the Chinese.

This theoretical conflict was reflected in the debates at the World Federation of Trade Unions Meeting in Peking on 5–9 June, and even more starkly in the debates at the third congress of the Romanian Workers' Party, held in Bucharest at the end of June. This was the first major international communist conference since the Moscow meeting of 1957 and each side used it to assail the other. Khrushchev stressed the horrors of nuclear war, and said that 'Lenin's propositions on imperialism were advanced and developed decades ago, when many factors that are now decisive for historical development, for the entire international situation, were not present'. In his speech two days later the Chinese delegate, Peng Chen, said that the major danger for the international communist movement was revisionism, and that 'the aggressive and predatory nature of imperialism will never change'. The secret debates at the congress provided Khrushchev with a more suitable occasion for attacking the Chinese, who later complained that at the Bucharest meeting Khrushchev launched

'an all-out and converging surprise attack on the Chinese
Communist Party'.

Khrushchev followed up his verbal polemic by withdrawing all
Russian technicians from China in August and by cancelling
many agreements between the two countries. In September he
went to New York to speak to the United Nations, and it was
while he was there that the Chinese gave a massive welcome to
Ferhat Abbas. Embarrassed as he was, Khrushchev was forced to
announce Russian recognition of the Provisional Government of
the Algerian Republic and to propose a referendum in Algeria
under U.N. supervision.

In an attempt to overcome the split in the international
communist movement a meeting of eighty-one Parties was held in
Moscow from 10 November to 1 December. The Moscow
Statement which was issued at the end of the conference did
represent a formal agreement by the contending forces, but this
was only very transient and disagreement was soon to break out
again. Each side accused the other of violating the Moscow
Statement and they disagreed about the interpretation of what it
said. Khrushchev had some chance of gaining new prestige by
achieving diplomatic success with the new Kennedy administration
which came to power in January 1961; but hopes of this were
destroyed when U.S.-trained Cuban exiles made an abortive
attempt to overthrow the Cuban government in April and were
routed in four days of fighting.

In the summer of 1961 the international situation worsened. In
Laos the Pathet Lao were making steady progress; nothing
substantial emerged from a meeting between Khrushchev and
Kennedy in Vienna early in June. Kennedy had announced a
considerable increase in U.S. defence expenditure, and the
Russians followed suit. Then on 21 June Khrushchev announced
that the time had come to sign a peace treaty with the German
Democratic Republic: tension rose and on 13 August the Berlin
wall went up.

In spite of this deterioration in Russo-American relations,
Moscow's relations with Peking got worse as well. This was most
obvious in the way China's ally Albania fell out with the Soviet
Union: in May a pro-Russian Admiral was tried and executed in
Tirana for conspiracy and the Russians withdrew all their
submarines from the naval base of Vlöre. By the end of the

summer the Russians had also withdrawn all their technicians and cancelled their aid. This appeared to the Chinese as a violation of the Moscow Statement, and the stage was now set for a further decline in Sino-Soviet relations at the Twenty-second Congress of the Soviet Party.

1 THE BUCHAREST CONGRESS

A wolf is a wolf, and its man-eating nature does not change. An ancient Chinese fable about the Chungshan Wolf tells the story of Schoolmaster Tungkuo who once found a wolf wounded by hunters and saved it by hiding it in his bag. After the hunters had left, he released the wolf from the bag. Instead of showing gratitude, the wolf wanted to devour him. Fortunately a peasant came along who understood well the man-eating nature of the wolf. He lured it back into the bag and beat it to death, and thus Schoolmaster Tungkuo was saved.

From Hongi (Red Flag of Peking)

During the latest Congress of the Romanian Communist Party Khrushchev addressed in private a select gathering of communist leaders from various countries and went over his differences with Mao. What he said in public carried only faint echoes of that secret speech. How much importance he attached to it can be seen from the fact that he urgently summoned Gomulka, who was just presiding in Warsaw over a session of the Polish Central Committee and was very reluctant to go to Bucharest. But so insistent was Khrushchev's summons that Gomulka had to close the Warsaw conference abruptly and leave for Romania. A fortnight earlier the General Council of the communist-led World Federation of Trade Unions met in Peking, and its conference was entirely taken up by a prolonged and passionate clash between Khrushchev's and Mao's adherents. The debates were more dramatic than in Bucharest, because the Chinese tabled their own motions in opposition to the Khrushchevite General Council and pressed for a formal vote, which they did not do in Bucharest. They were heavily outvoted but not altogether isolated.

This is the first time for exactly thirty-three years that such debates have been allowed to proceed at any international communist forum. The last time this occurred was in 1927, when Stalin and Trotsky presented their viewpoints before the Executive Committee of the Communist International and Trotsky was expelled. Thereafter heretics were excommunicated without being given the opportunity to state their case before the Comintern or the Cominform. Bukharin was disposed of in this way as early as 1928, and Tito twenty years later. Evidently Khrushchev cannot in this respect follow Stalin's example. He has had to meet heretical challenge with far greater toleration and to produce arguments rather than anathemas.

The communist movement is, in fact, divided between three distinct currents of opinion and ideology: the Left (or the 'ultra-Left') which is represented by Mao; the Right, for which Tito—but not he alone—speaks; and the Centre, led by Khrushchev.

The issues and arguments are clear enough. The Left sticks to what it regards as the orthodox Leninist view about imperialism and communism. It does not believe in the possibility of any genuine detente and considers all talk about ending the cold war as a 'dangerous illusion'. It suspects Khrushchev of taking his disarmament proposals quite seriously and endangering thereby the security of the communist bloc. It sees the chances of new communist revolutions, especially in the underdeveloped countries, as being far greater than Khrushchev cares to admit; and it thinks that Khrushchev compromises these chances in the interest of his diplomacy. Mao holds indeed that there is 'too much diplomacy and too little communism' in all that Khrushchev does. Finally, there are the differences over domestic policies, the Chinese communes, the treatment of consumer interests, and political 'liberalization'. On the other hand, the right-wing communists or revisionists discarded the Leninist view on imperialism as obsolete long before Khrushchev did so; and they reproach Khrushchev with not being consistent and persistent enough in striving for detente and disarmament.

Caught between two fires, Khrushchev has behaved as the middle-of-the-roader usually does: he has leaned leftwards and rightwards and leftwards again, hoping to meet and silence now one set of critics, now another. Consequently, Mao is accusing him of being a 'crypto-Titoist' and of refusing, to quote the Chinese *Red Flag*, 'to draw a clearcut line of division between [himself] and modern revisionism which is in the service of imperialism'. At best Mao looks upon Khrushchev as upon a well-intentioned but hopelessly muddled man, hardly worthy of occupying his high place in the communist world, as a sort of Schoolmaster Tungkuo, who does not know how to deal with the wolf of imperialism and can be saved only by the prudent firmness of Mao himself, the peasant of the parable about the

Chungshan Wolf. The revisionists take a rather unflattering view of Khrushchev for the opposite reason: they say that all too often he allows himself to be brow-beaten by the doctrinaires and dogmatists of Peking.

This controversy has been going on behind the scenes and in muted form ever since 1957. . . . There is little doubt that Chinese objections to Khrushchev's summitry had something to do with the breakdown of the Paris conference in May. Nowhere was Khrushchev's Paris performance applauded more wholeheartedly than in Peking. Why then have Russo-Chinese differences become further aggravated since then? One reason is that now, as in 1958, Khrushchev has not given up the idea that another summit meeting may yet be held. Nor has he altogether abandoned the hope of a degree of disarmament which would allow the Soviet Government to switch more investment to consumer industries. Even after Paris the Soviet government has actually increased budgetary allocations to Soviet consumer industries; and Peking has criticized precisely this decision.

But what is involved in all this is not merely Soviet diplomacy, but the trend of communist policy at large, which, the Chinese hold, is too much inhibited by Khrushchev's international game, too timid and too wobbly. On several occasions recently Mao's angry contempt for Khrushchev's policy must have exploded, for instance when he heard that the Italian communists welcomed President Eisenhower during his visit in Rome with the chant 'We, too, like Ike!'; and when it was reported to him that Khrushchev during the pre-summit visit to Paris told Frenchmen that if they want peace they must support General de Gaulle. This to Mao was a straight 'betrayal of communism'.

Ever since the Paris breakdown Khrushchev has been busy rallying foreign communist opinion against Mao; and at Bucharest he was out to demonstrate that he has the backing of the entire communist movement. On the face of it, he has succeeded in this; but the success may be more apparent than real. The divisions in communism remain as deep as ever; and some of those who have, for one reason or another, rallied to the Khrushchev line are by no means Khrushchevite middle-of-the roaders. Right-wing communism is represented not only by

Tito. Inside the Soviet bloc Gomulka and his adherents stand for it; they were rather worried by Khrushchev's behaviour in Paris; they pray for a detente and for trade with the West; and alone among the rulers of Eastern Europe they have not so far renewed the drive for the collectivization of farming. Outside the Soviet bloc Palmiro Togliatti is a right-wing communist; and during his present visit to Moscow the Russians are certainly telling him that he is only embarrassing them by showing an excess of zeal for peaceful coexistence.

On the other hand, 'ultra-left' and pro-Chinese tendencies have made themselves felt among the communists of East Germany, Czechoslovakia, Bulgaria, and Albania. In Bucharest the East Germans gave Khrushchev more than the normal dose of adulation, but what they had to say about the international situation came closer to the Chinese line than to the Russian. The Czechs continued to hedge; and only the Bulgarians joyfully joined the Khrushchevites. Yet all those assembled there were taken aback by the bluntness with which Khrushchev declared Lenin's teaching on imperialism to be out of date; and no one echoed him in this. Mao is meantime intensifying his bid for the leadership of Asian communism. Curiously enough, he has been cold-shouldered by his closest neighbours, the North Koreans; but he has succeeded in winning over the Indonesians and in neutralizing the North Vietnamese. And last but not least, there is no lack of either Maoists or revisionists in Moscow, in Khrushchev's own strongholds. The alignments are not fixed, and they are likely to shift as the controversy continues. And continue it will because neither side is in a position to call a halt to it. Khrushchev cannot afford to excommunicate Mao; nor can Mao pronounce anathema on Khrushchev. Both must, in their own interests, insist on the unity of the Soviet bloc. Paradoxically, Mao insists on it even more emphatically than Khrushchev does; and this is no mere tactical manoeuvre. Ever since the shock of the Hungarian rising, Mao has prompted all Communist Parties to re-acknowledge Soviet leadership of the communist bloc. He would like to see Moscow exercise that leadership in a manner tougher and more uncompromising than Khrushchev's. He wants to 'put teeth' into Soviet policy; but he does not want a breach with Moscow.

One obvious consequence of this state of affairs is that Moscow's foreign policy, exposed to such conflicting pressures, is becoming more unstable and unpredictable than it was over the last few years. Another, less obvious, consequence affects the communist movement as such. The growth of controversy, which cannot be concluded with the excommunications that were customary in the Stalin era, is shaking the whole 'monolithic' structure. Dissent and deviation, reprehensible though they still are in communist eyes, cease to be counter-revolution and treason. This in itself is bound to cause an upheaval in communist political habits. If dissent and deviation are no longer cardinal sins, if the leaders of the various Parties may engage in controversy, should dissent and argument not also be tolerated within each Party? Many communists in Russia, China, and elsewhere will soon ponder this question. What has happened in Bucharest and Peking tends to legitimize controversy in communist ranks. But once communists are allowed to disagree and to argue among themselves, the present methods of communist leadership will be shaken. No one can be an infallible and lifelong leader once a minority is allowed to criticize him and perhaps to persuade the majority. Thus, implied in the present debate is a threat to the position of the whole generation of leaders, which includes both Mao and Khrushchev, who have grown up in the Stalinist school of thought and are accustomed to rule their Parties (and countries) without any challenge either from rivals or from the ranks. Admittedly, this threat is still fairly remote. But it is distinct and large enough to trouble the Party machines even now, and to affect the fortunes if not of Mao and Khrushchev, then of their successors. In the years to come the communist movement is likely to experience upheavals far greater than those caused by the de-Stalinization of the 1950s.

28 June 1960

2 ALGERIA AND THE
   SINO-SOVIET DISPUTE

While the Soviet Prime Minister was busy making speeches in New York a significant political plot between Peking and Moscow was being played out behind his back, a plot which has given a new turn to the controversy between the two communist capitals, and as a result of which the Algerian war may well become *the* international crisis of the year 1961. Repercussions of this development reached Khrushchev in New York and accounted in part for his behaviour at the United Nations Assembly.

Only a couple of days after Khrushchev had landed on Manhattan Island, Ferhat Abbas, head of the Provisional Government of the Algerian Republic, accompanied by several of his ministers, set out from insurgent Algeria on a journey to Peking, where he had been invited by Premier Chou En-lai to attend the celebrations of the eleventh anniversary of the Chinese revolution. *En route* Ferhat Abbas and his companions stopped in Moscow. There they were received as scarcely more than private individuals—or as one of the many foreign delegations that nowadays stop in the Soviet capital—before embarking at the Sheremetev aerodrome on a Peking-bound Russian plane. No red carpet was spread out for the Algerians, no welcoming speeches awaited them, and no flowers. Even the whereabouts of Ferhat Abbas in the Soviet capital were obscure. Official Moscow, its eyes glued to reports on Khrushchev's doings in New York, belittled the head of a dubious and tiny government and his Chinese pilgrimage.

On 29 September Ferhat Abbas and his team landed in Peking. At once a dizzy change occurred around them: outlaws in their own country and 'clandestine travellers' in Moscow, they were welcomed at Peking airport by the Chinese Prime Minister and were cheered by large crowds. From the airport, amid the endless beating of drums and gongs and waving of Algerian and Chinese flags, Ferhat Abbas and Chou En-lai rode in an open car into the beflagged streets of Peking, where hundreds of thousands of troops, militias, and civilians lined up to hail them.

Another visitor in Peking was U Nu, the Burmese Prime Minister. His visit marked the end of the border dispute between his country and China, and he had arrived to sign a boundary treaty. In the absence of any top leaders from the Soviet bloc countries, U Nu and Ferhat Abbas were to be the two principal guests of honour at the anniversary celebrations. Ferhat Abbas, however, stole the show. At the great anniversary parade on 1 October he stood on the Tien An Men rostrum on Mao Tse-tung's right, between Mao and Chou En-lai, to receive the popular acclaim and the salute of the armed militia.

This was not a matter of mere pageantry. From the moment of his arrival Ferhat Abbas found himself at the very centre of Peking's political interest. He was closeted for hours with Mao Tse-tung and the other Party leaders and with the deputy Chief of Staff of the Chinese Army. He was guided all the time by Chou En-lai who, as member of the French Communist Party during the years of his exile in France, is more conversant with French-Algerian affairs than anyone else in Peking. The Chinese were obviously attaching quite extraordinary importance to this visit. Many Algerian delegations had been received in the Chinese capital in the last few years and had taken away with them advice, supplies, medical equipment, and assurances that they could count on more direct military assistance as well. (Algeria had also received such supplies and medical aid from the Soviet Union and even from Yugoslavia.) But until recently the Algerians had taken what they wanted and had not been anxious to get more, even though the Chinese had offered more. Ferhat Abbas had still hoped to obtain his objectives through negotiations with General de Gaulle. But since the failure of the French-Algerian talks at Melun last spring, he had been looking for fresh means towards a more vigorous prosecution of hostilities. Having been more or less cold-shouldered in Moscow, he turned towards Peking.

From the moment of his arrival in China Ferhat Abbas became involved in the controversy between Khrushchev and Mao. The Chinese made no bones about it: they considered Moscow's Algerian policy 'disgraceful' and they were going to put strong pressure on Khrushchev to change it. The reserve which Khrushchev has until quite recently shown *vis-à-vis* the Algerians has been dictated by a variety of motives. To side with Ferhat Abbas against de Gaulle was, in Khrushchev's eyes, tantamount to driving de Gaulle into Eisenhower's arms; and Khrushchev was more interested in playing de Gaulle against Eisenhower than in using Abbas against de Gaulle. He also feared that any form of communist intervention in Algeria would defeat his policy of detente. When some time ago Peking urged Moscow to grant the Abbas government *de facto* recognition, Moscow replied rather formalistically that this would be premature because Abbas held no definite territory under administrative control.

Mao and Chou En-lai decided to use the occasion of Ferhat Abbas's visit for a concerted attack on this Khrushchevite policy and for confronting Khrushchev with certain accomplished facts. On the first day of Abbas's visit, in a speech in his honour, Chou En-lai, recalling the 'century-old struggle of the Algerian people against French domination', stated: 'The establishment of the Provisional Government of the Republic of Algeria . . . signifies that this struggle has entered a new phase. We are glad to see that the Algerian National Liberation Army has already freed vast areas in Algeria inhabited by more than half of its population, and has established there its own organs of state power.' This was meant to dispose publicly of the official Soviet argument against the recognition of the Abbas government. Chou En-lai went on: 'This tremendous change in Algeria proves once again that a situation in which our enemies are strong while we are weak is only temporary—it is bound to be reversed. Decadent imperialism can be strong only in outward appearance; actually it is weak. Its temporary rampancy is merely a deathbed struggle.'

The controversial undertone of Chou En-lai's words was clear to those who were aware that the major issue between Moscow and Peking was the evaluation of the strategic power of the West, which Moscow refused to see as a mere 'paper tiger'. According to Chou En-lai then, the impotence of French arms in Algeria was just another particular illustration of the general Chinese contention that the communist bloc need not be afraid of the military power of the West and that Khrushchev approached the 'paper tiger of NATO' all too timidly and feebly. The burden of Chou En-lai's argument was that Algeria constituted at present one of the West's weakest spots and that communism must adjust its tactics to this fact. Moscow was not prepared to accept this view, still less its implications.

Ferhat Abbas, though a mere 'bourgeois nationalist', found himself drawn into this inner communist controversy; and guided by his own interests, he sided with the Chinese against the Russians, that is with the extreme left-wing of communism against 'the opportunists in Moscow'. Up to the last moment Moscow had advised the Algerians to seek a renewal of negotiations with de Gaulle. 'In this era of the great retreat of imperialism', it was said in Moscow, 'when so many colonial peoples are obtaining independence, de Gaulle will have to honour his promise of self-determination for Algeria. In any case, the Algerian conflict must not be used to estrange Gaullist France from the communist bloc and to cement the solidarity of the Atlantic Alliance.'

Ferhat Abbas, acclaimed by his Chinese hosts, now countered this Soviet argument point by point: 'To the Algerian people, suffering and dying each day, the vast controversies of the cold war are of no interest unless they concern the real solidarity of free men . . .', unless, that is, Moscow sides openly with Algeria. Aiming at Khrushchev's notion of peaceful coexistence based on the international *status quo*, Abbas continued: 'Similarly, peaceful coexistence is not compatible with territorial partition, with the *status quo*, with palliatives and with spheres of influence which would perpetuate any form of colonial servitude'. It was a mistake, he went on, to imagine that the war in Algeria was only a French war (as Khrushchev suggested it was). This was NATO's war, for without American equipment and aid the French would have long since been defeated. He who wants to weaken NATO, Abbas pointed out, must strike at it in Algeria; and it was foolish to imagine (as Khrushchev imagined) that one could weaken NATO by appeasing de Gaulle. It was time to stop lulling the 'peace-loving' and the colonial peoples with tales about the era of the retreat of imperialism when colonial peoples could gain independence more or less peacefully by negotiation. The truth was, Abbas asserted, that Western imperialism had embarked on a great war of colonial reconquest and was waging it 'within the framework of the Atlantic Pact'. The Algerians, he concluded, had therefore given up all idea of negotiations. Henceforth they would, on principle, refuse to parley with de Gaulle's govern-ment. Instead they would now work for 'the internationaliza-tion of the Algerian conflict'.

All this fitted in well with the Chinese attitude and with Chinese arguments against Moscow's 'opportunism'. But what were the means of this 'internationalization' of the Algerian conflict? This question loomed large in Abbas's talks with Mao Tse-tung and the other Chinese leaders. Abbas had, in the first instance, intended to appeal to the United Nations for an all-Algerian referendum conducted under the U.N.'s auspices; and for this he had apparently received some encouragement from Moscow. This idea did not, however, commend itself to his Chinese hosts, who held that in taking this initiative Abbas might be preparing the undoing of his own government. Had he learned nothing, they asked, from Lumumba's fate? Had not Lumumba been destroyed by that same United Nations force that he himself had summoned to Congo?

Ferhat Abbas became hesitant; and the discussion proceeded to alternative methods of 'internationalization'. The Chinese had for some time now been ready to send volunteers to Algeria, with an eye to the eventual formation of an International Brigade similar to the famous Brigade that fought in Spain in 1936–38. However, Khrushchev and the Russian Presidium had vetoed this project; and unless they withdrew the veto, the project could not be taken up again. The main thing then for the Chinese was to try and force Khrushchev's hand. But how? It was agreed in Peking that Ferhat Abbas should, in any case, seek to 'spread the Algerian war'; and that his first move in this direction was to be an appeal to all Arab countries for direct military assistance—the Algerian struggle must be proclaimed a holy Pan-Arab war. It was further agreed that Ferhat Abbas should on his return journey stop in Moscow and openly confront the Russians with his demands.

13 October 1960

3 THE CONFERENCE OF THE
EIGHTY-ONE PARTIES

The conference of the leaders of eighty-one Communist Parties, which was in session in Moscow for three weeks in November, was very nearly a revival of the old Communist International, which Stalin had dissolved in 1943. The Chinese communists, it seems, favoured a formal reconstitution of the International, whereas the Russians were against it, because they did not wish to give Western propagandists a handle for stepping up the anti-communist campaign.

Compared with this carefully prepared conference, the November 1957 meeting of communist leaders was a hastily improvised and tentative affair. This time an elaborate agenda was fixed well in advance, and theses and material for discussion were circulated among the participants a month beforehand, so that everyone knew the controversial issues and had time to make up his mind on them. It was indeed a matter of making up one's mind, for it was clear that what was being convened was not just another of those Cominform parades that used to be held between 1947 and 1953. The Cominform, with its eight or nine member Parties, was a relatively small, regional body, whereas the Moscow conference was representative of an almost world-wide movement. And there was this startling novelty: for the first time since the Lenin era the Russians came to an international communist gathering not to dictate their will and see it meekly accepted by all, but to defend and explain their policies against severe criticisms from 'fraternal Parties'. They had to reply to attacks not only from the Chinese, but even from Latin American and South-East Asian delegates. What an ironical situation this was!

In this respect the November conference was different even from the last congresses of the Stalinized Comintern, the congresses of 1935 and 1928, at which Stalin's infallibility was accepted without demur and he did not even deign to speak in person. No such Papal privileges were granted to Khrushchev; the Russo-Chinese dispute—the quarrel, that is, between the two Big Brothers—had the effect that neither was big enough to lay down the law.

At the conference the clash of opinion was genuine, prolonged, and sometimes passionate. It went on at the plenary sessions and in the various committees which had been constituted in almost parliamentary fashion. To the embarrassment and even alarm of Moscow's stiffer hierarchs, who were shocked by the unusual spectacle, the course of the debate was at times unpredictable; and there was no lack of stormy scenes.

Yet both the Russians and the Chinese had come to the conference willing to compromise and strike a quick bargain. Even before the conference both had dropped or toned down their most extreme formulas in order to narrow the gap between their respective viewpoints. The Chinese had ceased to repeat that 'war was inevitable' and to frown at 'peaceful coexistence'. The Russians had withdrawn the most indiscreet of their 'revisionist' statements: Khrushchev no longer repeated that Lenin's theory of imperialism was out of date, that world war was 'an impossibility', and that some Communist Parties in West and East could and should take the 'parliamentary road to socialism'. What then, after this preliminary *rapprochement*, kept the Chinese and the Russians at loggerheads for a full three weeks?

The fact is that the more both sides narrowed the gap between their ideological formulas, the more real did the gap show itself to be. Even though the Chinese had come to Moscow somewhat remorseful about their 'polemical excesses' and ready to admit that they had gone too far in ridiculing peaceful coexistence as a 'dangerous revisionist delusion', Moscow and Peking still had different things in mind when they spoke in favour of peaceful coexistence. To the Chinese this meant the avoidance of world war, but the continuation of the cold war and of the arms race. 'We are, of course, also for peaceful coexistence', they said in effect, 'but does this necessarily mean that Comrade Khrushchev has to climb up to the summit on all fours over and over again?' They were against Khrushchev's 'diplomatic initiatives'; and as the discussion heated up, they went over the record to show that he had sadly lacked in communist firmness and dignity, especially during the Camp David period. They also declared that they saw no necessary connection between peaceful coexistence and 'all that futile disarmament talk to which Western imperialism, in its insanity, does not and cannot respond, but which spreads illusions among our own peoples and causes them to relax more than it is safe for all of us'.

The Russian answer was that what the Chinese stood for was merely 'passive coexistence', whereas they, the Russians, were for 'an active policy of coexistence'. Passive coexistence, and this was the crux of the Khrushchevite argument, would be merely a drift into war. The state of world affairs, bad as it was, would have been far worse, so Khrushchev pointed out, if Soviet diplomacy had not actively striven for an international detente; and without this striving it might yet deteriorate rapidly and dangerously. Chinese 'irresponsibility' and 'criminal light-mindedness' in playing down the dangers of nuclear warfare came under angry attack. Khrushchev, admitting the failure of his disarmament efforts so far, nevertheless insisted on the need to continue these efforts. On this point, it is reported, he spoke with feeling, invoking the responsibility of the communist leaders 'before mankind and before history' who would not forgive them if they gave up the quest for disarmament. Were disarmament talks with the West altogether futile? The Chinese, in speaking of the 'insanity of decaying imperialism', overlooked the fact that 'the American bourgeoisie is divided against itself and one section of it sees clearly the folly of nuclear war and wants peace'.

Soviet diplomacy and the Communist Parties, Khrushchev went on, must bank on the 'sober elements of the Western bourgeoisie' and must by their own policy strengthen the hands of those elements against the 'insane imperialists'. It was easy for his critics to belittle the effects of his diplomatic moves; but should he sit back with folded arms when a new American administration was taking over? To the Chinese argument that the Democrats are no better than the Republicans and Kennedy is no better than Eisenhower, Khrushchev replied that this may be so, but that it would be an unforgivable error to take this for granted. He wanted at least to test the intentions of the new American administration, and, yes, to climb the summit once again. He is reported to have made an impassioned appeal to the conference not to obstruct his diplomacy, as the Chinese had done more than once. The conference was, it is alleged, greatly impressed by the gravity and urgency of his appeal.

If on this point Khrushchev carried his audience with him, the Chinese were more successful when they attacked his conduct of communist policy in the strict sense. They accused him of curbing the anti-imperialist struggle in Asia, Africa, and Latin America—especially in Iraq, Algeria, and India. They attacked his 'friendship' with Nasser, Kassem, Nehru, and Sukarno, and demanded that the Communist Parties in those countries should behave more aggressively towards those leaders and the 'national bourgeoisie' at large. In other words, they said that the Russians, in the interest of their diplomacy, had virtually sabotaged communist revolution in the underdeveloped countries. According to reports from Moscow, this charge was eagerly taken up by Latin American, Indian, and other communists, whose Parties are more or less divided between Khrushchevite and Maoist factions. The Russians countered these accusations with the thesis that the 'main form of class struggle' in the years ahead was to be economic competition between the Soviet bloc and NATO; and that all other methods of class struggle must be adjusted and, indeed, subordinated to this basic fact. Despite Sputniks and intercontinental missiles, they argued, the U.S.S.R. was still economically inferior to the U.S.A. As long as this was so, they insisted (that is, for another five to ten years), they could not afford to provoke the Western bourgeoisie unduly by committing themselves irrevocably to the support of every revolutionary movement in every corner of the world. The Chinese held that the Soviet bloc was, in fact, strategically far stronger than the Russians implied; but even if this were not so, it was just one more reason why the Soviet bloc should seek to compensate for its economic inferiority by throwing all its weight behind the revolutionary forces of Asia, Africa, and Latin America. Over this issue centred much of the three weeks' debate.

The Declaration of the Eighty-one Communist Parties, as it was finally adopted with many amendments and corrections, strikes a balance between the Russian and the Chinese viewpoints. In almost every passage it aims at a synthesis between a Russian thesis and a Chinese antithesis. Only this balancing secured for the document a unanimous adoption. The unanimity was not achieved mechanically; nor was it only apparent.

The disputants were anxious to present a common front to the outside world. The Chinese have not been out to challenge the Soviet leadership of the communist camp; but they have been determined to 'put teeth' into Soviet policy. In this they succeeded to some extent even before the conference, as could be seen from Khrushchev's behaviour at the United Nations, from his partial recognition of the Algerian government, and from the changed tenor of various Russian pronouncements.

The Moscow Declaration emphatically reacknowledges Soviet leadership, but even in so doing it bares quite a few Chinese teeth. Thus, it echoes Khrushchev in proclaiming that 'peaceful coexistence . . . or destructive war—this is the alternative today' and in rejecting American, and by implication also Chinese, brinkmanship as 'leading to thermo-nuclear catastrophe'. But against Khrushchev, the Declaration asserts that 'the aggressive nature of imperialism has not changed' (i.e. that Lenin's definition of it is still valid) and that 'imperialism . . . persists in preparing a new world war'. The eighty-one Parties accept the Russian thesis that the economic contest between the U.S.S.R. and the U.S.A. is 'the main form of the class struggle' at present; but they insist on the need to intensify the class struggle proper, especially in the underdeveloped countries. For the first time the 'national bourgeoisie' of those countries is openly described as a vacillating and undependable ally, liable to seek accommodation with the West; and for the first time Khrushchev's 'friends', Nasser and Kassem, have been attacked for suppressing communism in their countries. For all its elaborate character and stylistical *élan*, the Declaration is not likely to put an end to controversy. It will rather serve as one of those sacred texts which each disputant can, and undoubtedly will, quote in support of his own views and policies.

What then is going to be the effect of the Moscow conference on the international communist movement, and on Soviet diplomacy? The international communist movement remains divided into three wings: left, right, and centre. These are in *some* respects the indirect descendants of the three communist schools of thought—Trotskyist, Stalinist, and Bukharinist— which contended against each other in the 1920s. But whereas in the 1920s the contest ended in the establishment of a Stalinist monopoly and the suppression of all the other schools of thought,

the present struggle can hardly lead to a similar outcome. . . .
This relative tolerance is quite new to contemporary communism
which was formed in the monolithic mould of Stalinism. It
breaks up that mould; and it creates openings for viewpoints
other than the Maoist and the Khrushchevite. One may doubt
whether the conference would have been able to repeat, as it
has done, the condemnation of Titoism, if Tito and his Party
had not chosen to remain outside the organization. Within it,
the Poles, the Italians, and others form the right wing. In
Moscow this right preferred not to speak with its own voice;
it was glad to see that Khrushchev took the initiative for the
attack on the Chinese; and it lent its support to him. In the long
run, however, a three-cornered contest may well develop; and
the dispute, which ostensibly is still only between the Chinese
and the Russians, is already cutting across the various national
Parties. It is an *inner*-Party as well as an *inter*-Party affair: there
are 'revisionists' and 'dogmatists' in Russia and even in China,
and in quite a few other Parties. Among the South-East Asians
and Latin Americans the split between the Maoists and the
Khrushchevites has already become more or less open.

The decisions of the Moscow conference foreshadow little or
no change in the policies of the Communist Parties of the West,
especially of those of Western Europe, where the relative
stability of the existing regimes leaves little scope for revolutionary action in the near future. But the Parties of the underdeveloped nations are likely to become more active and
aggressive than hitherto. This may be of particular importance
for India, where the communists of West Bengal have, in
opposition to their national leadership, opted for the Maoist
line. Expecting to score a great success at the next election, the
Maoists of Calcutta are hoping to make a communist stronghold of West Bengal, and declare that they will not surrender to
Nehru and Congress as meekly as their comrades of Kerala
surrendered their stronghold. An intensification of revolutionary activity may also be expected in Latin America, where
Maoism has been gaining ground.

The effect of the conference on Soviet diplomacy may be
quite considerable. True, Khrushchev has been given a free
hand to make an approach to the new American administration;
and another journey to the summit is about to begin. But the

conference has also restricted Khrushchev's freedom of movement and of bargaining. This is not to say that the eighty-one
Communist Parties, big, small, and tiny, are, through a formal
resolution, dictating to the Soviet Premier what he has to do. It
is rather that he can no longer pursue any policy in overt
conflict with the Chinese or in defiance of the mood prevailing
in the communist movement at large. That mood allows
Khrushchev to pick up with President Kennedy the threads of
negotiation where he and President Eisenhower left them; but
it does not allow him to go back to the Camp David spirit with
all the hail-fellow-well-met *panache* so congenial to the Soviet
leader. The conference has told him that in any negotiations
with the West he must be, and must be seen to be, a much
tougher negotiator than he has been in the past. It has allowed
him to fly once again to the summit, but it has somewhat
clipped his wings before the flight. Whether Khrushchev will
act in the spirit of this instruction remains to be seen. If he does
not, the Chinese, and not only they, will turn on him all their
heavy guns—and the ideological barrage will be fiercer than
ever.

A real change has thus occurred in the background against
which the Soviet Government is going to confront the new
American administration. The relative ease and freedom of
initiative which Soviet diplomacy enjoyed between 1954 and
1960 is a thing of the past. Over those years Khrushchev rid
himself of his rivals Malenkov and Molotov and seemingly
became the sole master of Soviet diplomacy and policy. But
he has now come under pressures from within the communist
camp far more potent and severe than those to which he was
ever exposed from his Russian rivals. The growing momentum
of the communist 'one third of the world' has its impact even
on Moscow. It shows itself in the fact that, for all the renewed
emphasis on the Soviet leadership of the communist camp, the
Russians can now lead only on condition that they also allow
themselves to be led.

The ideological truce between Peking and Moscow is designed to cover the critical period during which Moscow will
be testing the intentions of the new American administration.
The results of the probes will have a decisive influence on the
further evolution of communist policy. Every move made by

the new American President and the Soviet Premier, every phase in their negotiations (if there are any), every bit of progress made, and every failure to make any progress, will be scrutinized throughout the communist world and eagerly evaluated as evidence in support either of the Khrushchevite or of the Maoist line. The Khrushchevites will dwell on every event and incident which they may be able to interpret as evidence in favour of their policy of 'active coexistence', while the Maoists will pick up every straw in the wind to prove that no genuine compact between East and West is possible, and that nothing but uninhibited global class struggle can resolve the fundamental conflict by which the world is torn. In a sense, therefore, Kennedy is going to be the unwitting arbiter of this inter-communist controversy.

7 and 8 December 1960

4 CUBA AND INDO-CHINA

Relations between the Soviet Union and China have in recent months been quite smooth—on the surface. The truce concluded at the Moscow conference of the Communist Parties last November is still on. The bitter and only slightly veiled attacks on Khrushchevite 'opportunism' that filled the Chinese press in 1959 and 1960 are not being repeated. Maoist policy has grown more 'moderate' and has ostensibly adjusted itself to Khrushchev's 'centrist' line. It appears that Mao has even made his apologies to Khrushchev and explained the vehemence of earlier criticisms by the circumstance that 'ultra-left' elements had temporarily gained the upper hand in Peking's political councils; and he has given the assurance that those elements have now been curbed and that the balance has been redressed. If this were true, Chinese policy would appear to be floundering in a welter of conflicting tendencies and factions on which Mao has not always been able to impose his will. Even Moscow is not quite sure whether to take this apology at its face value. Such is the secrecy which surrounds the Chinese Politbureau and Central Committee that the members of the Soviet Presidium do not know what the inner alignments are there, and in particular whether Mao himself inspired the attacks on Soviet policy or whether someone else (Liu Shao-chi?) did, despite Mao.

Officially, however, Moscow has accepted the apology and acknowledged that the Chinese Party 'has made a commendable effort to overcome dogmatism in its midst and to adopt a realistic and responsible attitude'. But behind this official acknowledgment doubt and suspicion have remained (and have been freshly aroused in the connection with the latest events). On the other hand, Soviet policy has partly yielded to the pressure of Chinese criticism and shifted somewhat 'to the left'. Khrushchev is far less sanguine than he used to be about summit diplomacy and the prospects of disarmament and detente, and more strongly committed to a militant anti-Western policy in the underdeveloped countries. Mutual Russo-Chinese adjustment has formed the basis of the ideological truce.

Until the Cuban crisis the truce was also helped by the relative lull in Soviet-American diplomatic activity, the lull which followed upon President Kennedy's demand for a waiting period to which Khrushchev had acceded. With the major issues of East-West diplomacy in abeyance, the Russians had little opportunity to 'sin' with the softness and opportunism which might have brought Chinese reprobation upon them. Yet, a difference between the Chinese and the Russian attitudes towards President Kennedy was all too evident. The Chinese treated Kennedy as an enemy as bad as Eisenhower or even worse, while the Russians gave him the benefit of the doubt, to say the least, and urged the other Communist Parties not to antagonize the new American administration unduly before it had shown its hand.

The Cuban crisis has to some extent strengthened the position of the Chinese within the communist bloc. (It has aroused much anti-American feeling even in 'revisionist' Poland.) It has placed a large question mark over some of Khrushchev's expectations and gestures of good will towards the new President, and has driven Khrushchev into his first public and hostile clash with Kennedy.

Moscow has nevertheless kept a cool head throughout the crisis and acted with caution. Khrushchev has not gone beyond the expression of moral and political solidarity with Castro's regime. He has not repeated his old threat that Soviet missiles would defend Cuba against American intervention. He hastened to reassure the American President that his government had no intention of establishing any military base in Cuba or of using Cuba as a jumping-off ground against the United States. He encouraged Castro to declare, after the collapse of the invasion, Cuban readiness for direct negotiations with Washington over a settlement of the Cuban-American conflict. Moreover, at the height of the crisis Khrushchev made his suggestions for at least a limited Soviet-American 'deal'. In arguing that 'it does not make sense to put out the fires smouldering in some parts of the world if new fires are kindled elsewhere' he in effect told the President that if the United States desisted from further intervention in Cuba, Russia would be prepared to bring under control the 'fires' in Laos and South Vietnam. The Chinese applauded the strong pro-Cuban tenor of Khrushchev's messages to the President; but the conciliatory undertone and the suggestion of this *quid pro quo* as the basis for a 'deal' were not to their taste. They saw no need for Moscow to offer such a *quid pro quo* after the setback the United States had suffered in Cuba. They repeated their conviction that Kennedy was a tougher adversary of the Soviet bloc and of communism than Eisenhower.

At the conclusion of the Cuban hostilities official Moscow was still puzzled by Kennedy's behaviour and not yet quite ready to deny him the benefit of the doubt. Khrushchev noted that the President had drawn a line between continued American support to the anti-Castro émigrés and direct American intervention in Cuba. This, in Khrushchev's view, promised Cuba a long period of respite, because the anti-Castro émigrés, demoralized by their debacle, would for a long time not be able to launch any new attack. Against this Peking holds that the American administration will end by intervening against Castro directly, with its own armed forces, and that only a more aggressive Soviet attitude can deter it. Moscow at first dismissed this forecast as groundless, but then it began to wonder. The Chinese remain convinced that the military superiority of the communist bloc should allow Khrushchev to treat American imperialism as a 'paper tiger', whereas Khrushchev is afraid of over-exploiting Soviet strength and underestimating the American capacity for retaliation.

This old difference in the evaluation of the international balance of power has been thrown into sharper relief by Major Gagarin's flight into outer space. Paradoxically, as far as the inner-communist alignments are concerned this Soviet triumph has played into Chinese rather than into Russian hands. The Chinese have made the most of the 'military consequences of Gagarin', insisting that the United States has no answer to Russia's new strategic advantage. President Kennedy's admission that in outer space the U.S.A. may lag behind the U.S.S.R. for a whole decade has given additional strength to this argument. The conclusion the Chinese draw is that communists have no need to pull their punches anywhere in Asia, Africa, and Latin America, if local circumstances favour them; that Cuba should serve them as an example; that as long as they can count on strong popular support on the spot they have nothing to fear from American or other intervention, because the NATO powers are paralyzed by their fear of a head-on collision with the Soviet Union.

Thus, despite all their mutual tactical adjustments, Moscow and Peking are still separated by this important difference: Moscow continues to base its policy on the assumption of an equilibrium of nuclear power in the world, while Peking holds that Russian missile technology has destroyed that equilibrium and given the Soviet bloc a strategic superiority which international communism should exploit to the utmost in order to advance on a broad front.

The Moscow conference made an attempt to bridge the difference between the Chinese and the Russian lines by a formula on the one hand committing the Communist Parties to refrain from any 'export of revolution' and, on the other, denying the NATO powers the right to 'export counter-revolution'. This formula implied, of course, that if any of the Western Powers were to 'export counter-revolution' the Soviet bloc would feel free to retaliate in kind. In the view of both Moscow and Peking the West has, under the cover of the United Nations, 'exported counter-revolution' to the Congo— only the remoteness of that country has excused the Russian and Chinese failure to intervene effectively on the spot. Cuba has been the next attempt at exporting counter-revolution; but as this was defeated by Castro's own forces, before any need for

Soviet and Chinese intervention arose, the policy adopted by the Moscow conference was not put to a test. Laos has been the first important test case; and the impact of the Cuban crisis on it has been unmistakable.

Up to the moment of the fighting in Cuba Moscow accepted with satisfaction President Kennedy's declared intention to modify American policy in Laos and to encourage the re-establishment of a neutralist regime there. Moscow was prepared to work for the same end, though not without strengthening militarily the bargaining position of Pathet Lao before a cease-fire and negotiations. To all intents and purposes Peking followed the Russian lead. However, to make sure that the situation in Laos did not get out of control, and probably to forestall any Chinese interference, the Soviet Union assumed the main responsibility for the supply of arms to the Pathet Lao and for communist tactics on the spot.

The Cuban affair changed the context within which Peking and Moscow have been viewing the situation in Laos. It has provided them with an alibi, if an alibi was needed, for a more aggressive policy not only in Laos but also in South Vietnam. In his April messages to the President Khrushchev intimated that if the United States felt entitled to intervene against 'unfriendly regimes' in countries situated on its borders, Russia and China might consider themselves free to do the same. The temptation for the communist powers to use the Cuban alibi in this way has been all the stronger because in Laos and Vietnam they have enjoyed a decisive local advantage—popular support—which was denied to the United States in Cuba. The pro-American elements in Laos and South Vietnam are discredited; the right-wing regimes are in a state of disintegration; and all that the native communist forces, allied with the neutralists, need to establish themselves in power is more arms, more effective military direction, and the green light from Moscow. All these could be provided with the maximum of discretion and without direct Russian or Chinese involvement. There can be little doubt that Peking is favouring such a policy, and that Moscow is stalling.

Khrushchev is wary of exploiting the local communist advantage in Laos to the full because this might provoke American or SEATO intervention and turn Laos into a new Korea. The

Chinese are not afraid of a new Korea. They might even welcome it. The Korean war was fought at a time when the Soviet bloc was weak, before the Soviet Union itself had recovered from the Second World War and before the communist regime had become consolidated in China. Yet the fighting ended in a stalemate which the United States did not dare to break by carrying hostilities beyond Korea and using its overwhelming nuclear superiority. The effect of the Korean stalemate was to make American policy in Asia far less confident than it had been and to give a fillip to communism in Indo-China. Why then—goes the Chinese argument—should the Soviet bloc be afraid of fighting another local war after an interval of nearly a decade, in circumstances so much more favourable to communism? If the United States did not dare to spread the Korean war in the hey-day of its nuclear superiority, it will certainly not turn a war over Laos into a world conflict now; and the fighting would end not in a stalemate but in an American defeat which would 'clear the air over Asia and beyond Asia' and give a powerful impulse to communism in all underdeveloped countries.

To Moscow the risks of such a gamble seem too great, despite all the accession of power from which the Soviet Union has benefited in the meantime and despite all the local advantages which communism enjoys in Laos and Vietnam. A new Korea would mark the final failure of Khrushchev's policy of detente. It might throw the Soviet Union and Eastern Europe back into the rigidity of a war economy and bring to a halt the expansion of consumer industries, with incalculable effects on civilian morale. It would shatter the foundations of Khrushchev's policies and perhaps his own position too. Khrushchev has therefore weighty reasons for seeking to avoid any military contest with the West, however local in scale.

Nor has he as yet given up the possibility of some future 'deal' with Kennedy. In parts of his Cuban messages to the President there was more sorrow than anger: he still appeared to view the Cuban affair as a momentary aberration on the part of a young and inexperienced President saddled with an awkward legacy; and he did not wish to make it more difficult for Kennedy to withdraw from the venture without too much loss of face. True, the strong terms in which the President has since addressed the communist world have come as a shock to

Moscow. The question is being asked there whether Kennedy is merely smarting under defeat but may yet return to the more conciliatory policy foreshadowed in his election campaign, or whether he is really seeing himself as the chosen leader of a new anti-communist crusade. Whatever the Chinese may say about this, Khrushchev still prefers to wait and see. The negotiations over Laos offer him, among other things, an opportunity to test American intentions. . . .

However, neither the Cuban crisis nor the situation in Laos have helped the Russians, because both have in communist eyes tended to strengthen the Chinese case. Both Cuba and Laos have also compelled Khrushchev to engage in complex manoeuvres designed to steal something of the Chinese thunder and yet to prevent a further exacerbation of Russo-American relations. It goes without saying that the more he succeeds in one of these purposes the less can he succeed in the other.

2 May 1961

5 THE SINO-SOVIET TRUCE
   BREAKS DOWN

A new and momentous quarrel has broken out between Russia and China. Khrushchev is now charging the leader of Chinese communism with 'disloyalty', 'subversive agitation', and nothing less than 'incitement to world war'. He is also threatening Mao that he will at last bring their protracted and hitherto secret or semi-secret dispute into the open. The charges and the threat are contained in an indictment of Mao's policy which has just been sent out from Khrushchev's offices in Moscow to the headquarters of several foreign Communist Parties. This still secret document claims that Mao and his comrades have 'violated the agreement of the eighty-one Communist Parties' concluded in Moscow only last November. . . .

The Moscow Declaration was hailed as an epoch-making event; and it was to be binding on all Communist Parties. The Chinese, it then seemed, had definitely accepted Soviet leadership, which meant that they would not seek to make their own influence felt in other Communist Parties. They obliged them-

selves to submit any new difference they might have with the
Russians to a sort of a comradely court. The conference of the
eighty-one Parties set up a special body to deal with such
disputes. Moscow now claims that the Chinese have violated
almost every point of this agreement. These are the charges:
first, 'The Chinese comrades have conducted surreptitious
agitation against the principles of the Moscow Declaration', in
the first instance against peaceful coexistence; secondly, they
'have not used the machinery for conciliation which the Moscow Conference has set up'; thirdly, they have continued to
'discredit the leadership of the Soviet Communist Party and
have sought to extend their influence to other Communist
Parties'. They have sent emissaries abroad who are building
up 'Chinese factions' in foreign Communist Parties, thereby
'grossly violating the Leninist principles of Party organization';
and finally, they have set up special centres in Europe, Asia,
and Africa from which they have been conducting their 'subversive intrigue' against Moscow.

Surveying the course of Russo-Chinese disputes over the
years, Moscow has now made several sensational disclosures
which throw new light on some important yet obscure events of
post-war history. Khrushchev blames Mao for being obsessed
with Taiwan and bent on 'liberating Taiwan' even at the risk
of world war. These are the actual terms of the charge: 'The
Chinese Communist Party does not know how to treat problems
in the order of their real importance; and it places Taiwan at
the centre of all its preoccupations, without bothering about the
development of the international situation. In this respect the
behaviour of the Chinese communists has been quite different
from that of the communists of the U.S.S.R. after the Peace of
Brest Litovsk, which deprived the U.S.S.R. of part of its
territories.'

Under the Brest Litovsk Peace, which Lenin's government
signed with Germany in 1918, Russia lost her former Baltic
possessions for the whole period between the two World Wars.
By invoking this example Khrushchev tells Mao that he should
have sought reconciliation with the United States and agreed
to Taiwan's formal detachment from Red China, instead of
making of the 'liberation of Taiwan' the condition for any
agreement with the United States. 'When our interests', Mos-

cow goes on to say, '. . . more than ever demanded from us a determined policy of coexistence with the countries hostile to socialism, the leadership of the Chinese Communist Parties denounced our every initiative in this direction as treason, as appeasing the invaders of Taiwan, or as a sacrifice of the interests of the people of China to those of the U.S.S.R.'

Moscow's most startling accusation and disclosure is that *Mao has ever since 1949 preached 'preventive war' against the West.* The document from which I am quoting refers ironically to a secret speech made by Mao as early as July 1949 in which 'he used beautiful but outdated and irrelevant Chinese legends and proverbs to advocate preventive war'. What this implies is that the communists fought the Korean war which followed next year on Mao's rather than on Stalin's initiative.

The root of the trouble, the document says, lies in the 'one-sided military character of the Chinese Party'. Because of peculiar conditions the Chinese Party 'has grown up as an army and not as a civilian organization like any other Communist Party'. A military organization the Chinese Party essentially still is. In the communist idiom, this amounts to a charge that Mao exercises a kind of Bonapartist military dictatorship. Here the indictment comes to its most dramatic point: 'One can understand that in 1949–50 the leaders of the Chinese Communist Party had to make allowance for the state of mind of their soldier-comrades still permeated by the experience of those terrible years [years of armed struggle against the Japanese and against the Kuomintang] and maintained such an attitude'. But what is shocking is that 'twelve years later (that is in 1961!) the position of the Chinese leaders has remained the same, while international developments have changed the basic elements of the situation'. Moscow is thus stating that even today Mao stands for preventive war. This is the first time that Moscow has advanced this accusation so explicitly.

I cannot say whether this charge is a polemical exaggeration or whether it is based on facts. Moscow refers to these Chinese arguments in favour of preventive war: 'An armed conflict between capitalism and communism is ultimately inevitable'; and consequently, 'the Soviet Union should use its present overwhelming superiority in missiles, rockets, and nuclear weapons' and dictate its terms to the United States, even if this means war. The Chinese want Khrushchev not only to 'go to the brink' but, if need be, to go beyond it. What is probably implied in their argument is that if Russia does not use her 'military superiority' now, or very soon, she may lose it because the United States may catch up with her in rocketry and space flight.

The Russians appear to take a more cautious and, at the same time, a more self-confident view. They counter-argue that 'world war between communism and capitalism is not inevitable—it can and should be avoided'; Soviet superiority in rocketry and space flight may not be as decisive a guarantee of victory as the Chinese assume; and the United States is not in a position to catch up with the U.S.S.R. in rocketry and space flight; and so the U.S.S.R. has nothing to lose but much to gain by playing for time instead of heading for war. Khrushchev is determined to use Russia's military advantages as bargaining counters in negotiation and even to go to the brink. But he will not go beyond it, unless (as he put it on another occasion) 'Western imperialism takes upon itself the odium of aggression' —unless, for instance, NATO armies or airfleets cross the frontier of Eastern Germany.

Moscow goes on to charge Mao and the Maoists with arrogance and 'dizziness with success', which overcomes them when they contemplate 'the territory occupied by the People's Republic of China, its enormous reserves of manpower, and its considerable influence . . . on the peoples of the Middle East and Africa'. But the size of a country and the teeming millions do not necessarily make for 'ideological reliability', Moscow warns. In their arrogance, the Chinese may provoke a schism in world communism comparable to the age-old schism between Eastern and Western Christianity. 'The leaders of the Chinese Communist Party have hatched, without daring to formulate it categorically, a sort of plan for the division of world communism into two zones, a so-called Western zone, for which the U.S.S.R. should be responsible . . . and a so-called Eastern zone under the People's Republic of China.' Moscow rejects this plan, saying that 'it has a flavour of racialism about it, because, if carried to logical conclusion, it would lead to a division between the white and the coloured races'. Such a division 'would not do away with the existing differences and disputes, and would be contrary to the principles of communism'.

The Khrushchevite indictment relates how the Chinese have tried to build up their 'zone' by turning the Communist Parties of Vietnam, Korea, and Indonesia into their domain; but it does not say whether they have succeeded. Instead Moscow exults in Mao's 'failure to get support from the leaders of European communism'; and it mocks at China's sole ally in Europe—tiny and backward Albania. Enver Hoxha, Albania's dictator, is charged with exterminating the Khrushchevites in his country, sending spies to Yugoslavia, and provoking dangerous frontier clashes between Yugoslavia and Albania. In the Albanian purges twelve members of the Politbureau have been imprisoned—three of them have been shot—and Soviet-trained commanders of the Albanian armed forces have been executed as 'American and Greek spies', for the sole reason that they were Russia's friends. Khrushchev reproaches Mao with aiding and abetting the Albanian dictator and warns that this policy may provoke an explosion in that little country similar to the Hungarian uprising of 1956.

Delighted though Moscow is with Mao's 'failure in Europe', it claims that the Chinese are working feverishly to make this good, to win the allegiance of Western European communists and to play them against Russia. Moscow complains bitterly that Mao is setting up pro-Chinese factions in the Western European Communist Parties and is using his diplomatic personnel for this 'subversive activity'. . . . Addressing itself especially to the French Communist Party, Moscow says that the Chinese have made common cause with those French communists who never made peace with Khrushchev's denunciation of Stalin at the Twentieth Congress, i.e. with the French Stalinist die-hards. Maurice Thorez, the French communist leader, and his wife Jeannette Vermeersch are taunted for their ambiguous behaviour and for turning a blind eye on the intrigues of the pro-Chinese elements in their Party.

This formidable list of accusations ends with the threat that if the Chinese do not mend their ways, Khrushchev will take the dispute out of the twilight of semi-secrecy and bluntly denounce them before international communist opinion. 'We have not been afraid of an open breach with the Yugoslav revisionists; and we shall not be afraid of an open breach with the Chinese dogmatists either'. . . .

The main question arising from all this is how the Russo-Chinese quarrel is going to affect Khrushchev's attitude to Berlin when the international tension over the Berlin issue mounts to a climax. The need to compete with Mao for leadership in the communist camp has been an important factor in Khrushchev's decision to take action over Berlin. He has to refute Mao's charges. He has to show himself tough and determined. He has to demonstrate that he is not 'appeasing Western imperialism'. He has to calculate his diplomatic moves with an eye to their effect on the intense Russo-Chinese contest for the allegiance of so many Communist Parties in Asia, Africa, Europe, and Latin America.

This makes it difficult for him to engage in genuine bargaining with the West, and imposes on him that diplomatic rigidity which so surprised President Kennedy in Vienna. On the other hand, Khrushchev is anxious to avoid the risk of war, because by courting it he would not only endanger Russia's interests, but virtually surrender to Mao. . . .

23 June 1961

13

The Twenty-second Congress and the End of the First Decade After Stalin

The Twenty-second Congress of the Soviet Communist Party met in Moscow from 17–31 October. On the domestic front it approved the new Party Programme announced in July in which economic targets for the next twenty years were set out. It proposed a 500 per cent rise in industrial output, a 250 per cent rise in agricultural output, and a 250 per cent rise in per capita income. It also envisaged rent-free housing, the abolition of taxation, and a reduction in the working week. The congress was also important because Stalin was denounced more explicitly than ever before; and because Khrushchev's attack on the Albanians and the Chinese walkout marked a new phase in Sino-Soviet hostility.

At the Twentieth Congress Khrushchev had denounced Stalin in secret, although the text of his speech had circulated widely among Party members; his condemnation at the Twenty-second Congress was open and undisguised. It was followed by various acts of symbolic importance that shocked an already startled Soviet opinion: Stalin's body was removed from the Red Square Mausoleum, his statues were pulled down, and towns called after him were renamed throughout the pro-Soviet communist world. Khrushchev also attacked the Anti-Party Group for opposing the decisions of the Twentieth Congress, and for the first time he named Voroshilov as a member of it. He accused the Albanians of resisting the agreements of 1957 and 1960, thus making the first public attack on another Communist Party since the Yugoslavs were expelled from the Cominform in 1948. Khrushchev also adopted a militant tone *vis-à-vis* the West and he announced that the Soviet Union would explode a 50-megaton bomb. However, he said that Russia would not insist on signing a peace treaty with the German Democratic Republic if the West showed 'a readiness to settle the German problem'. This vague formulation represented a retreat from his threats of the previous June.

Khrushchev's attack on the Albanians provoked the Chinese. Chou En-lai, who headed the Chinese delegation to the congress, deplored 'any public one-sided censure of a fraternal Party'; and he indicated his disapproval of Khrushchev's anti-Stalinism by laying a wreath on Stalin's tomb. The Chinese delegation then left for Peking before the congress had ended.

The congress was followed in December by the breaking off of Soviet diplomatic relations with Albania, and by a minor purge in Bulgaria where Dr. Vulko Chervenkov, Prime Minister from 1950 to 1956, was expelled from the Presidium for resisting de-Stalinization.

In 1962 Sino-Soviet relations worsened under the impact of three separate developments. First, the Soviet Union rebuilt its friendship with Tito which had been destroyed at the time of the Hungarian uprising. The Chinese had been particularly hostile to Tito and, as long as there was a chance of a Sino-Soviet *rapprochement*, the Russians kept their distance from him. But since hopes had faded for a Sino-Soviet reconciliation and since Russia had fallen out with Yugoslavia's traditional enemy Albania, there was no barrier to renewed contacts. In September the Soviet President, Leonid Brezhnev, visited Yugoslavia and in December Tito spent three weeks in Russia where he addressed the Supreme Soviet.

A second cause of Sino-Soviet bitterness was India. In August the Chinese announced that Russia had provided India with military aircraft, which, in view of increasing Sino-Indian tension, was tantamount to arming China's enemies. In October the Sino-Indian war broke out. At the same time there occurred the Cuba missile crisis. In September Ché Guevara had signed an agreement with the Russians on the installation of missiles in Cuba. This aroused the Americans and on 22 October Kennedy announced the blockade of all ships carrying military equipment to Cuba and threatened to take further action if existing missile installations were not removed. After a week of crisis, Khrushchev accepted Kennedy's demands in return for a U.S. promise not to invade the island. To the Chinese Khrushchev's actions appeared to be both too adventurous and then too timid and provided further justification for their hostility to his foreign policy.

1 THE TWENTY-SECOND
CONGRESS AND THE CULT
OF KHRUSHCHEV

With the Twenty-second Congress and the eviction of Stalin's mummy from the Mausoleum a new and much delayed phase of de-Stalinization has begun. . . . Only strong pressure from anti-Stalinist elements in the background has compelled Khrushchev to open this new chapter. Even if he had been out merely to gain popularity and enhance his position in a struggle for power, the fact that to do this he had to appeal to the anti-Stalinist element in the country itself testifies to the force of that sentiment. In the closed sessions of the congress an anti-Stalinism far more radical than Khrushchev's made itself felt: it was voiced by veteran Bolsheviks, victims of the Stalinist terror, and by young delegates who bore no responsibility for that terror.

The official, heavily edited and misleading reports of the congress create the impression that Khrushchev had to contend only against Molotov and the other Stalinist die-hards. The division was in fact between three large groups: the Stalinist die-hards, the radical anti-Stalinists, and the intermediate Khrushchevite tendency. Khrushchev has prevailed because he has been all things to all men: the anti-Stalinists supported him as the enemy of the die-hards; and many crypto-Stalinists have backed him, convinced that he will not carry de-Staliniza- tion 'too far'.

He has fought Stalinism with Stalinist methods (as Stalin himself fought the old Russian barbarism with barbarous methods). This contradiction has marked all his behaviour. He denounced Molotov and company as responsible for the great purges, and threatened them with exemplary punishment and even with a public trial. But having himself been one of the chief purgers, he is afraid of putting them in the dock lest they remind the country of his own role and demand his presence in the dock too. He promised to reveal the truth about the assassination of Kirov in 1934, the affair which served Stalin as the pretext for the purges. But he made the same promise six years ago, at the Twentieth Congress, and has failed to keep it.

He said that Molotov, Kaganovich, and Malenkov obstructed the investigation into the Kirov affair. But it is over four years now since Molotov and his associates were expelled from the Central Committee. What, if not Khrushchev's own complicity, has prevented him from revealing the full truth in these four years and even at the congress? He presented himself at the congress as the guardian of the country's and the Party's newly won freedom and warned that Molotov and company were out to bring back the Stalinist terror. Yet he himself denied Molotov, and even the senile Voroshilov, the freedom to state their case at the congress. He repudiated the cult of Stalin's personality. Yet at the congress the cult of Krushchev's personality flourished so grotesquely and ominously that it must have aroused protests from the radical anti-Stalinists. Khrushchev, who is in the habit of interrupting speakers on any trivial point, listened to all the eulogies and hymns in his honour without interrupting once. Only after protests against this new cult were made from the floor in closed sessions and in the Central Committee was he moved to come out with his repudiation of the Khrushchev cult. This is all to the good; but it remains to be seen whether the cult will really cease. He warned the Party that it must never allow any of its chiefs to place himself above criticism and control, and that it should jealously guard its right to depose any leader. Yet he himself remains above all criticism, for nothing said against him behind closed doors has been allowed to transpire into the press.

Yet the outcome of his struggle against Stalinism by Stalinist methods is relatively positive and beneficial. Though so much of Stalinism survives in Khrushchevism, there is progressively less and less of it. His call to the Party that it should beware of any new usurper like Stalin has sunk into people's minds and will not be forgotten. He has been able to consolidate his power only by restricting it. He has remained Number One, but only on the understanding that he is to be *primus inter pares*, all members of the Presidium being his equals. And most important of all, his half-hearted de-Stalinization is paving the way for those who will be able to liquidate Stalin's legacy (or rather its liabilities) without his inhibitions and mental reservations, frankly, consistently, in an un-Stalinist manner.

The greatest single liability of the Stalinist legacy and the greatest single barrier to Russia's further progress is the conception of the 'monolithic' Party, which, however torn by internal conflict, must never allow any open division of opinion and free debate, let alone the formation in its midst of any groups expounding their distinctive views. The 'monolith' is the real core of Stalinism, and Khrushchev seeks to preserve it by all means. All the votes at the congress as at the Central Committee have been unanimous, though it is clear that unanimity has been no more than a fiction throughout the post-Stalin years. And, as regards international communism, what is the worth of 'monolithicism' (on which Mao insists even more fervently than Khrushchev) when international communism too is obviously divided between various schools of thought which, instead of thrashing out their differences openly, play hide-and-seek with one another?

The most important event at the congress, an event which the official reports hide under a bushel and which has therefore not been noticed by outsiders, was an attack on the very principle of 'monolithicism'. It took the form of a demand, which Frol Kozlov, Khrushchev's present deputy, mentioned only *en passant* and with much equivocation, that the ban on the formation of groups and factions within the Party be lifted. That such a demand should have been raised at all is a fact of extraordinary consequence. The ban on inner Party groupings is over forty years old, and has behind it Lenin's authority. He proclaimed it in 1921, during the Kronstadt rising, as an emergency measure. On this ban Stalin subsequently built his 'monolith' and his autocracy, for by invoking the ban he was able to stifle and destroy any opposition. Yet not a single leader of any opposition, not even Trotsky, could bring himself to call for an end to that ban, precisely because it had behind it Lenin's authority.

Now, after so many decades someone has at last had the courage to call for its abolition. We do not know who it was; but whoever it was he spoke with the authentic voice of radical anti-Stalinism, which does not bow to the taboos even of the Lenin cult, a cult which Khrushchev exploits for his own purposes while he is smashing the Stalin cult. Amendments demanding an end to the ban on groupings have, of course, been defeated. But their appearance is to my mind a greater portent than the ejection of Stalin's body from the Mausoleum. The issue of the monolithic Party has been placed on the agenda and will remain there, whatever the formal vote of this congress.

1 November 1961

2 THE IMPACT OF THE TWENTY-SECOND CONGRESS ON THE U.S.S.R.

The impact of the Twenty-second Congress has been much stronger than that of the Twentieth; and its impact is different in kind. The Soviet Union is in a state of moral crisis, which has a far deeper significance than any mere quarrels or rivalries in the Kremlin could possibly have. The crisis affects the nation as a whole. The shock of 1956 was felt inside the Soviet Union mainly by the cadres of the Communist Party, who knew of Khrushchev's secret speech, but not by the mass of the people. The cadres were then dumbfounded and stunned; but for most of them the shock was softened by their sense of relief at having emerged at last from the historic chamber of horrors in which they had lived. The Twenty-second Congress has shaken the masses. All over the Soviet Union they argue about it, sometimes passionately and hotly. Party meetings, which used to be poorly attended and soporific, are now crowded, tense, and often end in uproar. Audiences ply the official agitators with searching questions; and when the agitators try to fob them off with routine answers, they boo and hiss and howl them down.

People feel that even now they are being told only part of the truth about the legacy of Stalinism. They are crying out for the full truth. Their relief at having left behind the terrors of the Stalin era is wearing thin. All the stronger is their irritation at the quasi-Stalinist tricks of official propaganda; at bureaucratic arbitrariness, muddle, and dishonesty; at shortages of consumer goods; and at restrictions of freedom of expression. Moreover, the masses have been allowed a glimpse of the gangster-like *mores* of the men who for so long made up the ruling group and partly still belong to it. This, no less than the revelations about Stalin's misdeeds, has made them acutely conscious of the moral degradation and of the political morass in which Stalinism has left Soviet society, despite all economic and educational progress.

The moral ferment is almost as intense as was the turmoil in Poland and Hungary in 1956, even though it is not so explosive. The more Khrushchev does to pacify it, the more he aggravates it. He has been sacking old Stalinist hands from official jobs *en masse*. But these dismissals make people realize how many of those old hands still remain and how little the changes in personnel mean without further and fundamental changes in the method of government. If the commotion is less explosive than it was in Hungary and Poland, this is so only because it lacks a political focus. In Poland and Hungary anti-Russian nationalism provided the focus; and the people there had not lived under Stalinism long enough to lose the habits of formulating programmes, putting forward slogans, and organizing for independent action. These factors are lacking in Russia. The political moods are therefore more complex and shapeless —a huge, whirling nebula through which no solid outlines can be seen. There are many new ideas in the air, but they fail to crystallize.

Nor are there any large and clear-cut political divisions— only shifting and turgid cross-currents. On the surface there is, of course, the division between those who hanker after the Stalin era and the de-Stalinizers. But on both sides there is a perplexing variety of shades and nuances. And underneath the surface, yet close to it, and cutting across this division, there are the conflicting trends of nationalism and internationalism, egalitarianism and anti-egalitarianism, centralization and de-centralization, conservatism and radicalism, and so on. Over these issues the de-Stalinizers are as much divided as are the epigones of Stalinism. And the shocks, the disillusionments, and the sense that the nation is still being fed with a big half-truth, if no longer with the old big lie—all this generates a sour cynicism which often turns into nihilism.

Yet there are in this ferment many elements that could coalesce into new and great currents of opinion—into something like a new left and a new right (though not in the Western sense of the terms). What is lacking, to judge by many reports from the Soviet Union, are centres of political thought and action capable of producing vital ideas that might inspire people and re-group them. As things are now, critics of official policy grumble a lot and unburden themselves in endless talk, but do not seem to formulate, let alone disseminate, any programmes of action. That such centres and groups and programmes will emerge eventually can, I think, be taken for granted. But the process is desperately slow. And because of this the search for a way out of the impasse tends to be as frantic as it is incoherent. Khrushchev is working hard to bring the turmoil under control, just as he did after the Twentieth Congress. This was the purpose of the latest conference of propagandists and Party organizers in Moscow. But it is far more difficult to stop a *malaise* than it is to crush a revolt. Tanks are of no use. The crisis can be met only with ideas and policies; and Khrushchev somehow seems to have run out of these. He is above all anxious to forestall the formation of any currents of opposition within the Party and without. He is seeking to cut short the nation-wide heart-searching and debating. But he can hardly succeed in this. He cannot stop de-Stalinization; yet he cannot easily proceed with it either. . . .

23 January 1962

5 THE CRISIS OVER THE
CUBAN MISSILES

The great inquest on Cuba is absorbing the attention of the entire communist world. The Soviet withdrawal from the Caribbean is giving rise to as much dispute and division as did the Soviet intervention in Hungary six years ago; and Khrushchev's position is not less affected than it was then. He survived the Hungarian shock, but only after having come under dangerous attack from Molotov and Kaganovich who were almost on the point of overthrowing him in June 1957. He may survive the Cuban shock too; but for the moment he has to sustain a severe trial of strength with his opponents.

His role in the Cuban affair is being hotly debated in Moscow, Peking, and in all communist-ruled capitals. Some may be wondering whether he did not needlessly play with fire in Cuba when he sought to establish a missile base there. But the main question discussed is whether he has proved himself a sober statesman and peacemaker and has averted nuclear catastrophe—or whether he has played the part of an 'appeaser' and allowed himself to be 'blackmailed by American imperialism into surrender'.

The official picture, exhibited in Moscow, shows him, of course, as the saviour of peace; and according to all reports, the Soviet man in the street is inclined to accept this image at its face value. The tributes that Lord Russell has paid to Khrushchev, saying that his presence of mind and magnanimity have saved mankind, undoubtedly made their impression on Soviet opinion. However, this flattering view of Khrushchev is not generally accepted by the politically-minded, especially by the communist hierarchy and the military. It is against attacks from these quarters that the Soviet leader has to defend himself if he is to hold his position. Significantly, in these quarters he is blamed for dismantling the missile base in Cuba rather than for trying to establish it. To many communists he appears as the author of a 'shameful communist Munich', as a kind of 'comrade Chamberlain', who deludes himself and others that by 'selling out' Cuba he has obtained 'peace for our generation'.

The anti-Khrushchevites are, of course, a mixed lot. There is the Molotov-Kaganovich Anti-Party Group, which, though long disgraced, has not yet been expelled from the Party and still has its sympathizers. There are further large groups in the Presidium and the Central Committee who all these years have been strong enough to protect the Anti-Party Group against the threat of further reprisals. In the background there is a formidable *pléiade* of famous marshals and generals more or less at loggerheads with Khrushchev—it is enough to name here Zhukov, Rokossovsky, Sokolovsky, Koniev, Golikov, and Moskalenko. Finally, in the days of the Cuban crisis a political divergency seemed to develop even between Khrushchev and his Ministry of Defence, for while he was holding out the olive branch to President Kennedy, Marshal Malinovsky was mobilizing and alerting the armed forces, especially the nuclear ones.

Outside the U.S.S.R. the Maoists and their sympathizers are

not at all willing to let Khrushchev get away with it, even though the truce between Peking and Moscow, concluded last April, is nominally still in force. Once again the Albanians, who loudly denounce the Khrushchevite 'betrayal of Cuba', express only what the Maoists and their friends have been saying in private. The Albanians have not been the only ones to re-open fire. It is now known that at the session of the Central Committee of the Bulgarian Party, which was held prior to the Twenty-second Congress, a large faction headed by Anton Yugov, the Prime Minister, came out openly against the 'Cuban surrender' and intended to carry the attack into the congress. Khrushchev was so alarmed that he struck back at once and got his critics expelled from the Central Committee overnight. However, expulsion now does not mean what it did in the Stalin era: those expelled are not necessarily reduced to political impotence; and the pro-Chinese faction has its adherents in most other East European Communist Parties, especially in Czechoslovakia and East Germany.

The latest recruit to the anti-Khrushchevite camp is Fidel Castro himself. He has been enraged to find himself used as a mere pawn and to hear Moscow propose a United Nations inspection of Cuba without even consulting Havana about it. His anger with Khrushchev might not matter much, especially in view of Cuba's continued economic dependence on Soviet aid. But it is within Castro's power to obstruct and render ineffective the Khrushchev-Kennedy agreement. Moreover, Soviet propaganda has over the last two years boosted Castro and assiduously built him up into the heroic figure of the Latin American revolution. If he were now to join Enver Hoxha in open rebellion—and the popular mood in Cuba may push him that way—Khrushchev would indeed be greatly embarrassed.

Thus the Soviet leader has been on the defensive *vis-à-vis* his communist critics as well as *vis-à-vis* President Kennedy. The argument which he is advancing in self-justification comes to this: he decided to set up the missile base in Cuba at Fidel Castro's request conveyed to him by Ché Guevara, the Cuban Minister, who came to Moscow in September. The Cubans were then in a panic, convinced that the Pentagon was bent on invading their country; and they asked for help. Khrushchev was prepared to come out with a statement that the U.S.S.R.

would treat an American invasion of Cuba as a *casus belli*. But the Cubans were not satisfied with this, saying that he had so many times made that statement and so many times watered it down that if he merely repeated it the American administration would not take it seriously. Only a visible and conspicuous token of Soviet readiness to go to war over Cuba, they held, could still deter an American invasion. The missile base was to be that deterrent. It lay in the nature of this project that the base should not be camouflaged, but that it should, on the contrary, be made to catch the American eye, and to catch it as soon as possible.

Khrushchev accepted the Cuban request and the underlying view of the situation. He did not, he claims, seek in Cuba to change the world balance of nuclear power; for he holds that the striking power of Soviet intercontinental missiles is enough to lay waste the U.S.A. and that it does not matter how many times over you are able to kill your enemy. It may be that the chiefs of the Soviet nuclear and missile forces did not quite share this view and attached greater operational value to the Cuban base. Whatever differences there may have been, the military and the Party Presidium agreed to meet the Cuban request. (In the Presidium Mikoyan alone seems to have had misgivings.) In taking the decision to install the base, Khrushchev and his advisers assumed that on 'discovering' it, Washington would react with an outburst of indignation; and that this would lead to a temporary aggravation of the cold war, but to nothing worse. They hoped that in the end Washington would have to bow to the accomplished fact and accept the presence of Soviet nuclear arms in Cuba; that this would free Castro from the threat of invasion, give the U.S.S.R. an enormous gain in prestige and propaganda, and weaken Washington's influence, thus stimulating the 'anti-imperialist revolution' throughout Latin America.

The miscalculation, it appears, was as incredibly and monumentally simple as this: neither Khrushchev nor Castro foresaw that the missile base, far from deterring an American invasion, would make the threat of the invasion real and imminent. This accounts for Khrushchev's behaviour in the critical week. In the first days of the crisis, even after President Kennedy had proclaimed the blockade of Cuba, Khrushchev still played his poker game coolly on the blissful assumption that his bluff would not be called. Not until 26 October did he suddenly realize that the U.S. was ready for the invasion and that the U.S.S.R. might be confronted with the stark choice between nuclear world war and acquiescence in the American occupation of Cuba. 'Not days but hours were left to us to forestall this danger', says Khrushchev to prove that he had to make his *volte-face* with the speed that the situation required; and that he had to order the dismantling of the base and accept all President Kennedy's conditions at once without consulting anyone, not even Castro. In these conditions he had to content himself with President Kennedy's pledge that there would be no invasion of Cuba.

When assessing the crisis Khrushchev and his supporters can point to the Presidential pledge as Cuba's and Russia's 'concrete gain'. The manoeuvre with the missile base, so they argue, has after all achieved its minimum objective: it has lifted the threat of invasion from Cuba. A wider and more imponderable gain is supposed to consist in showing the world how resolutely Moscow stands for peace, even if this involves considerable concessions and sacrifices. The anti-Khrushchevites reply that President Kennedy's pledge to respect Cuba's integrity is worth no more than were Hitler's assurances to respect the independence of Czechoslovakia. If anything, they argue, Khrushchev's surrender has encouraged the Pentagon to invade Cuba, even if for tactical reasons the invasion is slightly postponed. Khrushchev has made the Soviet deterrent quite incredible in the eyes of the West, say his critics. In effect he has strengthened the hands of those in NATO who wish to deal with the Soviet bloc only from positions of strength and who assume that Moscow may be forced to yield in other sectors too, perhaps even on Berlin. Khrushchev's critics conclude, that his Cuban 'capitulation', therefore, far from saving the peace has only rendered the threat of war more acute.

Both Khrushchevites and anti-Khrushchevites are now watching tensely the evolution of Washington's policy towards Cuba. This is going to be the test in the light of which the communist world will judge Khrushchev's performance in the Cuban crisis.

8 November 1962

The year 1962 has been a critical one for the Soviet government. For the first time in fifteen years or so there has been no substantial improvement in the standard of living. The food consumption curve has not moved upwards this year. Departing from the post-war practice of periodic reductions in prices of consumer goods, the government has raised the prices of meat and butter by thirty per cent. A rise of this order might enrage consumers in any country; and it has strained Soviet tempers. It brought home to many city dwellers the unpleasant fact that even in this age of Sputniks, they must go on living on an inferior bread-potato-and-cabbage diet. The high meat and butter prices, they were told, would enable the collective farmers to invest more money in machinery and fertilizers and so ultimately to increase the output of high quality food. In the meantime, however, the industrial worker has to finance the further development of farming out of his own pocket.

The situation has not been much better with regard to durable consumer goods. Housing remains scarce, for although much building is going on, the demand for housing is still greatly outstripping supply. The same is true of household goods, especially furniture, good quality clothing, shoes, etc. For the first time since the war the government has also failed to carry out a promised cut in taxation, or rather to abolish direct taxation for some of the lower income groups. (The abolition of such taxation had been much advertised as one of the features of the 'transition from socialism to communism'.) ... The key to any solution of Soviet economic troubles lies in an easing of the burden of armaments and Soviet opinion is more or less aware of this. Hence its pacifist mood and desire for some conciliation between East and West. To the Soviet man in the street peaceful coexistence is not merely the official slogan but much more than that—the promise of security and plenty. No wonder that Soviet opinion has received the peaceful settlement of the Cuban crisis with undisguised relief, hoping that this settlement will be followed by definite moves towards a wider detente.

However, as the Caribbean conflict recedes, the sense of

relief is tempered by a realization that the Soviet Union has suffered a severe setback and humiliation, that the wider detente may be as elusive as ever, and that Khrushchev's policy over Cuba may not have been quite as blameless and wise as the propagandists make it out to be. Just now many Russians must be pricking up their ears to what Khrushchev's foreign critics are saying about this; and for the first time they have been told explicitly that the critics are the Chinese and not just the Albanians. No doubt many dislike and distrust the Chinese, and for some time Party agitators and inspired gossip have subtly suggested that the Chinese are highly troublesome allies and that Mao Tse-tung may turn out to be as evil a spirit as Trotsky. On the other hand, the prospect of a break between Russia and her only great ally cannot fail to arouse uneasiness; and some may wonder whether all the blame for the Russo-Chinese 'misunderstandings' should be laid at the Chinese door.

Although Soviet newspapers do not reproduce the Chinese argument, some of it undoubtedly reaches the politically-minded in Moscow and elsewhere in the Soviet Union and has its effect. It should be said that the Chinese are now taking great care to prove that they are not the wild men, firebrands, and dogmatists their communist opponents portray them as. It is they, on the contrary, who now charge Khrushchev with being not merely an appeaser and defeatist, but also a 'reckless adventurer'. What they say now about Cuba, for instance, makes much more sense than their earlier pronouncements or Albanian vituperation. 'It is not China', the quotation is from Peking's *The People's Daily*, 'that has ever demanded that a nuclear missile base should be established in Cuba; and it is not China that has ever been opposed to the withdrawal of offensive weapons from that country.' The paper then goes on to say that 'some people . . . have been guilty of a double error, first of the error of recklessness because they use nuclear weapons as a means of retaliation or deterrence, which socialist countries have no need to do at all; and then of the error of defeatism when, veering from one extreme to another, they succumb to the imperialists' atomic blackmail and rush to capitulate'. This is a dangerous attack on Khrushchev's position, for the question is here openly raised, and raised for the first time within the communist camp, why and with what purpose in mind the Soviet leader had sent missiles to Cuba. Peking is attacking him not merely for 'appeasement' but, in the first place, for muddleheadedness and incompetence.

Khrushchev is seeking to strengthen his hands by a *rapprochement* with Yugoslavia. Nothing, indeed, could provide a more ironical comment on the schism between Maoism and Khrushchevism than did the rapturous ovations with which President Tito was welcomed in Moscow while Peking was heaping on him its most violent invective and abuse. The Yugoslav leader was accorded the privilege, not previously granted to any foreigner, of being invited to address the Supreme Soviet; and he used the rostrum of the Soviet to endorse fully, and perhaps with somewhat spurious ardour, Khrushchev's foreign policy and in particular his handling of the Cuban affair.

Thus something like a reversal of alliances is taking place within the communist camp. Before the eyes of the Supreme Soviet Khrushchev in effect tore up the solemn declarations of principle which eighty-one Communist Parties adopted at the Moscow Conference in 1960. These declarations, endorsed by all except the Yugoslavs, condemned and rejected the conflicting heresies of revisionism and dogmatism; but they also proclaimed the heresy of revisionism to be the more dangerous of the two and therefore deserving to be combatted with more uncompromising hostility. For about five years this seemed to be the canon of orthodoxy, common to both Khrushchev and Mao. Khrushchev now appears to have renounced the canon. Beaming at President Tito, he told the Supreme Soviet that the Yugoslav comrades had so markedly mended their ways that the danger of revisionism had almost vanished and that dogmatism had become the chief menace. As if to leave no doubt whom he had in mind, he ridiculed the wiseacres who were speaking about 'the paper tiger of American imperialism' and were forgetting that the tiger had 'nuclear teeth'—Khrushchev's audience knew, of course, that the author of the notorious metaphor was none other than Mao himself.

The realignment in the communist camp may be described as an attempt to replace the 'centre-left' coalition (i.e. the Khrushchev-Mao combination), which ideologically ruled the camp for these last five years, by a 'centre-right' coalition. The centre-left coalition was formed to maintain a common front against Yugoslavia and diverse brands of Titoism in other countries. The centre-right coalition is to keep at bay Maoism and its sympathizers. . . . Khrushchev evidently hopes to gain from this realignment important diplomatic advantages. He is convinced that his ideological alliance with Mao has hitherto severely limited his own freedom of diplomatic manoeuvre. He lets it be understood that Mao has ever since 1957 exercised the sort of a veto on his, Khrushchev's, foreign policy that Molotov and Kaganovich had exercised up to 1957.

To some extent this is true. The Chinese did in fact press Khrushchev to take up a more 'militant' attitude than he was willing to adopt during the crises in Iraq and the Lebanon in 1958–59. They made him the target of their attacks during his visits to France and the United States in 1959, when he sought to win the goodwill of de Gaulle and Eisenhower. They then used the U-2 incident to discredit the hopes he had placed on his Camp David talks with Eisenhower. To some extent, probably unwittingly, they provoked him into disrupting the Paris summit meeting in April 1960. And now they have spoken up once more against Khrushchevite 'appeasement'. Khrushchev is therefore impatient to free himself from the pressure of Chinese censoriousness. He believes that with the realignment within the communist camp he will be able to afford a more elastic and conciliatory line in his foreign policy; and that this may enable him to ease the burden of the arms' race and to earn thereby the confidence and the gratitude of the Soviet people. The decisive question is, of course, whether events will justify this belief and its underlying assumption. . . .

18 December 1962

5 THE SOVIET UNION ENTERS
THE SECOND DECADE AFTER
STALIN

The tenth anniversary of Stalin's death might be described as one of history's ironies. In the West press, radio, and television marked the occasion with a great profusion of comments on the enigma of Stalinism and the issues posed by de-Stalinization. In the U.S.S.R. oblivion and silence seemed to envelop the demi-god who had ruled the country for three decades. . . . The oblivion, however, was more apparent than real. Stalin is still weighing on Russia's memory; and in a sense he does so more than ever. The silence about him—so complete, so deliberate, so studious—testifies to a mental wrestling and an inner tension. More than ever Russia is obsessed by those nightmares of her recent past from which she is escaping. She is perhaps still too close to them to look back steadily, with eyes quite open. There is no doubt now about the reality of the de-Stalinization. But the job has so far been only half done; and it may be far more difficult for Russians to assess the record than it is for us in the West. . . .

As one surveys this first post-Stalin decade one is struck by a crucial imbalance between its various developments. As an industrial power, and as one of the world's leading technological forces, the Soviet Union has since 1953 advanced far more rapidly and decisively than one could have foretold even in a daring prognostication. The steady improvement in the Soviet standard of living, on the other hand, though remarkable, has not been so extraordinary as to surpass expectation. The main disproportion, however, appears between the material and the moral-political aspects of the post-Stalin years. True enough, the moral destitution in which Soviet society emerged from the Stalin era now also belongs to the past. The terror of an uncontrollable political police no longer pervades the air of the U.S.S.R. The huge concentration camps have been disbanded. The ideological Inquisition and the continuous witch-hunts have ceased. All this has happened not, as in post-Nazi Germany, under blows from *without*, under the impact of military defeat and foreign invasion, but under impulses which have come from *within* Soviet society itself, whose own striving for sanity and freedom has been strong and persistent enough to force such changes. Ten years ago it was an axiom with our political 'scientists' and moralists that no popular aspirations and pressures could ever prevail against any monolithic totalitarianism. To the Soviet people belongs the honour of having given the lie to that 'axiom'.

Yet it remains a fact that the moral-political evolution of the post-Stalinist Soviet Union has been lagging behind its economic growth. Soviet society is still far from having gained control of its political destiny—much further indeed than one hoped it would be ten years after Stalin's death. Despite limited freedom of debate in various fields of intellectual activity, and despite all the rebellious effervescence in literature, there is still no genuine freedom of expression and association. Khrushchev is the single leader; and even if he is not the tyrant and autocrat that Stalin was, he stands above all criticism, above truth, and above the law; and his word is both truth and law. The official outlook is still 'monolithic', even if the monolith is no more than a worn and battered façade. The deadweight of Stalinism has proved much heavier in politics than in any other sphere.

There is hardly any doubt about the basic cause of this. A nation that lived for over three decades under the weight of a monolithic orthodoxy and lost the habits of forming and expressing its political views independently, and of setting up its autonomous organizations, re-acquires these habits only slowly or by painful fits and starts. Only with great difficulty is Soviet political thinking recovering from the shapelessness and paralysis in which Stalinism left it; and only by slow degrees do the forward-looking elements of the nation gain the confidence and ability to formulate and raise demands and to draw together for any form of political action. The shocks of de-Stalinization have had a double effect: by their suddenness and apparent lack of clear motivation they have done much to confuse minds, even while they have stirred and stimulated political thought. In any case, nothing in the whole legacy of Stalinism has been as hard to overcome as the political atomization of society.

But time is doing its work; and the tempo of change is quickening in this respect too. The end of the first post-Stalin decade saw the Soviet Union debating many hitherto forbidden themes: the concentration camps, the extermination by Stalin of the oppositions, and the terrors of his collectivization. More and more taboos are subjected to desecration; and the urge for independent expression and organization is making itself felt overwhelmingly in the young generation. Heresies and non-conformist ideas may still be under an official ban; but the popular political instinct finds its ways to obviate any ban. In Moscow, Leningrad, Kiev, and many other cities, huge audiences, consisting sometimes of ten or fifteen thousand people, applaud ardently the Yevtushenkos and Voznessenskys, the young rebellious poets who confront officialdom with a distinctly political defiance. The significance of these events is not merely literary. These poetic meetings are substitutes for political debating clubs and for meetings of a quite different kind; and the re-awakened political passion of the people will not content itself with substitutes for long. In coming years the political meeting, which now exists only as a memory of the early 1920s or of 1917, will once again become a spectacular feature of public life; and not official spokesmen, nor even rebellious poets, will take the platform but genuine mouthpieces of popular aspirations.

Is this perhaps too sanguine a view of the future? It is now commonly agreed that what made a continuation of Stalinism impossible after 1953 was the modernization, and especially the intensive urbanization and education, of Soviet society. The needs of the new industrialized Russia had become incompatible with the backward and bizarre orthodoxy of Stalinism. But if that is true then the further, impressive progress which the Soviet Union has achieved since Stalin is going to necessitate many changes far wider in scope and far deeper than those that have taken place so far. During the first post-Stalin decade the urban population of the Soviet Union has grown from about eighty-two million people to nearly one hundred and fifteen million, that is from forty-three to fifty-two per cent of the total population. The educational advance has been even more sensational. In the early 1950s only one Soviet worker in ten had more than an elementary education; now nearly five industrial workers in ten have graduated from secondary schools. In 1953 only about fifty per cent of the intelligentsia and the white collar workers had secondary or university education; now the proportion is over ninety per cent. The number of men and women with academic degrees has doubled. About ten million people are employed in education, science, and medicine; altogether twenty-three million are occupied in the professions and as white collar workers— they form about one quarter of all those who are gainfully occupied.

The momentum of these latest changes in the structure and outlook of Soviet society will presently make itself felt. If after 1953 a relatively small minority of the people, consisting of the intelligentsia and educated workers, was strong enough to compel the ruling group to embark willy-nilly upon the road of de-Stalinization, then how much more powerful must be the pressures for further reform and progress which are coming from the far more numerous, more self-reliant, and better educated ranks of the new intelligentsia and the new working class! If Stalinism was too grotesquely archaic to survive in the Soviet Union of the past decade, Khrushchevism will turn out to be too primitive, backward, and outmoded for the Soviet Union of the coming decade. . . .

Western observers of the Soviet scene are often struck by what they describe as the gradual Americanization of the Soviet way of life. They notice a general preoccupation with material comfort, a weariness with ideology and a craving for entertainment, widespread profiteering and blackmarketing, cynicism and pessimism among the young, especially among the Soviet beatniks, who look sometimes like real cousins of their Western counterparts. These observers conclude that Soviet society, or at least its upper strata, are undergoing a process of *embourgeoisement*; and they express the hope that as the Soviet Union takes its place among the 'have-nations' (while China remains a 'have-not'), its revolutionary dynamism will subside, and then a genuine *rapprochement* and coexistence between East and West may become possible. This view seems to me erroneous. It contains a grain of truth, but no more. The general preoccupation with material comfort is real enough; and so (after half a century of wars, revolutions, and Stalinist terror) is the longing for a relaxed, easy-going life. Yet, the so-called Americanization is rather superficial and transient (although it is connected to some extent with the Soviet ambition to catch up with the U.S.A. industrially). The little profiteer, the beatnik, the *stilyaga*, and the enthusiastic admirer of the latest Western pop song and dance, who so quickly catch the eye of the Western visitor—all of these are marginal characters. The structure of society remains essentially dynamic and revolutionary. The basic elements of urban Russia, especially the workers, are recapturing the egalitarianism of the early years of the Revolution, while the peasantry, with its crippled individualism, is politically inert and declining. Even the privileged managerial groups have had to bow to the resurgent egalitarianism of the masses. All this is somehow incompatible with genuine 'Americanization'. One Western observer put the issue in a nutshell by saying that whereas in the West people normally try to keep *up* with the Joneses, in the Soviet Union the members of the privileged groups have to keep *down* with the Joneses, that is they have to respect and appease the egalitarian aspirations of the 'lower classes'. This testifies to a renascence of the revolutionary ethos and puts narrow limits to any *embourgeoisement*.

Over wide areas of social and political life, the open and latent conflict between the acquisitiveness of the few and the egalitarianism of the many is developing into a dominant factor, which is likely to determine the alignments and divisions of the coming period. One may say that a new Left and a new Right are emerging, although it may take years before they find shape and crystallize. To the extent to which both right and left accept the post-capitalist order of society, this new alignment can have little, if anything, in common with the party-political patterns of the West. The Soviet right stands for the preservation of as much managerial privilege as possible and for bureaucratic control of the body politic; whereas the new left is bound to struggle for more equality and more freedom. The centre group, for which Khrushchev speaks, has tried to act as umpire. The strength of this centre group so far has consisted in its ability to keep a relative and unstable balance between right and left, a balance made possible by the fact that while the right, associated as it is with the die-hards of Stalinism, has been discredited, the left has not yet gathered its strength and become articulate. But this state of affairs is not likely to last. The right is fighting losing battles and is in retreat, while the left will probably acquire enough weight to alter radically the political balance and to tear the ground from under the feet of the Khrushchevite (or post-Khrushchevite) centre.

Thus the prospect, as I see it, is not one of a nation which, overcoming material scarcity, settles into bourgeois moderation —it is rather of an increasingly dynamic society to which its growing wealth may give fresh stimuli for wreaking new revolutionary changes in its own midst and in its environment. Generally speaking, it is an historical half-truth, if not a complete *contre-verité*, that the 'have-nations' are always inclined to undisturbed enjoyment of satiety or to contentment and moderation. This has certainly not been true of the bourgeois West, where the wealthy and the powerful have, as a rule, shown the greatest urge to accumulate more wealth and more power. (Were the men who once built the British Empire 'have-nots'? And is the present United States a model of political self-restraint and moderation?) In the Soviet Union the accumulation of wealth and the growth of national self-confidence are coinciding with the re-emergence of radical-revolutionary currents of thought, which are bound to have their impact on Soviet foreign policy as well.

This is not to suggest that a more egalitarian or socialist-minded Soviet Union will seek war or will be more inclined to risk it. But it will be eager to reassert its basic antagonism to the bourgeois West. It will probably be less willing to drive power-political bargains in disregard of communist principle or at the expense of foreign revolutionary movements, bargains such as Stalin once drove with Hitler and Churchill and Roosevelt, and as Khrushchev has tried to strike with Eisenhower and Kennedy. The post-Khrushchev leadership is likely to seek to regain that uninhibited revolutionary initiative which Lenin and Trotsky once tried to exercise in the international field and which Russia's poverty and isolation did not allow them to take. Moscow will still proclaim that the 'peaceful coexistence of opposed social systems' is its major objective; but it will not be prepared to make ideological concessions in order to secure coexistence. This assessment of the future trend seems to me more realistic than hopes for a *rapprochement* between East and West based on the dubious prospect of the *embourgeoisement* of the Soviet Union.

In this context the Chinese challenge to Khrushchevism may acquire new significance. The Chinese are evidently banking on the radicalization of the social and political atmosphere in the U.S.S.R. Although their chances against Khrushchev are not at all promising at present, Mao and his men may be acting on a long-term calculation and in the hope that Soviet policy is bound to evolve in their direction. They may be right in this, although even if Soviet policy were to move closer to Maoism over the years, it would still reflect different national realities and would probably speak a different language. Mao's crude and coarse radicalism expresses China's poverty and backwardness and the mood of a state which the West has persisted in treating as an outlaw and which, in return, views the West not merely with contempt and hatred but with incomprehension. The new Russian radicalism, when it comes to the top, is likely to prove far more educated, intelligent, and subtle, far more strongly inspired by the tradition of classical Marxism, and far closer in touch with the complex realities of the second half of this century.

The long-term prospect outlined here seems to provide a frame also for the Russo-Chinese controversy. In the next few years that controversy is almost certain to grow in sharpness and to lead to dramatic crises—it may even assume the bitterness that the Soviet-Yugoslav feud had under Stalin. But the long-term trend in the Soviet Union may well render this controversy just as pointless as the Soviet-Yugoslav feud became after Stalin; and then the two communist giants may re-unite once again.

Finally, the condition in which the West finds itself during the middle and late 1960s will be of decisive importance for the developments in the communist world. If the West succeeds, by and large, in maintaining its economic prosperity, the new communist radicalism will hardly be able to overlap strongly into the West. Its playground would then remain more or less confined to Asia, Africa, and Latin America—this would in any case be a vast playground. But if the West were to be hit by deep slumps and mass unemployment, the second post-Stalin decade may see communism carrying the struggle back into its enemy's camp and throwing all its immensely enlarged resources into an onslaught on the social order of the West.

6 March 1963

14
Khrushchev's Troubles Increase

In 1963 and 1964 Russia encountered increasing difficulties, both foreign and domestic, and the failure of government policies, associated as they were with Khrushchev, led to his downfall in October 1964. Relations with China and East Europe got worse; there was no compensatory improvement in Russo-American affairs; at home, the Anti-Party Group attempted a comeback; and the crisis in agriculture increased popular and governmental discontent.

In 1963 the Sino-Soviet dispute came into the open. After much discussion, it was agreed to hold bilateral talks in Moscow but these were held in unfavourable circumstances. On 14 June the Chinese had sent the Russians a letter entitled 'A Proposal Concerning the General Line of the International Communist Movement' in which they set out twenty-five theses on communist strategy. This letter was a systematic restatement of known Chinese positions but the Russians refused to publish it and expelled five Chinese who distributed copies of it inside the Soviet Union. The Russians also exacerbated Chinese feelings by holding disarmament talks in Moscow while the bilateral talks were taking place. The bilateral talks began on 5 July but broke up inconclusively a fortnight later; the Chinese delegates, Teng Hsiao-ping and Peng Chen, went home. Five days later, the Nuclear Test Ban Treaty was initialled in Moscow by the representatives of Britain, the United States, and the Soviet Union. This treaty banned all nuclear testing apart from tests held underground. The Chinese and the French refused to sign it; and on 31 July Peking denounced it as a 'dirty fraud', and as an attempt by the U.S. and Russia to keep their nuclear monopoly. By signing it, the Chinese argued, Russia had betrayed the socialist camp. They also revealed that in 1959 the Russians had unilaterally broken a Sino-Soviet agreement on the sharing of nuclear technology.

Khrushchev's troubles increased: the virgin lands project, which had been started in 1954 and later expanded by Khrushchev, proved no solution to Russia's agricultural crisis; nor did the Test Ban Treaty open the way to an East-West detente. The Geneva disarmament talks were deadlocked by conflict over the proposed NATO Multilateral Force and the implications of West German membership of it; this impasse prevented agreement on the logical sequence of the Test Ban Treaty, a treaty on non-proliferation.

In January 1964 the Chinese made important diplomatic progress: they were recognized by France and Chou En-lai made a successful tour around Africa. It seemed at the time as if China was about to break out of her diplomatic isolation. In February Suslov presented a report to the Central Committee of the Soviet Party on the state of Sino-Soviet relations. He announced that Molotov, Malenkov, and Kaganovich had been expelled from the Party for conspiring with the Chinese, whom he accused of sabotaging Russia's attempts to prevent world war, of splitting the international communist movement, and of relying on armed risings rather than mass action to achieve revolution. The Russians were trying to convene another international communist conference to isolate the Chinese, but this was opposed not only by the Chinese and their allies but also by the Romanian and Italian Parties who did not want to finalize the break. The Romanians had been the only East European Party, apart from the Albanians, to publish the twenty-five-point Chinese letter and in March 1964 they sent a mission to Peking to mediate between the two conflicting Parties. This attempt was a failure. In April the Central Committee of the Romanian Party issued an open attack on Khrushchev's project for a joint planning body in Comecon: this proposal, they said, was 'not in keeping with the principles which underlie the relations between socialist countries'.

In spite of all this opposition the Russians arranged for the conference to be held in Moscow in December. The Chinese refused to come and told the Russians: 'the day your so-called conference takes place will be the day you step into your grave'. However, Khrushchev's fall postponed the conference and when it finally met in March 1965 it was a quiet and unimportant affair.

The last months of Khrushchev's rule were also marked by an escalation of the war in Vietnam. The Americans claimed that North Vietnamese torpedo boats had attacked their warships in the Gulf of Tonking on 2 and 4 August; and in reply they bombed North Vietnamese naval installations on 5 August. The U.S. Congress also passed a resolution enabling the President to increase the U.S. military commitment in Vietnam. The North Vietnamese reply was that the first incident had occurred while the U.S. destroyer *Maddox* was within North Vietnamese territorial waters, and that the second one had been invented by the American authorities. At Congressional hearings held in January 1968 witnesses cast considerable doubt on the validity of the American version of this incident.

1 THE COLLAPSE OF SINO-SOVIET TALKS

Over the last few years the Russians and the Chinese have agreed to disagree. Now they are evidently unable to agree even on this. Both sides profess that they aim at restoring their partnership, but both have done all they could to make divorce inescapable. In their 'Twenty-five Points' letter to the Soviet Central Committee the Chinese presented an ideological ultimatum which they knew the Russians could not accept. Khrushchev has refused to publish the letter and, rejecting it as slanderous, has prepared communist opinion for the storm about to break. At the International Congress of Women, just held in the Soviet capital, the division of the communist movement into right and left wings and a centre was openly revealed; and the Amazons of the right and the centre joined in a furious attack on their Chinese sisters. The congress witnessed extraordinary demonstrations of Chinese zealotry and repeated explosions of Russian hostility and hatred. All this was happening to the accompaniment of windows being smashed at the Chinese Embassy; and although the Soviet foreign office has apologized for this, it is clear that someone in Moscow was trying to unleash popular anger against the Maoists. Chinese diplomats and students have been expelled from the U.S.S.R. because they had distributed the subversive 'Twenty-five Points'. After all these public rows and quarrels what compromise can there still be? Even if the conference were to end with some more mildly-worded communiqué, the antagonism will remain and will grow more and more bitter.

It is pointless to compare this breach with the rupture between Stalin and Tito or between Khrushchev and Enver Hoxha. Other events in revolutionary history are brought to one's mind: the original split between Bolsheviks and Mensheviks in 1903; the collapse of the Second International in 1914; and the great feud between Trotsky and Stalin. But in the first case the schism occurred between two small circles of powerless and unknown emigré revolutionaries; in the second no constituted governments were directly involved; and, finally,

Trotsky, when he challenged Stalin, was a 'prophet unarmed' who opposed force only with ideas. Now two armed prophets confront one another, and two churches, two priesthoods, two great powers. Because of its immense scale and incalculable consequences the conflict is more directly comparable to the schism between Eastern and Western Christianity.

Paradoxically, the closer the breach, the more confused become the ostensibly ideological reasons for it. At the earlier stages of the controversy the issues seemed clear-cut and the positions well defined. Khrushchev spoke about peaceful co-existence between East and West with exuberant optimism, while Peking denied the very possibility of it. Khrushchev dwelt on the obsolescence of Lenin's theory of imperialism and of Lenin's conclusion that war, world war, is the inevitable concomitant of monopoly capitalism. The Chinese assiduously upheld the validity of every word Lenin had uttered on the subject. Khrushchev, Mikoyan, Togliatti, and Thorez, advocated the 'parliamentary road to socialism' for 'various countries'—peaceful revolution without bloodshed and civil war. Mao denounced this as new-fangled revisionism and renunciation of the revolutionary programme of communism. Moscow backed Nasser, Kassem, Sukarno, and other 'bourgeois' leaders of the anti-imperialist movement regardless of their anti-communism; Khrushchev even induced the communists of Iraq, India, and Indonesia, to give up any independent bid for power. The Chinese saw in this a betrayal of revolution. There were other secondary or temporary differences, for instance over the rural communes which the Chinese set up and which the Russians regarded as hopeless essays in Utopia.

With the progress of the controversy, however, the issues have become blurred. Each of the disputants has gradually given up his initial dogmatic sharpness; each has mixed water with his heady wine. Khrushchev, realizing the vulnerability of his frank revisionism, has become more wary, while Mao has been anxious to deprive him of any tactical advantage he was deriving from Peking's ultra-leftism. And so Khrushchev, while still preaching peaceful coexistence in diplomacy, politics, and trade, has opened fire against 'peaceful coexistence' in the sphere of ideology; and he points out that what he primarily seeks to promote through peaceful coexistence is world communism. He no longer dares to drop even a hint about Lenin's obsolescence and avoids mentioning the peaceful parliamentary road to socialism. Mao, on the other hand, no longer denies that peaceful coexistence with capitalism can be the legitimate pursuit of any communist government, provided that peaceful coexistence is not allowed to obstruct world revolution (and to this Khrushchev's plain answer is that it is not allowed to do so). Nor does Mao deny that the communists of one country or another may take a peaceful road to socialism—he adds however that this can be only an exception not the rule (a proposition which Moscow's ideologists dare not reject). Peking also accepts communist alliances with the 'bourgeois leaders of the anti-imperialist movements' in Asia and Africa.

Thus, on the face of it, the differences appear to have narrowed quite considerably or to have changed into a mere difference of emphasis. Khrushchev and his men argue: 'Of course, we must work for the ultimate victory of communism the world over; but let us do all we can to avoid world war and secure peaceful coexistence'. Mao and his followers reply: 'No doubt, we should avoid world war and work for peaceful coexistence; but world revolution must remain our prime objective'. Yet, the more similar and symmetrical the form of words, the more striking are the contrasts in articulation and emphasis; and the narrower the gap between the formulas, the wider the gulf between the disputants, and the more irrational and violent the dispute.

Anyone familiar with the great schisms in history will recognize here the strange situation, when the unity of a church or a political creed breaks down precisely at the moment when on formal dogmatic grounds it seems to be restored. Behind the trappings of doctrine and dogma are concealed the real issues of the conflict; and the deeper they are hidden the greater their explosiveness.

In their 'Twenty-five Points' the Chinese have for the first time bluntly and irrevocably repudiated Moscow's leadership of the socialist camp. That leadership, they say, was legitimate as long as the U.S.S.R. was the only victorious communist power, the sole country building socialism, the only fortress of proletarian revolution. Now, when thirteen countries (not counting Yugoslavia, of course) are under communist rule no one is entitled to impose his interest, will, or view on the others; the interest of the socialist camp as a whole must prevail. Yet, after the Twentieth Congress of the Soviet Communist Party and later, when Khrushchev was rather timid about reasserting the Soviet claim to leadership and Togliatti spoke of a 'polycentric' communist movement, it was the Chinese who urged and prodded Moscow to re-impose its supremacy on world communism and to exercise it with determination. On this point they have thus completely reversed their attitude. Henceforth, they say, Moscow must learn to subordinate itself to the 'camp as a whole'. But who is to determine where the interest of the camp lies at any particular moment? Who is to formulate the joint policy of the 'thirteen socialist countries'? Obviously each of the great antagonists identifies himself with the camp as a whole. Mao no less than Khrushchev might well say, paraphrasing the famous French monarch, '*Le camp c'est moi*'.

This is, however, not just a narrow rivalry of men hungry for power. Each of the contestants wants to lead the camp in a different direction and in a different spirit. To some extent we are confronted here with a division between the haves and the have-nots within the communist world, between those who have a stake in the preservation of the international *status quo* and those who want to overthrow it. Maoism proclaims the need for a new crusade of international communism. It holds that the net effect of Khrushchev's policies has been to break or brake the expansive momentum of communism, and that communism would have been much more advanced in Asia, Africa, Latin America, and perhaps even in Western Europe, if Moscow had not imposed on it moderate tactics designed to appease the West. Mao is convinced that without Khrushchev's meddling, Iraq at least would now have been under communist control, and India might already have been divided, as China was in the 1930s and up to 1948, between areas ruled by a bourgeois government and Red provinces. He does not propose that either Russia or China should go to war in order to further communism abroad, but that they should not discourage foreign communists from waging their class wars and that they should not be afraid of helping them morally and materially. He argues that the spread of communism, far from provoking the United States and NATO to world war, would weaken the imperialists and reduce their capacity for global counteraction.

It is clear enough that Khrushchev has no heart for any communist crusade. He rejects the idea as a desperate gamble. He has too much to lose. He holds that the revolutionary tide which followed the Second World War has ebbed away and that he acts in communism's best interest when he urges his comrades to exercise prudence and moderation. In theory he does not give up the hope for world revolution—has he not told the American capitalists: 'We shall bury you' and 'Your grandchildren will live under communism'? But he prefers to leave the matter precisely to the grandchildren. In the meantime he strives, as Stalin did between the two world wars, to gain a long respite, during which the Soviet Union and its associates can concentrate on economic development, on raising living standards, and on educational progress. To obtain these objectives he wishes to parley with the West, to reduce tensions, to slow down the armament race, to come to terms over partial issues, etc.

In this respect Khrushchev, despite his domestic de-Stalinization, is in fact pursuing the policy that Stalin followed at the time of the controversy with Trotsky. Stalin proclaimed socialism in one country and denounced Trotsky as a fomentor of permanent revolution. Khrushchev similarly denounces Mao Tse-tung (who otherwise has so few common features with Trotsky); and he declares himself to be content with socialism in one third of the world for the foreseeable future. . . .

In the long run the effect of the schism on the communist movement may be more important than the immediate diplomatic repercussions. The whole movement is in flux, as it has never been before. Indeed, an earthquake is shaking it, the full force of which was not foreseen in Moscow. Khrushchev seems to have imagined that, despite de-Stalinization, he could, like Stalin, break every communist heresy, or at least render it harmless, especially in the countries which depend on Soviet economic aid. Yet Stalin's strength *vis-à-vis* the heresies of his time consisted primarily in a moral factor: his regime represented the first and only victorious communist revolution; and so to communists everywhere their allegiance to their Party was identical with loyalty to the Russian revolution and with subservience to Stalinism. For any communist to oppose Stalin meant to cut himself off from his own Party and from the International. The 'heretics' of today are not confronted by any such excruciating dilemma. No anathema pronounced by Khrushchev, or by Mao, can now deny the heretic access to the communist world and isolate him morally. Ejected from one 'Church' he will find refuge in the rival 'Church', where he will be received with open arms as the true believer; he may even choose for himself an independent position in the no-man's-land between the two major Establishments. This new freedom of choice, which events have suddenly bestowed on communists, is already causing rapid shifts and startling realignments, which until quite recently seemed inconceivable. The monolith has in fact broken; and no one can put it together again.

It will take time for the new alignments to form, and for the possibilities open either to Khrushchevism or to Maoism to become quite clear. Khrushchev is anxious to score diplomatic successes while his position within the communist movement is relatively favourable. If it were to deteriorate gravely, his freedom to pursue his policy of peaceful coexistence would once again be limited, perhaps more severely than before. Mao, on the other hand, cannot start any communist crusade before the hosts of willing crusaders have been assembled and marshalled. He must also take into account the objective situation. The schism has come on an ebbing, not on a rising, tide of revolution. For nearly a decade the communists have benefited but little from the many upheavals in Asia and Africa, for these have resulted in the establishment of non-communist or anti-communist regimes. Latin America has not so far followed in Cuba's footsteps. In Europe all that Togliatti and Thorez have been doing is to conceal and embellish ideologically their Parties' basic *immobilisme*. Mao maintains that the 'demoralizing' influence of Khrushchevism has been largely responsible for this state of affairs; but he himself must now reckon with this state of affairs. He knows that he must wait for a new tide; but he is confident that he will not have to wait long, and that the revolutionary dynamic of the underdeveloped countries will presently create new openings for his militant brand of communism. Even in Western Europe, he believes, the stability of the bourgeois order is bound to be shaken with a change in the economic weather, when boom once again leads to depression or slump.

It is probable that the Chinese will seek to apply their militancy first to Vietnam, Laos, and perhaps also Korea. In Geneva, in 1955, they accepted the division of Vietnam, although at that time the Red Partisans could easily have taken control of the whole of that country. But Mao accepted the Geneva settlement because he had allowed himself to be persuaded by Khrushchev that the Indo-Chinese war might escalate into world war—and the late John Foster Dulles did indeed threaten escalation. Now Peking appears to be in a mood to go back on the Geneva agreement, no doubt with the argument that the Americans have anyhow repeatedly broken it. Much will depend on whether Ho Chi Minh and his comrades, who have opted for the Chinese line but with some reserve, are ready or willing to resume the 'war of liberation' in their country.

3 July 1963

2 BLACK DUST STORMS OVER RUSSIA

Recent news has brought to the world's attention a grave economic crisis in the U.S.S.R. This year's harvest has been poor. Bread has been virtually rationed; the Soviet government is sternly urging the population to save food; and queues have appeared at bakeries. Soviet envoys have been rummaging the grain markets of the West. They have bought nearly ten million tons of wheat and flour in Canada, Australia, and elsewhere. They want to buy more from the U.S.A.; but Washington has not yet authorized the sale, and Moscow is anxiously waiting for a decision. To meet an expected gap in their balance of payments, the Russians have drawn on their gold reserve; in September alone they sold gold for nearly 300 million dollars in London, Paris, and Zurich. The Soviet Union is clearly faced with an economic emergency which must affect every aspect of policy and is already reflected in diplomacy. What is the nature of this emergency, and what is its magnitude? Just how severe is the setback to Soviet agriculture? Is the crisis temporary or chronic? How and when can it be overcome? And what are the prospects before the Soviet economy at large?

Moscow has not yet published the statistics about the harvest, but I think it quite certain that the crop has amounted to not more than 120 million tons of grain, of which approximately one half is wheat. This is a very sharp drop from last year's harvest of nearly 150 million tons; it is well below even the bad harvests of 1959 and 1960, which yielded 125 and 134 million tons respectively. The total grain deficit amounts to 20–30 million tons, and the wheat deficit is of the order of 15 million tons. This determines the size of the purchases the Soviet government is making abroad. Insofar as the crisis has been due to exceptionally bad weather, it might be regarded as temporary. But a glance at the record of earlier years shows a striking frequency of poor harvests: of the last five years three years were very bad, one was mediocre, and only one was fairly good. The fact is that Soviet farming is abnormally vulnerable to the vagaries of climate; and this points to its weakness of structure. The present calamity has at a stroke obliterated a good half of the progress achieved since the end of the Stalin era. As the population has grown in the last ten years by nearly twenty per cent (i.e. by nearly 40 million), and as the urban population has been growing at almost double this rate, the supply of food is not going to be much more abundant than it was in Stalin's last years. Indeed, the *per capita* production of grain (about 500 kg. per head) is this year even lower than it was exactly half a century ago, in 1913!

This throws into sharp relief the long-term stagnation of Soviet farming. For a time it looked as if Khrushchev had managed to lift agriculture out of the rut. In the first period of his ascendancy, between 1953 and 1958 he showered reforms on the country: he denounced Stalin's maltreatment of the peasantry; put an end to requisitioning and rigid official control; sold the state-owned Machine Tractor Stations to the collective farms; raised the prices of all farm produce and enabled the farmers to double their earnings. In a word, he put away the stick with which Stalin drove the peasants, and he held out the carrot of incentives. His most startling move, however, was to initiate the ploughing up of the virgin lands in Soviet Asia and elsewhere so that within a few years about 100 million acres of those lands were brought under cultivation. He embarked upon this breathtaking improvisation in the teeth of opposition from Malenkov, who advocated intensive farming on the old lands and warned that Khrushchev's experiment would end in a disastrous soil erosion. Yet, during the first half of the post-Stalin decade the success in agriculture was so sensational that Khrushchev was able to wipe the floor with the critics of his policy. Agricultural output rose by nearly fifty per cent; and the food situation improved so radically that Khrushchev confidently predicted that within a few years the U.S.S.R. would catch up with the U.S.A. in farming and standards of nutrition. But in 1960–61 it was becoming clear that the stimulus which Khrushchev's reforms and improvisations had imparted to Soviet farming was exhausted, and that a new period of stagnation had set in.

Soviet economists then proposed new measures: some advocated a more 'liberal' policy, with new incentives to farmers and greater autonomy for the *kolkhozes*; others urged the government to bring agriculture under closer control and even to transform the *kolkhozes* into *sovkhozes*, that is state-owned farms. The Party leaders could not make up their minds, because no matter which course of action was adopted, new reforms required massive capital investment in agriculture and diversion of resources from armament and heavy industry. A heated controversy over this went on in the Presidium in 1960, after the breakdown of the Paris summit meeting, and at the beginning of 1961. Despite Khrushchev's misgivings, the Presidium then decided to raise defence expenditure and to cut allocations for farming. In the next three years, which brought the Berlin crisis and multi-megaton nuclear tests, this order of priorities was maintained. Khrushchev and his officialdom hoped that agriculture would somehow muddle through. Instead of further reforms, Khrushchev offered the farmers voluble but dubious agronomic advice in many speeches, which he has now collected and published in seven bulky volumes.

Thus the fortunes of Soviet farming and the people's standard of living have depended on the state of the arms race between East and West and on diplomacy. Now, conversely, the tempo of the arms race and the course of Soviet diplomacy are to some extent dictated by the condition of Soviet farming. In the middle of last summer, when Khrushchev resolved somewhat suddenly to come to terms with the U.S.A. over the test ban, and to seek a detente even at the price of a break with China, he must have taken this decision with an eye to the gloomy reports on the harvest that were piling up on his desk. Evidently these reports at last moved the Politbureau as well to endorse Khrushchev's initiative.

What has been brought to a head this year is the chronic crisis in agriculture; and its effects, even in the best of circumstances, must be felt for many years to come. It is a fact that, despite all the initial success and the boastful propaganda, Khrushchev's government (as the Stalinist regime before it) has failed to come to terms with the food producers. No longer afraid of the stick and disappointed at the meagreness of Khrushchev's carrot, farmers concentrate on tilling the small plots of land which they own privately, and they treat the needs of the collective farms with utter apathy or cynicism. The morale of rural Russia has sunk to a very deep low. The descriptions of rural life which one finds in recent Russian novels and periodicals suggest indeed an image of the Soviet peasantry amazingly similar to the image of the wretched French peasantry, so elemental in its individualistic greed, which Balzac drew 120 or 130 years ago! The Soviet government needs years of detente, of reduced defence budgets, reforms, and high investment in farming to cope with this issue and to raise the farmers' morale and productivity.

The most alarming feature of the present emergency is the disaster that has befallen the farms on the virgin lands in Soviet Asia. Khrushchev's gigantic and costly experiment there has ended in catastrophic soil erosion. Prolonged droughts and hot gales have turned vast areas of Kazakhstan and of the Altai Province into 'dust bowls'. Reports speak of black dust storms that have for months turned day into night and compelled travellers to drive with headlamps constantly on. Even the terrible soil erosion that various parts of the United States, especially Texas, experienced before 1933, seems small and mild by comparison. The extensive farms on the virgin lands, if they survive, will hardly be able to produce substantial crops in the next few years. They must first restore the top soil on their fields. This requires time and can be done only by careful use of a great mass of fertilizers. The government has ordered the managers of chemical plants to double the output of fertilizer, or at least to raise it from 20 to 35 million tons by 1965. But the chemical industry is one of the bottlenecks of the Soviet economy; and it remains to be seen whether the target can be attained. . . .

Politically, Khrushchev is suffering a signal defeat. Even quite recently he was still imprudent enough to poke fun at the Cassandras who had forecast the soil erosion in Kazakhstan; and all these years he has walked in the glory of his spurious success on the agricultural front. His prestige, just when it has risen in the West, is shattered at home. The perennial tension between town and country is mounting dangerously, after all his proclamations that it has vanished forever and that the Soviet Union is making its passage from socialism to communism. He is in no position to help with food the governments of Eastern Europe, and he tells them to buy what they can in the West. In his conflict with Mao he has just boasted of the contrast between his communist welfare state and poverty-stricken China and has said that Mao's wrong-headed agricultural policy has 'reduced the Chinese to their meagre rice rations, which they eat from the common bowl'. Peking is now going to have a resounding comeback; and Khrushchev is not going to have the best of the argument.

To restore his position Khrushchev needs not only the semblance of an international detente; he needs a real detente. He needs to cut drastically his defence expenditure in the next budget and in the budgets of the next few years and to throw immense resources into agriculture, and into the chemical industry and the consumer industries. He has to try to recover all the years since Stalin's death that he has wasted (as far as farming is concerned) on speechifying, bureaucratic fireworks, and improvisations. But can he recover those years? Will he have enough time for that? Or is he going to bequeath the predicament to his successor? In any case, it will take a long, long time before the black dust storms of 1963 have really blown over.

7 October 1963

3 THE RUSSO-CHINESE SCHISM DEEPENS

After a relatively uneventful interval of a few months, a new chapter has opened in the Russo-Chinese schism. The ideological 'truce' is at an end, and Peking is now calling for nothing less than the 'liquidation of Khrushchevism'. Neither side has in fact respected the truce, for although Moscow's newspapers have been more reticent than Peking's, the Soviet leaders have worked behind the scenes untiringly and incessantly to rob the Chinese of friends and allies in the communist camp. The Chinese felt that under these circumstances their own silence would only help the Russians; and they decided to do away with the pretence of the truce. In an ideological clash of this kind a crescendo of polemical vehemence is only to be expected. More important than this, however, are the new issues and the new attitudes that are coming to light with the resumption of the debate—issues and attitudes connected with the one important event of recent months, the recognition of Red China by France. This event is affecting Chinese ideology and diplomacy alike; and it is also creating new problems for the Russians.

That Maoist self-confidence has been heightened by diplomatic success goes without saying. The Chinese are now convinced that part of their diplomatic isolation from the world has been due to the fact that they remained under Moscow's wing for too long, that they did not use their own diplomatic initiative and relied instead on the efforts which Soviet diplomacy was supposed to make on their behalf in the United Nations and elsewhere, efforts which, they now believe, lacked resoluteness and sincerity. Peking now sees the French recognition as a decisive turn, after which recognition by other states is bound to follow. . . . In the meantime it is influencing Chinese policy more specifically. If until recently Peking opposed Moscow only in the field of ideology but felt no need to advance any diplomatic conceptions of its own, the situation has now changed in this respect too. The Chinese have come forward with their own diplomatic line, saying that Khrushchev's diplomacy lacks sense of direction and has no order of priorities. In other words, Mao is now seeking to beat Khrushchev on what was supposed to be Khrushchev's own ground—in diplomatic manoeuvring for 'peaceful coexistence'.

The 'new' diplomatic doctrine of the Chinese is simple enough. The socialist camp, they say, must see its chief enemy in the U.S.A. and ought to make common cause with any bourgeois governments prepared to resist American 'hegemony'. It is no use for communists to go on flogging the dead (or nearly dead) horses of French, British, or even Japanese imperialisms when the paramount task is to direct all blows against American imperialism. Peking maintains that Moscow, pursuing the hopeless aim of appeasing Washington, fails in fact to exploit those 'contradictions in the bourgeois camp', on the importance of which it likes to lecture the communist world. What the Chinese mean by this is clear from a few curious changes in their language and behaviour. Until recently, for instance, they would pick up every phrase coming from Moscow which could be interpreted as having pro-Gaullist connotations, and quote it as proof of Khrushchevite opportunism or venality. Now Peking's own propagandists speak with an undertone of shy admiration, almost of tenderness, about France's brave President who has dared to defy American imperialism. If the Maoists do not hail de Gaulle openly as a 'progressive hero', they nevertheless suggest that by proclaiming the right of every nation to rattle its own nuclear weapons, he does somehow champion the equality of all nations and all races. In any case, the time has passed when Peking castigated Khrushchev for making distinctions between the bad and the good (or the not so bad) leaders of Western imperialism, between the 'war-mongers' and the 'sober peace-loving statesmen'. The Chinese now also draw these distinctions; but whereas the Russians look for the sober bourgeois statesmen in Washington, Mao holds that it is both wicked and futile to look for them there—he has found them among America's restive and rebellious allies.

This attitude is already having curious practical consequences. Peking is now urging its adherents in the Afro-Asian countries to treat French nuclear tests, carried out either in the Sahara or in the Pacific, with considerable indulgence, to muffle their protests if not to cease protesting altogether, and to reserve full-throated indignation only for American nuclear armament. This is one of the issues now most hotly debated, especially by the communists of South-East Asia, for on this point too there is a sharp divergence between the Russian and the Chinese views. In pleading against too severe condemnations of French nuclear tests, Mao has undoubtedly been thinking of the day when China herself explodes her bomb and when she will claim for herself the indulgence now accorded to France.

Another curious twist can be seen in China's policy with regard to Malaysia. At first Malaysia was treated in all communist capitals, in Peking no less than in Moscow, as a sinister creation of British imperialism and as a provocation as bad as the war over Suez. In view of China's friendship with Indonesia, this attitude was not surprising. Meanwhile, however, Peking's policy-makers have changed their mind and have advised foreign communists to soften their opposition to Malaysia. The motive: British imperialism being the lesser evil, a British outpost in the Southern Pacific should from the communist viewpoint be regarded as preferable to yet another American base in that area. Peking reacted with the utmost hostility to the attempt of American mediation between Indonesia and Malaysia at the time of Robert Kennedy's visit to Jakarta, for in the Chinese view such a mediation would enhance American influence over both those countries and might even induce President Sukarno to break with the communists. The Chinese envoy in Jakarta has therefore done his best to curb Indonesian hostility towards the 'British puppet state of Malaysia'.

Such are the paradoxes arising out of China's changed position in the world. The Khrushchevites now turn accusations of opportunism and appeasement against the Maoists. The Russians may well point out that what the Chinese describe as their diplomatic doctrine is no novelty to them, that they, the Russians, have repeatedly tried to apply it and have never given it up altogether, but that they have repeatedly learned that attempts to play France or Britain against the United States were not very profitable and that a detente between the U.S.A. and the U.S.S.R. is of decisive importance for the peace of the world.

In the field of ideology the Maoists are also opening a new line of attack on Khrushchevism. They attack the Soviet leaders as the 'exploiters' of the whole socialist camp, as those out to grab wealth from all the other communist-ruled countries. The Chinese press has just published a report which V. G. Wilcox, a pro-Maoist communist of New Zealand, has given in China of negotiations he conducted with the Soviet leaders in Moscow. According to his own words Wilcox upbraided the Soviet leaders telling them that they imagined that the Soviet Union 'would advance to communism by exploiting the rest of the socialist world' and that they would grow fat and happy 'on the backs of the socialist peoples and the Communist Parties of other countries'. It may seem odd that the leader of the tiny Communist Party of New Zealand should have been chosen to make this grave accusation in public, an accusation at which the Chinese themselves had only hinted; but the Communist Party of New Zealand seems to be acting as a Chinese mouthpiece in a way in which the Albanian Party acted at an earlier stage. Here again it is ironical that it was the Yugoslavs who were first to speak of 'Soviet exploitation'; and they spoke of it in their controversy with Stalin around 1950. To Marxists-Leninists this charge has its deeper implication, because exploitation is to them an attribute of capitalism not of socialism. Whoever speaks of Soviet exploitation is therefore, in Marxist terms, bound to deny the U.S.S.R. the title of a workers' state and of a socialist country; and is bound to speak of Soviet 'state capitalism' or of the 'new class' dominating Soviet society. This is what Tito, Kardelj, and Djilas said about the Soviet Union in the heat of their common fight against Stalin—and what Djilas is still saying. That Mao, the arch-enemy of revisionism, should now attack Moscow from this old Titoist position is indeed somewhat paradoxical.

The cry 'Moscow is exploiting you' is calculated to incite Eastern Europe against the Russians. Khrushchev is far more vulnerable to such a threat than Stalin ever was. He cannot reply with terror and purges but has to convince the East Europeans that the U.S.S.R., far from exploiting them, is sensitive to their needs. This consideration is compelling Khrushchev to modify his economic policy *vis-à-vis* Eastern

Europe, sometimes to Soviet disadvantage, and to slow down the integration of the Soviet and the Eastern European industries. This is one of the unexpected results of the Russo-Chinese controversy. As it often happens in such ideological conflicts, neither side can foresee whither the logic of the dispute is leading, what positions he or his opponent is going to take up next, and what the final outcome will be.

30 March 1964

4 KHRUSHCHEV AT SEVENTY

When Stalin celebrated his seventieth birthday, in 1949, Moscow's Museum of the Revolution was turned into an 'All Union Exhibition of the Peoples' Gifts to Our Great and Beloved Leader'. The Stalin cult had reached the lowest depths of absurdity: every day for the next three years, until Stalin's death, *Pravda* filled its columns with the names of the institutions and individuals from whom the septuagenarian had received greetings and tributes. Compared with this the celebration of Khrushchev's birthday is, of course, a sober and modest affair.

Somehow, no myth or legend seems to stick to Khrushchev's figure, although several attempts have been made—somewhat timidly it is true—to fit a halo on his skull. He is perhaps too plump and chubby, and too much of a chatterbox to be dressed up as a remote, awe-inspiring hero. Myth-weaving is a slow job, in any case; and he has not been in power long enough. By Russian-Bolshevik standards, Khrushchev has been a quite exceptionally late developer, politically. In 1917 he was still a non-Party man; and throughout the civil war and the stormy decade of the 1920s he gained no distinction whatsoever. He began to rise from the low echelons of the Party only in the early 1930s. He was first elected to the Central Committee in 1934, at that 'Congress of Victors', the hundred per cent Stalinist Congress, most of whose participants were presently to be exterminated on Stalin's orders—only the most servile of the servile had any chance of survival.

Khrushchev's decisive promotion came with the Moscow Trials and great purges, when every slippery step up the Party ladder led over the corpses of comrades and friends. In 1938–39 he became Party boss of the Ukraine and member of the Politbureau in Moscow. Even by the end of the Stalin era his personality had impressed itself so little on the public mind that in March 1953 no one within Russia or without thought of him as of Stalin's successor. (Malenkov, Molotov, and Beria then formed the ruling triumvirate.) Life, it might be said, began for Khrushchev only at sixty. This circumstance was crucial for his subsequent fortunes. For one thing, it enabled him to lull the vigilance of the other candidates to power: while Molotov, Malenkov, and Beria eyed each other with intense suspicion, they feared little or nothing from Nikita Sergeyevich. And, secondly, being a junior member of the old Stalinist guard, a relative newcomer to it, Khrushchev could claim that he was not one of those who had elevated Stalin to his pinnacle of autocracy, thus incurring direct responsibility for what followed. He became a member of the Central Committee and of the Politbureau after all the basic policies had been determined and the course had been set for the great purges. A man in his position, if he was not ready to protest and die as a martyr, had to do what he did: dance his *gopak* before Stalin, chant 'Glory to our Great Leader', and attend to the bloody business of the purges. But, having been only an executor of his master's will, not a policy-maker, Khrushchev's stake in Stalinism was not as large as was the stake of a Molotov or a Kaganovich; and he was less bound to the Stalin legacy. This made it easier for him to come forward as the exponent of de-Stalinization. Yet he hesitated a long time, from 1953 till 1956, before he dared to raise his hand against his former idol; and, whenever he raises it again, his hand still trembles.

Thus, as an independent political character Khrushchev has existed only since 1953. What then is the record of his activity in this period? He is given, or he takes, full credit for all the recent feats of Soviet science, technology, and industry, for the nuclear experiments, the Sputniks, the Luniks, and for the world-wide prestige and admiration that have accrued to the Soviet Union. He also takes pride in the fact that the Soviet people are enjoying a rising standard of living and have more freedom than they could even dream of under Stalin. These achievements are real and impressive enough, even though the basis for much of them had been laid in the Stalin era thanks to the economic system, the national ownership of the means of production and planning, and to rapidly expanding mass education. Stalin before he died might well have dreamt, as one Roman Emperor did, that 'a golden hump sprouted from his back'—a portent that his people would be far wealthier and happier when he had gone.

Yet sober accounts of conditions in the U.S.S.R., including those given by Khrushchev himself, indicate only too clearly that the creative energies and resources of the U.S.S.R. are still shackled by bureaucratic fetters; that Soviet officialdom is still exercising power in a most arbitrary manner; that Party bosses and managers go on enjoying shocking privileges; that it is still rather risky for Soviet citizens to try and criticize those in power; and that all this has an adverse effect on the people's life and work, stifles initiative and spreads cynicism, disillusionment, and demoralization. What strikes one in the record of Khrushchevism is the great number of the vital issues that Khrushchev and his men have posed but not tackled, the chain of dilemmas they have brought to light but not resolved, and the numerous half-measures which they have half-heartedly initiated. To whatever field of Party or state activity one turns —labour relations or agriculture, the administration of justice or cultural policy—everywhere one notices the same deadlock between reform and the Stalinist *status quo*, or between the new trends and conservatism, a deadlock that seems to have settled on everything since the reformist ebullition of the middle 1950s.

If the Stalin regime entailed the dominance of the total lie, Khrushchev represents the triumph of the half-truth. Nowhere is this more striking than in the so-called 'return to socialist legality' and in the procedures of de-Stalinization. It is now eight years since Khrushchev at the Twentieth Congress pledged himself to reveal the results of the official investigations into the great purges and the resulting rehabilitations. Yet a fog of secrecy still surrounds the purges themselves and the whole train of events, beginning with the assassination of Kirov, that led to them. We know that Marshal Tukhachevsky and his colleagues have been rehabilitated, but we know nothing of the circumstances of and motives for their purge or of the reinvestigation of their trial. From a casual article in a Soviet newspaper one learns that Krestinsky, the eminent Trotskyist, has also been rehabilitated—Krestinsky, who was tried together with Rykov and Bukharin in 1938, and on whose confession the whole case against his co-defendants and against Trotsky was based. Yet Rykov, Bukharin, Trotsky, Zinoviev, Kamenev, Radek, Rakovsky, and so many others have not yet been formally cleared of the monstrous treason charges which served as the pretexts for their extermination. One could go on illustrating this strange state of affairs with very many such examples.

This is not merely a question of historical justice. The purges are still a festering sore on the Soviet body politic, a sore which cannot be healed as long as the regime remains 'monolithic', that is, as long as it allows no political criticism and no opposition to the infallible leader. If the full truth about the purges were to be revealed, the lesson which Soviet people would inevitably draw from it would be that the only alternative to the Stalinist terror was freedom of criticism and toleration of opposition. Khrushchev, who has the blood of the purges on his conscience, and who fears criticism and opposition, can hardly allow the whole truth about the Stalin epoch to be told. Yet there are many signs that Soviet people, especially the young, are growing as impatient with the Khrushchevite half-truth as they are with the Stalinist lie.

Khrushchev's remaining years will almost certainly be over-shadowed by the Russo-Chinese controversy. When all the polemical red herrings are brushed aside, what does Khrushchev stand for in that controversy? Insofar as he defends his own break with Stalinism against the Maoists and urges all communists to break with it, his position is one of overwhelming, almost unassailable, strength. There is not the slightest doubt that he has in this the moral support of the great majority of the Soviet people, of all the progressive forces of the U.S.S.R. and of Eastern Europe, and of most Western communists. The Maoists are blind not to see this and to identify their cause with a nostalgia for the Stalin epoch. Khrushchev's fault—and a grave fault it is—is not that he has carried de-Stalinization too far, but that he has not carried it far enough.

In some other respects, however, Khrushchev pursues an essentially Stalinist line, especially in foreign policy. He continues, in changed circumstances, Stalin's *Realpolitik*, even if he does it under the cloak of de-Stalinization. He seeks to subordinate international communism, and the revolutionary movements of Asia, Africa, and Latin America, to the purposes of Soviet policy and diplomacy. His *raison d'état* induces him to strive (in the name of 'peaceful coexistence') for something like a Russo-American nuclear world condominium, with all that this may imply in terms of power and ideology. The Maoists reject the condominium and the tacit standstill on revolution, which in their view it implies. Khrushchev is unavowedly working to stabilize the present division of the world into ideological spheres of influence; while Mao claims to reject the very idea that the present balance between communism and capitalism should or could be stabilized. . . .

10 April 1964

5 THE RUSSO-ROMANIAN QUARREL

Soviet Party leaders and economic planners are seriously perturbed over their—or is it Khrushchev's?—quarrel with the Romanians. It is not only the Romanian economic tie-up with the Soviet Union and the Comecon (Council for Mutual Economic Aid) that is at stake. If that were all Moscow would not be so worried. But behind the Russo-Romanian quarrel there is concealed a new and significant conflict between the U.S.S.R. and Yugoslavia, a conflict which imperils the whole Soviet power position in the Balkans and Eastern Europe at large. Not for nothing then did Khrushchev before his Scandinavian trip summon Marshal Tito for an urgent conference to Leningrad; and not for nothing did the Yugoslav leader then proceed to meet Georghiu-Dej and other members of the Romanian Politbureau near the Yugoslav frontier. Despite official assurances to the contrary, the Leningrad meeting between Khrushchev and Tito could not have been very friendly or cordial. There is reason to believe that the Soviet leader met his guest with bitter reproaches, telling him how disappointed he was at seeing Titoism undermining the Soviet influence in the Balkans just now when he, Khrushchev, is engaged in a heavy ideological and political contest with the Chinese.

The Russian argument is briefly this: the Romanians in their revolt against Comecon are not merely taking advantage of the Russo-Chinese controversy in order to strengthen their bargaining position, but they are definitely being incited against Comecon by the Yugoslavs. Moscow suspects that Titoism, which has never favoured the economic integration of Eastern Europe with the Soviet Union, is now obstructing it more than ever, both openly and surreptitiously. On quite a few occasions Soviet planners, trying to proceed with the integration of various Eastern European industries, have run into what may be described as 'Titoist-inspired opposition'. But the Yugoslavs have behaved in an elusive manner; and for tactical reasons Khrushchev preferred until quite recently to ignore his planners' complaints. Now, however, the issue has come to a head: the Russians and the Yugoslavs have clashed directly over their opposed Danube Development Schemes. Both schemes are concerned with navigation and with the construction of dams and hydro-electric plants and the distribution of electricity in the Danube Basin. The Russian plan, advanced through Comecon, envisages a single electrical grid for Romania, Bulgaria, Hungary, and the Soviet Ukraine, and also joint Bulgarian-Romanian-Soviet development of the lower reaches of the Danube. It is this scheme that the Romanian press has denounced as injurious to Romania's independence, a charge which the Russians have been refuting in awkward embarrassment. What both sides have preferred not to mention in this context is that the Romanians have already committed themselves to an alternative, Yugoslav scheme, which provides for joint Romanian-Yugoslav development of the Danube area. This scheme is designed to forge solid economic links between the two countries and to form something like a Yugoslav-Romanian bloc capable of exercising strong pressure on Bulgaria, Hungary, and Albania, and even of barring Russia's access to the Balkans. Paradoxically, such an alignment may look like a partial revival, under communist governments, of the Little Entente of the inter-war period. The

Little Entente had been formed under French auspices; and so it would not be surprising if the present Yugoslav-Romanian combination evoked a degree of sympathy in Gaullist diplomacy.

For the Russians their Danube Scheme is an essential part of a wider plan designed to deal with a serious crisis in Comecon. This consists in a chronic and acute imbalance between the manufacturing industries and the primary production of Eastern Europe. Since the foundation of Comecon in 1949 the manufacturing industries (especially engineering) of all member countries have expanded so rapidly that the output of fuel and metals has not been able to keep pace with the rate of the expansion. (For instance, machine building has grown nine to ten times in Romania, Poland, and Bulgaria, six times in the U.S.S.R. and Czechoslovakia, and five times in Hungary.) The resulting deficit of fuel, energy, and raw materials has already slowed down the tempo of industrialization. In some Comecon countries a chronic shortage of electricity forces the engineering industry to work at only seventy per cent of its capacity. East Germany, Hungary, Czechoslovakia, and Bulgaria have to import from thirty-five to ninety-five per cent of the coal, coke, iron ore, light metals, and oil which they need. So little hope have Comecon planners of overcoming the shortages, that in most of their long-term forecasts they assume that the fuel deficit in Eastern Europe will persist over the next twenty years. They nevertheless plan for a total Comecon steel output (including Soviet output) of 330 million tons by 1980. (The present output is about 110 million tons.) It is difficult to see how this target can be achieved if the deficits of fuel and iron ore persist for many years. To reduce these imbalances the leaders of Comecon are trying to slow down, at least for a couple of years, the expansion in engineering and to force up the growth of power generating capacity. The Romanians, we know, reject any limitation on the expansion of their industry and refuse to participate in any of the Comecon's regional development schemes. Yugoslav support has certainly encouraged them to defy Moscow; and it enables them also to cut off the Bulgarians from overland contact with the Soviet Union. They are thus dealing a heavy blow to Comecon which, having lost so much ground in the Danube Basin, must be greatly weakened in Poland, Hungary, and Czechoslovakia too.

Comecon finds itself, of course, weakened by the economic nationalism of Russia's old satellites, a nationalism of which the Romanians are now the most vociferous but not the only mouthpieces. In part this is the old, conventional, 'pre-communist' nationalism. In part, however, it is the echo of the Stalinist doctrine of socialism in a single country; it is that doctrine that both the Maoists and the Titoists still preach when they proclaim that it is the duty of each socialist country to attain economic self-sufficiency. Against them Khrushchev has advocated 'socialist integration' and supra-national planning; but faced with nationalist opposition he has had to beat a deep retreat. Nearly two years ago, in September 1962, Khrushchev came out in favour of a single Plan covering at first all Comecon countries and eventually also China. Since then he has, however, argued for the co-ordination of various national Plans rather than for a single international Plan; and he has had to restrict his demand for co-ordination only to fuel, metals, and some sectors of engineering, leaving the national sovereignty of the Comecon countries intact in all the major spheres of economic life. Yet, even after this deep retreat Khrushchev finds himself denounced by the Romanians as the enemy of their national sovereignty.

These then were the issues uppermost in Khrushchev's mind during his latest encounter with Marshal Tito. The irony of the situation consists in the fact that the Yugoslavs support the Romanians who, in their revolt against Moscow, have been flirting with the Chinese. Khrushchev might well have asked his Yugoslav guest whether he had not deserved more Yugoslav gratitude for defending the Titoist socialist honour against Chinese attacks. Have not Titoist revisionism and Maoist dogmatism co-operated tacitly—this may be a case of *les extrêmes se touchent*—to undermine the Soviet position? The argument could not have been altogether lost on Marshal Tito. But the Yugoslav leader is now steering between Scylla and Charibdis. On the one hand he does not like to see Soviet influence re-established in the Balkans to anything like its previous strength. On the other, he does not wish to weaken Khrushchevism *vis-à-vis* Maoism. Still less would he like to see Maoism, already entrenched in Albania, gaining another Balkan bridgehead—in Romania. And so Marshal Tito agreed in

Leningrad to intervene with the Romanians, to try to talk them out of their connection with the Chinese, if that is possible, and also to see whether the two rival, Russian and Yugoslav, Danube Development Schemes could not be somehow reconciled.

What effect, if any, is Marshal Tito's intervention going to have? The crisis in Comecon may have gone too deep and the centrifugal forces in Eastern Europe may have grown too strong for the situation to be retrieved. Eastern Europe is in disarray. Under Chinese blows Moscow's ideological supremacy is crumbling; and Soviet economic difficulties have accentuated the decline of Soviet prestige. Nothing has heightened Romanian self-confidence as much as the fact that last year they sent several hundred thousand tons of wheat across the Soviet frontier to alleviate the consequences of a bad harvest in the Soviet Ukraine. In Stalin's days far larger supplies of food, oil, and other goods were going to Russia; and no one in Bucharest dared to utter a disgruntled murmur. But times have changed . . .

If the weakening of Russia's position in Eastern Europe is in the main a result of the Russo-Chinese controversy, the developments in Eastern Europe are in their turn apt to weaken Khrushchev's position *vis-à-vis* Mao, and perhaps also *vis-à-vis* critics at home. There are certainly people in Moscow, in and around the Central Committee, who wonder whether Khrushchev's policy is not causing the Soviet Union too many losses in Europe as well as in Asia.

25 June 1964

6 THE TONKING GULF
INCIDENT

The storm in the Gulf of Tonking has once again sharply illumined the actual state of moral-political and military inequality between the U.S.S.R. and the U.S.A., an inequality that has been tacitly accepted by Moscow. When the Russians moved their missiles into Cuba, Washington confronted them with an ultimatum; and President Kennedy at once ordered

American warships and aircraft into the Caribbean Sea threatening to destroy the Soviet base in Cuba. Not for a single moment was the United States prepared to accept the Russian presence in Latin America, so close to its own borders. Khrushchev yielded and withdrew his missiles. By contrast, the action of the American naval units in the Gulf of Tonking did not bring forth any ultimatum either from China or from Russia. Both Peking and Moscow replied with verbal protests and indignation at 'American aggression'; but none of them threatened immediate retaliation. None even demanded an American military withdrawal. Both Peking and Moscow accept *de facto* the American presence in Vietnam, Laos, and in South-East Asia at large.

The widely-noticed Russian moderation during the crisis was calculated to demonstrate to electioneering Americans that they have nothing to fear from the U.S.S.R. Moscow has been trying to tell them that they should not allow Senator Goldwater to make their flesh creep once again with the old fear of communism. Will the American electorate be impressed by this Russian moderation? Will it heed Senator Fulbright's warning that the events in South-East Asia must not be allowed to imperil the detente between Russia and America? Or will the American electorate conclude that 'it pays to be firm with the communists' and that President Johnson achieved some success in Vietnam because he acted in Senator Goldwater's spirit? These are the important questions, for it is the result of the American elections that is going to affect Russo-American relations deeply one way or another. The bombardments in the Gulf of Tonking, if they are not followed up by new and more massive encounters, are not likely either to worsen or to improve the relations between the U.S.S.R. and the U.S.A.

But it is obvious that the events in Vietnam are grist to the Russo-Chinese controversy. Once again the Chinese are arguing that Khrushchevite appeasement is a standing invitation to American aggression, and that if Khrushchev acted over Vietnam with anything like the firmness with which President Kennedy acted over Cuba, the Americans would not dare to behave in South-East Asia as they do. Yet, despite this, and despite all their talk about the American 'paper tiger', the

Chinese themselves behaved during the crisis no less cautiously and no less moderately than did the Russians. They have not even threatened to send 'volunteers' across the border to help the North Vietnamese, although there has obviously been some demand in Peking for some such gesture of solidarity. The Soviet Union, the Chinese leaders say, is the only communist power which can deter American imperialism, but refuses to do so; it is all the more essential that in the communist world the power of (nuclear) deterrents should not remain a Russian monopoly. More than ever the Chinese now feel justified in their ambition to develop their own nuclear arsenal and to go on opposing Khrushchevite 'opportunism and capitulation'.

Although the Russians cannot afford any disengagement from South-East Asia in the long run, they may see definite short-term advantages in such a move. They fear that the protracted socio-political crisis in the successor states of Indo-China is coming to a head. They are finding it more and more difficult to curb the local communist forces, for in both Vietnam and Laos the communist-inspired guerrillas are powerful enough to overthrow their enemies in the south and rather impatient to carry the fighting to a victorious conclusion. To prevent total communist victory, the United States, who has backed the tottering southern regimes, is increasing its stakes and may feel compelled to carry the war to the north. The time for mediation between the warring parties seems over; and it was mainly as go-betweens that the Russians acted as co-chairmen of the International Commissions on Laos and Vietnam. This was all right as long as the local communists were inclined to heed Russian warnings and take Russian advice. But they no longer do so. They are all Maoists; and Ho Chi Minh, the Khrushchevite leader of North Vietnam, is allowed to hold office only because he plays along with the pro-Chinese majority in the Vietnamese Politbureau. The Russians resent this, behave moodily, threaten to withdraw, and some of them are in fact anxious to get out before the next flare-up, before the bigger and larger clash of arms begins, which the skirmishes in the Gulf of Tonking may have foreshadowed.

The pro-Chinese elements in Vietnam and Laos in reply accuse Moscow of trying to wash its hands of revolution in South-East Asia and of leaving communism there at the mercy of American imperialism. Whether they themselves take the Russian threat of disengagement seriously is another question. For one thing, the communist guerrillas in Laos and South Vietnam are so strongly entrenched that the Americans can hardly dislodge them; and after the Russian withdrawal they may feel far freer to launch offensive action. It may be feared that the Russians, in their disengagement manoeuvres, are playing with fire. The Americans may misinterpret the situation and conclude that after the Russian withdrawal South-East Asia is a vacuum which they are free to fill as they like. This would be a dangerous illusion and a dangerous temptation. For one thing, China is by no means as weak as it is supposed in the West; for another, American expansion or fear of American expansion is almost certain to force Russia back into South-East Asia; and then a major Russo-American clash may develop. Such, let me recall, was the pattern of events in Korea in 1949–50; only in Korea it was the United States that did the disengagement, that withdrew its occupation forces from South Korea only to return and fight the Korean war for two or three years. One cannot be sure that in South-East Asia a Russian disengagement will not entail comparable blunders and even graver complications. . . .

This is an edited version of an interview given on 11 August 1964 and published in L'Espresso.

15
The Fall of Khrushchev

On 15 October 1964 it was announced by *Tass* that 'in view of his advanced age and the deterioration of his health' Khrushchev had been released from his posts of First Secretary of the Party and Chairman of the Council of Ministers. He was replaced as First Secretary by Leonid Brezhnev and as Prime Minister by Alexei Kosygin. On 17 October *Pravda* published an article which, without mentioning Khrushchev, presented the case against him. The article denounced the cult of the personality and 'subjectivism and drifting in communist construction'; it also attacked what it called 'hare-brained scheming, immature conclusions, hasty decisions, actions divorced from reality, phrase-mongering, and commandism'. These were clearly the categories into which Khrushchev's policies were supposed to fall.[1]

The new leaders attempted to heal the Sino-Soviet breach. Khrushchev's overthrow coincided with the explosion of the first Chinese atom bomb, and in November Chou En-lai came to Moscow for talks with a bargaining position made stronger by China's nuclear advances. But although there was a temporary halt in inter-Party polemics this did not last: by the time the Russians held their international communist conference in March 1965 the Chinese were openly attacking 'Khrushchevism without Khrushchev' and the 'illegal and schismatic' Moscow meeting. Kosygin had made a trip to the Far East in February and visited Peking as well as Hanoi and Pyongyang; but he was unable to reach agreement with the Chinese despite the increased need for international communist solidarity in view of the Vietnam war. It was during Kosygin's visit to Hanoi that the Americans began their continuous bombing of North Vietnam;

[1] For a more detailed analysis of the fall of Khrushchev see 'The Failure of Khrushchevism' in *Ironies of History*.

and in the immediate post-Khrushchev period the focus of international affairs shifted to Vietnam and away from the nexus of European problems—disarmament, German reunification, access to Berlin—that had dominated world attention in the 1950s and early 1960s.

1 THE END OF THE KHRUSHCHEV INTERREGNUM

The downfall of Nikita Khrushchev and the almost simultaneous explosion of the first Chinese atom bomb are stupendous triumphs for Mao Tse-tung and communist China. Khrushchev is, metaphorically speaking, the first victim of the Chinese bomb. Far from resigning on grounds of ill-health, he has been overthrown by a palace revolt or a *coup d'état* which was being hatched carefully and with the utmost secrecy in the Kremlin at least since June. The initiators of the conspiracy were above all anxious to mend the breach between Moscow and Peking. They probably knew about the forthcoming nuclear explosion, and the foreknowledge induced them to speed up their action.

The pattern of the *coup* is now fairly clear. Last summer a series of apparently enigmatic developments occurred in Moscow, all of which can now be seen as pointing directly to Khrushchev's overthrow. In July Leonid Brezhnev, Chairman of the Presidium of the Supreme Soviet, that is the titular Head of State, suddenly resigned from his office and joined the Party Secretariat, where he was to serve as Khrushchev's first deputy. Mikoyan became Head of State. Through this re-shuffle the conspirators placed themselves in the two decisive strategic positions. With one hand Brezhnev gripped the steering wheel of the Party machine while he was getting ready to push over his superior with the other. Mikoyan's role was crucial. True, the office of the Soviet Head of State is not normally very important; but during a crisis of leadership it becomes, for a brief moment, decisive. After Stalin's death the change in the Presidency, where Shvernik was replaced by Marshal Voroshilov, opened a long series of important re-shuffles. The corresponding change occurred this time while Khrushchev was still in his seat of power. He evidently sensed no danger to himself in the July appointments. Both Mikoyan and Brezhnev had been his close and even intimate friends, or so he thought. He had repeatedly promoted Brezhnev, the last time over the head of Frol Kozlov, Brezhnev's rival, who was dismissed from the Presidium a couple of years ago because of his neo-Stalinist and pro-Chinese attitude. As to Mikoyan, he had until quite recently been Khrushchev's guardian angel, as it were, and the brain behind the Khrushchev regime.

Khrushchev's 'withdrawal' from office, we are told, occurred at a meeting of the Central Committee in Moscow on 14 October. Curiously, no such meeting had been on the agenda. The Committee had been officially convened for a session in the middle of November, at which Khrushchev was to make the report on the state of farming and propose 'new and vital reforms'. He was supposed to work on his brief in his retreat at Sochi, on the Black Sea. On the eve of the fateful event, M. Gaston Palewski, French Minister of Science, paid Khrushchev a courtesy visit at Sochi. Khrushchev, full of beans, told the visitor that he was in a hurry to leave for Moscow, because he had to act there as host to the crew of the *Voskhod* spaceship who were to be given a triumphal reception in the capital. He gave no hint of the forthcoming session of the Central Committee, the session that was to prevent him acting as host to the *Voskhod*. Apparently he still had no forebodings. Yet, at his side in Sochi there was Mikoyan—had he come there to lull Khrushchev's vigilance? That same day a curious incident occurred between them while Khrushchev was talking over the radio-telephone to the *Voskhod* cosmonauts who were just circling the globe. In the middle of the conversation Khrushchev suddenly shouted into the microphone: 'By my side here there is Comrade Mikoyan. He will not let me talk to you. He is pulling the telephone out of my hand.' In effect it was Mikoyan who delivered the solemn message of greetings to the *Voskhod* crew, while the crew (to judge from the text of their message published in *Pravda*) did not make the customary reverential bow to Khrushchev that Gagarin and all other cosmonauts had made. ('It is thanks to you and your wise leadership, Comrade Nikita Sergeyevich, that we are now conquering cosmic space . . .', etc.) While these comic incidents were taking place in Sochi, the Muscovite police had already received the order to remove Khrushchev's portraits from the processions, and from the public squares and official buildings.

When the Central Committee assembled on the 14th, Khrushchev's fate was sealed. Brezhnev, Mikoyan, Kosygin, and their allies had used against him the technique he first used against Malenkov in February 1955 and then against

Molotov, Kaganovich, and Malenkov again in June 1957. Benefiting by his absence and lack of vigilance, they mounted a majority against him, a majority made up of several groups each of which had reasons of its own to seek a change in the leadership. What were those reasons?

The feeling that Khrushchev had outstayed his time had rapidly gained ground in the ruling group and far beyond it. Qualities which endeared the former Soviet Premier to some people in the West—his incoherence, clownishness, irresponsibility, and unpredictability—increasingly worried and angered many communists, even erstwhile Khrushchevites. Mikoyan and his associates had supported Khrushchev in his rise to power because they had been anxious to debar Molotov and Malenkov. But they treated Khrushchev as a stopgap, and trusted him not to develop any autocratic ambition. They thought, as someone put it, that 'a clown like Nikita Sergeyevich cannot possibly aspire to become the *Vozhd*' (the Leader). With the exercise of power, however, Khrushchev's appetite for it grew; and he began to foster a 'legend' of his own. Even his well-wishers and supporters resented this. They were also shocked by the aura of nepotism that was beginning to surround him—witness the extraordinary career of Adzhubei, Khrushchev's son-in-law, his envoy extraordinary to the Pope and President Kennedy, and editor of *Izvestia*.

Men of the new educated and sophisticated élite had from the outset viewed Khrushchev as a rather archaic *muzhik* and semi-literate upstart; they wondered whether someone more worthy could not be found to represent Russia in the world. In the intelligentsia's eyes, however, his faults were partly redeemed by his role in 'liberalizing' the regime. Yet even in this they found him moody and unreliable: one moment he acted the de-Stalinizer, the patron of the young poets and writers and the guarantor of literary and artistic freedom; the next moment he was the quasi-Stalinist again and the enemy of any genuine freedom of expression.

Finally, there was the fiasco of Khrushchev's experiments in agriculture. These ended in disastrous soil erosion on the virgin lands, the cultivation of which he had promoted, against expert advice, at great cost to the nation. Acute food shortages followed; and last year there were long bread queues in the streets of the cities and towns. Amid so many discontents and frustrations the wonder is not that Khrushchev has fallen at last, but that he did not fall earlier.

However, in this crisis foreign policy has overshadowed all domestic factors, important though these are. The Russo-Chinese controversy has brought under attack the whole record of Khrushchev's foreign policy. No doubt the Chinese are unpopular in the U.S.S.R.; many Russians detest them for their sour austerity, dogmatism, and pride. But even those who hate them could not help reflecting whether the U.S.S.R. could in the long run afford to give up the advantages of the Chinese alliance. Mikoyan, for instance, who has been the real inspirer of post-Stalinist 'peaceful coexistence' and who is even more critical of Maoism than Khrushchev himself, has at several recent meetings with foreign communists openly shown his dislike of Khrushchev's 'reckless and brutal' methods in the struggle and the polemics against the Chinese. What has been even worse from the communist viewpoint is the utter disarray into which Khrushchev has thrown the whole international communist movement. Very few foreign communist leaders have shown any desire to attend, especially on Khrushchev's terms, the international conference he has convened for 15 December. If complete obedience and servility towards Moscow was the law of the communist movement under Stalin, utter defiance and universal rebellion against Moscow seemed to become the rule under Khrushchev. It is perhaps not surprising that this unheard of decline of Moscow's prestige among communists has caused acute anxiety in the Kremlin and has provoked a reaction.

The *coup de grâce* to Khrushchev was delivered by Palmiro Togliatti, the Italian communist leader, before he died in the Crimea in August leaving behind a highly controversial 'testament'. Togliatti had come to Russia in order to urge Khrushchev to postpone the international communist conference and to tone down the polemics against the Chinese. Khrushchev refused to receive him. While the famous Italian veteran, hitherto Khrushchev's staunch defender, was kept waiting in the antechambers of Soviet Party offices, Khrushchev left Moscow for a prolonged tour of farms, the tour during which *inter alia* he cordially entertained Lord Thompson, the British press magnate. Togliatti was furious; so were his numerous admirers in Moscow. Giving up the idea of a personal encounter with Khrushchev, he wrote the memorandum which was to become his testament. In it he reproached Khrushchev for his lack of candour, for his shilly-shallying de-Stalinization, and for his obstruction of free debate within the communist movement. He hinted also at the failure of much of Khrushchev's diplomacy and spoke 'pessimistically' about the danger of renewed international tension, in the face of which Moscow should not risk any final breach with Peking. *Pravda* reprinted these criticisms in full. Coming from the chief of the largest Communist Party in Western Europe, who was himself renowned for his moderation and anti-Maoism, Togliatti's arguments were a godsend to the anti-Khrushchevite factions. Posthumously, as it were, Togliatti helped them to mount the new majority in the Central Committee.

6 October 1964

2 THE CONSEQUENCES OF KHRUSHCHEV'S FALL

Exactly a month after Khrushchev's overthrow his former colleagues have completed the *coup* by making further changes at the top of the Party hierarchy. The Central Committee has appointed new men to its Presidium: Alexander Shelepin, one of the Party secretaries who had been in charge of state security, Pyotr Shelest, the Party boss of the Ukraine, and Pyotr Demichev, the former Party secretary of the Moscow organization (the latter is only a 'candidate member' of the Presidium). Within the Central Committee itself no fewer than eight 'candidates' have been promoted to full membership. Some familiar names, on the other hand, have been struck off the list: Frol Kozlov, reputed to be the leader of the 'conservatives' or neo-Stalinists, has disappeared from the Presidium on grounds of ill-health. Vassili Polyakov, head of the Party's agricultural branch, has been dismissed from his post, while A. Adzhubei, the disgraced leader's disgraced son-in-law, has been expelled from the Central Committee.

The new appointments are designed partly to fill gaps caused by dismissals and demotions and partly to establish a new balance between the various groups and factions. There is no question, of course, of Khrushchevites and anti-Khrushchevites, for they are all anti-Khrushchevites now, just as all were Khrushchevites until quite recently. However, the divisions between conservatives and reformers or neo-Stalinists and 'liberals' remain in force. So do the differences between those who are utterly hostile towards the Chinese and those eager for some compromise with them. At the moment the balance between the factions and groups is rather delicate; and uncertainty is heightened by the rather startling rejuvenation of the ruling circle. Most of the newcomers to the Presidium and the Central Committee are men in their middle forties. To this age group belong, for instance, Shelepin and Demichev. Among the new members of the Central Committee there is General Yepishev, who at the age of thirty-six heads the army's political administration. Thus leaders ten to twenty years younger than Brezhnev, Podgorny, and Suslov (themselves ten to fifteen years younger than Khrushchev, Mikoyan, and Molotov) are coming to the top. On the face of it, their rise ought to favour change and reform. Of course not all the younger men are necessarily ardent de-Stalinizers—some may be conservatives and disciplinarians. Shelepin has been supervisor of the political police; but he exercised this function at a time when the powers of the police were drastically cut. In any case, none of these young leaders was among Stalin's accomplices in the mass purges; and none has owed his promotion to the Stalinist terror. They should therefore be free from the sense of guilt, the fear, and the craving for self-exculpation which are so characteristic of the older leaders and which have so often impeded de-Stalinization.

It will take some time before the political character of the young newcomers shows itself. Meanwhile Messrs. Brezhnev, Suslov, and Podgorny, who have played so large a part in overthrowing Khrushchev, are behaving in a most embarrassed manner. Since the memorable communiqué about his dismissal, they have said nothing about him in public—not a word of praise and not a word of blame. His name has simply vanished. He has been attacked only by hint and allusion, though the hints have been quite transparent. It is mainly to Khrushchev's failures and mistakes in domestic policies that the allusions refer, although Chou En-lai's visit to Moscow and the resumption of negotiations with Peking show that the Russo-Chinese controversy was at least equally important in the crisis that led to Khrushchev's downfall. But his successors find it convenient to dwell exclusively on his failures at home, especially on the fiasco of his agricultural policy, for in so doing they hope to make their action against him acceptable to Soviet opinion; and at the same time this enables them to shrug off interventions by foreign communist leaders with the answer that the Khrushchev crisis is primarily an internal Soviet affair.

It was with these considerations in mind that the Central Committee, at its last session, placed the reorganization of the Party at the top of its agenda. This reorganization undoes the division of the Party into two separate, industrial and agricultural branches, a reform which Khrushchev had carried out only two years ago. The two branches are now being merged; at every level of the hierarchy, local, regional, and Republican, new Party committees are to be elected in December. In this way the Soviet people are being told that Khrushchev's scheme has failed to cope with the chronic crisis in agriculture; and that, moreover, by splitting the organization into two economic sectors, Khrushchev had sought to reduce the Party's political weight and so to enhance his own personal power and the cult of his own personality. But this again gives rise to the question why these charges are not made openly. Evidently Khrushchev's successors are as reluctant to wash the Party's dirty linen in public as Stalin's successors once were; and they too do not see eye to eye with each other over just how far they should go in denouncing the departed leader or over the motives of the denunciation.

Meanwhile, they keep on repeating emphatically that they stand by the decisions of the Twentieth and Twenty-second Congresses, the Congresses that were responsible for the most spectacular acts of de-Stalinization. Indeed, they are promising to press ahead with de-Stalinization and 'liberalization'. Yet even these promises are made only by hint and allusion. If until recently the Party ideologists claimed that the Twentieth and Twenty-second Congresses had '*achieved* a return to the Leninist principles of collective leadership and inner Party democracy', they now say that those Congresses had only *begun*, but not *achieved*, the salutary reform. Even of Khrushchev's overthrow it is said that it has carried the revival of inner Party democracy only 'a stage further', not that it has completed the process. Thus, by implication further instalments of de-Stalinization (and de-Khrushchevization) are being foreshadowed. This is evidently done in response to increased popular pressure for new 'liberal' reforms.

However, if the logic of the domestic situation calls for further de-Stalinization and liberalization, Moscow's evident desire for at least a partial agreement with Peking militates against this trend. The Chinese go on proclaiming their allegiance to the Stalin cult and denouncing the 'revisionists' opposed to it. This is one of the stumbling-blocks in the present Russo-Chinese negotiations. Behind it there are, of course, other stumbling-blocks. The Russians reaffirm the correctness of their policy of peaceful coexistence. They point to President Johnson's overwhelming electoral victory as evidence and justification for it, while the Chinese say that there is 'no difference between Johnson and Goldwater'. The Russians still stand by the Nuclear Test Ban, which remains unacceptable to the Chinese. The tenor of all Russian declarations is still 'moderate' and 'rightist'—it amounts indeed to something like Khrushchevism without Khrushchev; while Chinese propaganda remains 'leftish' or 'ultra-radical'. The various schools of thought in communism, the 'three currents',[1]—have not vanished with Khrushchev; nor are they likely to do so.

While the Russo-Chinese negotiations are on, the propagandists of both sides are observing a cease-fire. The formulas and the slogans have not changed on either side, but there have been some shifts of emphasis. Both the Russians and the Chinese are trying to find out whether they can go back to the compromise formulas adopted at the international communist conference in Moscow in 1960, or whether they can re-state those formulas in some new satisfactory version. The 1960 compromise broke down when Khrushchev allied himself (against the Chinese) with Tito and right-wing elements in

[1] See 'Three Currents in Communism' in *Ironies of History*.

other Communist Parties. Mao and his comrades therefore expect Khrushchev's successors at least to renew the attack against Titoism and the communist trends akin to it.

Behind these Party political issues looms the crisis in the relationship between the governments of the two great communist powers. Is Russia going to resume economic aid to China? And if so, on what terms? And is Russia going to view China's ascendancy as a nuclear power favourably and assist in it? So far not even a hint of these questions has been made in public; and the silence indicates how great the difficulties are and how much time it must take to reduce them, if reduced they can be. Khrushchev's successors probably feel that they have given sufficient proof of their intention to mend their relations with the Chinese; they now expect some ideological concession from Mao. They may be counting on moderate elements in Peking to speak up in favour of conciliation with Russia. This hope is certainly not groundless. Just as the Russians under Khrushchev were not unanimous in their policy towards China, so the Chinese under Mao differ in their attitudes towards Moscow; and the difference must have been stimulated by Khrushchev's overthrow. In all probability Chou En-lai speaks for those who favour a compromise with Moscow while Liu Shao-chi urges that the battle against 'Khrushchevism without Khrushchev' be pressed relentlessly to its conclusion. Thus, while officially the truce between Moscow and Peking lasts, the struggle between the factions is assuming fresh intensity in each of the two capitals and, indeed, in the entire communist movement.

17 November 1964

3 THE POLITICS OF
POST-KHRUSHCHEVITE RUSSIA

The most characteristic feature of the post-Khrushchev regime, now in its fifth month, is the unobtrusiveness and the taciturnity of its leaders. It looks as if they have taken an oath that none of them would seek popularity for himself so that none should be able to rise above his colleagues in the Presidium and establish his personal ascendancy. After the torrents of Khrushchev's loquacity, silence is once again considered golden, and only absolute political necessity entitles a leader to exchange it for the silver of a public speech. And so it took a storm over Asia for Kosygin, the new Prime Minister, to be able, on his Far Eastern tour, to make his first important political statements. At home he has so far spoken in public only once, at the Supreme Soviet in December; but he did this as chief economic planner rather than as Prime Minister, and he gave the Soviet an almost non-political annual routine report on the state of the Soviet economy. Brezhnev, the Party's new First Secretary, has not so far opened his mouth even once. He has not given even a hint of a public explanation of how and why he has taken his office and what are the differences, if any, between his and his predecessor's policies. There is more than a whiff of Stalinism in this secrecy; and perhaps even Stalin might have been less reticent in such circumstances. What is going on behind this thick veil of discretion?

Khrushchev's successors are still assessing the legacy they have taken over and trying to find out how much of it they can preserve and how much they must discard. They are also rearranging, re-distributing, and overhauling the levers and instruments of power. For the second time since Stalin an attempt is being made to separate to some extent the powers of Party and State—the previous attempt was made in 1953, when Malenkov was Prime Minister and Khrushchev became First Secretary. Many Soviet citizens hope that much good will result from a relative duality of power; some see in it the precondition for a genuine growth of civil liberties. The idea has a long history: in the early days of Stalin's autocracy. Bukharin, the great theorist of the 'Right Opposition', had already reached the conclusion that 'the root of all evil in our system of government is that Party and State are so completely merged'. It is remarkable that after nearly four decades people should arrive at this conclusion quite independently and are still trying to get at that 'root of all the evil'. Yet, while the prerogatives of Party and State are being disentangled, each, Party and State, is being remodelled and re-integrated so as to overcome the effects of some of Khrushchev's divisive and decentralizing decrees.

The real power continues to reside in the Party. The First Secretary still carries far more weight than does the Prime Minister. Yet so intense is his colleagues' fear and jealousy of his power that they have so far prevented Brezhnev from coming forward even as *primus inter pares*, the first among equals. The Presidium has, for the time being, done away with all order of precedence so that none of its members should be able to benefit from it. In these circumstances the slight pre-eminence which Kosygin has just gained by his appearances and utterances in Hanoi, Peking, and Pyongyang will not be welcome in Moscow. To counteract it, Brezhnev may well step into the limelight presently. From what has been said it is clear that the 'collective leadership', the diffusion of power among Khrushchev's successors, is real enough at present. The Presidium takes all important decisions on domestic and foreign policy. It meets frequently, once or twice a week. In an emergency or in a grave international crisis, it can be called together at a moment's notice. It can act swiftly and with determination, as long as it is not torn by a sharp internal division. In case of such a division the large and cumbersome Central Committee assumes its role as the Party's supreme authority; then the process of decision-making becomes complex and slow.

I am not proposing to indulge in the Kremlinologists' favourite game and to discuss here personalities or speculate on the chances of Podgorny, Suslov, or Novikov and on their respective attitudes towards either Brezhnev or Kosygin. The constellation of these Kremlin stars is highly capricious and elusive. It is also largely irrelevant, as those who so recently still saw Khrushchev as the irremovable dictator and Frol Kozlov as his heir apparent should have learnt by now. Far more stable, important, and clear are the basic alignments on which the men of the Presidium depend, for neither the Presidium nor the Central Committee act in a vacuum.

Within the Central Committee and around it there are powerful lobbies and pressure groups which represent multiple sectional interests in a perpetual interplay of conflict and common action. The spokesmen of the most powerful lobbies have direct access to the Presidium, whose sessions they often attend, if not as parties to conflicts, then as experts and consultants.

Here is a tentative listing of these lobbies and pressure groups in the approximate order of their importance. First come the nuclear scientists, managers of nuclear plants, heads of the military nuclear services, and the men in charge of outer space experiments. Compared with the other 'conventional' pressure groups, they are a small, though growing, body, much younger than the others, more compact, and quite exceptionally self-confident. As a group they handle between ten and fifteen per cent of the net national income, or between 17 and 25 billion roubles that are annually allocated to scientific research, nuclear armament, and outer space navigation. The members of this group are undogmatic or, combining Marxism with an ultra-modern scientific outlook, aware of how indispensable they are to Party and State, and completely unafraid of the Party bosses. It is, for instance, an open secret in Moscow that nuclear scientists are the chief patrons of the artistic *avant-garde*: they take under their wings the unorthodox poets; they buy abstract paintings and sculptures; and in this way they enable artists to stand up to the Ilyichevs and the other art censors.

Secondly, the chief planners and managers of heavy industry and engineering still represent the largest single economic interest in the state. The power of this lobby, however, has been weakened by the antagonism between its central Muscovite elements and the various republican and provincial managerial groups. The central managers suffered a signal defeat in 1957–58, when Khrushchev disbanded the All-Union economic ministries; now the balance seems to be shifting back in their favour. The men of this lobby work through the Central Planning Commission, the Councils of the National Economy, and, last but not least, through the Central Committee.

Thirdly, the trade union lobby, organized in the All-Union Council of the Trade Unions, also has an important say in economic planning, as far as it concerns issues of social policy and of national wage structure. Although the trade union bosses represent the interests of the employer-state *vis-à-vis* the workers, they must also, to some extent, voice the desiderata of their immense membership which comprises about 70 million workers and employees. The influence of this lobby has been responsible for the narrowing, in the course of the last decade, of the wide discrepancies between high and low wages and salaries, and for the shortening of working hours in industry.

Fourthly, the lobby of municipalities partly overlaps with the trade union lobby. Its importance arises from the fact that since Stalin's death, in only twelve years, the urban population of the U.S.S.R. has increased by about 50 million—by as much as the entire population of Great Britain, or France, or Italy. The demand for housing has grown stupendously and incomparably faster than the housing space provided; and the municipalities and the trade unions have had to press that demand on the ruling group, especially in the last few years, when construction has been falling short of the plan.

Fifthly, the agricultural interest is represented on the one hand by the well-organized and influential chiefs of the state-owned farms, the *sovkhozy*, and, on the other, by the timid and rather unrepresentative spokesmen of the collective farms, the *kolkhozes*. State farming gained much strength from Khrushchev's decision to bring under the plough vast areas of virgin land—the new farms on those lands are state-owned. Since the partial fiasco of that experiment, the *kolkhoz* lobby has been gaining some ground and it has been somewhat strengthened since Khrushchev's departure.

It is not quite clear where in this list the officer corps of the conventional military forces ought to be placed. Its influence has violently fluctuated in the post-Stalin era. Twice it acquired great importance: once at the moment of Beria's downfall, in the summer of 1953; and then again at the time of Molotov's and Kaganovich's demotion, in the summer of 1957. The phantom of a Soviet Bonaparte then hovered over the Soviet scene; but it was laid in the autumn of 1957 with Marshal Zhukov's eclipse. There are signs of a recent rise in the influence of the officer corps, possibly in connection with the recovery by the conventional forces of part of their old strategic importance. For a variety of reasons, however (such as the continuing predominance of the nuclear services and the ageing and exit of the famous Marshals of the last war), this lobby is not likely to recapture the power it had between 1953 and 1957.

The leaders of the many academic institutes and their *côteries* derive much influence from the relevance of their research to issues of national economy. In combination with the nuclear scientists and advanced managers, this lobby has been pressing hard for speeding up the tempo of automation, for the modernization of planning techniques, for the extensive and systematic use of computers, etc.

Finally, the journalistic and literary lobbies are important for propaganda; and so the Party leaders are sensitive to their pressure, but are also frightened of the dissent spreading among young writers. (The power of dissent showed itself lately in Moscow's Union of Writers, when in an election an over-whelming majority rejected the official candidates and elected 'heretics' to the Union's Board.)

Any classification and characterization of these lobbies is bound to be schematic; it cannot reproduce the immense reality of the pressures and counter-pressures that are active in a quasi-socialist state with nearly 230 million citizens. Across the lines of division described here run the divisions between the geographic regions and the nationalities: Great Russian, Ukrainian, Byelorussian, Georgian, Armenian, Kazakh, Uz-bekh, and others. All this produces an infinite complexity and variety of interests and aspirations. And the lobbies and pressure groups are themselves subjected to the pressures and counter-pressures coming from the depth of society, from the mass of workers and peasants.

Khrushchev's overthrow was brought about by the ex-ceptionally wide front which the lobbies and pressure groups had formed against him in the course of the last year of his government. The two major critical developments that brought about this situation were the disastrous state of agriculture and the consequent scarcity of food, and the steep decline in the course of the Russo-Chinese feud, of the Soviet influence over the communist camp. Another factor in the crisis was the widespread and explosive discontent in the working class, a discontent caused in the main by the wage freeze which Khrush-chev had been tacitly imposing on industry for four or five years. The full impact of this factor is becoming apparent in the light of the latest information from the U.S.S.R. According to certain Soviet opposition circles, which may be described as near Trotskyist, Khrushchev's downfall was preceded by a strike of all workers in Moscow's ZIS motor car factory and by many turbulent strikes all over the Donetz Coal Basin. In the

Donetz Basin troops were allegedly brought out, and bloody clashes followed, in which two hundred strikers were killed or wounded. I cannot vouch for the accuracy of the reports of the events in the Donetz Basin, but I have reason to believe in the complete truth of the information about the strike in Moscow. The strikes were economic, without, it seems, any political element in them; and they induced the trade union lobby to turn against Khrushchev and to assist in his overthrow.

While the Soviet press has not given to its readers even an inkling of these events, Khrushchev's successors have had to begin their term of office by quietly cancelling his wage freeze and promising an immediate and radical expansion of the housing programme. These are the real issues which shape Soviet policy. They are much larger and far more dramatic than any of the personal rivalries at the top of the Soviet hierarchy which fascinate most Western Sovietologists. These fundamental issues decide the outcome even of the personal rivalries for they determine how, in what direction, and in whose favour the lobbies and pressure groups exercise their influence at the level of the Central Committee. This fact accounts for the cagey behaviour and the silence of Khrushchev's successors: the situation is too tense and grave for them to speak out and take risks. The lobbies are far more powerful and active than they were under Stalin and Khrushchev; and there is no saying how they may be affected by the restive moods of the intelligentsia, the workers, and the peasants.

And, amid all the international alarums and domestic difficulties, a major political event is approaching: the Twenty-third Party Congress due to be convened in the second half of this year. Before the congress there must be some semblance of public debate, and the debate might even become real. At the congress the leaders would be expected to report on the Central Committee's work since 1961, to give some account of the Khrushchev crisis, to define their own attitude and policies, and to try and gain the prestige and public confidence, which they so urgently need and so conspicuously lack. The congress may, of course, be postponed beyond the statutory four-year term. But in that case the leaders would merely admit that they are daunted by their task; and such an admission would underline the lack of ideological and political authority in the hierarchy and would deepen and aggravate what is already a national crisis of confidence.

16 February 1965

16
The Policies of Brezhnev and Kosygin

In September 1965 important economic changes were announced by Kosygin at a Central Committee meeting. In the previous January it had already been announced that four hundred consumer goods industrial plants were to abandon production on the basis of planned targets and were to produce in response to consumer demand. This trend was continued in Kosygin's September report in which he said that 'Administrative methods have prevailed over economic ones'; a system of bonus payments for workers was introduced. At the same time the planning machinery was re-centralized: the *sovnarkhozy* which Khrushchev had set up in 1957 (see chapter 8) were abolished; and many All-Union Ministries for particular industries were re-established. Kosygin argued that a decentralized system of industrial planning 'has impeded the development of branch specialization and of rational industrial links between enterprises situated in different economic areas'. These decisions were ratified by a meeting of the Supreme Soviet held on 1–2 October.

The cancellation of Khrushchev's reforms was taken a step further at the Twenty-third Congress of the Soviet Communist Party, held in March 1966. Kosygin's speech concentrated on economic matters: he attacked Khrushchev's Five Year Plan for its 'economically unjustifiable' targets and for its 'amateurish contempt for the data of science and practical experience'. A more modest Five Year Plan, covering the period 1966–70, was proposed.

Brezhnev's speech dealt with foreign affairs. He announced that there would be no immediate full-scale international communist conference to discuss inter-Party differences. The Chinese and Albanians had refused to attend the 'revisionist' Twenty-third Congress, but in the preceding twelve months Chinese foreign

policy had reversed the trend of 1964 towards a less isolated
position. China had miscalculated during the Algerian *coup*
of June 1965 and her ally, the Indonesian Communist Party,
had been massacred by anti-Sukarno generals in the autumn; this
return to isolation was further confirmed by the Great Cultural
Revolution which was launched in May 1966, two months after
the Soviet congress. China's isolation was, of course, from the
governments of the world; whether she was also isolated from the
peoples of the world remained to be seen.

1 KOSYGIN'S ECONOMIC
COUNTER-REFORM

The Soviet Union has become the scene of a gigantic economic and administrative upheaval. The Party's Central Committee has at its last session decided to undo and obliterate most of the Khrushchev reforms of the 1950s. The whole structure of the Soviet economy is to be overhauled; and Kosygin, the Soviet Prime Minister, has made it clear that it is bound to take two or three years before the resulting disarray is brought under control. The overriding purpose of the changes is to re-invest in Moscow the strict central control over the economy that was once, before Khrushchev's days, exercised from the Kremlin.

It is over eight years now since Khrushchev struck a heavy blow against Moscow's bureaucracy, ordered the disbandment of scores of central economic ministries, and set up ninety-two *sovnarkhozy* or Economic Councils, each of which was to manage the affairs of the economic regions into which the country was divided. This reform was expected to break the rigidities of Stalinist super-centralization, to do justice to local interests, and to release local initiative and energy. In the years 1957 and 1958 Moscow witnessed the dispersal of its managerial aristocracy, whose members were leaving the capital to take up more modest posts in remote provinces. In vain did Molotov, Kaganovich, and Malenkov try to rally the disgraced industrial 'barons' and to preserve the central management of the economy. That was the hey-day of de-Stalinization; and Khrushchev then appeared to be the Soviet St. George slaying the dragon of bureaucracy. Now, a year after Khrushchev's downfall, the dragon seems to be reviving and returning in triumph. The central economic ministries are being re-created, while the regional *sovnarkhozy* are disbanded. A new migration of the bureaucracy is beginning: after a diaspora lasting eight years the barons of the industrial bureaucracy are about to return to the old seats of power in Moscow. Meanwhile, there is an interregnum in the immense realm of Soviet industry: the *sovnarkhozy* have lost power; the central ministries are not yet formed; and for the time being Gosplan, the State Planning Commission, which has no experience in the practical management of industry, is supposed to exercise authority.

It is with some obvious misgivings that the Soviet Prime Minister has launched this counter-reform. Between the lines of his long and grim speech at the Central Committee he tried to reassure the country that what it is experiencing is not a relapse into the absurdities of the Stalinist bureaucracy. While he insisted on the imperative need to restore central control of industry, he also dwelt on the need to restrict that control to a few selected but crucial areas, and to guarantee the rights and prerogatives of local managers and producers. A special Charter of the Socialist Factory is to rationalize the system of management on the spot and to protect it against arbitrary interference from the top. The new ministries, unlike their Stalinist predecessors, should avoid pressing managers and workers for mere quantative production records. They should judge the work of any factory not so much by its indices of gross output, which often conceal inferior produce, but by the indices of actual sales which measure more accurately the socio-economic value of the output. In this respect, Kosygin intimated, Soviet industry should move even further away from the Stalin era than it has done so far.

The state, Kosygin further announced, will gradually stop paying subsidies to all industrial concerns working at a deficit; henceforth every industrial unit should produce at a profit. This does not amount to the 'rehabilitation of the profit motive' predicted by some Western Sovietologists in connection with the so-called Lieberman Debate. For one thing, there has hardly been any need for any 'rehabilitation of profit'—in the last few years, for instance, profits shown by Soviet industry amounted annually to something like 40 billion roubles, between twenty and twenty-five per cent of the net national income. At present half of the national investment funds and of all other government expenditure is provided by industry's profits and half by indirect taxation. The proportions between the government's revenues from these two sources have been of decisive economic, political, and cultural significance. Throughout the decades of forced industrialization Stalin obtained most of the accummulation funds from indirect taxation, which he used in order to subsidize deficit industries, to expand industries which were growing much faster than their accumulation funds, and to keep down popular consumption. With the progress of industrialization, indirect taxation has played a decreasing part and industrial profits have played an increasing part in financing further economic development. (Therein, to put it in technical Marxist terms, consists the transition from 'primitive' to 'normal' socialist accumulation.)

Kosygin has announced that his government is carrying this policy much further. Henceforth Soviet industry is to ensure its continued expansion by means of self-finance, that is by drawing on its own profits. This implies a further relative reduction in indirect taxation and a relative increase in the population's purchasing power, which must find its counterpart in an increased volume of available consumer goods. In a state-owned economy, however, the question whether industry can draw on its profits is often a matter of book-keeping, for the profitability of an industry may depend on the prices it obtains for its produce; and it is the government that fixes the prices. A new Price Commission is now therefore to revise the entire price structure of the Soviet economy, with an eye to enabling producer industries to become financially self-supporting and consumer industries to expand faster than hitherto.

Anxious to justify the overhaul of the industrial machinery and the new policies, Kosygin spoke emphatically about the slowing down of Russia's rate of development in recent years. This has shown itself in the not quite satisfactory results of the Seven Year Plan now coming to a close. Although gross industrial output has risen by eighty-four per cent since 1958, this growth has been, according to the Soviet Prime Minister, far too slow in relation to investment in fixed capital; and similarly, the rise in productivity per man-hour has also been sluggish. The continued crisis in agriculture—this year has again brought poor harvests—limits the volume of available consumer goods and affects badly the morale and the efficiency of industrial workers. All this, Kosygin concludes, compels a re-centralization and a rationalization of economic management. The Soviet administration has not been able to cope with its mounting difficulties because Khrushchev, in his zeal for decentralization, has deprived it of the means of effective economic action.

There is undoubtedly some truth in all this. It has been clear for quite a long time now that the Khrushchevite reforms, far from curing the Soviet economy of too-rigid bureaucratic control, have added to it the drawbacks of an extreme decentralization. The regional *sovnarkhozy* have developed their own local interests and particularisms and have weakened the cohesiveness and the momentum of the national economy. Yet it is doubtful, to say the least, whether the present return to central control can provide the remedy. It is the curse of a bureaucratic regime that it cannot strike a sound balance between central control and local initiative; and Soviet management has floundered between the extremes of a despotic over-centralization and particularist-bureaucratic anarchy. There is also in Kosygin's counter-reform more than a mere reaction against the excesses and disappointments of the Khrushchevite decentralization. He has made a social appeal to the managerial groups with whom Khrushchev had been in some conflict. He is rehabilitating them; he is promising to raise them up again and to restore their privileges and prestige. He has pledged himself implicitly to resist the egalitarian trend that has been stirring in the U.S.S.R. in the post-Stalin era. His Charter of the Socialist Factory is to be above all the Charter of the Factory Manager, who is promised that he will be given the right—unheard of in the U.S.S.R.—to hire and fire workers, and also greater discretion than he hitherto enjoyed in distributing his wages funds among the workers. Nothing, apart from the much overwrought promise of a greater abundance of consumer goods in the future, is offered to sweeten the pill for the mass of the workers. It remains to be seen what the reaction to Kosygin's policies will be at the factory level and in the trade unions.

The adoption of these decisions has been a matter of political delicacy. It is not clear just how much support Kosygin has obtained for his moves either in the Presidium or in the Central Committee. His most influential colleagues have behaved in a non-committal manner. There must have been considerable opposition in the Central Committee if Kosygin had to reduce it to silence by the simple device of inviting many outsiders to

the Central Committee's session, a procedure which Khrushchev favoured and which was held out against him when he
fell. Nor is the postponement of the Party Congress till next
year, beyond the statutory time-limit, a good augury for the
present ruling group. Disregard for the Party's statutory rights
has too often and too loudly in recent years been denounced as
the hallmark of Stalinism!

There is indeed a distinct flavour of Stalinism in some of
Kosygin's moves; and it does not seem likely that the country
will easily swallow his counter-reforms. The workers are likely
to look askance at the increased powers of the managers. In
the capitals of the non-Russian nationalities people will resent
the renewed concentration of economic power in Moscow. The
country as a whole may suspect a shamefaced attempt at something like a bureaucratic restoration. . . .

30 September 1965

2 THE U.S.S.R. BETWEEN THE
TWENTIETH AND
TWENTY-THIRD CONGRESS

A year after Khrushchev's downfall, and nearly ten years after
his epoch-making speech at the Twentieth Congress, it is not
easy to see whither the U.S.S.R. is moving and what are its
prospects for the near future. The main issue with which its
government and people are occupied is how to overcome the
stagnation that makes itself felt in many spheres of national life;
how to break the various deadlocks Khrushchev's government
has left behind; and how to recapture the *élan* of the industrial
ascendancy and social advance of the first years after Stalin.

The sense of a general slowing down of national progress
has been widespread and acute. It was disillusionment with this
state of affairs that hastened Khrushchev's downfall: people had
realized that, after all its initial achievements, Khrushchev's
government had somehow lost initiative and tempo. The continuous rise in the popular standards of living, which he had
promised, failed to materialize; popular consumption was

declining. Food was scarce; in 1963–64 long bread queues appeared at the bakeries as in times of war and calamitous famine. The popular mood expressed itself in a certain crude nostalgia for the Stalin era and in bitter sarcasm about Stalin's successors. 'Do you know which was Stalin's gravest fault and crime?', ran, for instance, one characteristic comment of an anonymous Muscovite wit. 'I can tell you: it is that he did not lay in a stock of grain that would last us longer than the mere ten years after his death.' Popular memories are short; after fifteen or twenty years the hardships and terrors of the Stalin era may already appear less terrifying than they were. Unfortunately, the popular cynicism feeds on facts. According even to official statistics, there has been a steady decline in the annual growth rate of Soviet industrial production: in 1954 the rate was thirteen per cent, in 1964 it was only seven per cent. In consumer industries the decline has been even steeper. While such indices cause alarm in Moscow, they are naturally read with *Schadenfreude* in Washington, where some strategists conclude that the U.S.S.R., failing to 'catch up' with the U.S.A. industrially, is, like Britain and France before her, sinking to the rank of a second-class power, leaving the United States as the only super-power in the world.

This extreme conclusion is at least premature. Russia's industrial output still equals the combined output of Britain, France, and the Federal German Republic. It amounts to about sixty per cent of American production, according to Russian claims, or to about fifty per cent, according to American estimates. Even now the growth rate is well above Western rates so that the balance of industrial power is still shifting in Russia's favour, even if it does so more slowly than in the 1950s. Heavy industry in particular is still expanding by at least ten per cent a year. Since 1959 the annual output of steel has risen from 55 to 90 million tons; that of oil from 113 to 240 million tons; of electricity from 235 billion kilowatt-hours to over 500 billions; of cement from 33 to 66 million tons. Simultaneously the output of machine tools has risen by nearly one third, to 180 thousand units per year. When it is said that Soviet industrial production amounts to fifty or sixty per cent of the American, this means that the consumer industries still turn out only one quarter or less of the American output, whereas heavy industry produces three-quarters or more of American production, while the volume of heavy engineering is approximately the same in both countries.

The question now is whether the Soviet Union is going to maintain its present reduced tempo of growth? Or can it perhaps regain the higher tempo of the years between 1953 and 1958? Or is its pace of development going to slow down even further? The implications of each of these possible rates of development are clear enough. If the Russians could succeed in recapturing the higher rate of growth, they would be in a position to develop their economic and military potential rapidly, to raise their standard of living appreciably, and, indeed, to catch up with the U.S.A. If they were merely to maintain the present tempo, they might still be 'catching up', but more slowly than they hoped and at far greater cost to Soviet consumers. The question would then be whether Soviet consumers would consent to go on paying the cost. On the other hand, a further decline in the growth rate would aggravate all the difficulties with which the U.S.S.R. has been confronted; it would inflict on it a major international defeat with incalculable domestic repercussions.

We may, I think, assume that the industrialization of the U.S.S.R. will continue, at whatever pace; so will the urbanization of Soviet society and the progress of mass education. The long-term social trends, which have so mightily transformed the structure of Soviet society, are still at work. At the end of the Stalin era the Soviet Union was still predominantly a peasant country; only a little over forty per cent of its population lived in the cities and towns. At present the town dwellers already form fifty-five per cent of the population. This means that in the lifetime of one generation the urban population of the U.S.S.R. has grown by nearly 100 million (from twenty-odd million forty years ago to 122 million at present). And nearly half of this stupendous growth has occurred since the end of the Stalin era. For the first time in Russian history the working class now forms the majority of the nation, while the *kolkhoz* peasantry is a shrinking minority. This trend will continue, because millions of peasant children feel redundant on the farms and are attracted by opportunities in the towns. There has also been a phenomenal growth in the numbers of intellectuals and white-collar workers at large, who now form twenty-two per cent of the gainfully employed people. The U.S.S.R. is employing over 23 million technicians, teachers, doctors, scientists, and administrators—more than three times as many as it employed twenty years ago and on the eve of the Second World War.

This phenomenal and uniquely rapid transformation of society is for the Soviet Union a source of immense strength but also of some weakness. One of its consequences is the terrible overcrowding in the cities; the government's housing schemes have so far only slightly mitigated the desperate shortage of accommodation. What is worse, and far more dangerous, is that the state is now directly responsible for feeding the great majority of the nation. With the swelling of the urban population, this responsibility assumes gigantic dimensions; while the inertia of agriculture, which in some years produces not more than it did forty or fifty years ago, is becoming a national catastrophe. An industrial nation smaller than Russia might resolve the problem in the way Britain resolved it in the nineteenth century, by deliberately basing its economic policy upon systematic importation of foreign foodstuffs. But a nation of Russia's size, and in Russia's delicate international position, cannot regularly buy the bulk of its food in foreign markets. Its imports of grain and meat can provide only marginal additions to its own production. To encourage domestic food production Brezhnev and Kosygin are now doing what Khrushchev did a decade ago: they are offering incentives to the farmers, higher prices for foodstuffs, greater freedom to trade, and other 'liberal' concessions. By such means—but in the main by bringing under plough vast areas of virgin lands—Khrushchev obtained a spectacular, but only temporary, increase in the agricultural output. Can his successors achieve a comparable increase? And if they do, will their success not be as short-lived as Khrushchev's was?

But why has Soviet policy in this field continually moved from one costly failure to another, or, at best, from short-lived success to complete fiasco? Why have even the most hopeful administrative reforms proved ineffective in the end? This last question must be asked not only about agriculture, for the balance of the post-Stalin reforms in industry has also been negative. Only a few years ago Khrushchev, convinced that he had found the remedies for Russia's industrial troubles, was zealously decentralizing the administration, dismantling the economic ministries in Moscow, and setting up regional economic councils instead. Now his successors, mocking his 'projectomania', are busy recentralizing the economy, disbanding the regional councils, and re-creating the industrial ministries in Moscow. And economists and planners are once again exhibiting favourite panaceas and *nostrums*.

Unfortunately, the general atmosphere in which the Soviet economy is run is so unsound that its irrationality infects even the reformist work of the best economists and administrators. Whatever scheme is applied—whether it is based on 'socialist competition', Stakhanovism, or 'profitability'—is in practice reduced to a bureaucratic absurdity. This stems from a basically faulty relationship between politics and economics, from the lack of a common language and genuine contact between the ruling group and the great mass of producers in town and country. Any change in the pattern of economic administration introduces only a new variant of uncontrolled bureaucratic management, operating within closed circles of bureaucratic fictions. The Khrushchevian decentralization degraded the Moscow-based hierarchy in favour of the provincial bureaucracies. The present centralization re-establishes the supremacy of the central managerial hierarchy. Under the one scheme as under the other the mass of workers has no real share in the planning and in the running of the economy, and no chance to criticize and influence or depose those who plan and run it badly. Hence the pervasive corruption of the bureaucrats and managers. Hence the stubborn sullenness of the workers and farmers and their non-identification with the state and its purposes. Stalin's successors have sought to remedy this estrangement of the producers from the employer-state, one of the worst inheritances of the Stalin era, by means of 'reform from above'. The employer-state has given up most of the coercive practices by means of which it kept the workers and the peasants in subjection. But while some of the worst social evils have been removed in this way, the reform has not attained its positive objectives. The abatement of the terror has not amounted to a restitution of civil liberties; and the curbing of official arbitrariness has not sufficed to make workers and peasants identify themselves with the state or to give them a sense of responsibility for the national economy. It is still in terms of 'we' and 'they' that the ruled think of the rulers, the Party bosses and the industrial managers.

Thus, the record of these last ten or twelve years has unmistakably demonstrated the inadequacy of the post-Stalinist reforms from above. The bureaucracy has been unable to free the country from the absurdities and rigidities of its method of government. Its rule, though preferable to Stalin's autocracy, is still misrule. It is immensely wasteful; and it deadens or weakens all progressive impulses within the social organism. The chronic deadlocks in the economy cannot be broken by any schemes for 'profitability' or other administrative *nostrums*, because their main cause lies in politics and public morale. No matter what incentives the government offers to encourage production, the people at the factory benches and in the fields suspect, with good reason, that they will be cheated and never get the promised benefits. An uncontrolled bureaucracy is indeed an economic dis-incentive of quite devastating power. More than ever the Soviet Union needs, at every level of its existence, political freedom, the freedom of expression and association, the freedom for citizens to criticize the powers that be and, if need be, to replace them. Only this can give the mass of producers the sense that they are working for their own state and their own economy; and without that all talk about 'socialism and the transition to communism' is empty and hypocritical chatter.

This is by no means only a domestic Soviet problem, for bureaucratic irresponsibility has inevitably also affected the conduct of Soviet foreign policy. The fact that Moscow's moves —both those that concern the capitalist powers and those that concern other communist governments and Parties—are never open to public debate and criticism accounts for much of their irrationality. Without coming to terms with the U.S.A., without achieving an international detente that would really allow it to ease the burden of armament, the Soviet Union has lost its leading position in the communist camp, has dangerously offended its great Chinese ally, and has antagonized even its partners in Comecon, that is its Eastern European satellites. Soviet policy would hardly have run so disastrous a course if the Soviet government had to give an account of its moves, and to justify them before a truly representative Supreme Soviet, whose members were free to criticize and vote in accordance with their political conscience. But shielded by secrecy, immune from public criticism, and always assured of unanimous votes in their favour, the successive Party leaders and governments have been free to indulge in acts which would have aroused the hostility of a better-informed, more vocal and socialist-minded nation. Thus, in July 1960 Khrushchev cancelled all Soviet aid to China and recalled all Soviet engineers and technicians, inflicting thereby a most cruel and crippling blow on Russia's most important ally. Yet to the present day the Soviet people have not been officially informed of this event and its consequences! Clearly, Khrushchev would not have been able to pursue his futile 'personal diplomacy', to indulge alternately in a clownish wooing of American Presidents and then, in needless provocation, to embark on his Cuban adventure, to extol the 'socialism' of a Nasser or a Sukarno, and so on, if he had had to reckon with alert and quick-minded public attacks from critics at home. Nothing is as costly, incalculable, and potentially dangerous as is the secret diplomacy of uncontrolled governments. Once again: the Soviet Union needs civil liberties in order to rationalize its foreign policy and give it a truly socialist direction.

It would, however, be idle to expect that the present ruling group will restore civil liberties, unless it is forced to do so by a vigorous and articulate popular movement rising from below. It is because of the absence of any such movement, after decades of totalitarian suppression, that the Soviet Union has not so far been able to go beyond the half-hearted de-Stalinization and beyond the half-measures and palliatives of a half-reform. Will the popular energies of the U.S.S.R. awaken, assert themselves, and be able to cleanse the state, its economy, and its conduct of foreign affairs from the dry rot of bureaucracy? This is the momentous question which only the events of the coming years can answer.

3 SOVIET FOREIGN POLICY
IN 1965

The record of Soviet foreign policy in 1965 was not favourable to the Soviet Government. After Khrushchev's downfall, his successors blamed him for the tension between Russia and China, the anti-Russian uproar in Eastern Europe, the virtual dissolution of Comecon, and, last but not least, a deadlock in Russo-American relations. Brezhnev and Kosygin set out to correct Khrushchev's 'errors'; and, without abandoning the intention of cultivating the detente with the West, they hoped to repair the broken friendship with China. As a token of the peacefulness of their policy, they reduced military expenditure in their first budget, the budget for the year 1965. Towards China they made a gesture which was more than symbolic: they stopped all public polemic against the Chinese and resumed direct negotiations with them. None of these efforts, it appears, has met with striking success. After a year in office Kosygin speaks about a worsening in Russo-American relations and is raising defence expenditure; in his interview with James Reston of *The New York Times* he dismissed as untimely any suggestion of a meeting between himself and President Johnson. On the other hand, after a year during which the Russians (though not the Chinese) refrained from any public controversy over ideology, they are now again broadcasting their mutual polemics for the whole world to hear.

This simultaneous deterioration in Russia's relations with both the U.S.A. and China results to some extent from the course of the war in Vietnam. Peking and Moscow continue to disagree over policy there, although they have not so far defined any clear alternatives. The Chinese charge the Russians with being lukewarm and mean in allocating aid to the Vietcong; whereas the Russians accuse the Chinese of making a united communist front over Vietnam impossible. The Chinese have, in fact, obstructed any deep Russian involvement in Vietnam. They fear that if the Russians pour men and supplies into that country, they will rule it as their own province and then 'sell it down the river' to the Americans. But the Chinese, for all their verbal belligerency, have themselves also avoided military involvement in Vietnam. This situation—the aloofness of the two big brothers—may well suit Ho Chi Minh and the Hanoi government, but only for as long as American escalation has not made massive Russian, and/or Chinese, help a matter of life and death for North Vietnam. This point has evidently not yet been reached.

But are the Russians really prepared to sell the Vietnamese down the river? They are vigorously refuting the accusation and professing that they are second to none in their hostility towards American intervention. It is therefore still hardly possible to detect any significant differences between Russian and Chinese utterances on Vietnam. Both invoke the Geneva Agreements; both call for an end of American bombardments; both demand the withdrawal of American troops; and both know that the United States is in no mood to accept any of these demands. The supposed differences between Moscow's 'soft line' and Peking's 'tough line' may become more substantial and evident at a later stage of the war, when the United States has grown more weary of the fighting and more inclined to negotiate. Until then the complicated Russo-Chinese manoeuvres over Vietnam will to some extent consist of shadow-boxing.

The Soviet leaders are nevertheless careful not to plunge back into full-dress ideological controversy with Maoism; they avoid the theological fury that characterized the exchanges in Khrushchev's days. While Peking's anti-revisionist vehemence remains unabated, Moscow retorts only rarely and controls its language. This reticence and prudence have brought Brezhnev and Kosygin some dividends. By the time of Khrushchev's downfall Moscow was virtually isolated in the communist camp —even anti-Chinese communists thought that the Russians had gone too far in their attacks on Maoism. This is not the case at present. Moscow has regained much of the communist support in Europe and has managed to neutralize many Asian communists. Now the Chinese are increasingly isolated. It is they who bear the odium of persisting with the polemics; and as their accusations against the Russians grow wilder and wilder, they are becoming less and less convincing. Few communists can swallow, for instance, the Chinese allegations about capitalism in the U.S.S.R.

The Chinese have in addition committed a number of major

mistakes and suffered major defeats. They brought discredit upon themselves last summer when they rashly declared their support for Colonel Boumedienne, the new Algerian dictator, while most of the Algerian Left were still desperately resisting Boumedienne's *coup d'état*. The Chinese hoped to secure through Boumedienne the convocation of the Afro-Asian conference in Algiers and to exclude the Russians from it. These tactics appeared unprincipled and unscrupulous even to many pro-Chinese communists. Then, during the conflict between India and Pakistan, the moral support which Peking gave General Ayub Khan also outraged many of their leftish friends in Asia and Africa, who were inclined to say 'a plague on both your houses' to both Shastri and Ayub Khan. Most important has been the defeat which Chinese policy has suffered in Indonesia. For years the Indonesian communists, led by Aidit and strongly supported by the Chinese, cultivated the so-called Front of National Unity under General Sukarno, hailing the General as Indonesia's 'national and revolutionary hero'—with results that are now clear. Even at the height of the anticommunist terror in Jakarta, the Indonesian Communist Party did not cease to appeal to Sukarno for protection. The defeat of Indonesian communism has changed the political balance in Asia for quite a few years to come, even if the Communist Party eventually recovers. In the whole history of international communism there are only two comparable defeats: one suffered by the Chinese Party at Chiang Kai-shek's hands in 1927, and the other inflicted upon the German Party by Hitler in 1933. Aidit's policy *vis-à-vis* Sukarno was, by communist standards, extremely 'opportunistic' and rightist. Many communists have been puzzled by the fact that Peking supported it; and they have seen in this a reflection on the sincerity of the Maoist strictures at 'Khrushchevite opportunism'. The defeat of Indonesian communism is therefore Maoism's defeat as well.

The net result of these developments is a considerable improvement in Russia's tactical position *vis-à-vis* China. A parallel improvement is noticeable also in Russia's relations with Eastern Europe and with the Communist Parties of Western Europe. If the Russians manage to maintain or to improve further their position *vis-à-vis* the Chinese, they may well regain some of the elbow room they had lost; and they may show more initiative in international affairs than they could afford to show in the last few years. They may come to feel less cramped by fear of Chinese criticism and pressure; and in that case they may assume once again the role of peace-maker between the United States and communist Vietnam.

But again, the time for this has not yet come. And no Soviet Government can afford to ignore Chinese susceptibilities, as Khrushchev ignored them, without even being offered any *quid pro quo* by the American administration. Kosygin has made his terms fairly clear: the price of any new Russo-American accommodation is NATO's unequivocal refusal to allow the Federal German Republic any access, direct or indirect, to nuclear weapons. The fact that the American administration has in the last year repeatedly shelved this issue was probably received with sighs of relief in Moscow. But the deeper anxiety remains. It is always easier, the Russians reason, to stop a local war in South-East Asia than to wrest nuclear weapons from German hands, once the Germans have been allowed to get hold of them. For Russia, therefore, the latent crisis in Europe which grows with the new rise of German military power, overshadows the open crisis in Asia.

18 December 1965

4 THE TWENTY-THIRD CONGRESS: THE CRYPTO-STALINISTS RAISE THEIR HEADS

At the Twenty-third Congress, which ended in Moscow last week, the Soviet ruling group put a tombstone on Khrushchev's political grave, without mentioning his name even once. The inscription on the stone might run approximately like this:

Here lies a certain person (or rather an unperson), who by his arbitrary whims, conceits, and uncoordinated febrile activities did much harm to our Party and State, disorganized our industry, brought our farming to the brink of ruin, and nearly shook the morale of our people. He was eventually rendered harmless and put

into Limbo by the wisdom and vigilance of those who have succeeded him in office.

An almost identical method of anonymous denunciation, it may
be recalled, was applied to Stalin in the first two or three years
after his death. It is certain that at the closed session of the
congress, to which foreign communists—delegates from 'fraternal parties'—were not admitted, the de-Khrushchevization
was carried out quite explicitly.

What is clear is that the congress has either brought about or
merely revealed a swing from reform and de-Stalinization to
more rigid and authoritarian policies which may be described,
for the lack of a better term, as crypto- or neo-Stalinist. Most of
the reforms initiated by Khrushchev have been scrapped. The
congress was extremely reticent about the previously much
advertised projects of Soviet economists who urged the government to give wider scope in the national economy to the profit
motive. There is to be more central control over the administration and over industry. 'We want no more rocking of the
boat—we have had enough of that', the congress said in effect
to the 'liberals', 'de-Stalinizers', and advocates of further reform.
Stability, discipline, and caution were the watchwords. The
desire for stability and the fear of taking risks were such that the
authoritarians and crypto-Stalinists did not even dare to boast
of their indubitable success. They protested against the 'whole-
sale denigration of our heroic past' by novelists and writers of
memoirs; they called for stricter Party supervision over history
writing, literature, and the arts; but they did not come out
openly as the defenders of Stalin and Stalinism. Evidently no one
aspiring to play a role in Soviet political life can afford to do so.
This accounts for the fact that the congress did not rehabilitate
Molotov and Kaganovich, the Stalinist die-hards whom
Khrushchev had expelled from the Party; only their associates,
the old Marshal Voroshilov, has been brought back into the
Central Committee.

In the weeks preceding the opening of the congress the
possibility of a 'reassessment of Stalin' was hotly debated; and
the rumours of an impending rehabilitation of the great despot
caused alarm and led many eminent nuclear scientists, writers,
and Party veterans to express their misgivings and to protest in
public demonstrations, in collective letters to the Party leaders,

and in various other ways. These were almost factional activities, such as had not been tolerated for forty years, for in the Party, as in any army, collective protests of any kind are held to amount to mutiny. Those guilty of the mutinous acts have been reproved; but most of them are far too eminent to be punished; and their warnings have been heeded up to a point even by the crypto-Stalinists, who sensed that they might provoke a storm if they behave too provocatively.

The authoritarian trend in Party affairs has shown itself not so much in open pronouncements as in furtive manoeuvres and symbolic gestures. The Party's supreme authority, the Presidium, has been renamed Politbureau as it used to be called in the old days; and Brezhnev is no longer First Secretary but General Secretary, as Stalin was. The leaders of the three most powerful organizations, those of Moscow, Leningrad, and the Ukraine came forward with the demand for the restitution of the old title, which, they recalled, had been introduced by Lenin in 1922. This was no innocent playing with labels and historic memories, for although it is true that the Politbureau and the office of General Secretary had been formed on Lenin's initiative, it was only during the Stalin era that these exalted offices acquired their characteristic, awe-inspiring quality. To those old enough to remember this, it was evident that the leaders of Moscow, Leningrad, and the Ukraine were in fact calling for the man of the strong arm to take command of the Party once again and were hoping to impart strength to him by giving him Stalin's title. Yet no sooner had they raised this call than they had to mute it ambiguously and to reassure congress that they wanted strong leadership of the Leninist rather than of the Stalinist type.

The same ambiguity surrounded other decisions as well. Mikoyan, who had been the brain behind Khrushchev in the hey-day of de-Stalinization, was not re-elected to the Politbureau, ostensibly because of old age and ill-health. Yet he left the Party's ruling circle in silence, without even a vote of thanks for his forty years service in the Politbureau (and the Presidium). There is no doubt that his exit gave much satisfaction to the crypto-Stalinists. It was further decided to abolish the restrictions the previous congress had placed on the re-election of members to high office for second, third, or fourth terms. This reflected the hierarchy's fear that too much 'fresh blood' brought into it might result in too radical a change in the character and identity of the ruling group. The congress further resolved, again amid invocations of Leninist precedents, that so-called Party Conferences should be held in the intervals between Party Congresses. The difference consists in that delegates to congresses are elected by the rank and file, while participants of conferences are appointed from above. The difference may not amount to much in a country and a Party where the rank and file usually elect the nominees of those in authority. All the same, the conferences will more decidedly be the bureaucracy's own conventicles, immune against infiltration by undesirable influences; and they may be a good excuse for avoiding the convocation of congresses in critical situations. These measures and the all-round tightening of discipline indicate how anxious Brezhnev and his adherents are to reinforce the Party structure and its moral authority which have been so badly shaken by all the upsets of the post-Stalin years.

This indeed is the Time of Trouble for the Soviet Union. The prospects in agriculture remain uncertain. The standards of living are not rising or not rising fast enough. The economy has lost something of its momentum. Popular discontents have been boiling up. The ideological disarray, of which the Sinyavsky-Daniel affair is symptomatic, threatens to have a deep effect on national morale. And the outlook is rendered unsettled by the tensions between various generations and age groups. The old guilt-laden Stalinist generation is dying out; and the young who have not known Stalin are making their entry in every field of national life. It should be remarked that fifty per cent of the Soviet population are people under twenty-six years old, people for whom the last war is not even a childhood memory and to whom the taboos of the Stalin era are meaningless. Because of the immense losses the Soviet Union suffered in the last war—20 million dead—the middle generation is too weak and battered to fill the gap left by the old and to hold its ground against the young.

The next five or ten years are going to bring a dramatic rejuvenation of Soviet life, something like an explosion of youth and an irruption of new age groups into national politics and public affairs at large. The Party is physically and mentally much older than the nation. About fifty per cent of its members are over forty years old; and the average age of the hierarchy is around fifty. (The young are organized in the Komosomol, which offers them hardly any chance to influence national affairs.) A wide gap is thus yawning between the elderly conservative and frightened ruling group and the young, vigorous, but frustrated nation. Brezhnev is trying not so much to bridge the gap as to put up dams against the threatening irruption of new and unknown forces. It is doubtful whether the dams can hold and whether Brezhnev, even with the title of General Secretary, is the 'strong man' capable of controlling the gathering storms. He may well be the Party's new King Canute.

12 April 1966

5 THE TWENTY-THIRD
CONGRESS: THE SHADOW OF
VIETNAM

The Twenty-third Congress has left all the dilemmas of Soviet foreign policy in suspense, without daring to state them or discuss them. The pronouncements of the leaders were cagey, for they were designed to conceal differences within the ruling group and to avoid open controversy with other Communist Parties. Almost nothing was said about the Russo-Chinese conflict, although shortly before the congress Moscow assailed the Maoists heavily in confidential messages addressed to foreign communists, and although the Chinese had demonstratively refused to attend the Congress. The delegates had to content themselves with Brezhnev's benign assurances of good will towards China and of confidence in a happy resolution of the conflict. Between the lines one could almost hear sighs of relief at the absence of the Chinese. At the previous congress Chou En-lai, the notorious trouble-maker, demonstratively left after Khrushchev had launched an attack on the Albanians. No such scandalous scene could occur this time. The reason for the somewhat ostentatious 'prudence and self-restraint' the

Soviet leaders showed at the congress was their awareness that this tactic *vis-à-vis* China was bringing them handsome dividends. Some of the Parties that had until recently lined up with the Maoists were represented at the congress; and their delegates joined in the great unanimous hosannah for Khrushchev's successors. The Vietnamese (of North and South) also came with thanksgivings for the aid they were receiving from Russia; and in far-away Havana Fidel Castro was belabouring the Chinese with a rancour and a fury which even Khrushchev could not match. Brezhnev and Kosygin had some reason to be satisfied.

Yet, for all the prudence and caution, their speeches contained definite surprises; and so did the foreign policy deliberations at the congress. Brezhnev expressed himself in an idiom and in accents different from those used by Khrushchev. Although he spoke about Russia's desire to avoid war with the American imperialists, he did not dwell on 'peaceful coexistence': he played it down, and even tried to avoid using the term. 'Peaceful coexistence cannot flourish on the poisoned soil of American aggression', he and other speakers stated emphatically. The denunciations of American interventions in Vietnam and Latin America were unusually blunt; and, unlike Khrushchev, Brezhnev drew no distinction between the 'aggressive war-mongers' and the 'peace-loving and rational elements' in the American administration. His *leitmotif* was the Soviet Union's unconditional solidarity with all the revolutionary forces in the world struggling against neo-colonialism and striving for socialism. To be sure, Khrushchev also used to express such sentiments; and so it may be argued that there was nothing new in what Brezhnev said. However, the novelty consisted in quite a sharp shift of emphasis and in a conspicuous change of proportions. What used to be Khrushchev's main theme—'peaceful coexistence'—was only a minor note in Brezhnev's performance; and Khrushchev's secondary or even incidental theme—the Soviet Union's international revolutionary commitment—was Brezhnev's keynote. This was reflected in the whole composition and style of his *exposé*, and in its tenor which precluded any of those nostalgic references to the 'spirit of Geneva' and 'spirit of Camp David' which abounded in Khrushchevite pronouncements.

Nor did delegates at the congress, including those from foreign Communist Parties, speak about the possibility of a 'peaceful transition from capitalism to socialism' in some countries, which was another major theme in Khrushchev's days. These two notions—peaceful coexistence and the peaceful transition—have been the targets of all the Maoists attacks, for these were, in the Chinese eyes, the most important manifestations of 'Khrushchevite revisionism'. The present Soviet leaders were obviously anxious to remove these targets from sight. Thus, in a vague and cautious manner the congress was staged as a demonstration of a return to orthodoxy and to militancy. Characteristic of this mood was the fact that even the music that was transmitted into the congress hall from the Soviet satellite orbiting the moon was not the anthem of the Soviet Union, but the *Internationale*, the hymn of revolution and militant communism. This stage effect was carefully chosen.

The war in Vietnam undoubtedly cast its shadow on the congress. A special resolution on Vietnam commits the Soviet government to counter American escalation with increased aid to the Vietcong. The heightened vigilance and domestic discipline are all related to the tension in South-East Asia. This is reminiscent of the days of the Korean war about fifteen years ago, when Stalin was tightening the reins. But the alarms and the fears were much graver then, for the fighting was taking place much nearer the Soviet frontiers, and the threat of world war seemed more real and imminent. On the other hand, Brezhnev and Kosygin have to cope with difficulties by which Stalin was not embarrassed. They have to face the accusation that they are not doing enough to help the Vietcong and to defend North Vietnam against American bombardment. Not only the Chinese say this; even such staunch anti-Maoists as the Poles are reproaching Moscow for her inactivity and *immobilisme*. The Poles cannot help wondering, with a shudder, whether the Russians might not behave with similar phlegm in case of a conflict nearer home, if the Germans were one day to take up arms to reconquer the lands east of the Oder and Neisse. Generally speaking, Soviet passivity in face of an armed American attack on a 'fraternal socialist country' is causing anxious concern in all Communist Parties. At the congress this mood was expressed by the Cuban delegate who, despite his

Party's breach with the Chinese, delivered a somewhat vague but scathing attack on the Soviet position. Quoting Castro, he called the Soviet Party and government to 'take any risks that may be necessary to meet American aggression'. He held out the example of his own country, so small and so precariously placed, which was not afraid of any risks—why then should the Soviet colossus behave so gingerly over Vietnam? 'Very soon', he warned, 'there are going to be many other Vietnams' in various parts of the world, especially in Latin America. The Cuban delegate, and others besides him, were not impressed by Brezhnev's statement that Soviet aid to Vietnam last year amounted to half a billion dollars, which is very little indeed compared with the American expenditure. And uneasiness over the Soviet Government's behaviour is certainly shared by some sections of the Soviet people as well. This may be gathered from an event reported to have taken place just after the congress, when in the very centre of Moscow a young Ukrainian burned himself to death in protest against the authorities' refusal to let him go and fight as a volunteer in Vietnam. This demonstration was as unusual in Soviet circumstances as it was significant.

The resolutions of the congress and the reticence of the leaders *vis-à-vis* China conceal at least two conflicting attitudes. There are, on the one hand, those among the leaders who have in fact no desire for a reconciliation with China and are determined to continue the feud to the 'bitter end', but hold that it is good tactics for them to go on refraining from public polemics, to counter Chinese criticisms with insubstantial verbal concessions, and so to place the odium of the breach on the Chinese. Others, however, are genuinely anxious to come to terms with the Chinese, to co-ordinate policies and action, and to intervene more decisively in defence of North Vietnam. American escalation works to strengthen this latter group; and both groups fear that if the Russo-Chinese conflict is acted out in the open, the Americans may feel encouraged to attack China; and in that case the Soviet Union might find itself drawn into global conflict. It is difficult enough for the Soviet government to stand aloof while the American Air Force is bombing North Vietnam; but it would be quite impossible for it to do so if it bombarded China. (There was also much talk at the congress about the threat to peace in Europe coming from the Washington-Bonn axis, forming itself within NATO.) All this explains why Brezhnev and his adherents had to adopt at the congress the posture of 'moderation' *vis-à-vis* China. Behind the scenes, however, they attack the Chinese 'in secret', and continue a kind of an unpublicized war of nerves against Maoism.

13 April 1966

17
The Great Cultural Revolution

In 1966 China was convulsed by the Great Proletarian Cultural
Revolution. It began in April and May as an ideological
purification movement among the intellectuals and was centred
on Peking University. But in June and July it was clear that many
prominent political figures had been dismissed: Peng Chen, the
Mayor of Peking, Lu Ting-yi, the former propaganda chief, Chou
Yang, a prominent literary organizer, and Lo Jui-ching, the
Army Chief of Staff, were among them.

In August the Central Committee of the Communist Party met
in plenary session for the first time since 1962 and issued a
directive on the Great Cultural Revolution. It stated that 'The
aim of the Great Cultural Revolution is to revolutionize people's
ideology', and to combat old ideas and those in authority who
were 'taking the capitalist road'. It emphasized the need for study
of the Thought of Mao Tse-tung, for mass action, and for army
participation in the Cultural Revolution. These all became
important features of subsequent events: Mao's Thought was
issued in the form of a little red book of quotations, and,
following a mass demonstration by revolutionary youth on
18 August, young intellectuals, students, and workers were
organized into the 'Red Guards'. This was accompanied by the
emergence of Lin Piao, the Minister of Defence, as the 'close
comrade-in-arms' of Mao Tse-tung, 'the great helmsman'; and it
later emerged that the group of 'capitalist roaders' against whom
the Cultural Revolution was aimed included Liu Shao-chi, the
President of China, Teng Hsiao-ping, the Secretary of the Party,
and many less prominent officials in government and the Party.

THE MEANING OF THE 'CULTURAL REVOLUTION'

As one reads the endless official reports on the 'cultural upsurge of the masses' in China one may be tempted to dismiss the upsurge as mere farce. The Chinese News Agency has described in detail the 'fierce offensive against all old ideas, culture, customs, and habits' that the 'Red Guards have taken to the streets of Peking since 20 August'. But one looks in vain for any positive indication of what the new ideas and the new cultural customs and habits are. In the name of Marxism and Leninism the Guards have denounced Balzac and Hugo, and Shakespeare and Beethoven, as the products of a rotting bourgeois culture; they have defaced Pushkin's monument in Shanghai, and have vented their contempt for the works of Chernyshevsky and Herzen, the progenitors of the Russian revolutionary movement of the nineteenth century. Peking's 'cultural revolutionaries' are, it seems, quite unaware of Marx's lifelong admiration for Shakespeare and Balzac, of Lenin's love for Pushkin and Beethoven, and of the decisive formative influence Chernyshevsky had on him. We have been presented with long lists of streets and boulevards, the names of which have been changed from 'Eternal Peace' to 'The East is Red', from 'Well of the Prince's Palace' to 'Prevent Revisionism', from 'Glorious Square' to 'Support Vietnam', from 'Eastern Peace Market' to 'East Wind Market', and so on. We are asked to rejoice in the fact that certain culinary establishments are no longer called 'Collection of All Virtues', but 'Peking Roast Duck Restaurants'. Hosts of hairdressers and dressmakers have pledged themselves to produce no more outlandish haircuts, such as 'duck tail' and 'spiralling' hairdoes, or cowboy jeans and tight fitting shirts and blouses and various kinds of Hongkong-style skirts. 'We should not regard these matters lightly', the Chinese Agency says gravely, 'because it is here that the gates to capitalist restoration are wide open'. And so the floodwaters of the great proletarian cultural revolution are now pounding the various positions of the bourgeoisie; and the hotbeds of capitalism are no longer safe. Poor Karl Marx—he had no inkling, when, exactly a hundred years ago, he was preparing *Das*

Kapital for publication, where the real 'hotbeds of capitalism' were to be found.

Undertaking the all-too-easy task of ridiculing these exploits the Soviet press has recalled *Proletkult,* the Russian literary and artistic movement of the early years of the revolution, which renounced bourgeois art and promised to create a proletarian culture. A writer in *Pravda* has described Trotsky as *Proletkult*'s inspirer, which should presumably be enough to make both *Proletkult* and the Chinese 'cultural revolution' stink in our nostrils. The truth is that, by comparison with the Chinese riot, the Russian *Proletkult,* which was akin to Western European Futurism fashionable in those years, was a harmless and almost civilized affair; it was supported by Bukharin and Luna-charsky, while Trotsky, far from being its inspirer, wrote a whole book, *Literature and Revolution,* to repudiate it. *Pravda* could have found a much closer parallel to the latest events in China nearer home: in the Stalinist Russia of the late 1940s and early 1950s, when Stalin, Zhdanov, and *Pravda*'s writers 'disciplined' the intelligentsia, thundered against 'kowtowing to decadent Western culture', banned the works of Einstein, Freud, Mendel, and many other foreign thinkers, and indulged in a hysterical glorification of all things Russian. *Pravda* avoids drawing this parallel because even now Russia has not yet fully lived down the legacy of that period, and quite a few of the old bans are still in force. But the parallel is close enough; and it suggests that the Maoist 'cultural revolution' is a deadly serious affair. Its effect on China's spiritual and intellectual life is, in all probability, going to be just as devastating and lasting as were the consequences of the Stalinist witch-hunts. Its political meaning is also comparable. Like Russia in the last years of the Stalin era, so China has now plunged headlong into a self-centred isolationism and nationalism and has shut herself off more hermetically than ever from the outside world and from all its political and cultural influences. To achieve this Mao had to organize a pogrom of the intelligentsia, whom he suspects of being vulnerable to foreign especially 'revisionist' influences.

This is not to say that these developments foreshadow any new aggressive phase in China's foreign policy. True, in the last few weeks Peking and Shanghai have resounded with the cry for the liberation of Taiwan, Macao, and Hongkong. But nothing indicates that Marshal Lin Piao is preparing marching orders for the liberation campaigns (even though all Chinese, communists and anti-communists, Maoists and anti-Maoists alike, consider these territories as belonging to their country by right). China is even less ready than Russia was in Stalin's last years for war-like adventures or territorial expansion. Her ideological aggressiveness and her shrill contempt for Western cultural values are manifestations, no doubt morbid ones, of her intensely self-defensive mood and of her sense of complete isolation in a hostile world. Since Khrushchev withdrew, with utter ruthlessness, all economic assistance from China in 1960, that sense of isolation has grown heavy and stifling; and recent setbacks—above all the collapse of the pro-Maoist Communist Party of Indonesia and the slaughter of hundreds of thousands of its members—have aggravated it to the utmost. Despite Peking's thunderous rhetoric about the 'rising wave of revolution in Asia', the Indonesian events mark a deep ebb of revolution and a disaster for Maoism. The defection of the Japanese and North Korean Communist Parties from the Chinese camp have been further setbacks; and the ambiguous behaviour of the North Vietnamese, who are more than ever dependent on Soviet aid, is causing much discomfiture to Peking. Above all, the Chinese believe that the threat of an American attack on their country is real and imminent.

One way of getting out of the isolation would be to try a reconciliation with Khrushchev's successors in Moscow. But since Mao Tse-tung has ruled this out, he has had to contrive some extra-powerful booster to national morale. Three nuclear explosions have demonstrated China's new technological capacity to the nation and the world. But this feat is not enough to dispel the *malaise*; for many Chinese realize at what cost, and under what back-breaking handicaps their nation has entered, so belatedly, the nuclear arms race. Nor does Maoism offer China the pride in rapid industrialization that Stalinism once offered Russia—China's tempo of economic advance is relatively much slower. The 'cultural revolution' and an almost mystical apotheosis of Maoism are to provide a moral compensation for all these disappointments and frustrations.

It can be said in advance that the 'positive' effect of this booster on national morale will be short-lived, but that its adverse consequences will be felt for a long time. The Party, its hierarchy and cadres, will not recover quickly from the humiliation the 'Red Guards' have inflicted on them. The old intelligentsia—the scientists and the technicians, but more especially the writers and artists—who have been associated with the broad current of the Maoist revolution and have directed the educational work among the masses since 1949, are being degraded and ousted from their posts. They have not been destroyed as their counterparts were in Stalinist Russia; but they are forced to make room for a new intelligentsia, who have been brought up since the revolution and have far fewer ties either with their own native cultural tradition or with the cultural heritage of the outside world. To some extent this change of generations is inevitable in any post-revolutionary society. But when it is carried out as abruptly, brutally, and demagogically as it was in Stalinist Russia and as it is now being effected in China, the change entails an irreparable loss to the nation: a gap in its cultural consciousness, a lowering of standards, and an impoverishment of spiritual life. Post-Stalinist Russia is still smarting under the loss, and so will Maoist and post-Maoist China. . . .

What next? It remains to be seen whether Mao will proceed to stage purges in the Stalinist style or whether he will find a less bloody way of dealing with inner Party opposition. Beyond these immediate issues there loom the great unresolved problems of China's domestic and foreign policy. Dwelling on the dangers threatening the country from American imperialism, Mao is calling the nation to live the kind of Spartan life that the Red Partisans led during the heroic Yenan period. The newspapers have been quoting this sentence from the diary of a Maoist hero: 'I must remember Mao's teachings to set myself *high* political standards and *low* living standards'; and the mass of citizens are called upon to follow this maxim. The phrase sums up a programme. Yet it must be doubted whether the sentiment it expresses, admirable though it may be in heroic individuals, can animate an entire people and form the basis of national policy. It is an unwitting confession of how little Maoism has now to offer China. The countryside, though it no longer suffers from the mass famines so familiar under the *ancien régime*, remains backward, primitive, and terribly overpopulated; and in the cities industrialization is not progressing fast enough to absorb the surplus. This year a new Five Year Plan, the first since the economic disasters of 1958–62, has been put into effect; but its industrial targets have not been announced. Is it because production statistics are considered a military secret? Or because the targets are not inspiring enough for the propagandists to make much play of them? Either explanation may be correct.

In any case, the government is now placing far less emphasis on rapid economic development than it did in the 1950s and than Soviet governments have always done. Mao has not shown anything like Stalin's ruthlessness in harnessing the nation's manpower and resources and in forcing town and country alike to make the most terrible sacrifices for the sake of industrialization. Ever since the partial failure of the Great Leap, he has kept to the view that China's industrialization and modernization is a matter of many, many decades and that it may take the lifetime of two, three, or four generations to accomplish it. He does not call China 'to catch up with and to surpass the capitalist West', and he does not seek to dazzle the people with promises of quick successes. Realistic though this view may be basically, it holds out no solution to China's pressing needs, no method for dealing with her over-population, her open or latent unemployment, with the social antagonisms between town and country, and with the demands that the international situation places on China's economy.

Behind the call for 'high political standards and low living standards' is the desire and the hope of settling within the framework of what the Russians once described as 'War Communism'—on the basis, that is, of a roughly egalitarian distribution of extremely scarce economic resources. In Russia this policy led to an impasse and had to be abandoned only three years after the October Revolution. China is practising it—true, with considerable modifications—seventeen years after her revolution. But for how long can Party and government adhere to a policy which does not offer the people sufficient material incentives for development and growth? Yet, if China's rulers do not wish to embark upon forcible industrialization, they cannot initiate a more ambitious policy as long as China remains isolated and is denied foreign, especially Soviet, aid.

But this only means that all issues of policy, domestic as well as foreign, lead back to the same question, namely, whether China has any possibility of emerging from isolation in the foreseeable future. Has she any chance of resuming contact with the Soviet Union and regaining massive Soviet aid? We have seen that Mao has answered these questions in the negative, and that he urges China to 'go it alone' economically, politically, and militarily. This, however, implies virtual reconciliation with China's economic and social backwardness.

It is difficult to believe that political stabilization can be achieved on such a basis. Pressures for a more ambitious policy of economic progress will make themselves felt. A few years ago such pressures caused Mao and his colleagues to undertake the Great Leap. But the resulting disappointments brought about a pause in industrialization. Yet the slow tempo creates its own insurmountable difficulties and is certain to revive the demand for a more forward policy. Mao may then call for another Great Leap or else his entire approach will have to come under review. The fact is that, as a dynamic revolutionary power, China cannot 'go it alone'; and that the Maoist policy, committed as it is to isolationism, will be unable to cope with the crises to come. Whether these will develop in Mao's lifetime or later must, of course, remain an open question.

In the inner Party struggle the problem of the succession to Mao has loomed large behind the more topical issues. For the time being Lin Piao has emerged as the winner, and Liu Shao-chi looks like the loser. But it is perhaps too early to take the outcome of the struggle for granted. For one thing, in post-revolutionary regimes the heir apparent appointed in the dictator's lifetime is not necessarily the man who exercises power after the dictator's death. Stalin's heir apparent— Malenkov—did not succeed in imposing himself upon his colleagues; he had to yield his place to Khrushchev who had been well below him in the Party hierarchy. But even if Lin Piao were to be Mao's real successor, it does not follow that he will necessarily continue the policy with which he is at present associated. When the call for a revision and change of Mao's policy, the call now so furiously silenced, rises again, Lin Piao may well have to yield to it. Mao's departure, even though he may still be able to swim the Yangtse, is not likely to be far off;

and with it some reaction against the latest version of Maoism is all too likely to set in. The reaction need not be as severe as was the Russian revulsion against Stalinism, for Mao's place in the history of the Chinese revolution, whose presiding spirit he has been for so long, is much more solidly assured than Stalin's place was in Moscow's mausoleum. Mao has been in one person China's Lenin and Stalin. But at the end of his road he shows more and more similarity to Stalin; and the latest orgy of his personality cult underlines the likeness. It is as if he had outlived himself and is already a relic of the past, an embodiment of China's backwardness and isolationism. When the reaction against these aspects of Maoism comes, his successor or successors, whoever they are, will have to act as its mouthpieces and agents. *A la longue* China cannot keep up her ideological aspirations and 'go it alone'.

21 September 1966

CHRONOLOGY OF EVENTS

1953

5 March	Death of Stalin
3 April	Kremlin Doctors' Plot declared null and void
16–17 June	Rising in East Germany suppressed by Soviet tanks
10 July	Announcement of Beria's arrest
27 July	Korean Armistice signed
5–8 August	Meeting of the Supreme Soviet: Malenkov announces his pro-consumer policy
12 December	Trial of Beria and his associates begins
23 December	Beria sentenced and executed

1954

25 Jan.–18 Feb.	Berlin Conference of Foreign Ministers
26 Apr.–21 July	Geneva Conference on the Far East
7 May	Fall of Dien Bien Phu
30 August	French National Assembly vote against the E.D.C. Treaty
September	London discussions on German admission to NATO
29 Sept.–11 Oct.	Sino-Russian talks in Peking

1955

29 January	Mikoyan resigns from post of Minister of Internal Trade
3–9 February	Meeting of the Supreme Soviet: Bulganin becomes Prime Minister, Zhukov becomes Defence Minister
1 March	Mikoyan becomes a First Deputy Prime Minister
5 May	West Germany joins NATO
15 May	Signing of the Austrian State Treaty
26 May–3 June	Soviet leaders visit Yugoslavia
18–23 July	Geneva Summit Conference
27 September	Nasser announces the Czech arms deal
27 Oct.–16 Nov.	Geneva Foreign Ministers' Conference
18 Nov.–19 Dec.	Khrushchev and Bulganin visit India, Burma, and Afghanistan

1956

14–25 February	Twentieth Congress of the Soviet Communist Party

25 February	Khrushchev's secret speech
1 June	Molotov resigns post of Foreign Minister
2–23 June	Tito visits the Soviet Union
4 June	State Department publishes a text of Khrushchev's secret speech
28 June	Rioting in Poznan, Poland
26 July	Nasser nationalizes the Suez Canal
19–21 October	Crisis in Poland
23 Oct.–4 Nov.	Hungarian uprising
31 October	Tripartite attack on Egypt by Israel, Britain, and France
11 November	Tito criticizes Soviet policy in Hungary

1957

15 February	Gromyko replaces Shepilov as Foreign Minister
27 February	Mao Tse-tung's speech 'On the Correct Handling of Contradictions Among the People'
30 March	Khrushchev launches debate on economic reform
7 May	Supreme Soviet discusses Khrushchev's economic plans
3 July	Announcement of the dismissal of the Anti-Party Group
Aug.–Sept.	Syrian crisis
4 October	Russia launches *Sputnik I*, the first artificial satellite
8–26 October	Zhukov on a visit to Yugoslavia and Albania
26 October	Zhukov dismissed from Ministry of Defence
6–20 November	Meeting of the twelve ruling Communist Parties in Moscow

1958

26 February	Russian Central Committee abolishes the Machine Tractor Stations
27–31 March	Supreme Soviet meeting: Khrushchev becomes Prime Minister; unilateral Soviet cessation of nuclear tests
May	China begins the Great Leap Forward
14 July	Military *coup* in Iraq: General Kassem comes to power
15 July	U.S. troops land in the Lebanon
17 July	British troops occupy Jordan
31 July–3 Aug.	Khrushchev in China
3 September	Bulganin ousted from the Presidium

10 November	Khrushchev announces intention to sign a Peace Treaty with East Germany
15–19 December	Meeting of the Central Committee: Bulganin admits membership of the Anti-Party Group

1959

27 Jan.–5 Feb.	Twenty-first Congress of the Soviet Communist Party
21 Feb.–3 Mar.	Macmillan in Moscow
11 May–21 June	First session of the Geneva Foreign Ministers' Conference
13 July–5 Aug.	Geneva Foreign Ministers' Conference
15–28 September	Khrushchev visits the U.S.A.

1960

14 January	Supreme Soviet meeting: Khrushchev announces Soviet defence cuts
5 May	Khrushchev announces the shooting down of a U-2 plane
11 May	Eisenhower accepts responsibility for U-2 plane
18 May	Collapse of the Paris summit
20–25 June	Bucharest meeting of communist leaders
August	Soviet aid and technicians withdrawn from China
10 Nov.–1 Dec.	Moscow meeting of Eighty-one Communist Parties

1961

12 April	Yuri Gagarin makes the first manned space flight
17–20 April	Defeat of Cuban exiles' attempt to invade Cuba
3–4 June	Kennedy and Khrushchev meet in Vienna
30 July	New Draft Programme of the Soviet Communist Party published
13 August	East Germany builds a wall across their border with West Berlin
17–31 October	Twenty-second Congress of the Soviet Communist Party

1962

24 Sept.–4 Oct.	Brezhnev in Yugoslavia
22–28 October	Cuba Missiles Crisis
3 December	Russia recalls all embassy staff from Albania

1963

15–21 January	Khrushchev attacks China at the Congress of the East German Socialist Unity Party

14 June	Chinese send their twenty-five point letter to the Russians
27 July	Three Chinese officials expelled from the Soviet Union
5–20 July	Abortive unity talks between Chinese and Russian delegates in Moscow
5 August	Signing of the Nuclear Test Ban Treaty
22 November	President Kennedy assassinated in Dallas, Texas

1964

27 January	France and China establish diplomatic relations
14 February	Suslov presents report to Central Committee of Soviet Communist Party on Sino-Soviet relations
15–22 April	Meeting of the Central Committee of the Romanian Party takes up anti-Soviet position
15 July	Brezhnev replaces Mikoyan as President
15 October	*Tass* announces dismissal of Khrushchev
16 October	Chinese announce the explosion of their first atom bomb
5–13 November	Chou En-lai in Moscow

1965

6–10 February	Kosygin in Hanoi
7 February	U.S. begins continuous bombing of North Vietnam
1–5 March	Meeting of pro-Soviet Communist Parties in Moscow
19 June	Boumedienne ousts Ben Bella in Algeria
27–29 September	Meeting of the Central Committee of the Soviet Communist Party decides on recentralization of Soviet industry
30 September	Right-wing military seize power in Indonesia

1966

4–10 January	Tashkent meeting of Ayub Khan and Shastri
29 Mar.–8 Apr.	Twenty-third Congress of the Soviet Communist Party
April–May	Great Cultural Revolution begins in Peking University
8 August	Resolution of the Central Committee of the Communist Party of China on the Great Cultural Revolution leading to Red Guard movement

INDEX

More about Penguins
and Pelicans

Penguinews, which appears every month, contains details
of all the new books issued by Penguins as they are
published. From time to time it is supplemented by
Penguins in Print, which is a complete list of all books
published by Penguins which are in print. (There are well
over three thousand of these.)

A specimen copy of *Penguinews* will be sent to you free
on request, and you can become a subscriber for the
price of the postage. For a year's issues (including the
complete lists) please send 4s. if you live in the United
Kingdom, or 8s. if you live elsewhere. Just write to Dept
EP, Penguin Books Ltd, Harmondsworth, Middlesex,
enclosing a cheque or postal order, and your name will be
added to the mailing list.

Some other Pelican books are described on the following
pages.

Note: *Penguinews* and *Penguins in Print* are not
available in the U.S.A. or Canada.

The New Cold War

Edward Crankshaw

For several years a new Cold War has been simmering, almost unknown to the millions in both the West and East, between the two giants of the Communist world, Russia and China. Although most commentators until some two years ago were dismissing this new Cold War as a mere family squabble, Edward Crankshaw has been studying and writing about it since 1956.

In this Pelican he gives the first popular account of the conflict. He shows that the differences sprang initially from the differences between the Russian and Chinese revolutions – the one made by exiled intellectuals, the other by well-tried generals and administrators. He traces the first signs of open conflict to the famous 20th Party Congress of 1956, and goes on to give the inside story of the two critical conferences of world Communist Parties in Bucarest and Moscow in 1960.

What are the roots of the argument that is threatening to tear the Eastern *bloc* in two? Why does Albania mean China in Russian mouths, and Yugoslavia mean Russia when used by the Chinese? And what is the likely outcome of the battle of giants? It is these questions which this book sets out to answer. The answers will affect the whole world over the next ten years, for even though Khrushchev has gone, the basic cause of the conflict remains.

This book, originally a Penguin Special, has now been brought up to date with a postscript by the author.

'A veritable *tour de force* of condensation' – *Daily Telegraph*

The Making of Modern Russia

Lionel Kochan

'This is a history of Russia from the earliest times up to the outbreak of the Second World War. However, in keeping with his choice of title, Mr Kochan has concentrated on the modern period, devoting about as many pages to the eighty years following the Emancipation of the Serfs in 1861 as to the preceding 800-odd years. . . . The result is a straightforward account of a complicated story. A successful balance has been held between such conflicting themes as foreign policy . . . foreign influences and native intellectual trends. . . . His book could be a valuable introduction to the general reader in search of guidance . . . a commendable book' – *Sunday Times*

'He handles his material with skill and sympathy. I cannot think of a better short book for acquainting the general reader with the broad outlines of Russian history. I hope many will read it' – Edward Crankshaw in the *Observer*

'Gives proper weight to economic, geographical, and cultural, as well as political and military factors, and which, while giving long-term trends their place, manages very often to convey a sense of real events happening to real people' – Wright Miller in the *Guardian*

'It reads easily, it is the ideal book for the general reader' – *The Economist*

The Theory and Practice of Communism

R. N. Carew Hunt

'This is the best short account of Marxism and its
Russian consequences written from a highly critical
standpoint that has come my way' – Edward Crankshaw
in the *Observer*

R. N. Carew Hunt has come to be recognized as one of
the greatest western authorities on communism. This
concise and critical study of Marxism and its interpretation
in practice has quickly gained the standing of a classic.
The author clearly demonstrates that modern Marxism
is a synthesis, in which the basic creed of Karl Marx and
Engels has been tailored by Lenin and Stalin to fit the
twentieth century. In its analysis of the relationship and
the contrasts between Marx's predictions and the policies
of the communist governments of today the book provides
an excellent outline of the institutions and events which
have helped to shape the map of the contemporary
world – the Communist League, the First and Second
Internationals, the Russian Revolution, and developments
both inside and outside Russia between the time of Lenin
and Khrushchev.

Political Leaders of the Twentieth Century

Mao Tse-tung

Stuart Schram

These political biographies are intended to analyse in depth the real men lurking behind the personality cults of great contemporary statesmen. Their purpose is to explain how such political leaders of our times as Mao Tse-tung and Macmillan, de Gaulle and Stalin, Fidel Castro and Verwoerd formed their political outlooks, to examine how they gained power and how they held and exercised it, and to suggest what each of them has come to epitomize in the eyes of his own nation and of the world at large.

By any reckoning Mao Tse-tung must be regarded as one of the greatest and most remarkable statesmen of modern times. As a poet of distinction, as a political philosopher of major importance, and as a strategist whose 6000-mile trek across China has become a legend, Mao has devoted his life to China and the Chinese peasants. Indeed the Chinese People's Republic has shaped a whole pattern of revolution for poor peasant societies. In this new biography Stuart Schram sifts fact from fiction in the long story of Mao's struggle to free the greatness of China and to give a new meaning to Marxism.

The Culture Revolution in China

Joan Robinson

Most western journalists see China lurching to
self-destruction in an orgy of random violence, mad
adulation, inexplicable jargon and meticulous, meaningless
ritual. How, they ask, can the Red Guards believe their
own wall posters? What is the meaning of a 'party person
in authority taking the capitalist road'? And how can the
Thoughts of Mao make crops grow on a stony hill?

In this documentary investigation the author calls upon
the Chinese themselves to explain their revolution.
Joan Robinson, Professor of Economics at Cambridge
and author of the Pelican *Economic Philosophy*, has
recently visited China. From conversations, reported
here, and from the key documents, which have never
before been published in the West, she focuses attention
on the phenomenon most puzzling to those outside
China – a ruler so hostile to his own administration that
he incites and leads a nation-wide popular revolution
against it.

Soviet Communism and
Agrarian Revolution

Roy D. and Betty A. Laird

What has Communism to offer against the prospect of
world starvation? Larger and larger populations
everywhere demand more and more food: agricultural
production has to increase in all lands.

Professor Laird, assisted by his wife, has researched and
written about communist agriculture for some twenty
years: in this book he contends (with a wealth of proof
derived, often at first hand, from the areas examined)
that state and collective farming in the U.S.S.R. and
Eastern Europe is grossly inefficient. Not only have the
communist states failed, in practice, to produce enough
food, but their whole thinking is riddled with myths
which are bound to impede food-production.

In China and Cuba revolution was based on the land, not
on towns. Foreseeing that the developing nations may well
follow their examples, the Lairds argue that it will be a
human calamity if more of the earth's surface is subjected
to 'collectivization' and similar negative policies.

Moreover their views coincide largely with those which
have been canvassed by a significant minority of Russian
agronomists.

As one of the world's longest established ...rands, ...travel.

...rs our ...ecrets ...orld, ...lth of experience and a passion for travel.

Rely on Thomas Cook as your travelling companion on your next trip and benefit from our unique heritage.

Thomas Cook **pocket** guides

COLOGNE

Your travelling companion since 1873

Written by Jo Whittingham
Updated by Kate Hairsine

Published by Thomas Cook Publishing
A division of Thomas Cook Tour Operations Limited
Company registration No: 3772199 England
The Thomas Cook Business Park, 9 Coningsby Road
Peterborough PE3 8SB, United Kingdom
Email: books@thomascook.com, Tel: +44 (0)1733 416477
www.thomascookpublishing.com

Produced by The Content Works Ltd
Aston Court, Kingsmead Business Park, Frederick Place
High Wycombe, Bucks HP11 1LA
www.thecontentworks.com

Series design based on an original concept by Studio 183 Limited

ISBN: 978-1-84848-275-3

First edition © 2006 Thomas Cook Publishing
This third edition © 2009 Thomas Cook Publishing
Text © Thomas Cook Publishing
Maps © Thomas Cook Publishing/PCGraphics (UK) Limited
Transport map © Communicarta Limited

Series Editor: Lucy Armstrong
Production/DTP: Steven Collins

Printed and bound in Spain by GraphyCems

Cover photography (4711 eau de cologne) © Walter Bibikow/awl images

CONTENTS

SYMBOLS KEY

The following symbols are used throughout this book:

ⓐ address ① telephone Ⓦ website address
Ⓛ opening times Ⓝ public transport connections

The following symbols are used on the maps:

ℹ️	information office	◾	points of interest
✈️	airport	○	city
➕	hospital	○	large town
🛡️	police station	○	small town
🚌	bus station	=	motorway
🚆	railway station	—	main road
Ⓤ	U-Bahn	—	minor road
Ⓢ	S-Bahn	—	railway
✝️	cathedral		
❶	numbers denote featured cafés & restaurants		

Hotels and restaurants are graded by approximate price as follows:
£ budget price **££** mid-range price **£££** expensive

Abbreviations used in addresses:
Str., -str.   Straße, Strasse, -strasse (street, road)
Pl., -pl.   Platz, -platz (square)

▶ *Morning view of Cologne town houses*

INTRODUCING
Cologne

Introduction

As well as having Germany's most visited tourist attraction –
the imposing cathedral, the biggest Gothic building in the world –
Cologne is a thriving metropolis with world-class art galleries,
fabulous shopping, cosy Christmas markets, a fun-loving population,
good beer and a vibrant alternative scene. But despite being an
excellent city-break destination, Cologne is a surprisingly well-kept
travel secret.

With a population of just under a million, Cologne is Germany's
fourth largest city, and the economic and cultural capital of the
Rhineland region. Its inhabitants have a reputation for being laid-
back and tolerant, one of the reasons why Cologne has a large gay
community and is a magnet for many artists and musicians.

The city's history stretches back more than 2,000 years to its Roman
founders and plenty of evidence of their influence can still be found
on the streets and in museums. More recent history can be felt in
the old town's cobbled alleyways, the majority of which were rebuilt,
along with the churches, after devastating World War II bombing.
The surviving historic architecture is set against mostly attractive
modern neighbours.

Art and culture are in plentiful supply in Cologne. Its galleries are
full of important international works and superb collections by famous
local artists. This, combined with the huge selection of theatres,
concert halls and music venues, makes it difficult for even the most
dedicated cultural tourist to do more than scratch the surface of
the city's cultural riches in a short break.

Cologne is one of Germany's leading gastronomic centres, boasting
more than 3,000 restaurants and pubs, and food from almost all
corners of the globe can be enjoyed here, alongside hearty traditional

German fare. Cologne's café culture seems almost Mediterranean during the summer, when the streets are filled with people relaxing over coffee, lunch or enormous ice creams. But it's at night that the city really comes to life, with local *Kölsch* beer consumed enthusiastically in traditional pubs, and cocktails prepared at trendy bars and clubs every night of the week.

The friendly people of Cologne save their best for the annual festivals, however, when they, along with hundreds of thousands of visitors, throng the streets for the colourful *Rosenmontag* (Rose Monday) and Christopher Street Day parades, as well as the awe-inspiring *Kölner Lichter* (Cologne Lights) firework display.

⬛ *The cathedral is visible from kilometres away*

When to go

SEASONS & CLIMATE

During the summer, life moves outdoors and everyone drinks and dines at tables under huge parasols in the streets and squares, come rain or shine. There are usually spells when summer temperatures reach about 30°C (86°F), but the norm is a more comfortable 18–25°C (65–77°F).

Winter rarely brings heavy snow to the city although there can be cold snaps. It is best to expect mild and wet weather from winter into spring, but in a vibrant city like Cologne a little rain needn't get in the way of a good time (see pages 46–7).

ANNUAL EVENTS

Cologne regards itself as a festival city, and rightly so because it hosts events that attract millions of visitors throughout the year. Some are steeped in tradition; the rest just involve having a good time.

February–March

Karneval Carnival in Cologne is one of Europe's biggest street festivals and a good excuse to don fancy dress and party from the Thursday before Ash Wednesday through to *Rosenmontag* (Rose Monday) without sobering up. But be warned, if you aren't into massive drunken crowds and 24 hours a day of oompah music reverberating around every corner of the city, then carnival isn't for you (for more about *Karneval*, see pages 12–13). ⓦ www.koelnerkarneval.de

---

⊙ *Christopher Street Day is one of Europe's biggest Gay Pride events*

April

Art Cologne Germany's most important art fair is attended by more than 250 international galleries and dealers, showing the best modern and contemporary works the world has to offer. Open to the public as well as to trade, this five-day fair is packed full of exhibits, performances and events. Ⓦ www.artcologne.de

July

Christopher Street Day More than just a day, this Gay Pride gathering has taken over the first weekend in July, when there is an open-air stage in the old town and the city's most vivacious parade, as up to 35,000 lavishly costumed lesbians and gays party through the streets and on late into the night.
Ⓦ www.csd-cologne.de

Kölner Lichter (Cologne Lights) A spectacular firework display above the Rhine, set to music and watched by hundreds of thousands of revellers from the river's banks and bridges. Due to construction works on the Rhine, the fireworks are set off in front of the Tanzbrunnen (see page 115) between the Hohenzollernbrücke and the Zoobrücke. Arrive early to bag a good spot. Ⓦ www.koelner-lichter.de

Summerjam Germany's largest reggae festival, this three-day event is held in July every year on Cologne's Fühlinger Lake, less than half an hour out of the city on public transport. Ⓦ www.summerjam.de

July–August

SOMA – Summer of Music and Arts Festival Held on the banks of the Rhine, this three-day festival is an insider tip for chilling out and hearing great alternative music at open-air stages and in club tents. There's a great kids' area and free camping.
Ⓦ www.soma-festival.de

November–December

Christmas markets From the last weekend in November to
23 December, several markets fill Cologne with festive spirit and
are ideal for finding traditional German Christmas decorations,
toys, nutcrackers and treats. The huge market in Roncalliplatz
is watched over by a gigantic Christmas tree and the immense
cathedral. This, and the other city centre markets in Alter Markt,
Neumarkt and Rudolfplatz, are free to visit; the floating market
moored at Rheinpromenade and the Medieval Market next to
the Chocolate Museum charge admission.

PUBLIC HOLIDAYS
New Year's Day 1 Jan
Good Friday 2 Apr 2010, 22 Apr 2011, 6 Apr 2012
Easter Monday 5 Apr 2010, 25 Apr 2011, 9 Apr 2012
Labour Day 1 May
Ascension Day 13 May 2010, 2 June 2011, 17 May 2012
Whit Monday 24 May 2010, 13 June 2011, 28 May 2012
Corpus Christi 3 June 2010, 23 June 2011, 7 June 2012
German Unification Day 3 Oct
All Saints' Day 1 Nov
Christmas 25 & 26 Dec

There is some regional variation in German public holidays, but the
dates above are correct for Cologne. Most shops and businesses in
the city close in the afternoon of: *Weiberfastnacht* (the Thursday
before Rose Monday), Rose Monday, Christmas Eve and New Year's
Eve, as well as the whole day on the public holidays shown above.

Karneval

Karneval (carnival) in Cologne is considered to be the 'fifth season' and kicks off on 11 November at 11.11 sharp at the Heumarkt square in the old town, followed by a day of fancy dress and drinking. But it's the six days before the start of Lent on Ash Wednesday that mark Cologne's real party season. On *Weiberfastnacht* (Women's Carnival) on the Thursday before Ash Wednesday, thousands of costumed merrymakers, mainly women, gather at Heumarkt for the official opening of celebrations by the Carnival Prince, Peasant and Maiden at exactly 11.11. Be warned – on this day women traditionally run around with scissors and cut off men's ties as trophies, giving them a kiss as recompense.

On the Friday and Saturday, the party frenzy continues in Cologne's pubs and spills out into the street. It you don't want to stand out as a tourist, don't forget to bring a costume with you (most supermarkets and stores sell face paint and masks during carnival, so there's no excuse not to enter into the carnival spirit).

Joining in the alternative *Geisterzug*, or Ghost parade, is a fun option on Saturday night. Unlike the Rose Monday procession, anyone can parade in the *Geisterzug*, which every year weaves and dances its way through a different part of the city, accompanied by hundreds of drummers. For more information on the route, ask at the tourist office or take a look at ⓦ www.geisterzug.de (in German).

On Carnival Sunday at 11.00, Cologne's children and district clubs parade in costume through the city's streets. It's smaller than the Rose Monday procession, but takes virtually the same route.

Rosenmontag (Rose Monday) is the highlight of Cologne's carnival, when the kilometre-long parade twists through town. More than a million people line the streets to cheer on the decorated floats and scramble for sweets and flowers. Many of the carnival groups spend the whole year preparing their floats, often topped with huge figures satirising topical events. The tourist office publishes a free map of the parade route, and you need to get up early to secure a good viewing spot.

The fifth season wraps up with the burning of the *Nubbel* (the spirit of carnival) to atone for the sins of the past five days. Many pubs and restaurants will torch a straw figure at midnight on Tuesday, before the city returns to normal on Ash Wednesday.

Large parts of Cologne are closed to traffic on Carnival Sunday and Rose Monday, and it is an exercise in futility to attempt to drive anywhere in the city centre on those days. Allow plenty of time if you are planning on taking the U- or S-Bahn: the public transport system virtually grinds to a halt during carnival. And if you plan on sleeping at some stage in the five days, don't forget to bring earplugs – in many parts of the city, carnival music blares incessantly during the fifth season. And don't forget to say, 'Kölle Alaaf' – 'Cologne above all'.

⬤ *Dressing up for* Rosenmontag

History

It was the Romans who realised that this spot on the Rhine would be a good place to settle, and in 33 BC Colonia was born. Thanks to the fact that a local girl later married the Emperor Claudius, it was elevated to city status by 50 AD. As well as their engineering expertise and military might, the Romans also later brought Christianity to the city, which went on to become a centre of ecclesiastical importance over the centuries.

The emblem of the city's prosperity and power, the huge cathedral (the Dom) was to be the 'largest structure north of the Alps' when it was started in 1248. It was the archbishops of Cologne who wielded much of this power, not only within the church, but also in secular matters. However, by the 15th century the citizens had driven the archbishops out and Cologne was one of the wealthiest German-speaking cities, but the gigantic cathedral construction project would not be completed for hundreds of years yet (see page 61).

● *The giant Dom, over 600 years in the making*

In 1794, the city was occupied by French soldiers, who chose to renumber the houses according to their own system. They happened to mark the house of the Muelhens family 4711, and the name of their famous brand of eau de cologne was born. This concoction had been made in the city since the early 18th century and was originally sold as medicinal water, but in 1810 Napoleon decreed that the formulas of medicines should be made known for the benefit of the poor, so to retain their secret the manufacturers reneged on their medicinal claims and reclassified it as a toilet water. The scent was popular with bath-shy aristocrats, who used it to mask their own unpleasant odour.

Cologne and the Rhineland were annexed in 1815 by the kings of Prussia, under whose rule the city continued to prosper, becoming a hub of the new railways in the mid-19th century and finally completing its cathedral in 1880. This success as an industrial and communications centre continued into the 20th century, only to be abruptly halted by World War II.

Hitler's army occupied the previously demilitarised Rhineland in 1936, but in early 1940 troops gathered in Cologne to launch an invasion of the Netherlands, Belgium and France. This prompted the first Allied bombing raid on the city and subsequent raids on military and industrial targets intensified until the last, most devastating attack on 2 March 1945. Cologne was reduced to a pile of rubble, with as many as 90 per cent of its buildings and all of its bridges destroyed, although the cathedral survived.

Immediately after the war the resilient population began the reconstruction of their city and managed to restore something of the historical character to the old town area, painstakingly rebuilding and repairing the ancient Romanesque churches. Despite its turbulent past at the heart of Europe, Cologne has again grown into a prosperous media and industrial centre, and a beautiful city.

Lifestyle

Germans think of Cologne as a fun-loving city and local *Kölsch* people are renowned for their openness, laid-back attitude and sharp sense of humour. A cynic might say that such stereotypes are manufactured by tourist officials to draw in the crowds, but in Cologne such claims seem to have considerably more than a grain of truth. The patient locals do their best to help tourists who can't speak German and are not easily offended. In fact if you adopt the local habit of sitting in busy cafés or beer gardens, you'll find it easy to get chatting with the locals, who will be happy to give their tips for good bars, clubs and places to visit. People of all ages spend a lot of their time socialising on terraces in front of cafés and restaurants in summer and in cosy bars in winter. Although alcoholic drinks are available during the day and late into the night, the atmosphere in bars and on the streets remains friendly rather than intimidating.

Cologne is an important centre for Germany's media and arts, and it has a large university and music colleges, all of which may account for the bohemian lifestyle that many of its inhabitants seem to enjoy, hanging out in cafés and bars until late and frequenting theatres and galleries. Spending sunny Sundays in the park picnicking and working on their tan is another popular pastime, and it is normal to see bikini-clad women on any patch of grass.

Germany has recycling its rubbish down to a fine art and Cologne's litter bins have separate sections for paper, plastic and general waste, so take care that your rubbish goes in the right place and whatever you do don't drop litter – nobody else does.

⬤ *Cologne café society – laid-back and sociable*

The only downside is that Cologne is not a particularly cheap place to stay, shop or eat. The demand for hotel rooms is high during the festivals and the many trade fairs and conferences held in the city, so prices are inflated over these periods. Although visitors from the UK might still find Germany a little cheaper than home, for those from the US it will seem expensive.

Culture

For outsiders, the perception of Cologne as an industrial city sits comfortably with the assumption that it has little culture to offer. Nothing could be further from the truth, because the city's long history provides ample material for museums and its wealthy art collectors have left a world-class legacy for its galleries.

In just two of the old town galleries – Museum Ludwig and the Wallraf-Richartz Museum – spectacular art collections cover everything from medieval triptychs to still lifes by Dutch masters, Impressionist landscapes to pop art, right up to contemporary German pieces. All of this can be found inside the box-like buildings of these two museums (see pages 64 & 67), which, despite their severe appearance, provide beautiful, sensitive and well-lit gallery space inside. Unsurpassed bodies of work by well-known local artists Käthe Kollwitz (see page 79) and Max Ernst (located in Brühl, see page 138) fill entire galleries of their own, providing incredible insight into their fascinating lives and their art. There are other art venues spread around Cologne, devoted to ecclesiastical, Asian and applied art, that are all worth visiting if time allows. Most galleries and museums are closed on Mondays but open on public holidays (with the exception of Christmas and New Year's Day) when opening hours are the same as for Sundays.

Those interested in Roman artefacts will be captivated by the relics of old Colonia on display in the main Römisch-Germanisches Museum (see page 66), including the famous Dionysus mosaic, but should not miss a walk through a Roman sewer and the foundations of the Roman governor's palace in the Praetorium under the town hall (see page 66).

After suitable quiet contemplation of art and history, this energetic population likes to be entertained. All kinds of theatre,

The Philharmonie is just one of Cologne's many cultural venues

usually performed in German, from traditional regional humour to experimental new German and international productions, and huge international musicals and stage shows, can be found in venues of all sizes around the city. The quality of classical music in Cologne is extremely high and the city is home to a number of music schools. Performances by the Gürzenich-Orchestra Cologne, which can trace its origins back to the 15th century, and the WDR Symphony Orchestra Cologne, with its great reputation for performing the work of 20th-century composers, are always in demand. These are the two resident orchestras at the Kölner Philharmonie (Philharmonic Hall) (see page 64), where performances are given almost daily. Popular classical concerts are also given in the city's 12 Romanesque churches, which provide a wonderful atmosphere in which to enjoy the work of famous composers. While perhaps not renowned for opera, Cologne does have an excellent Opera House, which hosts a varied repertoire of modern and classical operas, along with frequent ballet performances.

Many of Cologne's cultural highlights are in or near the centre of the city, so even on a short visit you will be able to sample a few. Theatre and concert listings and tickets can be obtained at individual venues or from **Köln Ticket** (🕾 (0221) 2801 Ⓦ www.koelnticket.de).

Another option is to buy a Cologne Welcome Card, which gives discounts to many museums, theatres and other venues, as well as free travel on the combined public transport network. Available from the tourist office (see page 152).

▶ *Statue of Kaiser Friedrich Wilhelm III near the Hohenzollernbrücke*

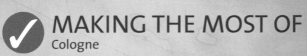

MAKING THE MOST OF
Cologne

Shopping

Germany has deregulated its shopping hours, so while many stores and supermarkets in Cologne close at 20.00 Monday to Saturday, some of the bigger chains are in the process of extending their hours. Most shops in Germany are closed on Sundays, although Cologne has a multitude of small kiosks where it's possible to buy everything from beer to bread rolls seven days a week.

The city has a maze of shopping streets reserved just for pedestrians and once you get started it will be a while before you want to find your way out. International and German designer names are well represented, as are stores packed with cheap up-to-the-minute fashion and brightly lit shops loaded with top cosmetic brands. Head to the city centre streets of Hohe Strasse and Schildergasse, just a short walk from the cathedral, for the big names, and wind your way out towards the ring road to find the trendy clothes and shoe stores on Ehrenstrasse, and individually designed jewellery on Friesenstrasse.

Goods are generally just slightly cheaper than they are in UK shops, a notable example being the luxurious German-made Dr Hauschka cosmetics, which are more widely available and reasonably priced here. Another fashionable souvenir is a pair of Birkenstock sandals from the brand's own shop on Breite Strasse.

Fortunately the regular souvenir shops are almost entirely confined to the cathedral square, so if you want to take home a model of the cathedral, some pretty handmade Christmas decorations or a magnificent nutcracker you will find your quarry here. There is also a little *Kölsch* emporium on Alter Markt, selling everything related to the city's best-loved beer, including the slim, straight-sided glasses (*Stangen*) from which it is always consumed. Of course, by far the best souvenir from this city is a bottle of the scent that bears its name – *Kölnwasser* or eau de cologne. The best-known brand is 4711, so-called after the number of its inventor's house and packaged in pretty turquoise-labelled bottles. A reconstruction of that very building, on its original site at the corner of Glockengasse, is dedicated to the sale of the famous fragrance and though its fashionable days have long gone, taking a sniff here is an essential Cologne experience.

USEFUL SHOPPING PHRASES

What time do the shops open/close?
Um wieviel Uhr öffnen/schliessen die Geschäfte?
Oom veefeel oor erffnen/shleessen dee geshefter?

How much is this?	**Can I try this on?**
Wieviel kostet das?	Kann ich das anprobieren?
Veefeel kostet das?	*Can ikh das anprobeeren?*

My size is ...	**I'll take this one, thank you**
Ich habe Grösse ...	Ich nehme das, danke schön
Ikh haber grerser ...	*Ikh neymer das, danker shern*

Can you show me the one in the window/this one, please?
Zeigen Sie mir bitte das im Fenster/dieses da?
Tsyegen zee mere bitter dass im fenster/deezess dar?

This is too large/too small/too expensive
Es ist zu gross/zu klein/zu teuer
Es ist tsu gross/tsu kline/tsu toyer

Eating & drinking

In recent years Germans, like the British, have become more open-minded about their food and today Cologne is bursting with great places to eat. As a result of its ethnic diversity, the city boasts many fine Turkish, Italian and Japanese restaurants. British diners will note the scarcity of Indian restaurants, but the few around the centre serve excellent curries and anyone desperate for a spicy hit could try a *Currywurst* (sliced sausage in curry sauce) instead. Also, at the first sign of the sun, people of all ages will be out under parasols eating outrageously large sundaes in Italian ice cream parlours.

Many of the café/bistro-style places that line Cologne's streets open early enough to serve a German breakfast of bread, meat and cheese to locals and tourists, while the bakeries also open early for coffee and pastries. Both these options provide a cheap alternative to hotel buffets.

The city normally breaks for lunch between noon and 15.00, when anything from a sandwich or pasta dish in a café to a full-blown restaurant meal is tucked away. There are very few take-away sandwich shops, as people generally sit down to eat. Most cafés and bars, along with many restaurants, then stay open through the afternoon until late, perhaps 23.00 or midnight. Restaurants often double as bars and

PRICE CATEGORIES

The restaurant price guides used in the book indicate the approximate cost of a three-course meal for one person, excluding drinks.

£ up to €20   ££ €20–30   £££ over €30

diners will linger after dinner over a few drinks. Restaurant and bar closing hours are much more flexible than in Britain and the US, and places will often stay open later than their advertised hours if there is a crowd.

⬥ Cologne's streets and squares are lined with cafés and bistros

There are some things you shouldn't leave Cologne without trying. Cologne's lifeblood is its *Kölsch*, a light and tasty top-fermented beer (where the yeast rises instead of sinking), brewed to a special recipe by numerous local breweries. Everyone, male and female, drinks *Kölsch* from special straight 0.2 litre glasses, known as *Stangen*. It is served almost everywhere, but for an authentic experience of *Kölsch* drinking go to a traditional brewery pub (*Brauhaus*) – a misnomer today, as no brewing goes on in them. The old town has many to choose from and they are distinguished by their dark wood-panelled interiors, plain sanded table tops and slightly over-confident waiters, who will swap your empty glass for a full one, sometimes without asking, until you tell them to stop. When you pay the bill, they will also more than likely rummage round for change in their black wallet until you tell them to keep it.

The *Brauhäuser* are also good places to sample local delicacies, but because of their popularity with locals and tourists alike, it is often a good idea to book a table, especially on weekends.

A long-standing Cologne joke, born out of a story about a cheapskate host, is the dish *Halve Hahn*, which, although it means half a chicken, is actually a rye bread roll and cheese. A more serious meal is pork knuckle with pickled cabbage and mashed potato (*Haxe mit Sauerkraut und Kartoffelpüree*), definitely the dish of choice for meat-lovers.

Table service is universal in cafés and bars as well as restaurants, where generally service is not included and a tip of up to 10 per cent is normal, as long as you were satisfied with your meal. Beware that credit cards are not widely accepted, so it is advisable before you order to check that your card will pay the bill.

▶ Kölsch *isn't* Kölsch *unless it's served in a* Stange

In summer Cologne is perfect for a picnic and its many busy parks, particularly Rheinpark, Stadtgarten and Volksgarten, are inviting places for lunch. A respectable spread can be assembled from the bakeries and fruit stalls around Hohe Strasse, where you can pick up cakes, sandwiches and pretzels. For something more luxurious try the Kaufhof department store's basement supermarket, with its tempting deli counters and wine selection.

Vegetarians travelling to Cologne might not be optimistic about their opportunities for fine dining given Germany's reputation as a nation of carnivores, but if you pick the right restaurants you may be pleasantly surprised. The menus in traditional restaurants and *Brauhäuser* are heavily meat-based, and even if you order a salad you will need to make sure it comes without *Speck* (bacon pieces). However, the city's diverse ethnic restaurants are much better options for vegetarian fare. Italian places serve plenty of meat-free pasta and pizza, while most Thai, Chinese and Vietnamese restaurants have a small selection of vegetarian dishes.

A safe bet for vegetarians is to follow the students to the streets around Zülpicher Platz, where there are lots of falafel restaurants and all the cafés have vegetarian options. There are even some dedicated vegetarian restaurants around, including the stylish **Osho's Place** near Friesenplatz (ⓐ Venloer Str. 5–7 ⓣ (0221) 800 0581 ⓦ www.oshos-place.de ⓛ 08.00–00.00 Sun–Thur, 08.00–01.00 Fri & Sat). This relaxed, informal place serves up internationally inspired vegetarian food and has a great salad bar.

USEFUL DINING PHRASES

I would like a table for ... people, please
Ein Tisch für ... Personen, bitte
Ine teesh foor ... perzohnen, bitter

Waiter/waitress!
Herr Ober/Fräulein, bitte!
Hair ohber/froyline, bitter!

May I have the bill, please?
Die Rechnung, bitte?
Dee rekhnung, bitter?

Could I have it well-cooked/medium/rare please?
Ich möchte es bitte durch/halb durch/englisch gebraten?
Ikh merkhter es bitter doorkh/halb doorkh/eng-lish gebrarten?

I am a vegetarian. Does this contain meat?
Ich bin Vegetarier (Vegetarierin fem.). Enthält das hier Fleisch?
Ish bin veggetaareer (veggetaareerin). Enthelt dass heer flyshe?

Where is the toilet (restroom) please?
Wo sind die Toiletten, bitte?
Voo zeent dee toletten, bitter?

I would like a cup of/two cups of/another coffee/tea, please
Ich möchte eine Tasse/zwei Tassen/noch eine Tasse Kaffee/
Tee, bitte
*Ikh merkhter iner tasser/tsvy tassen/nokh iner tasser kafey/
tey, bitter*

I would like a beer/two beers, please
Ich möchte ein Bier/zwei Biere, bitte
Ikh merkhter ine beer/tsvy beerer, bitter

Entertainment & nightlife

Cologne loves a good time. It is a youthful city, with a large student population, but people of all ages can be found enjoying a drink in one of the city's myriad bars, some of which stay open until 05.00. For those who fancy a dance, there are also plenty of trendy clubs to choose from, with DJs playing everything from rap and hip-hop to house and Latin beats.

As with most cities, different areas have their own style of bars and clubs and attract different crowds accordingly. The bars and traditional *Brauhäuser* in the old town are the standard tourist haunts, where *Kölsch* is consumed from lunchtime well into the early hours, particularly at the weekend. Meanwhile the locals hang out in the trendier bars and nightclubs on and around the ring road on any night of the week. Students congregate in bars and restaurants near Zülpicher Platz, and more fashionable types head north to the flash cocktail bars and expensive restaurants close to Friesenplatz.

Any norms are completely disrupted, however, when one of the city's festivals begins and the whole place gets party fever. This happens regularly and begins with the *Karneval* season on 11 November, which reaches its climax in February/March with the Rose Monday parade, when the streets and bars are filled with two million revellers. July brings the Christopher Street Day parade, which is a huge Gay Pride event that draws almost as many visitors as *Karneval*, many of them in the most outlandish outfits imaginable. Later that month, the Cologne Lights, a fantastic firework display over the river, brings yet more crowds and provides another excuse to party. In between all this mayhem the city also has a vibrant live music scene, with its stadium and arena hosting famous international pop acts and rock

TICKETS & LISTINGS
Each venue has its own box office, but there are also conveniently located ticket shops in the city centre, which have comprehensive events listings and friendly staff to help you decide what to see.

KölnMusik Ticket ❷ Roncallipl. (next to cathedral)
❶ (0221) 2040 8160 ❸ 10.00–19.00 Mon–Fri, until 16.00 Sat
KölnMusik Event ❸ Mayersche Bookshop, Neumarkt
❶ (0221) 2040 8333 ❸ 09.00–20.00 Mon–Fri, until 21.00 Sat
Köln Ticket has an excellent listings website where you can also purchase tickets. It's in German, but is easy to work out.
❶ (0221) 2801 ❿ www.koelnticket.de

groups. Bands with smaller audiences also have plenty of venues to play in Cologne, and jazz is popular and easy to find in bars and the famous Stadtgarten venue in a city park. You can even hear excellent musicians, often students from local music schools, performing classical music around the cathedral square to help pay their fees.

After all this activity, sitting in a darkened room might appeal and a trip to one of the many cinemas in town will cost you less than in the UK. Most blockbuster movies are dubbed into German, but several cinemas screen films in their original version with, or sometimes even without, subtitles. The website ❿ www.choices.de gives an overview of all movies on in Cologne. It's in German, but scroll to the bottom of the page and click on 'Originalversionen' to see what's offered in English. The Metropolis in Cologne's Südstadt (see page 118) specialises in English-language films and even has an English-language website and telephone line, making it easy to find out screening times.

Sport & relaxation

SPECTATOR SPORTS

The RheinEnergie Stadium is home to the city's football heroes, FC Köln. Across the Rhine, in the Deutz district, the Kölner Haie (Cologne Sharks) play their ice hockey at Kölnarena. German league champions an amazing eight times, they have huge support in the city and the action-packed games make great entertainment.

While some may like to participate, most people probably prefer to watch the Ford Cologne Marathon, which starts from Mindenstrasse in Deutz late September/early October and sees 14,000 runners snake their way across the bridge and around the city. There is also an event for inline skaters, which you have to hope avoids the cobbles.

FC Köln ⓐ RheinEnergie Stadion, Aachener Str. 999 ❶ (0221) 8021 ⓦ Tickets and listings www.koelnticket.de ⓥ U-Bahn: Rheinenergie-Stadion

Kölner Haie/Cologne Sharks (ice hockey) ⓐ Kölnarena, Willy-Brand-Pl. 2, Deutz ❶ (0221) 8020 ⓦ Tickets and listings www.koelnticket.de or www.haie.de ⓥ U-Bahn: Deutz/Messe

🔺 *Cologne Sharks – the ice hockey team with bite*

Ford Cologne Marathon For route and entry information check the website. Ⓦ www.koeln-marathon.de

PARTICIPATION SPORTS
Cycling
Cycling is popular with Cologne's residents and is a good way to see the city. If you hire a bike, stick to the clearly marked cycle lanes in town and the many large parks.

Radstation Köln Hbf is the place to hire bikes. ❸ Breslauer Pl. (main railway station) ❶ (0221) 139 7190 Ⓦ www.radstationkoeln.de
🕓 05.30–22.30 Mon–Fri, 06.30–20.00 Sat, 08.00–20.00 Sun (open until 22.00 Sat & Sun, April–Sept)

Swimming
Unfortunately the only outdoor pool in central Cologne is closed for renovations until 2011, but the **Weidenbad** (❸ Ostlandstr. 39 ❶ (0221) 431 040 🕓 10.00–20.00 Mon–Fri, 09.00–20.00 Sat & Sun Ⓝ U-Bahn: Rhein-Energie-Stadion), a 25-minute U-Bahn ride from the central station, is a good alternative. The pool opens around the middle of May until the end of August.

RELAXATION
Spas
Holidays are all about pampering, so treat yourself to a trip to a thermal spa where you can spend all day soaking in health-giving, mineral-rich waters and taking time out for a sauna, a massage or a beauty treatment.

Claudius Therme ❸ Sachsenburgstr. 1 (Rheinpark) ❶ (0221) 981 440 Ⓦ www.claudius-therme.de 🕓 09.00–00.00 Ⓝ Shuttle Bus 150 from Deutzer Bahnhof; U-Bahn: Zoo/Flora and cable car. Admission charge

Accommodation

This city relies on its trade fairs as much as tourism to fill its thousands of hotel rooms, so although there are many hotels to chose from they tend to cater to the needs and budget of the business customer rather than those travelling for pleasure. That said, if your visit to Cologne does not coincide with a trade fair or one of the major festivals you can pick up rooms quite cheaply, but if you descend with the hordes for a popular event, book as far in advance as possible and be prepared to pay a premium. In the city centre the only options apart from hotels are a few serviced apartments and backpacker hostels, which are also in demand during events.

Many tourists choose to base themselves in the Altstadt (old town) and this is sensible because it allows you to visit all the major sights on foot and means that there is only a short totter back to bed from the *Brauhäuser*. Therein lies one of the area's downfalls, however; it can be noisy well into the early hours of the morning, especially at the weekend, so if you don't plan to be out partying it would be wise to check your hotel's proximity to bars and nightclubs or find a room a little out of the centre. Staying away from the old town in Cologne's business or residential districts around the ring road, or across the river in Deutz, should be quieter and is certainly no less convenient

PRICE CATEGORIES
The ratings below indicate the approximate cost of a room for two people for one night.
£ up to €100 **££** €100–200 **£££** over €200

because the S-Bahn and U-Bahn system, along with the buses, will get you wherever you need to go cheaply and efficiently. Bear in mind that there are also numerous bars and nightclubs around the ring road between Rudolfplatz and Friesenplatz, so booming late-night bass could be an issue here too.

Cologne's star classification system for its hotels is voluntary, so while the ratings between 1 and 5 stars are good, if slightly generous, indicators of the facilities available, they are only displayed by some of the city's hotels, which is less than helpful.

The price categories box (unrelated to the official star system) gives an indication of the maximum rates that tourists in Cologne should expect to pay per night for a double room with a shower and toilet. The price is per room rather than per person. Breakfast is often included, but beware of expensive hotel breakfast buffets where it is not.

HOTELS

Am Rathaus £ Rather bare, but clean and functional rooms, right in the middle of the old town. ➋ Bürgerstr. 6 (The Altstadt) ➊ (0221) 257 7624 ➍ www.hotel-am-rathaus-koeln.de

City Pension Storch £ Each of the simple, clean rooms in this small hotel comes with a kitchenette. Only a five-minute walk to the Dom. ➋ Steinfelder Gasse 26 (The Innenstadt) ➊ (0221) 326 993 ➍ www.city-pension-storch.de ➎ U-Bahn: Appellhofplatz

Domgarten £ This pretty, old building has traditionally furnished rooms and a central location near the railway station. ➋ Domstr. 26 (The Altstadt) ➊ (0221) 168 0080 ➎ U-Bahn: Dom/Hbf

Dom Hotel Am Römerbrunnen £ Budget accommodation with small rooms but friendly service right in the city centre. ❸ Komoedienstr. 54 (The Altstadt) ❶ (0221) 16 094 Ⓦ www.am-roemerbrunnen.de Ⓝ U-Bahn: Appellhofplatz

Hotel Alter Römer £ Good value 12-room hotel over a pub. Many of the rooms have a view of the Rhine. ❸ Am Bollwerk 23 (The Altstadt) ❶ (0221) 258 1885

Rhein-Hotel St Martin £ Right on the riverfront and at the centre of the old town, this is a good base from which to explore Cologne. ❸ Frankenwerft 31–33 (The Altstadt) ❶ (0221) 257 7955 Ⓦ www.koeln-altstadt.de/rheinhotel

Antik Hotel Bristol ££ Furnished with charming antiques, this reliable hotel is close to the MediaPark. ❸ Kaiser-Wilhelm-Ring 48 (Outside the centre) ❶ (0221) 120 195 Ⓦ www.antik-hotel-bristol.de Ⓝ U-Bahn: Christophstrasse/MediaPark

Esplanade Hotel ££ Conveniently situated on the ring road, this friendly hotel has crisp, clean rooms and an excellent breakfast buffet. ❸ Hohenstaufenring 56 (Around the Ringstrassen) ❶ (0221) 921 5570 Ⓦ www.hotelesplanade.de Ⓝ U-Bahn: Mauritiuskirche

Hopper Hotel Et Cetera ££ This former monastery, located in the fashionable Belgian quarter, has stylishly furnished rooms. ❸ Brüsseler Str. 26 (Around the Ringstrassen) ❶ (0221) 924 400 Ⓦ www.hopper.de Ⓝ U-Bahn: Rudolfplatz

----

❶ *The Dom Hotel, comfort next to the cathedral*

Hotel Allegro ££ Well-priced hotel with excellent views of the Rhine River and excellent staff. ⓐ Thurnmarkt 1–7 (The Altstadt) ⓣ (0221) 240 826 ⓦ www.hotel-allegro-koeln.de Ⓝ U-Bahn: Heumarkt

Im Kupferkessel ££ On a quiet side-street off Christophstrasse, this friendly, family-run place has a traditional, beamed dining area and clean rooms. ⓐ Probsteigasse 6 (Outside the centre) ⓣ (0221) 270 7960 ⓦ www.im-kupferkessel.de Ⓝ U-Bahn: Christophstrasse/MediaPark

Barcelo Cologne City Center £££ Friendly service, comfortable rooms and a good location near Rudolfplatz make this a great choice. ⓐ Habsburgerring 9–13 (The Innenstadt) ⓣ (0221) 2280 ⓦ www.barcelocolognecitycenter.com Ⓝ U-Bahn: Rudolfplatz

Dom Hotel £££ This excellent hotel, a member of the Le Meridien group, sits in the shadow of the cathedral. ⓐ Domkloster 2A (The Altstadt) ⓣ (0221) 20 240 ⓦ www.koeln.lemeridien.de Ⓝ U-Bahn: Dom/Hbf; S-Bahn: Köln Hbf

Hotel im Wasserturm £££ This extraordinary hotel, with luxurious designer rooms, fills a 130-year-old water tower, close to the centre. ⓐ Kaygasse 2 (The Innenstadt) ⓣ (0221) 20 080 ⓦ www.hotel-im-wasserturm.de Ⓝ U-Bahn: Poststrasse

SERVICED APARTMENTS

Domicilium £ Only 3 km (less than 2 miles) from the city centre, these stylish modern apartments are clean and comfortable. ⓐ Scheidtweiler Str. 15A (Outside the centre) ⓣ (0221) 546 3301 ⓦ www.domicilium-koeln.de Ⓝ U-Bahn: Aachener Strasse/Gurtel

Lyskirchen Altstadthotel £ Just south of the old town, eight well-appointed apartments are part of a standard hotel. ⓐ Filzengraben 26–32 (The Altstadt) ⓣ (0221) 20 970 ⓦ www.hotel-lyskirchen.com ⓝ U-Bahn: Heumarkt

HOSTELS

Jugendherberge Köln-Deutz £ This modern youth hostel has twin and group rooms with en-suite facilities. A Youth Hostel Association or Hostelling International membership card is required ⓐ Siegesstr. 5 (Outside the centre) ⓣ (0221) 814 711 ⓦ www.koeln-deutz.jugendherberge.de ⓝ Train/tram: Köln Deutz

Station-Hostel for Backpackers £ Right next to the railway station, this basic but clean hostel has a great location, no curfew and some en-suite rooms. ⓐ Marzellenstr. 44–56 (The Altstadt) ⓣ (0221) 912 5301 ⓦ www.hostel-cologne.de ⓝ U-Bahn: Dom/Hbf; S-Bahn: Köln Hbf

CAMPSITES

Camping Berger £ A well-equipped site with hot showers, shop and restaurant, situated on the bank of the Rhine about 7 km (4 miles) from the city centre. ⓐ Uferstr. 73, Köln-Rodenkirchen (Outside the centre) ⓣ (0221) 935 5240 ⓦ www.camping-berger-koeln.de ⓝ U-Bahn: Rodenkirchen, then bus 135 to Uferstrasse

THE BEST OF COLOGNE

To get a true sense of the history and culture of this ancient city, stick to the Altstadt (old town), where many of the major attractions are located. It has the immense cathedral, churches, some of the best museums and galleries, views along the Rhine and many *Brauhäuser* where you can sample the famous *Kölsch* beer and a liberal helping of Cologne's laid-back lifestyle. If you want to dash around many of the museums and galleries in a few days it may be worth buying a Welcome Card, which affords individuals or groups reduced admission to many cultural attractions and free use of public transport. The cards are available from Cologne tourist information offices (see page 152) and many city hotels.

TOP 10 ATTRACTIONS

- **Dom (Cathedral)** An awe-inspiring Gothic masterpiece from outside, inside and the tower top (see page 61)

- *Karneval* Costumes, parades and partying descend on Cologne (see page 12)

- **Christmas markets** A festive hoard of traditional German toys, decorations and gifts (see page 11)

- **A tour of the *Brauhäuser*** (guided or otherwise) *Kölsch* drinking for research purposes (see page 70)

- **Museum Ludwig** A formidable collection of modern art in a beautiful interior (see page 64)

- **Schokoladenmuseum (Chocolate Museum)** Learn about your favourite food and eat it (see page 77)

- **Shopping** Cologne is an excellent place to find a special gift or trendy piece of clothing, with everything from huge department stores to the quirkiest of boutiques (see page 22)

- **Römisch-Germanisches Museum (Roman Germanic Museum)** Packed with impressive and fragile artefacts, this museum is a must for anyone interested in Roman history (see page 66)

- **Kölner Seilbahn (Cable car)** Probably the best view over the Rhine and the old town skyline (see page 111)

- **Thermal spa** Pamper yourself in the natural thermal waters of Claudius Therme, with its numerous pools, saunas and steam baths (see page 104)

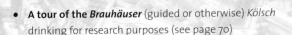

⬤ *The exterior of the Dom, Cologne's Cathedral*

Suggested itineraries

HALF-DAY: COLOGNE IN A HURRY

If a few hours are all you have, head to the Altstadt (old town). Stand outside the cathedral and marvel at its size, venture inside to see the exquisite gold Shrine of the Magi, then dash up the tower's 509 steps for a panoramic view of the city. Catch your breath over a *Kölsch* or ice cream in the cathedral square and choose to visit one of the Roncalliplatz museums: the Museum Ludwig for modern art or the Römisch-Germanisches Museum to discover Roman Cologne. Finally wind your way through the old town to a *Brauhaus* with a river view and enjoy a traditional meal.

1 DAY: TIME TO SEE A LITTLE MORE

As long as it isn't Sunday, add some shopping to the half-day highlights; in Hohe Strasse and Schildergasse if you are a chain-store devotee, or on Ehrenstrasse and Breite Strasse if boutiques are your style. There might just be time to squeeze in a trip to the chocolate museum.

2–3 DAYS: TIME TO SEE MUCH MORE

Once you have had your fill of the old town sights and the shops, pack a picnic, escape the city centre and get to Cologne zoo early for feeding time. When hunger gets the better of you take the cable car across the Rhine and find a spot with a view in the Rheinpark, where you can tuck in to lunch and relax. Spend more than you should on a slap-up meal on Friesenstrasse and sip cocktails in a trendy bar until late.

LONGER: ENJOYING COLOGNE TO THE FULL

If you have more than three days available, you have time to soak up the atmosphere and embrace the café culture in the stylish areas around the ring road at your leisure; explore the Belgian quarter and stop for refreshments under the imposing medieval gate in Rudolfplatz. For evening entertainment, experience some traditional Cologne humour at Volkstheater Millowitsch or dress to impress and party at one of the sleek clubs on Friesenplatz. There might also be time to board a scenic cruise on the Rhine to see the city from a different angle and some of the beautiful scenery that lines the river banks outside Cologne. You should also take at least one trip out of town, to Bonn or Brühl (see pages 120 & 134).

● *Make time to relax at the Botanischer Garten*

Something for nothing

If it's free entertainment that you are after, then Cologne is your ideal destination, because throughout the year the city hosts all kinds of events and festivals that bring thousands of people onto the streets to enjoy a friendly party atmosphere. The biggest day is *Rosenmontag*

🔺 *Cologne lit by the Cologne Lights*

(Rose Monday), when the Carnival season reaches its climax and a gigantic procession of floats, bands and city-dwellers in fancy dress makes its way through the streets, with people throwing sweets and chocolate bars to spectators as they pass.

Christopher Street Day (Gay Pride) in July has become the summer carnival and brings the crowds out again for another colourful parade of fabulous costumes, music and dancers. The following weekend usually brings Kölner Lichter (Cologne Lights), a huge firework display over the river, played out in time to classic pop anthems, which sees the river banks, bridges and tour boats crammed with eager spectators. All of these events see the old town bars packed to capacity, so that revellers spill out onto the streets and keep the party going into the early hours of the morning.

Rather more sedate, but with a wonderful festive atmosphere, four of Cologne's Christmas markets, in the old town squares from the end of November through December, are free to look round, although you will most likely be tempted to buy the traditional decorations, toys, gingerbread and mulled wine.

Even when there is no festival on there is a great atmosphere in the old town, and a walk through its streets and along the river will take you past entertainers, historic sights and fabulous views. The city's many parks are also ideal for a stroll or even a picnic. Sunday is when the locals descend on their green spaces, so if you want to make up an extra player for a game of football or just want to see how locals relax, do the same.

One more freebie that might appeal: if you visit Phantasialand (see page 135) on your birthday and you can prove your date of birth, you get in for nothing.

When it rains

Think of rain as an opportunity rather than a disaster, a chance
to stop dashing between the sights and linger in the places that you
like the most. This is a city where you can really immerse yourself in
art, so spend a few hours contemplating the masterpieces of modern
art in Museum Ludwig, or perhaps moving up the chronologically
arranged floors of the Wallraf-Richartz Museum from the glowing
gold of medieval works to the bold brush strokes of the Impressionists
(see pages 64 & 67). There are few places where so many great
collections of paintings are this close together, so take the
opportunity to enjoy them.

Guaranteed to cheer up even the dullest day for adults and
children, the Chocolate Museum (see page 77) is full of interesting
exhibits explaining the origins and manufacture of everyone's
favourite pick-me-up, with a chocolate fountain that is as good as
it sounds. Rain could also be the perfect excuse to spoil yourself
with a day pass to the thermal spa (see page 104), where you can
bathe in naturally mineral-rich water or keep out the chill in
a sauna.

Another way to stay dry is to explore Cologne's huge potential
for shopping – all under one roof. The truly massive Galeria Kaufhof
department store (see page 81) alone should keep even a half-hearted
shopper busy for an hour or so, with a basement full of deli counters,
chocolates, wines and little bars to stop for a drink and a snack, and
floors overflowing with fashion, cosmetics and shoes. There is also
the Neumarkt Galerie shopping centre, with its distinctive upside
down ice cream on the roof, which is full of all kinds of shops, cafés
and restaurants in the dry (see page 85).

For a cosy atmosphere on a miserable day, look no further than the old town's *Brauhäuser*, which will instantly warm you with their wood-panelled walls, free-flowing *Kölsch* and some of the heartiest, most comforting food in the world. If it's really horrible outside they might even have an open fire burning to make for an extra cosy experience. For listings of *Brauhaüser* in the old town, see page 70.

▲ *Check out the exhibits at Cologne's Chocolate Museum*

On arrival

There is no need to worry about your arrival in Cologne. It is a safe city with an efficient, well-signposted public transport system and a friendly population that is usually happy to help visitors.

TIME DIFFERENCES

German clocks follow Central European Time (CET). During Daylight Saving Time (end Mar–end Oct), the clocks are put ahead one hour.

ARRIVING

By air

It is likely that you will arrive into the modern, glass terminal buildings at **Köln/Bonn Airport** (❶ (02203) 404 001 Ⓦ www.koeln-bonn-airport.de), since this is the regional centre for low-cost airlines. This airport has excellent facilities and travel links to Cologne, which is only 15 km (9 miles) away. Both the arrivals and departures areas have plenty of restaurants and cafés, including 24-hour buffet bars. Bureaux de change and ATMs can only be found in the departures areas, however, so bring euros with you to avoid any inconvenience. If any problems arise there are information desks located in the departures area of Terminal 1 (between areas B and C) and Terminal 2 (area D), where you will find assistance.

It takes less than 20 minutes to reach Cologne city centre by rail. Trains are frequent and cheap, with a single fare to the city centre station (Köln Hbf) on the S-Bahn costing €2.40. The airport's train station, Köln/Bonn Flughafen, is situated downstairs between Terminals 1 and 2.

Shuttle buses nos. 670 or 161 run to the bus ranks behind the station and cost the same as the train, but take 25 minutes.

Taxis usually take 15 mins (depending on the traffic) but are by far the most expensive option, as the fare into the city is €25. Taxis are conveniently located outside Terminals 1 and 2.

By rail

Cologne's main train station, Köln Hauptbahnhof (usually written as Köln Hbf), is the arrival station for most visitors, and its doors bring you out in front of the magnificent cathedral. The main corridor serves as the Colonnaden shopping centre, with food outlets and shops. The entrance to the Dom/Hbf U-Bahn station is to the left of the main door and there are taxi ranks outside both entrances. S-Bahns (inner-city trains) also stop at Köln Hbf. An information desk faces the front door, underneath the departures board.

🔺 *You're never far away from a tram in Cologne*

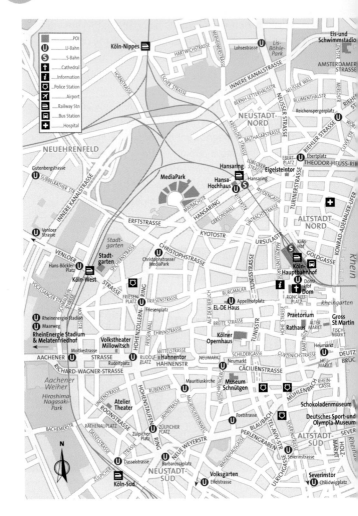

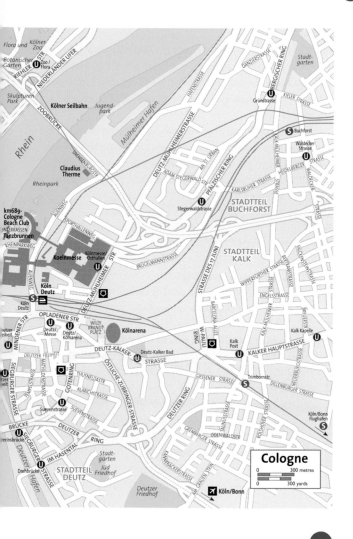

Cologne

0 _____ 300 metres
0 _____ 300 yards

By road

The city's bus station lurks behind Köln Hauptbahnhof and has little in the way of facilities, apart from a ticket office, but it is right in the centre of town. For journeys to other parts of Cologne hop in a taxi in front of the train station or walk through the Colonnaden to catch the U-Bahn.

It is best to avoid driving into Cologne, because the roads are congested, poorly signposted and there are many one-way streets, making it easy to get lost. Parking in the city centre can also be difficult and expensive, and if you are caught parked illegally there is a fine of at least €30.

IF YOU GET LOST, TRY ...

Excuse me, do you speak English?
Entschuldigen Sie, sprechen Sie Englisch?
Entshuldigen zee, shprekhen zee english?

Excuse me, is this the right way to the old town/the city centre/the tourist office/the station/the bus station?
Entschuldigung, geht es hier zur Altstadt/zur Stadtmitte/ zur Touristeninformation/zum Bahnhof/zum Busbahnhof?
Entshuldeegoong, gayt es here tsoor altshtat/tsoor shtatmitter/ tsoor touristeninformation/tsoom baanhof/tsoom busbaanhof?

Can you point to it on my map, please?
Können Sie es mir bitte auf der Karte zeigen?
Kernen see es meer bitter owf der kaarte tsygen?

If you are arriving by car familiarise yourself with the main streets beforehand. The city is enclosed by several ring roads, running from the Rhine bank in the north round to the river again in the south. Straight streets run out to this semi-circle like spokes from the city centre.

FINDING YOUR FEET

Cologne's old town is a busy place, but the pace of life is relaxed. The local people are well-known for their outgoing nature and are happy to help tourists. This is also a safe city with a low crime rate, although pickpockets do operate in busy areas around the cathedral, so keep any valuables safe. Most of the main shopping and tourist streets are closed to traffic, but it is worth remembering that Germans drive on the right and that trams run along some streets too. Cyclists are probably more of a hazard, particularly around the ring road, where parallel white lines on the pavement mark the busy cycle lane, which pedestrians should steer clear of.

ORIENTATION

On-foot navigation round Cologne is easy, because the cathedral towers are visible from almost everywhere and are the perfect landmark to head for. There are also plenty of large maps located around the tourist areas and U-Bahn stations.

The narrow streets of the old town between the cathedral and Heumarkt run gently downhill to the river. All the main shopping areas, Hohe Strasse, Schildergasse and the square at Neumarkt, are easily recognisable pedestrian streets that will direct you back to the old town or out to the ring road. The size of the ring road and its volume of traffic make it unmistakable, so you will not cross it unless you mean to. The medieval gate in the square at Rudolfplatz is another landmark you can't miss.

The maps in this book are up to date and show all the main sights and streets in each area, but many of the restaurants, clubs and shops that we list are on smaller streets for which you will need a larger street plan. If you are planning to stay in Cologne for longer than a couple of days, it's a good idea to acquire a detailed map of the city, preferably one with a street index, from a local newsstand or bookshop or from the tourist office.

GETTING AROUND

The best way of exploring the city and surrounding towns is on the integrated bus, U-Bahn (subway/tram) and S-Bahn network. When a tram travels underground in Cologne it is called a U-Bahn; above the ground it is known as a tram (*Stadtbahn* or *Strassenbahn*). For ease of use, we have referred to all U-Bahn or tram stops in this guide as U-Bahn stops. *S-Bahnen* are rapid suburban trains. Routes are simple to navigate, each vehicle clearly displays its line number and there are announcements for each stop. Tickets can be purchased from machines and kiosks in stations and must be validated (stamped) when you board.

If you are only travelling a short distance, buy a *Kurzstreckenticket* (short-trip ticket), which is valid for four stops. A single trip (1b) ticket

ß VERSUS SS

The German letter "ß", called *scharfes S* (sharp S), is represented in English by "ss". For ease of use, all German names and words in this guide have been written using "ss". Be aware, however, that you may come across "ß" when travelling in Germany; common uses include *Straße* (street) and *Grüße* (greetings).

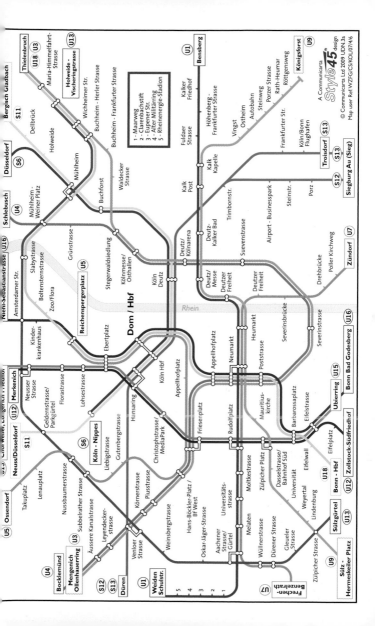

will take you anywhere in the city and is valid for 90 minutes (though you can only use it in one direction of travel). A cheap option is the *Tagesticket* (day ticket) for Cologne, which lasts until 03.00 the next day.

For those travelling in a group, a five-person *Tagesticket 5 Personen* is the way to go. It's cheaper than buying two single day tickets, but you can only travel after 09.00 on weekdays. For travel outside the city, the U-Bahn, S-Bahn and bus network is often cheaper (although slower) than using the train. A 2b CityPlus ticket will take you all the way to Brühl or Bonn. For ticket and timetable information, call ☎ 0180 3504 030 or check Ⓦ www.vrsinfo.de.

Licensed taxis usually come in the form of cream-coloured Mercedes and are easy to find day and night at the city's numerous taxi ranks or can be hailed when their light indicates that they are free. There is a minimum charge of €3, and the fares can tick up quite fast, so it might be wise to ask the driver how much the trip will cost before setting off. ☎ (0221) 19410 or (0221) 2882 Ⓦ www.taxiruf.de

CAR HIRE

It is only worthwhile hiring a car if you are heading out of town to explore and there are plenty of rental companies at Köln/Bonn Airport, the main railway station and around town. Pre-booking via your chosen airline's affiliates should secure you reduced rates.

Avis ⓐ Äussere Kanalstr. 86 ☎ (0221) 234 333
ⓐ Köln Hauptbahnhof ☎ (0221) 913 0063
ⓐ Köln/Bonn Airport ☎ 02203 402 343
Europcar ⓐ 26 Christophstr. ☎ (0221) 912 6010
ⓐ Dom/Hauptbahnhof, Trankgasse 11 ☎ (0221) 139 2748
ⓐ Köln/Bonn Airport, Mietwagencenter ☎ 02203 955 880

❯ *Cologne's streets are a mix of architectural styles*

THE CITY OF
Cologne

The Altstadt (old town)

Every trip to Cologne should start in the old town, which sits on the banks of the Rhine, between the impressive cathedral and Heumarkt square. Packed with character and culture, street life and nightlife, it has enough to keep the most energetic sightseer busy and amply fed and watered. The area is largely pedestrianised, so it is easy to explore the maze of cobbled streets on foot and there is no danger of getting lost with the cathedral towers to use as a landmark. The old town has the railway and S-Bahn station Köln Hbf, and the U-Bahn station Dom/Hbf, right at its centre.

SIGHTS & ATTRACTIONS

The old town is a great place to discover on foot and, while there are many world-class galleries and museums to visit, spare some time for sitting with a coffee or a *Kölsch* and soaking up the relaxed atmosphere. Wandering from the cathedral to the cobbled square of Alter Markt, with its view of the town hall and busy street cafés and *Brauhäuser*, will take less than 20 minutes. From here you can wind your way through cobbled streets towards the river until you reach the colourful old town houses in Fischmarkt, built between the 14th and 17th centuries, overlooked by the church tower of Gross St Martin. If the river-view cafés here don't tempt you to sit down, then continue along the river and make your way onto either the railway or road bridge for excellent views back to the old town and along the Rhine.

Cologne is well used to tourists and any warm day will find the square beneath the cathedral's façade full of street artists and performers, whose favourite trick is to pretend to be a statue, only to leap forward and surprise unsuspecting passers-by. Small groups of

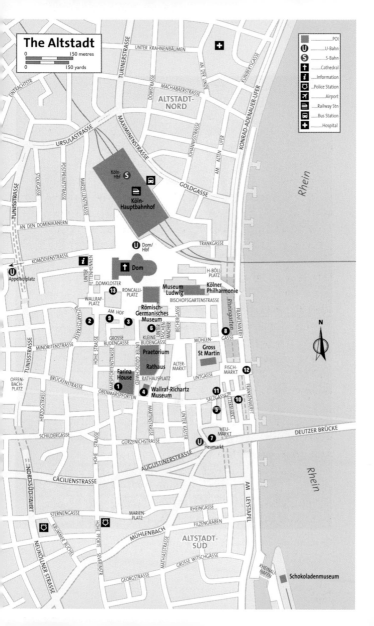

◆ *Stained glass windows in Cologne's cathedral*

musicians also perform in the pedestrian areas around the cathedral, as close to the appreciative audiences of outdoor drinkers and diners as they can get. In December this square also plays host to one of the city's intensely festive Christmas markets.

Dom (Cathedral)

Testament to the fact that it is impossible to ignore the looming presence of the city's cathedral are the two million visitors who pass through its doors each year, making it Germany's most visited attraction. This masterpiece of high Gothic architecture has been at the heart of Cologne since its construction began in 1248, but took an incredible 632 years to complete. Work stopped in 1560 and only restarted in the 19th century, when a revival of the Gothic style rekindled interest in the building. When it was finished in 1880, the two 157 m (480 ft) high towers made it the tallest building in the world, until the construction of the Eiffel Tower nine years later. In 1996 the cathedral was designated a World Heritage Site by UNESCO and remains a powerful religious and architectural focal point for the city.

Fabulous views of the cathedral can be found all over the city, but nothing beats the impact that the blackened stone structure has from the doors of the main rail station, which is at a lower level. From here the spires appear never-ending and there are always tourists struggling to fit their friends and the building into the same photograph. Entering the cathedral through a huge door, which is completely dwarfed by the vast façade, is suitably humbling but does little to prepare the visitor for the scale of the vaulted nave.

Many artworks reside in the cathedral, including a 15th-century altar painting of the city's patron saints and the luminous shrine of the Magi, crafted by German goldsmiths around 1200 and reputed to contain the bones of the Nativity's three kings. More of the cathedral's ecclesiastical riches are on display in the vaulted treasure chamber on the north side of the chancel. The swallow's nest organ, seemingly precariously hanging on the wall of the central nave since 1998, also deserves a moment's contemplation when you realise it weighs 30 tons.

Perhaps one of the best ways to orientate yourself in Cologne (or disorientate yourself if you do not enjoy spiral staircases) is to climb the 509 steps to an observation platform in one of the towers. Although the stairs are in good condition they are only recommended for the fit and fearless, because they can be hot and crowded with people going down as well as up. Whether or not you need a rest, take a break about halfway up to see the bells, one of which is the largest free-swinging bell in the world. Once at the top, if the weather is clear, a panorama of Cologne and the Rhine stretches out beneath you and you can try to spot a good *Brauhaus* to visit for a well-earned *Kölsch* after your descent.

Cathedral 🕐 For information about tours (which are usually held in German), call (0221) 9258 4730 between 10.00–12.00 and 13.00–15.00 🌐 www.koelner-dom.de 🕐 06.00–19.30, no viewing during services **Treasure chamber** 🕐 10.00–18.00 **Tower ascent** 🕐 09.00–16.00 Nov–Feb; 09.00–17.00 Mar, Apr & Oct; 09.00–18.00 May–Sept 🚇 U-Bahn: Dom/Hbf; S-Bahn: Köln Hbf. Admission charge

Gross St Martin (Great St Martin's Church)

Almost standing in the cathedral's shadow is Gross St Martin, one of Cologne's 12 Romanesque churches. Built in the 12th and 13th centuries this, like the other churches, was badly damaged during World War II, but had been lovingly repaired by 1963. Its beautiful tower and steeple, flanked by four smaller towers, are hard to miss from the Fischmarkt, where they look out onto the river from behind the square's cafés. Although it is an impressive space, the interior of the church is disconcertingly bare, so may only really appeal to religious visitors and those of an architectural persuasion. ❸ An Gross St. Martin 9, off Mühlengasse ❶ (0221) 1642 5650 ❷ 10.00–12.00, 15.00–17.00 Tues–Fri, 10.00–12.30, 13.30–17.00 Sat, 14.00–16.00 Sun ⓦ U-Bahn: Dom/Hbf or Heumarkt; S-Bahn: Köln Hbf

Rathausplatz (Town Hall Square)

It is well worth taking some time to look round Rathausplatz, especially if you are planning a visit to the Wallraf-Richartz Museum, which takes up one side of the leafy square. The benches shaded by trees provide a welcome rest for tired feet and a great view of Cologne's historic town hall (Rathaus). Its 15th-century church-like tower and wonderful 16th-century loggia are evidence of the city's affluent past and contrast with the 20th-century section of the complex, built after bomb damage. The Rathaus is not freely open to the public but tours can be booked through the Cologne Tourist Board (see page 152). The foundations of the Praetorium (Roman governor's palace) can also be seen underneath the town hall (see page 66). In the centre of the square, protected by a glass roof that the curious can peer through, is the Mikwe. This is an excavation of a medieval Jewish ritual bath dating from about 1170 and has a steep staircase leading down about 15m to a pool. ❸ Rathauspl., near Alter Markt ⓦ U-Bahn: Dom/Hbf or Heumarkt

CULTURE

Cologne prides itself on being a city of art and culture, and many of its major galleries, museums and venues can be found in the old town. These exhibitions are all housed in modern, purpose-built venues, where there is plenty of space, light and air. Most museums have cloakrooms, and visitors are required to leave bulky bags in lockers. Many of Cologne's museums are closed on Mondays.

Farina House

The home of the world's oldest eau de cologne factory named after perfumer Giovanni Maria Farina, who invented the original Cologne water in 1709. The museum looks at the history of this city's famous perfume and the Farina family. It's very popular with tourists and can get a little crowded. The factory sells one of the two brands of eau de cologne available in the city today; the other is the better-known 4711 (see page 86). ⓐ Obenmarspforten 21 ⓣ (0221) 3998 9941 ⓦ www.farinagegenueber.de ⓛ 09.00–18.00 Mon–Sat, 11.00–16.00 Sun ⓝ U-Bahn: Heumarkt. Admission charge

Kölner Philharmonie (Philharmonic Hall)

Located in the city centre, just down the steps from Museum Ludwig, is one of Cologne's finest music venues. Opened in 1986, the Philharmonic Hall hosts a huge variety of concerts from traditional and modern classical performances to jazz, folk and pop music. Concerts are held almost daily and there are often as many as three a day on Sundays and public holidays. The design of the concert hall itself is based on an amphitheatre, with the stage almost in the centre of the space, affording the audience uninterrupted views of the orchestra. Concert listings can be found on the website or in the Köln Musik ticket office, next door to the Römisch-Germanisches Museum. ⓐ Bischofgartenstr. 1 ⓣ (0221) 204 080 ⓦ www.koelner-philharmonie.de ⓝ U-Bahn: Dom/Hbf; S-Bahn: Köln Hbf

Museum Ludwig

An art gallery rather than a museum, this fabulously light and airy

◔ *The Renaissance façade of the Rathaus*

building behind the cathedral houses the city's collection of 20th- and 21st-century art. Spread over four floors are icons of American Pop Art, masterpieces of German Expressionism, Surrealism, Russian avant-garde and contemporary art. The first-floor galleries boast a collection of Picasso paintings and sculpture, as well as works by Dalí and Magritte. Special exhibitions, which change regularly, are displayed on the floor below the entrance hall and admission to them is included in the entrance fee. An English audio-guide is available at the ticket desk for €3, but for those who do not need in-depth analysis all exhibits are labelled in German and English. ⓐ Bischofsgartenstr. 1 ⓣ (0221) 2212 6165 ⓦ www.museenkoeln.de/museum-ludwig ⓛ 10.00–18.00 Tues–Sun, 10.00–22.00 first Thur of the month ⓜ U-Bahn: Dom/Hbf; S-Bahn: Köln Hbf. Admission charge

Römisch-Germanisches Museum (Roman-Germanic Museum)

Also next door to the cathedral, this museum is a must for anyone

PRAETORIUM EXCAVATIONS

Another taste of Roman influence in Cologne is beneath the Rathaus (town hall), where the foundations of the first–fourth-century AD Roman governor's palace are preserved. In its time this was the most important building on the Rhine and is now complemented with an exhibition of Roman monuments and art, along with a well-preserved section of a Roman sewer that visitors can walk through, marvelling at the skills of the ancient engineers. ⓐ Entrance: Kleine Budengasse ⓛ 10.00–17.00 Tues–Sun ⓜ U-Bahn: Heumarkt; bus: Rathaus or Gürzenich. Admission charge with even the slightest interest in Roman history. Go downstairs first to view the impressive Dionysius mosaic, which was found in the city in 1941 during excavations for an air-raid shelter. Exhibits cover every aspect of Roman life, from shoes and jewellery to amphorae and bridge foundations. Roman Colonia was a centre for glass production, famous for its exquisite pieces with 'snake thread' decoration, and the volume of pristine local finds on display is fascinating. Although English labelling is not comprehensive, there is enough information available to understand the exhibits and room for some fun filling in the gaps for yourself. ⓐ Roncallipl. 4 ⓣ (0221) 2212 4438 ⓦ www.museenkoeln.de ⓛ 10.00–17.00 Tues–Sun ⓝ U-Bahn: Dom/Hbf; S-Bahn: Köln Hbf. Admission charge

Wallraf-Richartz Museum/Fondation Corboud

This museum, the sister gallery to Museum Ludwig, is home to Western painting from the 13th to the 19th centuries, and should cater to most tastes. The medieval paintings assembled on the second floor are astonishingly vibrant and many of them are from Cologne. In fact, *The Martyrdom of St Ursula at the City of Cologne* (1411) is the earliest identifiable depiction of the city. The third floor boasts a huge range of 17th-century Dutch and Flemish paintings, including pieces by Rembrandt, Rubens and Van Dyck, while the fifth floor is reserved for 18th- and 19th-century art. Here, the ever-popular Impressionists are represented by Renoir, Monet and Sisley, while paintings by Van Gogh, Cèzanne and Munch are the icing on the cake. Widely publicised temporary exhibitions are also held in the gallery and can be visited on payment of an additional fee. ⓐ Obenmarspforten ⓣ (0221) 2212 1119 ⓦ www.museenkoeln.de/wallraf-richartz-museum ⓛ 10.00–18.00 Tues, Wed & Fri, 10.00–22.00 Thur, 11.00–18.00 Sat & Sun ⓝ U-Bahn: Heumarkt; bus: Rathaus or Gürzenich. Admission charge

RETAIL THERAPY

For serious shoppers the short walk to nearby Hohe Strasse (see page 81) would probably be worthwhile, but if it is a kitsch memento of your visit you need then the old town is the right place to find it. The brazen souvenir outlets in the streets surrounding the cathedral, selling postcards and models of the famous building, could not contrast more with the upmarket boutiques nearby, nestled next to the Dom Hotel. There is also a shopping centre in the main railway station, with everything from bookshops to pharmacies.

CCAA Glasgalerie A great shop for stylish souvenirs, this gallery sells original reproductions of Roman glass artefacts as well as modern creations by contemporary artists. ③ Auf dem Berlich 30, west of Komödienstr. ① (0221) 257 6191 ⑩ www.ccaa.de ⓛ 10.00–13.00, 14.00–18.00 Tues–Fri, 10.00–16.00 Sat ⓝ U-Bahn: Appellhofplatz

Chopard Boutique Exclusive jewellery and watches in a classically styled store. ③ Domkloster 2 ① (0221) 925 7990 ⓛ 10.30–19.00 Mon–Fri, 10.30–18.00 Sat ⓝ U-Bahn: Dom/Hbf; S-Bahn: Köln Hbf

Gaffel Kölsch Shop Wedged between two *Brauhäuser* is a shop selling everything you need to set up your own *Brauhaus* at home, including *Stangen*, the small straight-sided glasses. ③ Alter Markt 20–22 ① (0221) 257 7818 ⑩ www.gaffel-haus.de ⓛ 11.00–01.00 Tues–Thur, 11.00–03.00 Fri & Sat ⓝ U-Bahn: Heumarkt

Louis Vuitton Luxurious surroundings and excellent service will please fans of this top-quality brand of luggage and shoes. ③ Domkloster 2

📞 (0221) 257 6828 🌐 www.louisvuitton.com 🕐 10.00–19.00 Mon–Fri, 10.00–18.00 Sat 🚇 U-Bahn: Dom/Hbf; S-Bahn: Köln Hbf

Rhine Gold Individually designed jewellery, made by local goldsmiths.
📍 Frankenwerft 11 📞 (0221) 257 8708 🕐 10.00–18.30 Tues–Fri, 10.00–18.00 Sat 🚇 U-Bahn: Heumarkt

TAKING A BREAK

Whatever your tonic – ice cream, coffee, *Kölsch* – there are plenty of places in the old town to sit down and recharge. Most *Brauhäuser* (see page 70) serve drinks and food throughout the day, as do the following establishments if you fancy something different.

Café Jansen £ ❶ A remnant of a bygone era, this café (which is dearly loved by elderly women) offers peace and quiet, old-fashioned cream cakes and respectful service. 📍 Obenmarspforten 7–11
📞 (0221) 272 7390 🕐 08.30–18.00 Mon–Fri, 09.00–18.00 Sat, 11.00–18.00 Sun 🚇 U-Bahn: Heumarkt

Eis-Café Sagui £ ❷ This excellent ice cream parlour is tucked round the corner from the Dom Hotel and serves ridiculously indulgent sundaes, as well as coffee, with ruthless efficiency.
📍 Hohe Str. 164–8 📞 (0221) 258 0440 🕐 09.30–00.00 🚇 U-Bahn: Heumarkt

Raffaello £ ❸ Another good ice cream parlour, with views of the cathedral, Raffaello excels at tall sundaes loaded with fruit.
📍 Am Hof 28 📞 (0221) 420 7960 🕐 09.30–23.00 Sun–Thur, 10.00–00.00 Fri & Sat 🚇 U-Bahn: Dom/Hbf; S-Bahn: Köln Hbf

Richartz Café Restaurant £ ❹ On the ground floor of the Wallraf-Richartz Museum, this stylish spot serves great coffee and cake, as well as tasty soups and other snacks. ⓐ Martinstr. 39 ❶ (0221) 992 3759 Ⓦ www.richartz-koeln.de ❶ 10.00–18.00 Tues–Thur, 10.00–22.00 Fri, 11.00–18.00 Sat & Sun Ⓝ U-Bahn: Heumarkt; bus: Rathaus or Gürzenich

AFTER DARK

BRAUHÄUSER (BREWERY PUBS)

Brauerei zum Pfaffen £ ❺ Housed in the beautiful orange building on the corner of Heumarkt, with an interior filled with carved wood and stained glass. Serves delicious Pfaffen *Kölsch* and substantial regional dishes. ⓐ Heumarkt 62 ❶ (0221) 257 7765 Ⓦ www.max-paeffgen.de ❶ 11.00–00.00 Tues–Sun; warm dishes stop an hour before closing Ⓝ U-Bahn: Heumarkt

Brauhaus Sion £ ❻ With its dark wooden panelling, bags of hops decorating the walls and ceilings made from old beer barrel staves, this is a comfortable place to while away a rainy evening. The terrace in summer is perfect for people-watching while enjoying a *Kölsch* or two. ⓐ Unter Taschenmacher 5–7 ❶ (0221) 257 8540 Ⓦ www.brauhaus-sion.de ❶ 10.00–00.30 Sun–Thur, 10.00–01.00 Fri & Sat Ⓝ U-Bahn: Dom/Hbf; S-Bahn: Köln Hbf

Malzmühle £ ❼ As well as being famous for its local brew, this *Brauhaus* also serves traditional Cologne fare with a heavy emphasis on meat. Can get packed with locals and tourists. ⓐ Heumarkt 6 ❶ (0221) 210 117 Ⓦ www.muehlenkoelsch.de ❶ 10.00–00.00 Mon–Sat, 11.00–00.00 Sun Ⓝ U-Bahn: Heumarkt

Peters Brauhaus £ 8 Friendly, traditional tavern that serves good food and a range of schnapps as well as *Kölsch*. The huge stained-glass ceiling light is also worth a look. ⓐ Mühlengasse 1 ⓣ (0221) 257 3950 ⓦ www.peters-brauhaus.de ⓛ 11.00–00.30 ⓝ U-Bahn: Dom/Hbf; S-Bahn: Köln Hbf

As evening falls the crowds make for the Brauhäuser

Früh am Dom ££ A popular place from breakfast until late, with a vaulted cellar bar, a traditional *Brauhaus* and more subdued first-floor restaurant, as well as outside tables. Credit cards accepted in restaurant. ⓐ Am Hof 12–18 ⓣ (0221) 261 3211 ⓦ www.frueh.de ⓒ *Brauhaus:* 08.00–00.00; restaurant: 12.00–00.00 ⓝ U-Bahn: Dom/Hbf; S-Bahn: Köln Hbf

RESTAURANTS

Restaurant Beirut £ Centrally placed, this restaurant serves tasty Lebanese specialities. Every meal comes with a smile and a complimentary peppermint tea. ⓐ Buttermarkt 3 ⓣ (0221) 258 1539 ⓦ www.beirut-restaurant.de ⓒ 11.30–00.00 ⓝ U-Bahn: Heumarkt

Ristorante da Pino £ A reasonably priced Italian restaurant that cooks up tasty pizza, antipasti, meat and fish dishes from lunch until late. Seating outside in a quiet square. ⓐ Salzgasse 4 ⓣ (0221) 257 7769 ⓒ 11.00–01.00 ⓝ U-Bahn: Heumarkt

Das Kleine Stapelhäuschen ££ Its traditional decor, Rhine-side setting, top-notch German food and good wine list make this a great choice for lunch or dinner. ⓐ Fischmarkt 1–3 ⓣ (0221) 257 7862 ⓦ www.koeln-altstadt.de/stapelhaeuschen ⓒ 06.30–00.00 ⓝ U-Bahn: Heumarkt

Le Merou £££ This is primarily a seafood restaurant, with exquisite lobster and oyster specialities and an extensive wine list. ⓐ Dom Hotel, Domkloster 2A ⓣ (0221) 20240 ⓦ www.lemerou.de ⓒ 12.00–22.00 ⓝ U-Bahn: Dom/Hbf; S-Bahn: Köln Hbf

BARS

Barney Valley's Irish Pub A small bar, cluttered with Irish ephemera,

playing loud music and pouring stouts and whiskies as well as *Kölsch*.
🅰 Kleine Budengasse 7–9 🅣 (0221) 257 0820 🅛 11.00–03.00 Sun–Thur,
11.00–04.00 Fri & Sat 🅝 U-Bahn: Dom/Hbf; S-Bahn: Köln Hbf

Em Streckstrum Relax with a *Kölsch* in suitably dingy surroundings
and listen to live jazz daily. 🅐 Buttermarkt 37 🅣 (0221) 257 7931
🅦 www.papajoes.de 🅛 20.00–03.00 Mon–Sat, 16.00–03.00 Sun
🅝 U-Bahn: Heumarkt

Klimperkasten 1920s style, hundreds of old photos on the walls,
soggy sofas, and old-fashioned music from dancehall to chansons
make this place a favourite with young and old. 🅐 Alter Markt 50–52
🅣 (0221) 258 132 🅦 www.papajoes.de 🅛 11.00–03.00 🅝 U-Bahn: Heumarkt

Sonderbar One of the few trendy bars in the old town, with regular DJs,
stylish lighting and a huge mirrorball. 🅐 Lintgasse 28 🅣 (0221) 257 7857
🅦 www.sonderbar-koeln.de 🅛 17.00–03.00 🅝 U-Bahn: Heumarkt

Taberna Flamenca A friendly Spanish restaurant and bar that's a
meeting place for Spaniards and Latinos. Good food and live music every
evening (except Monday) from 21.00. 🅐 Salzgasse 8 🅣 (0221) 942 4352
🅦 www.taberna-flamenca.net 🅛 19.00–05.00 Tues–Sun 🅝 U-Bahn:
Heumarkt

CLUBS
Alter Wartesaal A stylish art deco restaurant, bar and club, playing
mainly R&B, funk and soul, set in the old waiting rooms of the former
train station. Also hosts gay and lesbian parties. 🅐 Johannisstr. 11
🅣 (0221) 912 8850 🅦 www.wartesaal.de 🅛 Restaurant: 12.00–01.00;
bar: until 02.00; club: hours vary 🅝 U-Bahn: Dom/Hbf; S-Bahn: Köln Hbf

The Innenstadt (city centre)

When you've had your fill of culture and *Kölsch* in the old town, head for Cologne's busiest shopping streets, only a short walk from the Rhine, beginning on crowded Hohe Strasse, along Schildergasse, and on to the U-Bahn hub at Neumarkt

This is not the most visually attractive part of the city, but serious shoppers will only have eyes for the vast range of consumables on offer, and the fact that the bulk of the streets are pedestrianised makes it an enjoyable place to browse. Hohe Strasse and Schildergasse hold few surprises as they're full of international chain stores, although some of the German brand names will be new to tourists. Enclosed shopping centres off Neumarkt and Appellhofplatz are good places to aim for if it's raining, as are the huge department stores on Schildergasse.

Not much happens in the city centre in the evening, as it sits between the much livelier old town and the cooler local haunts near the ring road. It is, however, safe to walk in, and if you're passing through or are tired after a long day of retail therapy there are a few bars worth stopping off at.

SIGHTS & ATTRACTIONS

If you need a break from all the clothes and shoes, or have companions who don't want to shop, there are several attractions in this part of town that will keep anyone entertained for a few hours. By far the most popular is the Chocolate Museum, perched right on the bank of the Rhine, which is just a pleasant, well-signposted walk or short U-Bahn-ride away.

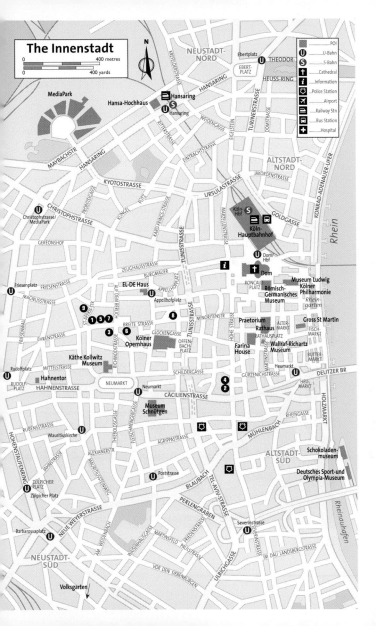

Deutsches Sport & Olympia Museum
(German Sport & Olympic Museum)

This museum charts the development of sports through the ages, from the athletes of ancient Greece to the ever-changing technology of today's Formula 1 cars. A treasure trove for sports fanatics, the museum is full of memorabilia, including examples of the kit and equipment that have helped champions to victory. There are also displays focusing on the German Olympic games held in Berlin in 1936 and Munich in 1972. All of the main explanations are in English as well as German and most of the exhibits themselves need little introduction. If you have some extra energy to burn off you can try your hand at racing a cycle through a wind tunnel, throwing your best right hook at punch bags in a boxing ring, or squeezing into

🔺 *The Formula 1 exhibition at the Sport Museum is popular with kids*

a four-man bobsleigh. Another highlight could be a game of
football on Cologne's highest sports field on the museum's roof.
ⓐ Rheinauhafen 1 ❶ (0221) 336 090 Ⓦ www.sportmuseum.info
🕐 10.00–18.00 Tues–Fri, 11.00–19.00 Sat & Sun Ⓝ U-Bahn: Heumarkt
or Severinstrasse. Admission charge

Schokoladenmuseum (Imhoff-Stollwerck-Museum) (Chocolate Museum)

Since 2000, this former customs office has been the place for
chocoholics of every age to discover the history of their favourite
treat and try a few samples – in the name of research, of course.

After walking through a grove of cacao trees in the tropical
greenhouse, you can go on to see how the raw cacao is roasted,
melted, moulded and packaged by following a real production line,
all clearly explained in English. Once you've got to grips with that,
find out how truffles and novelty shapes are created and delve into
chocolate's long history. If you are flagging after all this hard work,
a sip from the chocolate fountain might keep you going long enough
to reach the shop, which is overflowing with chocolate goodies to take
home. It would be easy to while away a few hours here, particularly
if you stop for coffee or lunch in the glass-fronted café and take
in the views of the Rhine from the roof. ⓐ Rheinauhafen 1A
❶ (0221) 931 8880 Ⓦ www.schokoladenmuseum.de 🕐 10.00–18.00
Tues–Fri, 11.00–19.00 Sat & Sun Ⓝ U-Bahn: Heumarkt or
Severinstrasse. Admission charge

CULTURE

Art, music, history and religion can all be found in the city centre at
four venues that could not be more different.

EL-DE Haus

Cologne's former Gestapo headquarters now house the National Socialist Documentation Centre along with a museum tracing the history of the Nazi party in the city. The ten torture chambers and cells with their graffiti from prisoners on their way to death camps are at the centre of the exhibition. In 2006, EL-DE Haus was given the prestigious 'Best in Heritage' award by the European Heritage Association. Incidentally, the museum's name comes from the initials of Leopold Dahmen, who ran the jewellery shop in the building when it was seized by the Nazis in 1934. ⓐ Appellhofpl. 23–25 ⓣ (0221) 2212 6331 ⓦ www.museenkoeln.de/ns-dok ⓛ 10.00–16.00 Tues, Wed & Fri, 10.00–18.00 Thur, 11.00–16.00 Sat & Sun ⓝ U-Bahn: Appellhofplatz. Admission charge

● *The Chocolate Museum by night*

Käthe Kollwitz Museum

This gallery on the upper level of the Neumarkt Galerie shopping arcade holds the largest collection of Kollwitz's often dark and emotional drawings, prints, posters and sculptures. One of Germany's most important Expressionist artists of the early 20th century, her work echoes her difficult and tragic life, spent mostly in Berlin. The museum is owned by the Kreissparkasse Köln bank and was opened in 1985. ⓐ Neumarkt 18–24 ⓣ (0221) 227 2899 ⓦ www.kollwitz.de ⓛ 10.00–18.00 Tues–Fri, 11.00–18.00 Sat & Sun ⓜ U-Bahn: Neumarkt. Admission charge

Kölner Opernhaus (Cologne Opera House)

If all the singing in the *Brauhäuser* has left you yearning for something more refined, a trip to Cologne's famous opera house might be just the ticket. Situated in Germany's largest theatre

⬆ *A performance of* Rigoletto *at the Opera House*

complex, along with the Schauspielhaus, which hosts modern and classical theatre, and the tiny West End Theater, home to modern productions, the opera house can seat an audience of 1,300. Every year it has a varied repertoire of 20th-century and classical works and ballet features heavily, too. Tickets are also available through Köln Ticket (see page 31). ⓐ Offenbachpl. ⓣ (0221) 2212 8400 ⓦ www.buehnenkoeln.de ⓛ Box office: 10.00–19.30 Mon–Fri, 11.00–19.30 Sat ⓝ U-Bahn: Appellhofplatz

Museum Schnütgen

A welcome oasis of calm after the tourist frenzy of the cathedral. The museum holds one of Europe's most important medieval religious collections, covering 1,000 years of art history from the early Middle Ages to the end of the baroque period. It's all displayed in the original setting of Cäcilienkirche (St Cecilia's), a Romanesque church dating back to the 10th century. Some 700 items are on show, including carvings in wood, stone and ivory, as well as tapestries and glasswork. A new cultural centre has recently been built onto the entrance of the church, greatly extending its exhibition space. ⓐ Cäcilienstr. 29 ⓣ (0221) 2212 3620 ⓦ www.museenkoeln.de/museum-schnuetgen ⓛ 10.00–17.00 Tues–Fri, 11.00–17.00 Sat & Sun ⓝ U-Bahn: Neumarkt. Admission charge

RETAIL THERAPY

You could easily spend a day exploring the city centre's shops and department stores, so get your walking shoes on (or make the Birkenstock shop first on your list) and get started. All stores are closed on Sundays, and many of the larger shops stay open longer on Fridays.

HOHE STRASSE

Germany's first pedestrian shopping street is not Cologne's most glamorous, but is packed with international clothing brands such as H&M, Zara and Mango, alongside The Body Shop, Foot Locker and various fast-food giants.

Galeria Kaufhof You can't miss this massive department store. It sells anything you could ever want, but is particularly good for fashion, cosmetics and jewellery. The basement food hall is also a treat, crammed with chocolate, deli counters, fresh produce and a huge selection of wine and beer. ⓐ Hohe Str. 41–53 ⓣ (0221) 2230 ⓦ www.galeria-kaufhof.de ⓛ 09.30–20.00 Mon–Thur & Sat, 09.30–21.00 Fri ⓝ U-Bahn: Heumarkt

SCHILDERGASSE

Leading off Hohe Strasse, this is a wider, more attractive thoroughfare, with space for bag-laden shoppers and street cafés. Big stores such as Benetton vie for your attention, as do international fast-food chains.

Douglas An oasis of beauty products in a lovely, softly lit space. There's occasional live music downstairs next to the coffee bar. ⓐ Schildergasse 39 ⓣ (0221) 920 860 ⓦ www.douglas.de ⓛ 10.00–20.00 Mon–Thur & Sat, 10.00–21.00 Fri ⓝ U-Bahn: Heumarkt

Humanic More shoes than you could ever imagine, for men, women and children, over three floors. Also Playstations in the basement and a first-floor café for the easily bored. ⓐ Schildergasse 94–96A ⓣ (0221) 925 9450 ⓦ www.shoemanic.com ⓛ 10.00–20.00 Mon–Thur, 10.00–21.00 Fri & Sat ⓝ U-Bahn: Neumarkt

Sport Scheck A gigantic sports superstore on six floors stuffed with sportswear, shoes and equipment for every activity. ⓐ Schildergasse 38 ⓣ (0221) 920 1000 ⓦ www.sportscheck.com ⓛ 10.00–20.00 Mon–Sat ⓝ U-Bahn: Heumarkt

NEUMARKT

The square at the end of Schildergasse, bustling with trams and people heading for the U-Bahn station, is the place to go for under-cover shopping when the weather is bad. The modern glass and steel façade of the Neumarkt Galerie is easy to spot from a distance as there's a giant, upside-down ice cream cone melting over one of its corners, the precise significance of which remains unclear.

🔺 *Schildergasse is just one of the city's many pedestrianised shopping streets*

NEUMARKT GALERIE

Cologne's largest shopping centre is smart and airy, with a vast range of outlets selling health food, jewellery, clothes, books and shoes. Abundant restaurants, coffee shops and ice cream parlours are an added temptation. Well worth a visit is **Mayersche Buchhandlung**, which holds half a million books, including some in English, on three floors; there's also a large reading area with tables and sockets for laptops. English magazines can also be found on the ground floor. **Sinn Leffer** is yet another giant store selling a massive range of brand-name fashion for men and women, including Tommy Hilfiger, Mexx and Esprit. 🅰 Neumarkt 2 🆆 www.neumarkt-galerie.de 🕒 Most shops open 09.30–20.00 Mon–Sat

Daniels Extremely sleek and stylish menswear store stocked with designer gear including Armani, Boss and Ralph Lauren. 🅰 Neumarkt 18 🅣 (0221) 257 7115 🆆 www.daniels-mode.de 🕒 10.00–20.00 Mon–Sat 🅝 U-Bahn: Neumarkt

Globetrotter With four floors of everything you could ever need in the outdoors, Globetrotter is gear-freak heaven. Try out scuba equipment or a kayak in the pool, test a sleeping bag in the cool room, and check if a jacket is really waterproof in the rain room. An adventure in itself. 🅰 Olivenhaindorf Richmodstr. 10 🅣 (0221) 277 2880 🆆 www.globetrotter.de 🕒 10.00–20.00 Mon–Thur & Sat, 10.00–21.00 Fri 🅝 U-Bahn: Neumarkt

◀ *Globetrotter: feel like having a paddle?*

BREITE STRASSE

Parallel to Schildergasse and close to the opera house, this is another relaxed, pedestrianised street with shops selling interior goods, clothes, footwear, jewellery and leather goods.

4711 Haus Just a few steps from Breite Strasse, this beautiful building, rebuilt after the original was destroyed during the war, is home to the

🔻 *The home of authentic cologne*

famous 4711 eau de cologne in its turquoise bottles. The scent used to be manufactured here by the Mulhens family, but today the site serves as a perfume boutique and exhibition. ⓐ Glockengasse 4711 ⓦ www.4711.com ⓛ 09.00–19.00 Mon–Fri, 09.00–18.00 Sat ⓝ U-Bahn: Heumarkt

Galerie Karstadt Another of Cologne's huge department stores, with a gourmet supermarket in the basement, a music store on the top floor and everything from books to clothes to cosmetics in between. ⓐ Breite Str. 103 ⓣ (0221) 20390 ⓦ www.karstadt.de ⓛ 10.00–20.00 Mon–Sat ⓝ U-Bahn: Appellhofplatz

Heubel Antique and modern furniture, accessories and jewellery. Heaven for browsers. ⓐ Breite Str. 118 ⓣ (0221) 257 6013 ⓦ www.heubel.de ⓛ 10.00–19.00 Mon–Fri, 10.00–18.00 Sat ⓝ U-Bahn: Appellhofplatz

Maus & Co Dedicated to Germany's most famous TV mouse and filled with soft toys, clothes and endless items featuring the cuddly orange character. ⓐ Breite Str. 6–26 (in the WDR arcade) ⓛ 10.00–19.00 Mon–Fri, 10.00–18.00 Sat ⓝ U-Bahn: Appellhofplatz

TAKING A BREAK

Crowds of hungry and thirsty shoppers mean there are many options for drinks and lunch in the city centre. All of the shopping streets are scattered with coffee shops, and the malls and department stores provide plenty of good and varied places to eat, so you don't need to stray far if your retail therapy is set to continue. There are also little market stalls selling fresh fruit on Hohe Strasse, where you could grab something on the go.

Café Fromme £ ❶ Modern café and patisserie with handmade cakes, pastries and chocolates. ⓐ Breite Str. 122 ❶ (0221) 257 6157 Ⓦ www.cafe-fromme.net ❶ 08.30–19.00 Mon–Fri, 08.30–18.30 Sat, 10.30–18.00 Sun Ⓝ U-Bahn: Appellhofplatz

Galeria Kaufhof £ ❷ Visit the food hall in the basement of this department store and take the weight off your feet at the little Italian café or wine bar, both of which serve good, moderately priced light lunches. ⓐ Hohe Str. 41–53 ❶ (0221) 2230 Ⓦ www.galeria-kaufhof.de ❶ 09.30–20.00 Mon–Thur & Sat, 09.30–21.00 Fri Ⓝ U-Bahn: Heumarkt

Galerie Karstadt £ ❸ The store's restaurant is a good choice for lunch, provided you can make it to the top floor without being distracted. ⓐ Breite Str. 103 ❶ (0221) 20390 Ⓦ www.karstadt.de ❶ 10.00–20.00 Mon–Sat Ⓝ U-Bahn: Appellhofplatz

Sky Beach £ ❹ Relax in a deckchair under palm trees and let the sand trickle through your toes right in the middle of Cologne. The beach bar is on the top floor of the Galeria Kaufhof department store (enter at the P2 car park). ⓐ Galeria Kaufhof, Hohe Str. Ⓦ www.skybeach.de ❶ 12.00–late Mon–Fri, 11.00–late Sat & Sun, May–Sept only Ⓝ U-Bahn: Heumarkt

AFTER DARK

This is not Cologne's party district, so don't expect to find much more than a few friendly bars. That said, many of the restaurants geared towards hungry shoppers during the day also stay open into the evening and might make a welcome change from the busy tourist spots of the old town. Otherwise, unless you're going to the theatre or the opera, there is little to keep the visitor in the city centre after the shops have closed.

Bento Box £ ⑤ Busy, reasonably priced Japanese sushi and noodle bar, with clean minimalist décor and an open kitchen so you can watch the chefs at work. Further branches at Ubierring 33 and Neusserstr 41. ⓐ Breite Str. 116 ⓣ (0221) 420 7740 ⓦ www.bentobox.de ⓛ 11.30–22.30 Mon–Sat ⓝ U-Bahn: Appellhofplatz

Bei Bepi ££ ⑥ With its ever-changing menu and pasta specialities, this vibrant Italian restaurant remains popular after nearly 40 years. ⓐ Breite Str. 85 ⓣ (0221) 257 6370 ⓛ 11.00–23.00 Mon–Sat ⓝ U-Bahn: Appellhofplatz

Bier-Esel ££ ⑦ This *Brauhaus* serves *Kölsch*, as you might expect, but is also known locally for its good mussel dishes. ⓐ Breite Str. 114 ⓣ (0221) 257 6090 ⓛ 11.30–00.00 ⓝ U-Bahn: Appellhofplatz

Gaststätte 'La päd' ££ ⑧ A cosy bar, cluttered with heavy, dark furniture and copper pots, that stretches back from a small front on the street. Shared by locals and tourists enjoying *Kölsch* and comforting hot drinks including *Glühwein* (mulled wine) and tea with rum. ⓐ Breite Str. 32 ⓣ (0221) 257 8412 ⓛ 16.00–01.00 Mon–Sat ⓝ U-Bahn: Appellhofplatz

Hase ££ ⑨ Creative and delicious Mediterranean food that makes a welcome change from the more usual heavy Cologne fare. It attracts a chic shopping crowd on a Saturday afternoon. ⓐ St.-Apern-Str. 17 ⓣ (0221) 254 375 ⓛ 12.00–01.00 Mon–Sat (Kitchen: 12.00–16.00, 19.00–23.00) ⓝ U-Bahn: Appellhofplatz

Around the Ringstrassen (ring road)

Once you pass Neumarkt and move through progressively quirkier
and cooler shopping streets towards Cologne's ring road, it feels
distinctly as if you are stepping off the tourist trail and into the real
city where people live and work. Fortunately, because the pace of life
in Cologne is so laid-back, the whole area around Zülpicher Platz,
Rudolfplatz and Friesenplatz is an ideal place to wander, shop and
stop off at cafés during the day, and go clubbing all night. This is
the part of town that the students, professionals, artists and media-
types frequent, which makes it vibrant, busy and, best of all, a great
place to people-watch. Getting there and getting around are no
problem, as there are convenient U-Bahn stops at Zülpicher Platz,
Rudolfplatz and Friesenplatz.

SIGHTS & ATTRACTIONS

The semi-circle of Cologne's ring road follows the line of the
medieval city wall, which was demolished to make way for it.
Remnants of the old wall can still be found, however, the most
obvious being the imposing gates at Rudolfplatz (Hahnentor),
Ebertplatz to the north (Eigelsteintor) and Chlodwigplatz to the
south (Severinstor), which are all easily accessible.

The ring road itself is dominated by traffic for much of the day,
but comes alive at night with fun-lovers flocking to its multitude
of bars, restaurants and cinemas. If you visit during daytime, it's
worth ducking off the ring road to explore the smaller and more
interesting streets around it. Heading back towards the centre, the
area between Friesenstrasse and Mittelstrasse contains a maze of
trendy shopping streets, where cool clothes and shoes, both new

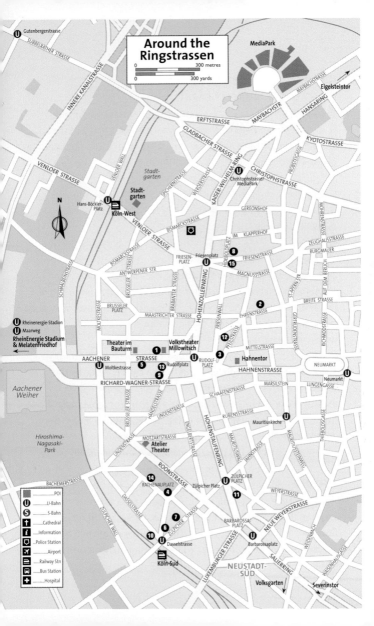

Around the Ringstrassen

0		300 metres
0		300 yards

MediaPark

Eigelsteintor

Gutenbergerstrasse

SUBBELRATHER STRASSE

INNERE KANALSTRASSE

ERFTSTRASSE

MAYBACHSTR

HANSARING

GLADBACHER STRASSE

KAISER-WILHELM-RING

KYOTOSTRASSE

VENLOER STRASSE

Stadt-garten

CHRISTOPHSTRASSE

Christophstrasse
MediaPark

Hans-Böckler-Platz

Stadtgarten

Köln-West

GEREONSHOF

VENLOER STRASSE

BISMARCKSTRASSE

IM KLAPPERHOF

BURGMAUER

ZEUGHAUSSTRASSE

FRIESEN-PLATZ

Friesenplatz

FRIESENSTRASSE

ANTWERPENER STR

MAGNUSSTRASSE

BRÜSSELER

BRABANTER STRASSE

HOHENZOLLERNRING

BREITE STRASSE

BRUSSELER PLATZ

MAASTRICHTER STRASSE

EHRENSTRASSE

Rheinenergie-Stadion

Maarweg

RheinEnergie Stadium & Melatenfriedhof

Theater im Bauturm

Volkstheater Millowitsch

MITTELSTRASSE

Hahnentor

NEUMARKT

AACHENER STRASSE

Moltkestrasse

Rudolfplatz

RUDOLF-PLATZ

HAHNENSTRASSE

Neumarkt

Aachener Weiher

RICHARD-WAGNER-STRASSE

MARSILSTEIN

LUNGENGASSE

Hiroshima-Nagasaki-Park

MOTZARTSTRASSE

Atelier Theater

SCHAAFENSTRASSE

RUBENSSTRASSE

Mauritiuskirche

HOHENSTAUFENRING

ROONSTRASSE

RATHENAUPLATZ

Zülpicher Platz

ZÜLPICHER PLATZ

WEYERSTRASSE

BACHEMERSTRASSE

BARBAROSSA PLATZ

NEUE WEYERSTRASSE

Dasselstrasse

Barbarossaplatz

Köln-Süd

LUXEMBURGER STRASSE

SALIERRING

NEUSTADT-SÜD

Volksgarten

Severinstor

▪	POI
Ⓤ	U-Bahn
Ⓢ	S-Bahn
✝	Cathedral
𝑖	Information
⚔	Police Station
✈	Airport
🚆	Railway Stn
🚌	Bus Station
✚	Hospital

STADTGARTEN (CITY PARK)

If the bustle of the city is getting too much for you then just a short walk away on Venloer Strasse is Cologne's oldest park, the Stadtgarten. Laid out in 1827–9, its tall mature trees and well-kept lawns create a peaceful green bubble, where locals go to walk, relax and sunbathe. More than that, it also has an excellent café-restaurant and beer garden and is home to – and shares its name with – one of the city's best-known music venues.

and second-hand, can be found alongside cafés, restaurants and clubs. This district also has a historical site, at the city-centre end of Friesenstrasse, in the form of the round, castellated tower that stood on the northwestern corner of the Roman city walls, which houses a well-preserved mosaic.

On the other side of the ring road, to the west of Friesenplatz and Rudolfplatz, is the Belgian quarter, easily identified by the street names. If you have time for a walk here, you'll soon discover the attractive old buildings and expensive apartments that make it one of the most fashionable places to live in the city. This area is also home to some classier and inevitably more expensive bars and restaurants, making it a good choice for a romantic meal.

CULTURE

Jazz and theatre are two of the city's passions and this area has its fair share of music venues and theatres. Both modern and traditional productions are frequently staged, and although most are in German

🔺 *Acres of space to unwind in the Stadtgarten*

they will undoubtedly provide some insight into the city's famous sense of humour.

Atelier Theater Cabaret and satire are the specialities here, sometimes accompanied by live music. The 99 seats tend to sell out fast and the programme usually changes weekly. Open until 01.00, the theatre's café-bar is a great place for a pre- and post-performance drink. ⓐ Roonstr. 78 ⓣ (0221) 242 485 ⓦ www.ateliertheater.de ⓛ Shows: 20.30; box office: 18.00–20.00 Ⓝ U-Bahn: Zülpicher Platz

Stadtgarten The venue at the Venloer Strasse side of the Stadtgarten shares its name with the park and has been a well-known jazz stronghold in the city since the 1970s. Today it remains one of the best places in Cologne to hear jazz, although it also plays host to all kinds of contemporary music. The on-site café-restaurant also holds monthly changing exhibitions of new German art. ⓐ Venloer Str. 40 ⓣ (0221) 952 9940 ⓦ www.stadtgarten.de Ⓝ U-Bahn: Hans-Böckler-Platz

Theater im Bauturm Energetic and ambitious contemporary works are performed at this small, modern theatre. ⓐ Aachener Str. 24 ⓣ (0221) 524 242 ⓦ www.theater-im-bauturm.de ⓛ Box office: 17.00–20.00 Mon–Fri Ⓝ U-Bahn: Rudolfplatz

Volkstheater Millowitsch Something of a Cologne institution, this traditional theatre, with its plush red seats, is home to the city's favourite folk theatre. The Millowitsch family has performed here, in comedic tales of everyday life, for 200 years, and Peter, the seventh generation, is as enthusiastic as ever. His late father Willy took his acclaimed performances from the stage to the wider

🔺 *Memorial to the much-loved Willy Millowitsch*

TV audience and was considered to be the personification of everything
Kölsch. 🅰 Aachener Str. 5 ❶ (0221) 251 747 🅦 www.millowitsch.de
🕒 Box office open three hours prior to performances
Ⓝ U-Bahn: Rudolfplatz

RETAIL THERAPY

Shopping in this part of town is more of an adventure than in the giant chain stores a 15-minute walk away. Quirky emporiums full of ethnic goods and cheap jewellery rub shoulders with slick stores selling skateboarding gear on the more affordable Ehrenstrasse, while exclusive boutiques line Mittelstrasse. Frequented by a young and disconcertingly good-looking crowd, these are the streets on which to see and be seen.

Apropos One of those shops that gives you plenty of warning you can't afford anything in it before you even get through the door. Turn off the street into a fuchsia tunnel, which leads into a covered leafy square with a chic café. From here you enter the shop itself, which is packed with collections from many designer names and has an enviable selection of jeans. ⓐ Mittelstr. 3 ① (0221) 272 5190 ⓦ www.apropos-coeln.de ① 10.00–19.00 Mon–Sat ⓝ U-Bahn: Rudolfplatz

Carhartt Baggy skateboard gear for men and women. ⓐ Ehrenstr. 73 ① (0221) 258 9529 ⓦ www.carhartt.com ① 11.00–20.00 Mon–Fri, 11.00–18.00 Sat ⓝ U-Bahn: Rudolfplatz or Friesenplatz

Crumpler Hardwearing, funky bags for your back, camera and laptop. Designed by two Australian bike couriers, Crumpler has become a cult hit in the street scene. ⓐ Ehrenstr. 71 ① (0221) 258 9404 ⓦ www.crumpler.eu ① 11.00–14.30, 15.00–19.30 Mon–Fri, 10.00–19.30 Sat ⓝ U-Bahn: Rudolfplatz or Friesenplatz

Diesel Jeans and casual wear for men and women. ⓐ Ehrenstr. 69 ① (0221) 272 4550 ① 11.00–20.00 Mon–Sat ⓝ U-Bahn: Rudolfplatz

Doubleight Cool skater and surf clothing, plus helpful staff.
🅐 Ehrenstr. 65 🕿 (0221) 272 5672 🕐 12.00–20.00 Mon–Fri,
11.00–20.00 Sat Ⓝ U-Bahn: Rudolfplatz or Friesenplatz

Hört Hört Everything percussion, including tambourines, bongos
and steel drums. Not surprisingly, it can be noisy. 🅐 Engelbertstr. 46
🕿 (0221) 236 789 🕐 11.00–19.00 Mon–Fri, 11.00–16.00 Sat Ⓝ U-Bahn:
Rudolfplatz

Lapis Independent jewellers specialising in modern designs with lapis
lazuli set in gold and silver. 🅐 Friesenstr. 73–75 🕿 (0221) 258 9798
🕐 10.30–13.30, 14.30–18.30 Tues–Fri, 10.30–16.00 Sat Ⓝ U-Bahn:
Friesenplatz

MAC Modern, bold cosmetics in a sleek white boutique.
🅐 Ehrenstr. 44 🕿 (0221) 258 5724 🅦 www.maccosmetics.com
🕐 11.00–19.30 Mon–Fri, 11.00–18.00 Sat Ⓝ U-Bahn: Rudolfplatz
or Friesenplatz

Made In With street wear that's out of the ordinary and a
wide range of skate goods. 🅐 Hahnenstr. 20 🕿 (0221) 255 466
🅦 www.madeincorp.com 🕐 11.00–19.00 Mon–Fri, 11.00–18.00 Sat
Ⓝ U-Bahn: Rudolfplatz

Papelito An Aladdin's cave of beautiful stationery, paper
models, decorations, books, photo albums and unique postcards.
🅐 Zülpicher Str. 22 🕿 (0221) 240 9786 🅦 http://papelito-koeln.de
🕐 12.00–20.00 Mon–Fri, 12.00–16.30 Sat Ⓝ U-Bahn: Zülpicher Platz

Tausend Fliegende Fische Popular new and used clothes shop, with some wild designs that aren't always cheap. Huge mirror and velvet-curtained changing rooms make trying on all the more tempting. ⓐ Roonstr. 18 ⓣ (0221) 240 0233 ⓛ 11.00–20.00 Mon–Fri, 10.00–19.00 Sat ⓜ U-Bahn: Barbarossaplatz

TAKING A BREAK

There are so many enticing and eccentrically themed cafés, ice cream parlours and bars in this part of town that the chances are sightseeing will provide a break from them rather than the other way round. That's no bad thing, and the locals, especially the students, seem to find as much time to spend sipping their drinks and chatting with friends as the tourists do.

Café Bauturm £ ❶ Eclectic interior with book pages papering the ceiling and chandeliers made from broken bottles. Frequented by artistic types and serving coffee, alcohol and good food from early until late. ⓐ Aachner Str. 24 ⓣ (0221) 528 984 ⓦ http://cafe-bauturm.de ⓛ 08.00–03.00 Mon–Fri, 09.00–03.00 Sat & Sun ⓜ U-Bahn: Rudolfplatz

Café Waschsalon £ ❷ Full of launderette chic, with washing machine drums serving as light shades. Drinks, snacks and light meals all day. ⓐ Ehrenstr. 77 ⓣ (0221) 133 378 ⓛ 10.00–01.00 Mon–Thur & Sun, 10.00–03.00 Fri & Sat ⓜ U-Bahn: Rudolfplatz or Friesenplatz

Eis Café Breda £ ❸ Sit out on Rudolfplatz on a sunny day and enjoy indulgent ice creams, coffees and snacks. ⓐ Pfeilstr. 2–4 ⓣ (0221) 257 3164 ⓛ 10.00–22.00 ⓜ U-Bahn: Rudolfplatz

Feysinn £ ❹ Slightly studenty bar-bistro, with an attractive mirrored bar, street seating and cheap, tasty lunches. ➌ Rathenaupl. 7 ❶ (0221) 240 9210 Ⓦ www.cafe-feynsinn.de ⏱ 09.00–01.00 Mon–Thur, 09.00–02.00 Fri, 09.30–02.00 Sat, 10.00–01.00 Sun Ⓝ U-Bahn: Dasselstrasse; train: Köln-Süd

Kaffee Storch £ ❺ Relaxed café that often plays old jazz tracks. It's a popular hang-out – Mondays from 23.30 feature open-mike poetry readings, while from the same time on Tuesdays anyone can show off their latest video artwork. ➌ Aachener Str. 17 ❶ (0221) 251 717 ⏱ 14.00–02.00 Ⓝ U-Bahn: Rudolfplatz

Magnus £ ❻ A big café-bar with a brightly painted interior, varied menu and generous portions. Come here for cocktails in the evening. ➌ Zülpicher Str. 48 ❶ (0221) 241 469 Ⓦ www.cafemagnus.de ⏱ 09.00–01.00 Sun & Mon, 09.00–02.00 Tues–Thur, 09.00–04.00 Fri & Sat Ⓝ U-Bahn: Zülpicher Platz

AFTER DARK

The area around the ring road really comes to life in the evening, with a huge range of excellent bars, restaurants and clubs frequented by locals every night of the week. On the ring road itself are the big bar-restaurants, many with live music or their own party atmosphere, which are a good place to start before hitting the clubs, none of which open before 22.00. In the smaller streets between Rudolfplatz and Friesenplatz you'll find more intimate restaurants and fashionable cocktail bars that often stay open until 05.00 at the weekend. There's no reason to ignore the student area, either: centred on Zülpicher Strasse, it is filled with lively bars, and good, reasonably priced restaurants. The ultra-stylish Rathenauplatz nearby is home to romantic restaurants, which are popular with the city's Porsche-driving set, as well as a busy park with a beer garden and children's playground.

RESTAURANTS

Habibi £ ❼ Cheap, freshly prepared Arabic food, including great falafel, that you can eat at the small mosaic covered tables or take away. Free cinnamon tea and freshly squeezed juices. ⓐ Zülpicher Str. 28 ❶ (0221) 271 7141 ⓦ www.habibi-koeln.de ● 11.00–01.00 Sun–Thur, 11.00–03.00 Fri & Sat ⓝ U-Bahn: Zülpicher Platz

Sushi Nara 2 £ ❽ The best kind of sushi bar, with a central conveyor belt surrounded by high stools. Also serves noodle dishes. Reasonable prices. ⓐ Friesenstr. 57 ❶ (0221) 120 170 ● 10.30–15.00, 17.30–23.30 Mon–Sat, 17.00–22.00 Sun ⓝ U-Bahn: Friesenplatz

Türkiye Pazari £ ❾ An informal diner that's always packed with people enjoying kebabs and Turkish specialities from the hotplate that's visible through the window. ⓐ Händelstr. 51 ❶ (0221) 252 674 ● 08.00–02.00 ⓝ U-Bahn: Rudolfplatz

Zarathustra £ ❿ Popular Persian restaurant with incredibly fragrant kebab and meat dishes cooked in a traditional oven. Also does take-away. ⓐ Dasselstr. 4 ❶ (0221) 240 7660 ⓦ www.zarathustra-persischekueche.de ● 12.00–00.00 ⓝ U-Bahn: Dasselstrasse

Al Salam £–££ ⓫ The ground-floor is an oriental bar replete with cushions and hookahs; upstairs is an opulently decorated restaurant offering fine Arabic and oriental food at moderate prices.

ⓐ Hohenstaufenring 22 ⓣ (0221) 216 713 ⓛ 18.00–01.00 Tues–Fri & Sun, 18.00–02.00 Sat ⓝ U-Bahn: Zülpicher Platz

Spitz £–££ ⓬ Café, bar and restaurant rolled into one offering tasty fresh food using regional ingredients and an enormous choice of German wines. ⓐ Pfeilstr. 31–37 ⓣ (0221) 1690 9848 ⓦ www.spitzsystem.com ⓛ 09.00–01.00 ⓝ U-Bahn: Rudolfplatz

Tandoor Palace £–££ ⓭ A classy Indian restaurant with a crisp clean interior and walls decorated with painted flowers. Friendly, family-run place producing consistently good food. ⓐ Händelstr. 33 ⓣ (0221) 236 855 ⓦ www.tandoorpalace.de ⓛ 12.00–15.00, 19.00–00.00 ⓝ U-Bahn: Rudolfplatz

Weinstube Bacchus ££ ⓮ Busy and friendly, this excellent bistro has a cosy wood-panelled interior, a well-chosen wine list and perfectly

🔺 *It's a moveable feast*

cooked meat and fish dishes. Rathenaupl. 17 (0221) 217 986
www.weinstubebacchus.de 17.00–01.00 Mon–Fri, 18.00–01.00
Sat & Sun U-Bahn: Dasselstrasse; train: Köln-Süd

Heising & Adelmann £££ **⑮** Cologne's in-crowd flock to this stylish
(if pricey) bar-restaurant for its meat- and fish-based menu, which
is more creative than many others in the city. Friesenstr. 58–60
(0221) 130 9424 www.heising-und-adelmann.de 18.00–03.00
Mon–Sat U-Bahn: Friesenplatz

BARS & CLUBS
Breugel Brasserie Cocktail bar and restaurant with a moody,
dark interior and grand piano. Musicians perform every night.
Hohenzollering 17 (0221) 252 579 www.bruegel.de 12.00–03.00
Mon–Fri, 18.00–03.00 Sat & Sun U-Bahn: Rudolfplatz

Diamonds Club Classy white interior and cool lighting make this
the ideal destination for fans of house music. Hohenzollering 90
www.club-diamonds.de 22.00–05.00 Fri, Sat & eve before
public holiday U-Bahn: Friesenplatz. Admission charge

Hallmackenreuther Two-storey bar with DJs and chic 1960s
decor. Popular with students by day and a trendy crowd at night.
Brüsseler Platz 9 (0221) 517 970 11.00–01.00 U-Bahn:
Moltkestrasse

Jameson's Irish Pub Huge Irish theme bar, with sports events
shown on two big screens, live music on Thursday and Saturday, and
karaoke on Friday and Sunday. Friesenstr. 30–40 (0221) 912 3323
www.jamesonpubs.com 12.00–01.00 Mon–Thur, 12.00–03.00

Fri & Sat, 11.00–01.00 Sun ⓝ U-Bahn: Friesenplatz

Päff A great place to kick back and relax, with a laid-back atmosphere and equally cool clientele. For the (slightly) more energetic there's a dance floor in the basement. ⓐ Friesenwall 130 ⓣ (0221) 121 060 ⓦ www.paeff.com ⓛ 20.00–02.00 Sun–Thur, 20.00–03.00 Fri & Sat ⓝ U-Bahn: Friesenplatz

Scheinbar Retro-style bar replete with lava lamps and low lighting. The mixed relaxed crowd enjoys funk, electro and anything in between. The cosy corner tables fill up quickly, so arrive early. ⓐ Brüsselerstr. 10 ⓣ (0221) 923 2048 ⓛ 20.00–03.00 Mon–Thur, 20.00–05.00 Fri & Sat ⓝ U-Bahn: Moltkestrasse

Triple A Ranked among Germany's top clubs, with different DJs every night of the week, playing everything from chart sounds and techno to soul and classic disco. ⓐ An d'r Hahnepooz 8 (Rudolfplatz) ⓦ www.triplea-club.de ⓛ 23.00–late ⓝ U-Bahn: Rudolfplatz. Admission charge

Umbruch Small, atmospheric bar with seats at the front and a dance floor at the back. Plays hip-hop, funk, techno and house and is popular with the local students. ⓐ Zülpicher Str. 11 ⓣ (0221) 240 6622 ⓛ 20.00–02.00 Sun–Thur, 20.00–03.00 Fri & Sat ⓝ U-Bahn: Zulpicher Platz

CINEMAS

Off Broadway Set back from the street through an archway, this small art-house cinema shows films (including British and American) in their original version, subtitled in German. ⓐ Zülpicher Str. 24 ⓣ (0221) 232 418 ⓦ www.off-broadway.de ⓝ U-Bahn: Zulpicher Platz

Outside the centre

As you move away from the city centre, Cologne rapidly gets greener, as it's almost completely encircled by well-kept, well-used parks. Other attractions, such as the zoo, Rhine cable car and MediaPark, are easy to reach by public transport and will occupy adults and kids alike for hours. However, places to stop for lunch and a snack are not as forthcoming as they are in the centre, so if you're planning a day in the park, a picnic would be the perfect solution. Remember to pack your swimming kit, too, as there is a great thermal bath with multiple pools and massage parlours in which to relax and unwind.

SIGHTS & ATTRACTIONS

Many of these attractions could happily take up a whole day if you let them. Some, especially the zoo, thermal baths and Rheinpark, can get busy at weekends, when local families swell the tourist numbers. Don't let that put you off, though: it just adds to the atmosphere.

Claudius Therme (Thermal baths)

To take relaxation to another level, try this luxurious spa, located in the Rheinpark close to the cable car. A natural thermal mineral spring provides the complex's numerous indoor and outdoor pools with therapeutic water, which you can soak and swim in. There are solariums, saunas and steam baths, and you can also hire towels and swimming costumes. Day tickets to use all the facilities are quite expensive, but you will probably want to stay that long. Massages and beauty treatments are available for an extra charge, although they need to be pre-booked. ⓐ Sachsenburgstr. 1 ❶ (0221) 981 440

ⓦ www.claudius-therme.de ⓛ 09.00–00.00 ⓝ Bus: 150; U-Bahn:
Zoo/Flora then cable car. Admission charge

Flora & Botanischer Garten (Botanic Garden)

Head through the archway past the zoo ticket office and cross the
road to reach the magnificent wrought-iron gates at the entrance to
this garden. Once you are through them stop to admire the brightly
planted parterre, sparkling fountain and the grand Flora building
beyond. This 19th-century park is a beautiful, colourful place to take
a stroll on a sunny day. A network of paths runs between the mature
trees, past statues and sculptures, to the small, natural-looking lake
featuring a statue of Neptune and terrapins. There are also several
glasshouses, with an amazing selection of cacti. The café (see page 116)
in the central building serves light lunch, ice creams and cold drinks
– at a price. ⓐ Amsterdamer Str. 34 ⓣ (0221) 560 890 ⓛ 08.00–21.00
summer; 08.00–dusk winter ⓝ U-Bahn: Zoo/Flora

Hansa-Hochhaus (Hansa skyscraper)

Just a stone's throw from the MediaPark is another of Cologne's
highest buildings. The slightly forbidding Hansa-Hochhaus was
Europe's tallest skyscraper in the 1920s, reaching a height of 65 m
(200 ft), although that looks diminutive by today's standards. It now
houses the huge Saturn music store over several of its floors, which
stocks CDs in every genre. Warning: once you start listening to sample
tracks on the headphones, it's hard to stop. **Saturn** ⓐ Am Hansaring
ⓣ (0221) 161 6260 ⓦ www.saturn.de ⓛ 10.00–20.00 Mon–Sat
ⓝ U-Bahn: Hansaring

km689 – Cologne Beach Club

If you prefer to lie on sand rather than grass, then stop by Rheinpark's

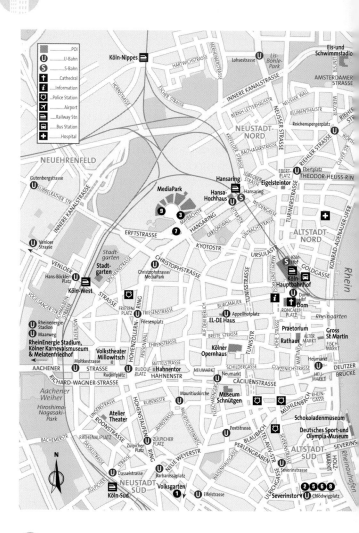

THE CITY

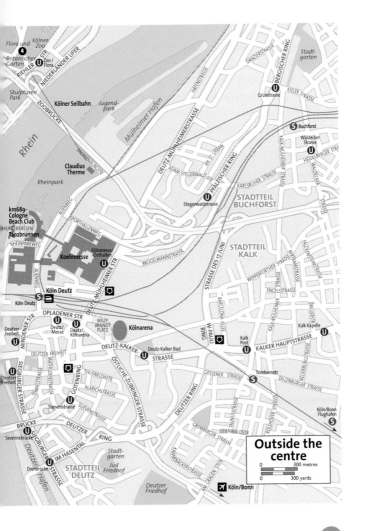

Outside the centre

| 0 | | 300 metres |
| 0 | | 300 yards |

lively beach venue, whose entrance is opposite the café. A huge area of safe, clean sand runs down to the riverbank and there are hammocks and deckchairs as well as DJs and bars serving cocktails and snacks. When the sun is out this place is very popular, so get there early to bag the best spot. ⓐ Rheinterrassen 1 ⓘ (0221) 650 0430 ⓦ www.km689.rhein-terrassen.de ⓛ 12.00–01.00 May–Sept ⓝ Bus: 150 to Tanzbrunnen. Admission charge

Kölnarena

This impressive stadium, with its glass façade spanned by a 76 m (250 ft) high steel arc, is known locally as the 'lunch basket'. It uses its full potential to host huge pop concerts and stage shows with audiences of up to 19,000. It's also home to the city's ice hockey, basketball and handball teams and serves as a venue for prestigious sporting events, such as the Ice Hockey World Championship back in 2001. ⓐ Willy Brandt Pl. 1 ⓘ (0221) 8020 for tickets ⓦ www.koelnarena.de ⓝ U-Bahn: Deutz/Messe or Deutz-Kalker Bad; S-Bahn: Köln Deutz

Kölner Zoo (Cologne Zoo)

Extremely popular with animal lovers of all ages, this zoo keeps more than 500 species in total, representing every continent and ocean. The enormous *Elefantenpark* is a highlight, as it allows the elephants space to behave and interact more as they might in the wild. It's also fascinating to watch the group of 150 baboons on their own island, doing what baboons do. There are also great apes, reptiles and insects, as well as a huge aquarium and steamy Southeast Asian jungle, complete with free-flying birds. Feeding times for the different animals are posted near the entrance, and if you're hungry yourself there are snack bars, a café and a restaurant where you can refuel. Outside the zoo, between the ticket office and U-Bahn station, there are also good pretzel stands and a kiosk selling sweets and drinks. ❸ Riehler Str. 173 ❶ 0180 5280101 ⓦ www.zoo-koeln.de ⏰ 09.00–18.00 summer; 09.00–17.00 winter ⓝ U-Bahn: Zoo/Flora. Admission charge

MediaPark

For a taste of modern Cologne, visit the newly developed MediaPark in the north of the city, just outside the ring road. This former freight depot is now covered with sleek offices, which house TV and radio stations and media giants like EMI and Sony Music. A new landmark is the rather beautiful KölnTurm, a tapering glass skyscraper that is reflected in the park's lake. There are many restaurants and shops here, as well as the *Cinedom*, Cologne's biggest and busiest cinema, with a terrace café on its roof that boasts good views. ⓦ www.mediapark.de ⓝ U-Bahn: Christophstrasse/MediaPark

● *The basket-shaped Kölnarena doubles as a stadium and a concert venue*

◐ *If you've got a head for heights the cable car is a great way to see Cologne*

KÖLNER SEILBAHN (CABLE CAR)

By far the most scenic way to cross the Rhine, the cable car runs from opposite the zoo, high above the river, over to the Rheinpark. From this vantage point you get a brilliant view back over the Cologne skyline, where the cathedral towers soar above everything else. If you're afraid of heights and have second thoughts, note that there's a walkway across the bridge below, which gives easy access to the Rheinpark. ❸ Riehler Str. 180 ☎ (0221) 547 4183 ⓦ www.koelner-seilbahn.de 🕙 10.00–18.00 late Mar–early Nov Ⓝ U-Bahn: Zoo/Flora. Admission charge

Melatenfriedhof (Melaten Cemetery)

This huge public cemetery, which is more like a park than a burial ground, lies just three U-Bahn stops from Rudolfsplatz. The old trees, grassy meadows and elaborate gravestones make it a perfect resting place for the living as well as the dead. Melaten was built in the early 1800s after Napoleon ordered that all burials should take place outside the city, in accordance with the traditions of ancient Rome. The name comes from the French *malade* (sick), and is a reference to the disused lepers' colony that the cemetery was built on. ❸ Aachener Str. ⓦ www.melatenfriedhof.de 🕙 07.00–20.00 Apr–Oct; 08.00–17.00 Nov–Mar Ⓝ U-Bahn: Melaten

RheinEnergie Stadium

Home to the Bundesliga team FC Köln, who play in red and white, the former Müngersdorfer stadium, built in 1975, was transformed into a state of the art venue for the 2006 FIFA World Cup. Guided

tours take place several times a day, except when FC Köln are playing at home or when the stadium is being used for a pop concert. Call for tour times and to register for an English speaking tour guide.
 Aachener Str. 999 (0221) 7161 6104 www.stadion-koeln.de
 Tours: 17.00–19.00 Mon–Fri U-Bahn: Rheinenergie-Stadion.
Admission charge

Rheinpark

At about 50 hectares (125 acres), this is Cologne's largest park and is so big that there's a miniature railway to carry you from one end to the other, although cycling and rollerblading are popular alternatives. Local families flock here on sunny days, especially Sundays, for picnics, barbecues, football, fun on the big adventure playground and general relaxation. There are also great views along the Rhine back to the city, and the cathedral towers are always visible through the treetops. At the opposite end of the park from the cable car is a café selling drinks and snacks. The nearby stage, surrounded by a famous dancing fountain (Tanzbrunnen), hosts concerts in the evening (see page 115). U-Bahn: Zoo/Flora, then cable car

Volksgarten (People's Park)

In the south of the city, another of the city's great parks, Volksgarten, is notable for its large, tranquil lake. Pedalos and rowing boats are available for hire, so the water is never still for long. Among the well-kept grass and mature trees is a beer garden, which has been in the same spot since 1891 and serves excellent *Kölsch* and snacks.
 U-Bahn: Eifelplatz

● *The RheinEnergie Stadium is home to the city's football heroes*

CULTURE

As you get into the fringes of Cologne, the art and culture of the centre begins to dry up. If you're passing, the Sculpture Park is worth a visit, if only to put your art critic hat on for a while, or you could keep your eye out for it as you glide over in the cable car. The Tanzbrunnen concerts aren't regular, so check listings for details.

Kölner Karnevalsmuseum (Cologne Carnival Museum)

This museum details the history of the traditional festival from Roman times to the present day. The documents showing minutes from historical carnival club meetings probably aren't that exciting for non-Kölners, but the costumes, and music and videos give a good idea of the event for those who aren't lucky enough to see the real thing. ❸ Maarweg 134–136 ❶ (0221) 574 0076 Ⓦ www.kk-museum.de ⏰ 10.00–20.00 Thur, 10.00–17.00 Fri, 11.00–17.00 Sat & Sun, open for groups Tues, Wed on request & during carnival Ⓝ U-Bahn: Maarweg. Admission charge

Skulpturen Park (Sculpture Park)

Close to the zoo, this green space on the banks of the Rhine is scattered with an exhibition of contemporary sculpture by internationally renowned artists. Running since 1999, part of the exhibition changes every two years and seventeen new works have been acquired for Köln Sculpture 5, which runs until 2011. The sculptures vary in media, including aluminium, bronze, stone, iron and concrete. There is a guided tour (small fee) on the first Saturday of each month at 15.00. ❸ Riehler Str., next to the Zoobrücke bridge Ⓦ www.skulpturenparkkoeln.de ⏰ 10.30–19.00 Apr–Sept; 10.30–18.30 Oct–Mar Ⓝ U-Bahn: Zoo/Flora

Tanzbrunnen

Clustered at the opposite end of the Rheinpark from the cable car is a range of venues hosting various kinds of entertainment throughout the year. Look out for the circular stage that shelters under a winged, tent-like structure and is surrounded by water. The fountains in the pool are illuminated and perform their own dance during the classical and pop concerts that take place on the stage. There's another, larger, outdoor stage and a big indoor venue which hosts music and comedy performanmces and club nights. Listings magazines and ticket offices have programme details. ❸ Rheinparkweg 1 ❶ (0221) 821 2121 Tickets available from Köln Tickets ❶ (0221) 2801 Ⓦ www.koelnticket.de Ⓝ U-Bahn: Deutz/Messe; S-Bahn: Köln Deutz

TAKING A BREAK

If the weather's nice, pack a picnic. Otherwise, there's a selection of places to get a drink or have lunch, as well as the catering facilities in the zoo. Many of the bars and restaurants listed below in the After Dark section also serve food and drinks during the day.

Biergarten Volksgarten £ ❶ A leafy spot to drink beer, lunch on pizza and salad and indulge in homemade cakes in the afternoon. ⓐ Volksgartenstr. 27 ❶ (0221) 382 626 Ⓦ www.hellers-volksgarten.de ❶ 11.30–01.00 Ⓝ U-Bahn: Eifelplatz

Café Zikade £ ❷ Lovely café tucked behind Chlodwigplatz, offering mostly vegetarian snacks and meals, including a great breakfast and freshly pressed juices. ❸ Kurfürstenstr. 2A ❶ (0221) 311 591 Ⓦ www.cafezikade.de ❶ 08.30–20.00 Mon–Fri, 08.30–19.00 Sat Ⓝ U-Bahn: Chlodwigplatz

La Gelateria – Eiscafé Paradiso £ ❸ Italian-style ice creams, coffee and snacks, with a panoramic view of the MediaPark from the roof of the Cinedom. ❷ Im MediaPark 1 ❶ (0221) 9519 5226 🕐 14.00–00.00 Mon–Fri, 12.00–00.00 Sat & Sun Ⓝ U-Bahn: Christophstrasse/MediaPark

Garten Restaurant am Zoo-Eck £–££ ❹ Conveniently nestled between the zoo and the botanic garden, this is the place for steaks, big mixed grills and salads. ❷ Stammheimerstr. 2 ❶ (0221) 765 391 🕐 11.00–23.00 Ⓝ U-Bahn: Zoo/Flora

AFTER DARK

There is still plenty of nightlife outside the city centre, and one of the best places to be in summer is sipping a drink on Köln beach watching the sun set over the old town. Indeed, walking along the Deutz bank of the Rhine at night gives some great views over to the illuminated cathedral. There are also lively bars and restaurants in the MediaPark, in the north of the city (Nordstadt) near Ebertplatz, and in the south (Südstadt) near Chlodwigplatz.

RESTAURANTS

Kajtek £ ❺ Family-run Polish restaurant and bar offering hearty and tasty traditional dishes in a homely Eastern European atmosphere. Large vodka menu and Polish beer on tap. ❷ Im Ferkulum 10–14 ❶ (0221) 429 2622 Ⓦ www.restaurant-kajtek.de 🕐 19.00–01.00 Tues–Thur, 19.00–04.00 Fri & Sat, 19.00–23.00 Sun (kitchen closes 22.00) Ⓝ U-Bahn: Chlodwigplatz

Keimaks £ ❻ A charming mix of modern fusion food and

old-fashioned furniture in this cosy restaurant and bar just off Chlodwigplatz. Worth reserving as it gets booked out quickly at the weekend. ⓐ Kurfürstenstr. 27 ⓣ (0221) 312 670 ⓛ 18.30–01.30 ⓝ U-Bahn: Chlodwigplatz

Pantanal Rodizio ££ ❼ Make sure you're hungry before coming to this Nordstadt restaurant because waiters will keep bringing the delicious Brazilian *rodizio* salad buffet and meat kebabs until you tell them to stop. ⓐ Maybachstr. 22 ⓣ (0221) 130 1767 ⓦ www.pantanal-rodizio.de ⓛ 18.00–00.00 Mon–Sat, 12.00–00.00 Sun ⓝ U-Bahn: Christophstrasse/MediaPark

La Patata ££ ❽ Tiny, almost cramped, traditional family-run Spanish restaurant in Südstadt, serving some of the best tapas in town. Worth a visit. ⓐ Kurfürstenstr. 24 ⓣ (0221) 316 902 ⓦ www.lapatata-laplata.de ⓛ 17.00–00.00 ⓝ U-Bahn: Chlodwigplatz

Osman 30 ££–£££ ❾ This chic top-scale restaurant on the 30th floor of the MediaPark has an amazing view over Cologne's skyscrapers and cathedral. The food is excellent and the wine list extensive. Great on sunny Sundays, when brunch is served on the enormous terrace. ⓐ Im Mediapark 8 ⓣ (0221) 5005 2080 ⓦ www.osman-cologne.de ⓛ 18.00–01.00 Mon–Thur, 18.00–04.00 Fri & Sat, 11.00–19.00 Sun ⓝ U-Bahn: Christophstrasse/MediaPark

BARS
Elektra Stylish but cosy retro bar with a very mixed crowd and different music to the standard electronic fare. ⓐ Gereonswall 12–14 ⓦ www.elektrabar.de ⓛ 19.00–02.00 Sun–Thur, 19.00–04.00 Fri & Sat ⓝ U-Bahn: Hansaring

Fiffi Bar A mad, dog-themed bar not far from the Volksgarten. To get there follow Seveninstr. south to Bonner Strasse, then turn right. **ⓐ** Rolandstr. 99 **ⓣ** (0221) 340 6211 **ⓦ** www.fiffibar.de **ⓛ** 21.00–02.00 Sun–Thur, 21.00–04.00 Fri & Sat **ⓝ** U-Bahn: Chlodwigplatz

Laubraub This simply decorated wine bar serves a wide selection of German reds and whites. In autumn, don't miss out on the traditional *Federweisser* (fermented grape juice) and *Zwiebelkuchen* (onion quiche). **ⓐ** Im Ferkulum 30 **ⓣ** (0221) 2716 2049 **ⓦ** www.laubraub.de **ⓛ** 19.00–late Mon–Sat **ⓝ** U-Bahn: Chlodwigplatz

Underground If you're into heavy metal, rock and punk, then this historic club is for you. Pub, concert rooms and beer garden in a former warehouse. **ⓐ** Vogelsangerstr. 200 **ⓣ** (0221) 542 326 or (0221) 954 2990 **ⓦ** www.underground-cologne.de **ⓛ** Pub: 18.30–late; club: 22.00–late **ⓝ** U-Bahn: Venloer Strasse

CINEMAS
Cinedom Cologne's largest and busiest cinema has 14 screens and regularly hosts film premieres. For some visitors the gloss will be lost as movies are screened in German. **ⓐ** Im MediaPark 1 **ⓣ** (0221) 9519 5195 **ⓦ** www.cinedom.de **ⓝ** U-Bahn: Christophstrasse/MediaPark

Metropolis The best English-language cinema option in the city, this venue shows current films in their original form, often not even subtitled. **ⓐ** Ebertpl. 19 **ⓣ** Info: (0221) 739 1245 (wait for English after German); tickets: (0221) 722 436 **ⓦ** www.metropolis-koeln.de **ⓝ** U-Bahn: Ebertplatz

---

ⓞ *Schloss Augustusburg in Brühl*

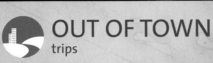

OUT OF TOWN
trips

Bonn

Just 30 km (19 miles) south of Cologne on the banks of the Rhine is Bonn, the perfect destination for a fascinating day trip. The capital of the Federal Republic of Germany between 1949 and 1991, Bonn is an energetic place filled with beautiful buildings, museums and art galleries, as well as great shops and colourful festivals. As it was the birthplace of Beethoven, classical music is also at the cultural heart of the city.

GETTING THERE

By rail
Transport links between Cologne and Bonn are excellent and depending on the type of train, the trip takes between 20 minutes and half an hour from Cologne's main railway station. You can also hop on the train

to Bonn from Köln-West (near U-Bahn Venloer Strasse) and Köln-Süd (near U-Bahn Dasselstrasse) stations. For a cheaper but longer ride, a southbound U-Bahn on line 18 will take you to Bonn in an hour (for a one-way trip to Bonn, you will need to buy a City Plus 2b ticket).

By road

A hassle-free drive down the A555 Autobahn takes around 40 minutes, although for the visitor, parking and navigating Bonn's one-way streets can be a challenge.

By water

A leisurely way to reach Bonn and see the lovely landscapes along the Rhine is to take a tour boat from Cologne. Depending on which boat you take, the trip can take between two and three and a half

◗ *On a sunny day, it can be difficult to find a free table at Bonn's Marktplatz*

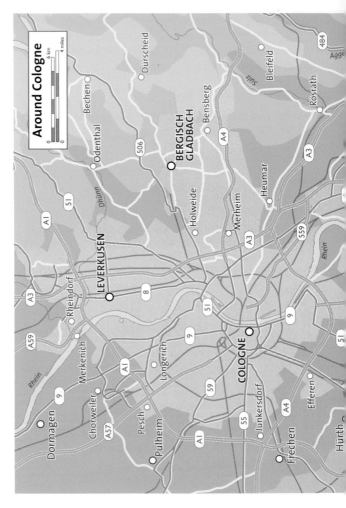

Around Cologne

hours, so a one-way boat ticket and a train ride back will save time if necessary. Most cruises leave in the morning, so it can be worth checking times the day before. The company, **Köln Düsseldorfer** (📍 Frankenwerft 35 ☎ (0221) 208 8318 🌐 www.k-d.com) leaves from near the Fischmarkt on the Rhine, whereas **Bonner Personen Schifffahrt** (☎ (0228) 636 363 🌐 www.b-p-s.de) departs from under the Hohenzollernbrücke, just behind the Dom.

SIGHTS & ATTRACTIONS

Visitors who travel by train will arrive at the main station in the centre of Bonn's old town, and many of the top sights are only a short walk away. A five-minute walk from the station is the **tourist information office** (📍 Windeckstr. 1, off Münsterplatz ☎ (0228) 775 000 🕐 09.00–18.30 Mon–Fri, 09.00–16.00 Sat, 10.00–14.00 Sun), where you can pick up useful maps and guides.

Altes Rathaus (Old Town Hall)

The marketplace is dominated by this imposing baroque building, completed in 1738 and visited by many dignitaries over the centuries. Numerous speeches have been given from the steps out front, including a welcome from President John F Kennedy in 1963. 📍 Am Markt ☎ (0228) 774 288 🕐 12.00–16.00 first Sat of month, May–Oct

Beethoven-Denkmal (Beethoven statue)

Bonn's favourite son is immortalised in bronze on Münsterplatz. The statue was unveiled in 1845 to commemorate the composer's 75th birthday (18 years after his death) and stands in front of the magnificent central post-office building, which was once a royal palace. (For the Beethoven Museum, see page 127.)

Marktplatz (Market Square)

A short walk along Remigiusstrasse brings you to Bonn's triangular market square, which still hosts thriving fruit and vegetable stalls, alongside cafés, shops and restaurants, making it an interesting place to linger and watch the world go by.

Münsterbasilika

The unmistakable spires of Bonn's biggest church are the first landmark to head for. Built between the 11th and 13th centuries on the graves of the city's patrons Cassius and Florentius, the basilica is a combination of Romanesque and Gothic architectural styles. Like so many buildings along the Rhine, it was damaged by World War II bombs, but has been fully restored. Tours in English can be booked through the tourist office (see opposite). ⓐ Münsterpl. ⓣ (0228) 985 8810 (10.00–12.00 Mon–Fri, 16.00–19.00 Thur only) ⓦ www.bonner-muenster.de ⓛ 07.00–19.00

POPPELSDORF DISTRICT

Heading away from Münsterplatz as you leave the main railway station will take you down the grand, tree-lined Poppelsdorfer Allee towards the spectacular Poppelsdorf Palace. This is a fashionable residential area with some beautiful art nouveau houses built in the 1870s, plus plenty of good cafés and restaurants.

Botanische Gärten (Botanical Gardens)

Formerly the castle gardens, this 6-hectare (15-acre) plot was assigned to the university in 1818 and today is filled with interesting plants and tropical greenhouses – and people relaxing. ⓐ Meckheimer Allee 171 ⓣ (0228) 735 523 ⓦ www.botgart.uni-bonn.de ⓛ 09.00–18.00 Mon–Fri & Sun, Apr–Oct; 09.00–16.00 Mon–Fri, 09.00–18.00 Sun,

Nov–Mar (conservatories shorter hours). Admission charge Sun & public holidays

Freizeitpark Rheinaue (Rheinaue Leisure Park)

This vast park south of the old town contains sports facilities, playgrounds, barbecue areas and a meadow lake where you can hire pedalos and rowing boats. It's ideal for walking, sunbathing, picnicking or just watching the rollerbladers and model boat fanatics. The park also hosts the **Rheinkultur** (Ⓦ www.rheinkultur.com) music festival in July, where huge crowds gather for free rock, pop, hip-hop and jazz concerts. Another July event is the **Bonner Bierbörse** (Bonn Beer Festival Ⓦ www.bierboerse.com), with more than 90 exhibitors offering international beers and open-air entertainment.

Poppelsdorfer Schloss (Poppelsdorf Palace)

Completed in 1753, this rococo pleasure palace is more reminiscent of a French château than a castle, but is impressive nonetheless. In 1818 it was assigned to house scientific collections from Bonn University and as such is now home to the rock and crystal collection of its mineralogical museum. ⓐ Meckenheimer Allee 171 ① (0228) 732 761 ⓛ Mineralogical Museum: 15.00–17.00 Wed, 10.00–12.00 Sun

CULTURE

Arithmeum

Science and technology museum focusing on the history of counting, with the world's largest collection of historical mechanical calculating machines. It also features contemporary art inspired by geometrical patterns. Great for scientifically minded kids and adults.

SPOILT FOR CHOICE
There are so many museums, art galleries and music venues in Bonn that if you're only here for a short time the biggest problem will be deciding what to see. If you're planning on visiting several museums, you might want to invest in a Bonn Regio WelcomeCard (available from the tourist office), which provides free and reduced admission to some museums and galleries.

ⓐ Lennéstr. 2 ❶ (0228) 738 790 ⓦ www.arithmeum.uni-bonn.de
🕐 11.00–18.00 Tues–Sun

Beethoven-Haus

An exhibition of the great composer's manuscripts, musical instruments and possessions, along with a tour of the house he was born in, give an insight into Beethoven's life and work. The attached Chamber Music Hall hosts concerts weekly in summer (see the website for details).
ⓐ Bonngasse 18–26 ❶ (0228) 981 7525 ⓦ www.beethoven-haus-bonn.de
🕐 10.00–18.00 Mon–Sat, 11.00–18.00 Sun, Apr–Oct; 10.00–17.00 Mon–Sat, 11.00–17.00 Sun, Nov–Mar. Admission charge

Deutsches Museum Bonn (German Museum)

If you like the monorail in front of the entrance, you'll spend hours in this museum of science and technology discovering the details behind everything from ship-building to space travel. Kids especially will love it. ⓐ Ahrstr. 45 ❶ (0228) 302 252 ⓦ www.deutsches-museum.de 🕐 10.00–18.00 Tues–Sun

Kunstmuseum Bonn (Art Museum)

The arresting contemporary building that is home to Bonn's modern art museum was designed by Axel Schultes and is an attraction in itself. That is not to belittle the impressive collection of 20th-century art that hangs in the museum, particularly works by Ernst and Klee

◭ *The art in Bonn isn't just hidden away inside museums*

and those of the Rheinish Expressionists. 🅐 Friedrich-Ebert-Allee 2
🅣 (0228) 776 260 🅦 http://kunstmuseum.bonn.de 🅛 09.00–19.00
Tues–Sun

Rheinisches Landesmuseum (Rhine Regional Museum)

Explore the Rhine region's history, art and culture from the Stone Age
to the present day in this recently revamped exhibition divided into
various sections, from trade and tools to influential local individuals
and artists. It's a good place to get an overview of this fascinating
region. 🅐 Colmantstr. 14–18 🅣 (0228) 20700 🅦 www.rlmb.lvr.de

RETAIL THERAPY

Strolling around the shops in Bonn's car-free old town is an excellent
way to spend the day and see some of the city's historic buildings, too.
Many of the shops are concentrated around the squares at Münsterplatz
and Marktplatz and spill over down Sternstrasse and Remigiusstrasse
in between. There are some particularly good designer boutiques for
men and women, but if you prefer a bargain why not try Germany's
biggest flea market, held on the third Sunday of the month between
April and October in the Rheinaue park.

Body Gear Don't let the name put you off: this chic boutique
sells exclusive designer menswear to the discerning gentlemen
of Bonn. 🅐 Sternstr. 54 (in Einkaufpassage) 🅣 (0228) 694 444
🅦 www.bodygear.de 🅛 10.30–19.00 Mon–Sat

Gentile Shoes, bags and accessories that will make you stand out
from the crowd. 🅐 Am Dreleck 11 🅣 (0228) 659 688 🅛 10.00–19.00
Mon–Wed, 10.00–20.00 Thur & Fri, 10.00–16.00 Sat

Kaufhof Bonn's biggest department store stocks everything from artisan food in the basement to cosmetics, clothing, jewellery and kitchenware. ⓐ Münsterpl. ⓣ (0228) 5160 ⓦ www.kaufhof.de ⓛ 09.30–20.00 Mon–Thur, 09.30–21.00 Fri & Sat

Room Nine A bit pricey, but the unusual mix of interesting clothes, shoes and accessories includes many one-off items. ⓐ Sterntorbrücke 9 ⓣ (0228) 981 4730 ⓛ 10.00–19.00 Mon–Fri, 10.00–18.00 Sat

Senfgarten Tucked away in a side street, this small shop stocks over 140 different types of mustard, as well as marmalades and oils. Many of the products are available for tasting. ⓐ Acherstr. 12 ⓣ (0228) 390 7536 ⓛ 10.00–18.00 Mon–Sat

TAKING A BREAK

As in Cologne, café culture is alive and well in Bonn, particularly during summer, so there's plenty of choice.

Am Alten Zoll £ This incredibly popular beer garden has great views of the Rhine and shady trees for warm summer days. Cheap pizza and beer are the attractions. ⓐ Am Brassertufer ⓛ 11.00–23.00

Café im Kunstmuseum £ At the end of a visit to this modern art gallery, head to its café, with art on the walls, Italian coffee and delicious cakes. ⓐ Friedrich-Ebert-Allee 2 ⓣ (0228) 230 059 ⓦ www.cafekumu.de ⓛ 10.00–19.00 Tues–Sun

Pendel £ A great place to relax while shopping, this café-bistro serves toasties, light lunches, coffee and cocktails. ⓐ Vivatsgasse 2A

◑ (0228) 976 6064 **Ⓦ** www.cafe-bistro-pendel.de **◐** 09.00–01.00 Mon–Thur, 09.00–02.00 Fri, 10.00–02.00 Sat, 10.00–01.00 Sun

Bon(n) Gout £–££ Trendy two-storey cafe with a wide-range of cakes and coffee, plus snacks and full meals. **ⓐ** Remigiuspl. 2 (at the flower market) **◑** (0228) 658 988 **◐** 09.00–23.00 Mon–Fri, 09.00–01.00 Sat, 10.00–23.00 Sun

Miebach £–££ Sit out on this café's marketplace terrace with drinks, cake or breakfast; the latter is served until 14.00. **ⓐ** Markt 8 **◑** (0228) 692 500 **Ⓦ** www.miebachs.com **◐** 09.00–00.00

AFTER DARK

Bonn is lively at night and stays open late, which suits the city's students and tourists well. Even if you don't venture beyond the centre, there are many restaurants to choose from and if you're looking for culture then you're in luck, too: theatres, cinemas and open-air music cater to every taste. Theatre and music listings in English can be found in *Rhine Magazine*, available in bookshops.

RESTAURANTS

Brauhaus Bönnsch £ In addition to serving its own home-brewed beer, this pub is a great place for traditional German fare that's heavy on the meat. **ⓐ** Sterntorbrücke 4 **◑** (0228) 650 610 **Ⓦ** www.boennsch.de **◐** 11.00–01.00 Mon–Thur, 11.00–03.00 Fri & Sat, 12.00–00.00 Sun

San Telmo £ Good Spanish restaurant with great atmosphere and friendly service in Bonn's old town, not far from the centre. **ⓐ** Breite Str. 55 **◑** (0228) 638 663 **Ⓦ** www.san-telmo.de **◐** 18.00–23.00

Ichiban Sushi Bar £–££ Fantastic sushi bar in the town centre, but so popular that you may have to wait for a table. ⓐ Stockenstr. 14 ① (0228) 410 9789 Ⓦ www.ichiban-sushibar.de Ⓛ 12.00–22.00 Mon–Sat, 15.00–21.00 Sun

BARS & CLUBS

Blow-up After midnight, it can be hard to move in this small bar, set in a former brothel. Old couches, mirrors, red lights and little-known grooves from the 1960s and 1970s make it a relaxed place to hang out. ⓐ Rathausgasse 10 ① (0228) 659 750 Ⓛ 22.00–late

Casa del Gatto Cosy cellar bar that's popular for its cheap beer and food and its sunny terrace in summer. ⓐ Kaiserpl. 20 ① (0228) 695 522 Ⓦ http://casadelgatto.de Ⓛ 11.00–01.00 Mon–Thur & Sun, 11.00–02.00 Fri & Sat

James Joyce Irish Pub Located in a 300-year-old building with low-beamed ceilings, this pub is hard to beat. Big screen and pool tables as well as hundreds of books and cosy corners make it the perfect choice for a rainy day. ⓐ Mauspfad 6–10 ① (0228) 369 5671 Ⓦ www.jamesjoyce-bonn.de Ⓛ 16.00–01.00 Sun–Thur, 16.00–03.00 Fri, 14.00–03.00 Sat

Pawlow In the heart of Bonn's alternative Altstadt (old town), this casual bar attracts arts students, old-school lefties and locals. It's worth the 15-minute walk from the station to sit at one of their outside beer benches and watch the world go by. ⓐ Heerstr. 64 ① (0228) 653 603 Ⓛ 11.00–01.00 Sun–Thur, 11.00–late Fri & Sat

ENTERTAINMENT

Beethovenfest Bonn Held usually from late August to late September, this internationally renowned festival doesn't just showcase Beethoven, but also focuses on contemporary composers. ➊ Information: (0228) 201 0345; tickets: 0180 500 1812 ➌ www.beethovenfest.de

Kammerspiele Bonn Stages a range of traditional theatre, music and dance productions throughout the year. ➋ Am Michaelshof 9 ➊ (0228) 778 008 ➌ www.theater-bonn.de ➍ Box office: 10.00–15.30 Mon–Fri, 09.30–12.00 Sat

Poppelsdorfer Schlosskonzerte In July and August this magnificent building becomes a backdrop for classical concerts. ➋ Meckenheimer Allee 171 ➊ (0228) 654 965 ➌ www.klassische-philharmonie-bonn.de

ACCOMMODATION

Many hotels in Bonn also get booked out when trade fairs are being held in Cologne, and prices tend to be higher during these times.

Hotel Aigner £ Located in a quiet side street in Bonn's old town, this small family-run hotel is close to the area's restaurant and bars. ➋ Dorotheenstr. 12 ➊ (0228) 604 060 ➌ www.hotel-aigner.de

Hotel Ibis £ Basic, reliable rooms at reasonable rates, just north of the city centre. ➋ Vorgebirgstr. 33 ➊ (0228) 72660 ➌ www.ibishotel.com

Günnewig Hotel Bristol ££ This comfortable hotel is conveniently located between Poppelsdorf Schlosskonzerte and the university. ➋ Prinz-Albert-Str. 2 ➊ (0228) 26980 ➌ www.guennewig.de

Brühl & Phantasialand

Brühl is an attractive town, only 20 km (12 miles) southwest of Cologne, popular with commuters because of its good shops and restaurants, without the hectic pace of city life. It makes it onto the tourist trail because it is home to the incredible Augustusburg Palace and Falkenlust hunting lodge, which were designated World Heritage Sites more than 20 years ago by UNESCO, but the town has other attractions worth seeing that many of the coach parties miss. Another draw to the area is one of Europe's biggest theme parks, Phantasialand.

GETTING THERE

By rail

A train from Cologne's main railway station takes 15 minutes to Brühl, less if you are getting on at Köln-West (near U-Bahn Venloer Strasse) or Köln Süd (near U-Bahn Dasselstrasse) stations. The southbound U-Bahn line 18 is slightly cheaper and takes 30 minutes

BRÜHL OLD TOWN

Spare some time on your trip to enjoy Brühl's picturesque old town, which is closed to cars and full of busy street cafés and entertainers. Keep an eye out for the Rathaus (town hall), which is located in a former Franciscan monastery established in the 15th century. A number of half-timbered buildings and pretty churches give Brühl a more rustic and old-fashioned feel than either of its larger neighbouring cities.

(for a one-way trip to Brühl, you will need a City Plus 2b ticket). The best tram stop for the Augustusburg Palace is Brühl-Mitte.

By road

It's no more than a 30-minute drive from Cologne on the A553 Autobahn into Brühl.

SIGHTS & ATTRACTIONS

Phantasialand

Escape from reality for the day when you walk through the gates of Phantasialand, Germany's biggest and best theme park, just a few

🔵 *Thrills and spills in Germany's biggest theme park*

miles southwest of Brühl. Built on the Disney model, the huge park is split into themed areas that take the form of a street in old Berlin, a scene from the Wild West and Chinatown, to name just a few. The all-important rides are spread across the whole site and range from the child-friendly in Kinderland to the distinctly unfriendly Mystery Castle, with a spooky laboratory and scary 65 m (215 ft) drop.

Water rides are popular on hot, sunny days and the big round rafts of River Quest spin through tunnels and through white-water rapids, while the aptly named Wildwash Creek sends the brave around in a hollowed-out log at breakneck speed over various drops, so everyone gets a thorough soaking. Colorado Adventure is drier, but has you racing through tunnels and round sharp bends in a runaway train. The IMAX cinema technology used in Galaxy allows you to fly through space and survive meteor showers without moving (much).

It might be best to save a meal in one of the themed restaurants until after you've finished the rides. Perhaps one of the cinema or live shows would suit those who have just eaten.

If your children are less than 1 m (39 in) tall, they get in free, as does anyone visiting on their birthday (proof of date of birth required). **ⓣ** (02232) 36200 **ⓦ** www.phantasialand.de **ⓛ** 09.00–18.00 late Mar–early Nov. Admission charge

Schloss Augustusburg & Jagdschloss Falkenlust (Augustusburg Palace & Falkenlust hunting lodge)

Brühl's 'must see' sight, the Augustusburg Palace is a beautiful baroque building set in exceptionally well-maintained gardens, which remain in their original 18th-century French parterre design around vast lakes. Construction of the palace began in 1725 for the Archbishop of Cologne, Clemens August, but wasn't completed until 1769, eight years after his death. Among the gems inside the palace

🔻 *The staircase is a masterpiece of Rococo overstatement*

are 18th-century frescoes and the magnificent marble staircase dating from 1740.

The Falkenlust hunting lodge stands proud at the end of a straight avenue leading from the palace and was originally built by Clemens August as a place to practise his beloved falconry. Visitors should note that the palace closes for 90 minutes at lunchtime on weekdays.
ⓐ Schlossstr. 6 ⓣ (02232) 44000 ⓦ www.schlossbruehl.de

🕙 09.00–12.00, 13.30–16.00 Tues–Fri, 10.00–17.00 Sat & Sun, Feb–Nov. Admission charge

CULTURE

Max Ernst Museum

Opened in 2005, this 19th-century building in a parkland setting, just a ten-minute walk from the old town, provides the perfect venue for Brühl to display the work of its most famous son. Max Ernst was born on Schlossstrasse in 1891 and went on to become famous throughout the world for his 20th-century Dadaist and Surrealist art. Many of his paintings, along with the majority of his graphic works and bronze sculptures, are now housed in this museum. There is also a collection of Ernst's photography, which provides an interesting perspective on his contemporary artists and friends. ⓐ Comestr. 42 ❶ 0180 5743 465 Ⓦ www.maxernstmuseum.de 🕙 11.00–18.00 Tues–Sun, 11.00–21.00 first Thur of the month. Admission charge

Museum für Alltagsgeschichte (Museum of Everyday Life)

This faithfully restored half-timbered house is home to a cleverly displayed selection of artefacts that aren't normally found in museums, such as tools, clothing and dishes. Surprisingly engaging. ⓐ Kempishofstr. 15 ❶ (02232) 42642 Ⓦ www.bruehler-museumsinsel.de 🕙 15.00–17.00 Wed & Sat, 11.00–13.00, 15.00–17.00 Sun. Admission charge

TAKING A BREAK

Brauhaus Brühler Hof £ Traditional hearty local food and

thirst-quenching beer that will keep you going through the day.
ⓐ Uhlstr. 30 **ⓣ** (02232) 410 132 **ⓦ** www.bruehlerhof.de **ⓛ** 10.00–01.00

Café Buschheuer's This traditional family-run café and bistro has
top notch coffee and homemade cakes, as well as light snacks
and meals. **ⓐ** Uhlstr. 21 **ⓣ** (02232) 149 636 **ⓦ** www.buschheuers.de
ⓛ 08.30–18.00 Mon–Sat, 10.00–18.00 Sun

Caico Eiscafe il Gelato The place for indulgent ice-cream and
a decent Italian coffee. **ⓐ** Uhlstr. 59 **ⓣ** (02232) 943 738 **ⓛ** 10.00–21.00
Tues–Sat, 10.00–20.00 Sun

Hof-Café £ Sit in the marketplace and eat delicious waffles,
breakfasts and home-baked cakes while you sip coffee. **ⓐ** Markt 24
ⓣ (02232) 42976 **ⓛ** 08.30–18.00

AFTER DARK

RESTAURANTS
China Palast £ A good Chinese restaurant in a handy central location.
ⓐ Markt 6 **ⓣ** (02232) 49795 **ⓛ** 11.30–15.00, 17.30–23.30

La Locanda £ Enjoy delicious Tuscan meat and fish dishes in this
simple, rustic place, which has a log fire in winter. **ⓐ** Bonnstr. 73
ⓣ (02232) 42075 **ⓦ** www.lalocanda.de **ⓛ** 17.00–00.00 Tues–Sun

Don Pancho £–££ This Argentinian restaurant does great grilled steak
and fish, and always seems to be busy. **ⓐ** Kölnstr. 55 **ⓣ** (02232) 43835
ⓦ www.don-pancho.de **ⓛ** 11.30–14.30, 17.30–23.30 Mon–Fri,
17.30–23.30 Sat

Balthasar Neumann ££ Classic German and French cuisine with flair, plus an extensive wine list. ⓐ Wallstr. 30 ⓣ (02232) 993 367 ⓦ www.balthasar-neumann.de ⓛ 09.30–23.00 Tues–Sat, 10.00–17.00 Sun

CINEMA

Zoom Kino Not your standard big screen, but a huge sheet stretched across the town hall on summer evenings. Films are shown in the original version with German subtitles. ⓐ Uhlstr. 3 ⓣ (02232) 792 170 ⓦ www.zoomkino.de ⓛ Screenings at 20.00

ACCOMMODATION

Hotel Bonprix £ Rooms furnished in the most basic way, but comfortable and convenient for Brühl as well as Cologne and Bonn. ⓐ Hamburgerstr. 18 ⓣ (02232) 15030 ⓦ www.hotel-bonprix.de

Hotel Ling Bao ££ Part of the Phantasialand theme park, this luxury family hotel is a large replica Chinese building. ⓐ Berggeiststr. 31–41 ⓣ (02232) 36666 ⓦ www.phantasialand.de

Ramada Hotel Brühl-Köln ££ Comfortable rooms to the west of town. ⓐ Römerstr. 1–7 ⓣ (02232) 2040 ⓦ www.ramada.de

ⓞ *A tour boat moored near the Hohenzollernbrücke rail bridge*

 PRACTICAL
information

Directory

GETTING THERE

By air

Köln/Bonn Airport has become a hub for low-cost airlines
flying from destinations all over Europe and within Germany.
Reasonably priced flights from airports around the UK are easy to
find and take between 1 hour 15 minutes and 1 hour 30 minutes.
EasyJet (W www.easyjet.com) flies from London Gatwick. **TUIfly**
(W www.tuifly.com) has flights from Manchester. **German Wings**
(W www.germanwings.com) flies from Dublin, Edinburgh, and
London Stansted. **British Airways** (W www.britishairways.com) and
Lufthansa (W www.lufthansa.com) flights leave from London Heathrow.

Scheduled flights from various cities in North America, South
Africa and Australia fly into Düsseldorf and Frankfurt airports, which
are 60 km (37 miles) and 180 km (112 miles) from Cologne respectively.

Many people are aware that air travel emits CO_2, which
contributes to climate change. You may be interested in the
possibility of lessening the environmental impact of your flight
through the charity **Climate Care** (W www.climatecare.org),
which offsets your CO_2 by funding environmental projects
around the world.

By rail

A practical alternative to air travel, particularly if you live in the
southeast of England, is to catch the **Eurostar** (W www.eurostar.com)
to Brussels Midi and take a high-speed Thalys train to Cologne from
there. The journey time from London Waterloo to Brussels is 2 hours
40 minutes and the second leg from Brussels to Cologne takes 2 hours
20 minutes. This combination of trains has the advantage that it brings

you directly into the centre of Cologne, to the main railway station just next to the cathedral. Total journey time is approximately 6½ hrs. The monthly **Thomas Cook European Rail Timetable** (Ⓦ www.thomascookpublishing.com) has up-to-date schedules for European international and national train services. For timetables and tickets, see also **Euro Railways** (Ⓦ www.eurorailways.com).

🔽 *The Intercity Express (ICE) train in Cologne station*

By road

If you're coming from Britain and prefer the independence of driving your own car abroad, then Cologne, in the northwest of Germany, is a surprisingly short trip. Once you've made the hop across the English Channel by ferry or through the **Eurotunnel** ( www.eurotunnel.com) to Calais, you should be able to cover the 400 km (250 miles) to Cologne in less than four hours. The E40 motorway will take you through France, into Belgium, past Brussels and Liège up to the Dutch border, when you should join the E314 motorway. This goes all the way to the German border, where it is best to turn onto the A4 Autobahn and then the A1 for the last few miles into Cologne.

Alternatives to the Eurotunnel include **P&O Ferries** (www.poferries.com), and **SeaFrance** (www.seafrance.com), both of which sail from Dover to Calais.

Another possibility from the UK is coach travel. It's quite cheap to take the overnight coach from London Victoria, but so is a low-cost airline fare booked well in advance, and the coach journey takes a lot longer – between 11 hours 30 minutes and 13 hours; sometimes a change is required in Brussels. The coach arrives at Cologne's city centre bus station, behind the main railway station in Breslauer Platz. Eurolines buses can be booked through **National Express** in the UK (www.nationalexpress.com).

Of course, an entirely hassle-free way of arranging your holiday transport and accommodation is by booking a ready-made package break to Cologne with your travel agent. Booking your holiday in this way also gives you extra legal protection should unforeseen circumstances arise. If you choose to travel independently, it's worth paying the extra for travel insurance.

TRAVEL INSURANCE

However you book your city break, it is important to take out adequate personal travel insurance for the trip. For peace of mind, the policy should give cover for medical expenses, loss, theft, repatriation, personal liability and cancellation expenses. If you are travelling in your own vehicle you should also check that you are appropriately insured, make sure that you bring the relevant insurance documents and your driving licence with you.

ENTRY FORMALITIES

Citizens of the UK, Republic of Ireland and other EU countries, the USA, Canada, Australia and New Zealand are all permitted to enter Germany with a valid passport. A visa is only required if the duration of the stay is more than 90 days. Visitors from South Africa need to ensure that they have a valid passport and visa, return or onward travel tickets and sufficient funds for their stay.

Visitors to Germany from within the EU are entitled to bring their personal effects and goods for personal consumption and not for resale, which can be up to 800 cigarettes and ten litres of spirits. Those entering the country from outside the EU may bring 200 cigarettes (50 cigars, 250g tobacco), two litres of wine and one litre of spirits. No meat or milk products are permitted to be brought into the country from inside or outside the EU. For those flying in or out of Köln/Bonn Airport, customs can be contacted on ℹ (02203) 955 7919

MONEY

Since 2002 the currency in Germany has been the euro, divided into 100 cents. Easily distinguishable notes are available in denominations of 5, 10, 20, 50 and 100 euros, while coins worth 1, 2, 5, 10, 20 and 50 cents, as well as 1 and 2 euros, are widely used. The Germans like to carry cash and in Cologne it's a good idea to do the same, because, as many tourists find out to their embarrassment, credit cards are not widely accepted.

Bureaux de change are few and far between in Cologne, so if you're worried about getting hold of cash it's a good idea to obtain some euros before you arrive. Two bureaux de change are located opposite the cathedral:

American Express ❷ Burgmauer 14 🕐 09.00–18.00 Mon–Fri, 10.00–13.00 Sat

Travelex ❷ Burgmauer 4 🕐 09.00–18.00 Mon–Fri, 09.00–14.00 Sat, Mar–Oct; 09.00–18.00 Mon–Fri, 10.00–13.00 Sat, Nov & Dec; 09.00–18.00 Mon–Fri, Jan & Feb

Look for the words 'International Geldautomat' on ATMs to show that they will take international credit and debit cards. There are few ATMs in the old town, but the shopping streets and the ring road have plenty of banks with 24-hour cash machines. Some German banks are affiliated to either MasterCard or Visa, so if your card does not work in one machine try one attached to a different bank.

Even some large shops and restaurants in Cologne will not take credit cards, so check the payment methods available before you order a meal or run up a bar bill. The Eurocard is the most commonly accepted card, but it is rarely issued by UK banks these days.

HEALTH, SAFETY & CRIME

Cologne's food and drinking water are safe for visitors to consume and should present no problems, except perhaps to vegetarians, who will find menus heavily meat-based.

Germany's healthcare system is excellent and European Union members are entitled to free or reduced cost emergency medical treatment in Germany on presentation of a valid European Health Insurance Card (EHIC). You will be charged a practice fee of €10 if you visit the doctor or dentist. If you are hospitalised, you will be charged a fee of €10 a day for a maximum of 28 days. Apply for the EHIC online at ⓦ www.nhs.uk/Healthcareabroad and allow at least a week to receive the card.

It is important to remember that the EHIC is not an alternative to travel insurance (see page 145) and will not cover aspects such as repatriation back to your home country.

Crime is not a big problem in Cologne, but keep an eye on your valuables in busy tourist areas, as pickpockets are always on the lookout for an easy target. The local police, with their slightly military-looking green uniform, are not a common sight in the tourist areas except during big events, when they are always present in large numbers. See Emergencies (pages 154–5) for more details.

OPENING HOURS

Germany deregulated store opening hours in 2007, so opening times in Cologne are fairly flexible. In general, most supermarkets are open from 08.00–20.00, Monday to Saturday. Other types of stores tend to open around 10.00 and close anywhere between 18.00 and 20.00. Many small shops are closed on Saturday afternoons. All of the city's shops are closed on Sundays, except for bakeries, which

open Sunday mornings, and kiosks. If you need anything from newspapers to beer outside regular hours, your best bet is one of the many kiosks or *Büdchen*, which open from the early hours until late at night and are also a popular source of cheap beer during festivals.

Most banks are open 08.00–16.00 Monday to Friday and are closed on Saturdays. Most post offices are open from 08.00–18.00 Monday to Friday and 09.00–12.00 on Saturday, but some of the bigger branches have longer opening hours.

All of the city's museums are closed on Mondays, but open on most public holidays (including public holidays that fall on a Monday) except Christmas and New Year's Day.

TOILETS

Public toilets in the city are few and far between, and you normally have to pay €0.50 to use them. There are good facilities in all the major museums and department stores.

CHILDREN

Kids are very welcome throughout Germany. Restaurants, cafés and even bars will generally be happy to cater for children and the preference for outdoor seating in summer removes any concerns about smoky air and fidgeting. The following sights and activities are guaranteed to keep youngsters entertained:

Climb the cathedral tower Ideal for burning off some energy, the 509 steps to a great view of the city are safe and a big challenge to count. See page 61 for details of the Dom's contact details and opening times.

Chocolate Museum (see page 77) Fun, educational and delicious – a treat for children and adults alike.

Deutsches Sport & Olympia Museum (see page 76) Packed with sports memorabilia, interactive exhibits and information about the two German-hosted Olympic games.

City parks (see pages 92 & 112) Stadtgarten, Rheinpark and Volksgarten are all great green spaces for football, picnics and fun. Rheinpark has a miniature train to ride and Volksgarten has pedalos on the lake.

Kölner Zoo (see page 108) See animals from every continent, including elephants, bears, gorillas, insects and fish. Watch out for notices displaying feeding times to find out what the inhabitants like for lunch.

Cable car (see page 111) Views are always more exciting when you are dangling from a wire high above a river.

Phantasialand (see page 135) One of Germany's largest theme parks is just 20 km (12 miles) from Cologne and filled with all kinds of rides from white-knuckle rollercoasters and flumes to more sedate carousels.

Ice cream parlours These friendly Italian places can be found all over the city and their huge sundaes are a favourite with young and old, from morning until night.

COMMUNICATIONS
Internet
See Ⓦ www.willkommeninkoeln.de for a list of WLAN hotspots in Cologne, and click on the drop-down menu next to the search option.

There are also plenty of internet cafés around the city, including a 24-hour one in the six-storey Giga-Center gambling, gaming and internet centre.

Giga-Center Köln Ⓐ Hohenzollern Ring 7–11 Ⓣ (0221) 6502 6444 Ⓦ www.giga-center.info Ⓛ 24 hrs Ⓝ U-Bahn: Rudolfplatz

Phone
Most public phones in Cologne – look out for a pink and grey kiosk marked with a T – take coins, phone cards and credit cards and have instructions for their use in English; basically, lift the receiver, insert your payment method and dial the number. Phone cards can be purchased from post offices and many other shops.

TELEPHONING GERMANY
To call Cologne from abroad, dial your international access code (usually oo), then the national code for Germany (49), followed by the area code (221 for Cologne) and the number you require, which will be anything from four to nine digits long.

TELEPHONING ABROAD
To phone home from Cologne, dial the international access code (oo) followed by the relevant country code: UK 44, USA and Canada 1, Australia 61, New Zealand 64, Republic of Ireland 353, South Africa 27.

Germany has a good mobile phone network, but before you travel, check with your service provider that you will be able to access the relevant network.

Post

The German postal service (Deutsche Post) is efficient and reliable. The bright yellow post offices and postboxes are easy to spot and it's best to buy stamps from a post office or an official machine outside. The German word for 'stamps' is *Briefmarken*. There is

⊙ *The bright yellow stamp machines are hard to miss*

a post office in the main railway station and at Auf de Ruhr 90, just off Breite Strasse.

ELECTRICITY

The electricity supply in Germany is 230 volts, 50Hz. European style two-pins plugs are standard and continental adaptors are suitable. Visitors with 110-volt appliances will need to use a voltage transformer.

TRAVELLERS WITH DISABILITIES

While the relatively modern buildings of most of Cologne's major museums provide good access for those with disabilities, much of the old town is full of steps and cobbles that will make getting around in a wheelchair difficult. Disabled access to the tram system is generally good, and while lifts down to U-Bahn stations are progressively being installed only those marked on the official maps are accessible. The city's taxis are mostly Mercedes and will not accommodate wheelchairs. The more modern hotels have the most appropriate facilities for disabled guests, but it's best to phone ahead and check that any specific requirements can be met.

A useful source of advice on accessible accommodation, restaurants and attractions in Germany and Cologne is Ⓦ www.cometogermany.com – click on 'Travelers with Disabilities' and select Cologne from the list.

TOURIST INFORMATION

The English-speaking staff at the Cologne Tourist Board office in front of the cathedral towers are a useful source of maps, accommodation and event information.

Cologne Tourist Board
Old town ⓐ Unter Fettenhennen 19 ⓣ (0221) 2213 0400
🕐 09.00–20.00 Mon–Sat, 10.00–17.00 Sun
Köln/Bonn Airport ⓐ Arrivals hall terminal 2 🕐 07.00–20.00
Mon–Fri, 08.00–20.00 Sat, 09.30–18.00 Sun

   There are three official tourism websites that are crammed
with information in English about the city and its history, events
and facilities, as well as finding accommodation. They are:
Cologne Tourist Board ⓦ www.koeln.de/tourismus/koelntourismus/en
German National Tourist Board ⓦ www.koelntourismus.de
Cologne City Council ⓦ www.stadt-koeln.de

BACKGROUND READING

The Lost Honour of Katherina Blum by Heinrich Böll. Probably
his best-known novel outside Germany, this is a powerful and
prophetic account of the power of the tabloid press and the state.
One of Germany's foremost post-1945 writers, Böll was born and
lived in Cologne. He won the Nobel Prize for Literature in 1972 and
his novels and essays reflect his horrific experiences of war and
the typical, resilient *Rheinisch* humour that Cologne's population
is famous for. An archive of his work, in German only, is held at
Cologne Library on Antwerpener Strasse.

Emergencies

If you need an ambulance or paramedics, call the fire service number and request an ambulance (*Krankenwagen*).

Police ☎ 110
Fire service (and ambulance) ☎ 112

MEDICAL SERVICES

Lists of local doctors and dentists can be found in telephone directories, local newspapers or by contacting the relevant embassy. In an emergency your hotel should be able to summon a doctor. Lists of hospitals appear in local phone directories, too. In emergencies tourists with EHIC cards (see page 147) can receive treatment at any of these establishments at a charge of €10 per day for a maximum of 28 days.

Hospitals with an outpatient emergency department (*Notaufnahme*) include **Kliniken der Stadt Köln Krankenhaus Merheim** (☎ Ostmerheimer Str. 200 ☎ (0221) 89070), **Kliniken der Stadt Köln Krankenhaus Holweide** (☎ Neufelder Str. 32 ☎ (0221) 89070), **Krankenhaus der Augustinerinnen Köln** (☎ Jakobstr. 27–31 ☎ (0221) 33080) and **Evangelisches Krankenhaus Köln-Weyertal** (☎ Weyertal 76 ☎ (0221) 4790).

POLICE

All of the city-centre police stations are open 24 hours a day and can be contacted on ☎ (0221) 2290. In cases of theft you will have to report it to the police to obtain documentation for your insurance claim.

There are police stations located at Maximinstrasse 6 (close to the main railway station), Waidmarkt 1, Bismarckstrasse 9 and Elsassstrasse 27.

EMERGENCY PHRASES

Help!	**Fire!**	**Stop!**
Hilfe!	Feuer!	Halt!
Heelfe!	*Foy-er!*	*Halt!*

Please call an ambulance/a doctor/the police/the fire service!
Rufen Sie bitte einen Krankenwagen/einen Arzt/die Polizei/
die Feuerwehr!
*Roofen zee bitter inen krankenvaagen/inen artst/dee politsye/
dee foyervair!*

EMBASSIES & CONSULATES

Australian Embassy 🅰 Wallstr. 76-79, 10179 Berlin 📞 (030) 700 129 129
🌐 www.germany.embassy.gov.au

British Embassy 🅰 Yorckstr. 19, 40476 Düsseldorf 📞 (0211) 94480
🌐 http://ukingermany.fco.gov.uk

Canadian Embassy 🅰 Benrather Str. 8, 40213 Düsseldorf 📞 (0211) 172 170
🌐 www.international.gc.ca

New Zealand Embassy 🅰 Friedrichstr. 60, 10117 Berlin 📞 (030) 206 210
🌐 www.nzembassy.com/germany

South African Consul General 🅰 Tiergartenstr. 18, 10785 Berlin
📞 (030) 220 730 🌐 www.suedafrika.org

United States Embassy 🅰 Willi-Becker-Allee 10, 40227 Düsseldorf
📞 (0211) 788 8927 🌐 http://duesseldorf.usconsulate.gov

Editorial/project management: Lisa Plumridge
Copy editor: Monica Guy
Layout/DTP: Alison Rayner

The publishers would like to thank the following individuals and organisations for supplying their copyright photographs for this book: Martin Boose, page 7; Grant Bourne, pages 27, 37 & 101; Robert Brands, page 13; Inge Decker/Stadt Köln, page 95; Diedrich Dettmann/CSD Cologne, page 9; FC Köln, page 113; Globetrotter, page 84; Kate Hairsine, pages 120–1 & 128; iStockphoto.com (Kermarrec Aurelien, page 60; Timothy Ball, page 119; Luke Daniek, page 21; Anton Dimitrov, page 40–1; Hans Klamm, page 5); Valerij Kalyuzhnyy/BigStockPhoto.com, page 141; Kölner Haie, page 32; Köln Lichter, page 44; Kölner Seilbahn, page 110; Kölner Verkehrs-Betriebe, page 49;

Send your thoughts to
books@thomascook.com

- Found a great bar, club, shop or must-see sight that we don't feature?
- Like to tip us off about any information that needs a little updating?
- Want to tell us what you love about this handy little guidebook and more importantly how we can make it even handier?

Then here's your chance to tell all! Send us ideas, discoveries and recommendations today and then look out for your valuable input in the next edition of this title.

Email the above address (stating the title) or write to: pocket guides Series Editor, Thomas Cook Publishing, PO Box 227, Coningsby Road, Peterborough PE3 8SB, UK.

WHAT'S IN YOUR GUIDEBOOK?

Independent authors Impartial up-to-date information from our travel experts who meticulously source local knowledge.

Experience Thomas Cook's 165 years in the travel industry and guidebook publishing enriches every word with expertise you can trust.

Travel know-how Thomas Cook has thousands of staff working around the globe, all living and breathing travel.

Editors Travel-publishing professionals, pulling everything together to craft a perfect blend of words, pictures, maps and design.

You, the traveller We deliver a practical, no-nonsense approach to information, geared to how you really use it.

Useful phrases

English	German	Approx pronunciation
BASICS		
Yes	Ja	Yah
No	Nein	Nine
Please	Bitte	Bitter
Thank you	Danke	Danker
Hello	Hallo	Hallo
Goodbye	Auf Wiedersehen	Owf veederzeyhen
Excuse me	Entschuldigen Sie	Entshuldigen zee
Sorry	Entschuldigung	Entshuldigoong
That's okay	Das stimmt	Das shtimt
To	Nach	Nakh
From	Von	Fon
I don't speak German	Ich spreche kein Deutsch	Ikh shprekher kine doitsh
Do you speak English?	Sprechen Sie Englisch?	Shprekhen zee eng-lish?
Good morning	Guten Morgen	Gooten morgen
Good afternoon	Guten Tag	Guten tag
Good evening	Guten Abend	Guten abend
Goodnight	Gute Nacht	Gute nacht
My name is ...	Mein Name ist ...	Mine naamer ist ...
NUMBERS		
One	Eins	Ines
Two	Zwei	Tsvy
Three	Drei	Dry
Four	Vier	Feer
Five	Fünf	Foonf
Six	Sechs	Zex
Seven	Sieben	Zeeben
Eight	Acht	Akht
Nine	Neun	Noyn
Ten	Zehn	Tseyn
Twenty	Zwanzig	Tvantsikh
Fifty	Fünfzig	Foonftsikh
One hundred	Hundert	Hoondert
SIGNS & NOTICES		
Airport	Flughafen	Floogharfen
Rail station/Platform	Bahnhof/Bahnsteig	Baanhof/Baanshtykh
Smoking/Non-smoking	Raucher/Nichtraucher	Raukher/Nikhtraukher
Toilets	Toiletten	Toletten
Ladies/Gentlemen	Damen/Herren	Daamen/Herren
Subway	Die U-Bahn	Dee Oo-baan